Sappho and Catullus
in Twentieth-Century Italian
and North American Poetry

Also available from Bloomsbury

Antipodean Antiquities: Classical Reception Down Under,
edited by Marguerite Johnson
Kinaesthesia and Classical Antiquity 1750–1820: Moved by Stone, Helen Slaney
Virgil's Map: Geography, Empire, and the Georgics, Charlie Kerrigan

Sappho and Catullus in Twentieth-Century Italian and North American Poetry

Cecilia Piantanida

BLOOMSBURY ACADEMIC
LONDON • NEW YORK • OXFORD • NEW DELHI • SYDNEY

BLOOMSBURY ACADEMIC
Bloomsbury Publishing Plc
50 Bedford Square, London, WC1B 3DP, UK
1385 Broadway, New York, NY 10018, USA
29 Earlsfort Terrace, Dublin 2, Ireland

BLOOMSBURY, BLOOMSBURY ACADEMIC and the Diana logo are trademarks
of Bloomsbury Publishing Plc

First published in Great Britain 2021
This paperback edition published 2022

Copyright © Cecilia Piantanida, 2021

Cecilia Piantanida has asserted her right under the Copyright, Designs and
Patents Act, 1988, to be identified as Author of this work.

For legal purposes the Acknowledgements on p. ix constitute an extension of this copyright page.

Cover design: Terry Woodley
Cover image © Jonathan Knowles/Getty

All rights reserved. No part of this publication may be reproduced or transmitted in any form or by any
means, electronic or mechanical, including photocopying, recording, or any information storage or
retrieval system, without prior permission in writing from the publishers.

Bloomsbury Publishing Plc does not have any control over, or responsibility for, any third-party websites
referred to or in this book. All internet addresses given in this
book were correct at the time of going to press. The author and publisher regret
any inconvenience caused if addresses have changed or sites have ceased to
exist but can accept no responsibility for any such changes.

A catalogue record for this book is available from the British Library.

Library of Congress Cataloging-in-Publication Data
Names: Piantanida, Cecilia, 1985- author.
Title: Sappho and Catullus in twentieth-century Italian and
North American poetry / Cecilia Piantanida.
Other titles: Bloomsbury studies in classical reception.
Description: London ; New York : Bloomsbury Academic, 2021. | Series: Bloomsbury studies in classical reception | Includes bibliographical references and index. | Summary: "Going beyond exclusively national perspectives, this volume considers the reception of the ancient Greek poet Sappho and her first Latin translator, Catullus, as a literary pair who transmit poetic culture across the world from the early 20th century to the present. Sappho's and Catullus' reception has shaped a transnational network of poets and intellectuals, helping to define ideas of origins, gender, sexuality and national identities. This book shows that across time and cultures translations and rewritings of Sappho and Catullus articulate modernist poetics of myth and fragmentation, forms of confessionalism and post-modern pastiche. The inquiry focuses on Italian and North American poetry as two central yet understudied hubs of Sappho's and Catullus' modern reception, also linked by a rich mutual intellectual exchange: key case-studies include Giovanni Pascoli, Ezra Pound, H.D., Salvatore Quasimodo, Robert Lowell, Rosita Copioli and Anne Carson, and cover a wide range of unpublished archival material. Texts are analysed and compared through reception and translation theories and inserted within the current debate on the Classics as World Literature, demonstrating how sustained transnational poetic discourse employs the ancient pair to expand notions of literary origins and redefine poetry's relationship to human existence"– Provided by publisher.
Identifiers: LCCN 2020034501 (print) | LCCN 2020034502 (ebook) | ISBN 9781350101890 (hardcover) | ISBN 9781350101906 (ebook) | ISBN 9781350101913 (epub)
Subjects: LCSH: Sappho–Influence. | Catullus, Gaius Valerius–Influence. | Poetry, Modern–20th century–History and criticism. | Italian poetry–20th century–History and criticism. | English poetry–North America–20th century–History and criticism. | Italian poetry–20th century–Classical influences. | English poetry–North America–20th century–Classical influences.
Classification: LCC PN1271 .P53 2021 (print) | LCC PN1271 (ebook) | DDC 884/.0109–dc23
LC record available at https://lccn.loc.gov/2020034501
LC ebook record available at https://lccn.loc.gov/2020034502

ISBN: HB: 978-1-3501-0189-0
PB: 978-1-3501-9168-6
ePDF: 978-1-3501-0190-6
eBook: 978-1-3501-0191-3

Typeset by RefineCatch Limited, Bungay, Suffolk

To find out more about our authors and books visit www.bloomsbury.com
and sign up for our newsletters

Ai miei genitori

Contents

Acknowledgements	ix
Introduction: The Slow Fire	1
The poets and their texts	4
World reception/world authors	8
Global palimpsests	8
Poetry is Sappho and Catullus	12
The 'translocal stretch'	13
From Italy to North America and Back	14
Who? What? When? And Why?	17
1 Mythical Rewritings	23
Sappho and Catullus at the origins: Pascoli's poetic laboratory	
(1877–84)	26
Sappho	26
Catullus	33
Modern myths: 1895–1899	36
Sappho and the blooming flowers of dusk	36
Catullus and the perpetual ritual of lyric	42
2 Modernist Rites	53
Sappho and Catullus *Imagistes*	56
Angels and drabs in Pound's *Lustra* (1917)	58
H.D.'s Sappho in the Imagist period	66
Sappho and Catullus beyond Imagism	70
Erotic ritualism: H.D.'s *Hymen* (1921) and *Heliodora* (1924)	70
The second phase in Pound's reception: The two masks of Eros	79
The third phase in Pound's reception: Private and public poetry	81
3 Classical Hermeticism	85
Tradition and translation toward a lyric absolute	90
Sappho as a lyric abstraction: Poetic voice in *Lirici greci*	97
Quasimodo's elegiac Catullus	102
Lirici greci's reception	108

4	The Self and the Object	113
	Rewriting the self with Catullus: Lowell's *Life Studies*	117
	Sappho through a prism	122
	Objectivist Catullus: The Zukofskys' translations	130
5	Body vs Soul	141
	Ceronetti's anti-establishment Catullus	147
	The brightness of Sappho and Catullus	153
	Copioli's spiritual eroticism	156
6	Postmodern Sappho and Catullus	169
	Triangulating eros	172
	(Un)Knowing Sappho and Catullus: *Men in the Off Hours* (2000)	174
	Sappho disappears	174
	Catullus beyond himself	178
	Floating with Sappho	185
	Giving thanatos back to eros: Catullus in *Nox* (2010)	191

Epilogue	195
Notes	201
List of Manuscripts	219
Audio-visual Material	220
Works Cited	221
Index	243

Acknowledgements

I gratefully acknowledge a Jermyn Brooks Graduate Award, a Lord Crewe Graduate Scholarship, and funding received from Lincoln College (Oxford), which allowed the project at the core of this book to take shape during my doctoral studies at the University of Oxford. I am also honoured to have received from the Isaiah Berlin Fund and the Faculty of Medieval and Modern Languages of the University of Oxford a scholarship and several travel grants to spend three months of extremely productive research in Italian libraries and archives.

Several publishers have kindly granted permissions to print extracts or images:

Extracts from 'Canto IV' By Ezra Pound, from *The Cantos of Ezra Pound*, ©1934 by Ezra Pound. Reprinted by permission of New Directions Publishing Corp.

Extracts from 'Canto V' By Ezra Pound, from *The Cantos of Ezra Pound*, ©1934 by Ezra Pound. Reprinted by permission of New Directions Publishing Corp.

'April – 12. Sappho', excerpts from 'Afterthought' from *Notebook* by Robert Lowell; 'Words for Hart Crane', 'Sappho to a Girl', excerpts from 'Preface', 'Three Letters to Anaktoria' and 'Hamlet in Russia, A Soliloquy' from *Imitations* from *Collected Poems* by Robert Lowell, © 2003 by Harriet Lowell and Sheridan Lowell. Reprinted by permission of Farrar, Straus and Giroux.

'Catullus: Carmina', 'TV Men: Sappho (1)', and 'TV Men: Sappho (2)' from *Men in the Off Hours* © 2000 by Anne Carson. Used by permission of Alfred A. Knopf, an imprint of the Knopf Doubleday Publishing Group, a division of Penguin Random House LLC. All rights reserved. Extracts from *Men in the Off Hours* by Anne Carson published by Jonathan Cape, reprinted by permission of The Random House Group Limited © 2000. Extracts from *Nox*, © 2010 by Anne Carson. Reprinted by permission of New Directions Publishing Corp.

Egidio Fiorin very helpfully sent, and gave me permission to print, the image of Merini, A. and E. Baj (1999–2000), *L'uovo di Saffo*, © Colophonarte.

I wish to thank some of the people who were crucial to this project. My most sincere thanks to Anne Carson for kindly participating in an e-mail interview in January 2011, and to Rosita Copioli for hosting me at her house and answering my questions so generously during an in-person interview in July 2019. Both Anne Carson and Rosita Copioli gave permission to print excerpts of the interviews in this book. I am greatly indebted to Alessandro Quasimodo, Giovanni Anceschi, Università La Sapienza and the Biblioteca Comunale dell'Archiginnasio in Bologna for allowing me to publish several documents from the correspondence between Salvatore Quasimodo and Luciano Anceschi in this volume. Professor Gian Luigi Ruggio, Elisabetta Gianasi, Maria Elisa Caproni and Stefano Crudeli of the Archivio of Casa Pascoli opened the archive especially for me during a very hot August, generously assisting me with all aspects of my research on Giovanni Pascoli's papers. Dr.ssa Marina Venier introduced me to the Biblioteca Nazionale Centrale di Roma. Dr.ssa Anna Manfron of the Biblioteca Comunale dell'Archiginnasio in Bologna, Dr. Alessandro Taddei of the Archivio del Novecento at Università La Sapienza in Rome, and Ilaria Spadolini of Archivio Contemporaneo 'A. Bonsanti' at Gabinetto G.P. Vieusseux in Florence helped me navigate many and various archival collections.

I have learned much from numerous colleagues, with whom I have exchanged ideas over the years. This book reflects a deep and ongoing collaboration with Nicola Gardini, my mentor and friend, who contributed to this project from its inception. My unreserved gratitude goes to him, for the time spent on many stimulating discussions and for urging me to dig deeper into the heart of the matter, while maintaining the broader perspective of history. Without his guidance, intellectual support and encouragement, this book would not have been written. I am also deeply indebted to the insights and guidance of Carlo Caruso and Martin McLaughlin, who went far beyond their duties as doctoral examiners and whose advice greatly helped me to refine the project behind this book. Francesco Citti's comments on my edition of Pascoli's autograph translations, which I discuss in the first chapter, were invaluable. Oliver Taplin, Silvio Bär and Andrea Rodighiero generously gave me some of their time to discuss Sappho and her reception in Italy and Europe. Jaś Elsner, Barbara Graziosi and Sarah Shaw shared precious advice and extremely helpful comments at various stages of the project. I wish to thank Patrick Finglass and Adrian Kelly for giving me the opportunity to contribute to their exciting project on Sappho, which gave me many ideas for this book. I am grateful to them as editors of the *Cambridge Companion to Sappho* and to Barbara Goff and Katherine Harloe for kindly sharing their work with me ahead of publication. My sincere thanks to Guido Furci and Université Paris III-Sorbonne Nouvelle for inviting me to Paris to present and discuss my research in a very inspiring seminar. My colleagues at Durham University created a friendly and supportive work environment – I am particularly indebted to Charles Burdett and Annalisa Cipollone for their generous comments on early drafts of my work. Alice Wright, Georgina Leighton and Lily Mac Mahon at Bloomsbury believed in this book and facilitated its coming to life.

Many other colleagues and friends helped this project see the light and supported me every step of the way. I am very grateful to Gregory Ariail, for our conversations on poetry and writing and for his invaluable close reading and advice; to Teresa Franco for her precious intellectual partnership on all matters related to translation, poetry and publishing; to Caterina Paoli for the endlessly stimulating discussions on poetry and the classics and for letting me read and cite her doctoral thesis; to Alberica Bazzoni for her theoretical outlook on the world; to Claudia Dellacasa, Anne-Claire Michoux and my father, Antonio Piantanida, for reading so judiciously various parts of this book and for their encouragement; to Jérémie Wenger for many productive 'philo-poetic' coffees. My most sincere thanks also to Silvia, Maria Grazia and Fulvio Dobrovich for generously welcoming me in Rome, and to Ursula Wunderli for opening her house to me when I was in Prato.

Finally, my wholehearted gratitude goes to my family. To Filippo, Sara and Margherita for their moral support and for putting me up in Milan during my many trips to the library. To Stefano, who has accompanied me throughout this journey, holding my hand when I most needed it. And, most of all, to my parents, Anna and Antonio, without whom none of this would have been possible. Thank you for unconditionally believing in me and for your unfailing support.

Introduction: The Slow Fire

'Along my veins / runs the slow fire'. It is 1917, London. The American Ezra Pound translates Catullus's rewriting of Sappho, musing: 'That was the way of love, *flamma dimanat*' (1917: 182). Sappho, the seventh-century BC lyricist from the Greek island of Lesbos, and her first Latin translator, Catullus, are called upon to ponder love in the poetic laboratory of Pound's magnum opus to be, *The Cantos*. Pulled from the past by way of misquotation – 'dimanat' stands for 'demanat' (*Cat.* 51.10)[1] – as a slow but constant fire, Sappho and Catullus release new poetic possibilities: 'So the murk opens' (1917: 182).

In one of the earliest representations of eros' blissful affliction,[2] the lyric voice of Sappho's fr. 31 expresses her desire for a girl, who sits and laughs with a man; enraptured by the effects of desire on her body, she feels near to death. Notoriously, Catullus loosely translates Sappho's ode in his poem 51. He rewrites the lyric in his own voice addressing it directly to his beloved Lesbia, with clear references to Sappho herself. As the Catullan persona becomes aware of his own weakness before Lesbia's beauty, he makes Sappho's erotic lyricism the object of his poetic aspirations. Translating Catullus's translation, Pound invokes the archetypal bond between source text and translator, model and innovator that legislates tradition and defines the relationship between Sappho and Catullus as a literary pair. An idea of love seals the poetic triangle.

The erotic and the poetic have defined Sappho's and Catullus's reception since their interwoven rediscoveries in the Renaissance. From the very beginning the two poets have often travelled together.[3] Catullus's poem was in circulation for a long time before Sappho 31 came to light in Marc-Antoine de Muret's 1554 edition of Catullus. She is saluted as a model of poetic perfection: 'But now I think there is no one who is not impatient to listen to the Tenth Muse' (Muret, quoted in Michelakis 2009: 346).[4] Sixteenth-century poets approached Sappho by revisiting Catullus 51's strategies of appropriation. As DeJean notes, Sappho's fortune was facilitated by a process of mediated desire – poets entered in a contest for the best translation, driven less by interest in Sappho's lyrics than by ambition to emulate their Roman predecessor. Poets such as Ronsard and Jean Antone de Baïf called themselves the 'new Catullus' and the Lesbian poet was made into an object of male literary desire (1989: 33). By the seventeenth century Sappho and Catullus had developed their own independent traditions, but the success of Sappho 31 and Catullus 51, two of the most translated and imitated poems in modern western literature, cemented their long-lasting relationship. Steadily making their way through time and space, the literary pair shifted to the centre of literary culture in the twentieth century. Since the early 1900s, an industry of poetic translations and rewritings of Sappho's and Catullus's poetry and biographies has enabled the two ancient poets to move into contemporary world literature.[5]

The literary pair has kindled the imagination of modern poets, igniting the development of various poetics that became central to the twentieth century, such as modernist poetics of myth and fragmentation, forms of confessionalism and postmodern pastiche. Their modern reception has expanded the discourse on literary origins and contributed to the conceptualization of the relationship of poetry to human existence.

This process has unfolded across different countries and literary cultures. Just a few years before Pound's translations in 'Three Cantos' (1917), the poet-scholar Giovanni Pascoli was opening his new collection *Poemi conviviali* (Convivial poems) (1904) with a mythical rewriting of Sappho's life in the poem 'Solon'. He had recently published a long neo-Latin poem based on Catullus 50, *Catullocalvos* (1897).[6] In the same years, the Bohemian-Austrian poet Reiner Maria Rilke picked up a sense of the fragmentary and intense eroticism from Sappho's works in a few lyrics dedicated to her in *Neue Gedichte* (New Poetry) (1907); a pattern that returned with Anglo-American *Imagism*, where both Sappho and Catullus took on modernist personas in the poems of Ezra Pound and H.D.[7] In Paris, Sappho was particularly favoured by the 'Sappho 1900' group led by Natalie Barney, Renée Vivien and Colette, who, inspired by the homoeroticism of her lyrics, tried to recreate a lesbian society at Barney's literary salon.[8] Already in 1929, in 'The Scholars', Yeats complained of how misunderstood Catullus was by the critics.[9] As fascism raged in Europe, the lyric fragment became again the focus of Sappho's and Catullus's reception in the hands of the Nobel Prize winner Salvatore Quasimodo, who published translation anthologies of Sappho ([1940]2004) and Catullus (1945 and 1955) to advance a form of neo-humanism.[10] Five years later, the Bostonian Robert Lowell's rewritings chastised the literary establishment in *Life Studies* (1959) and *Imitations* (1961),[11] where Sappho and Catullus speak of their ordinary 1950s lives. Over in Brooklyn in

1969, Louis Zukofsky, although not knowing Latin, decided to 'breathe' with Catullus, embarking on a homophonic translation of his entire *liber*.[12] In the same year in Italy, Guido Ceronetti, who did know Latin, published the most explicit translation ever written in Italian ([1969]1991), with Catullus speaking to *épater le bourgeois* (shock the bourgeois); his Sappho, much politer, was made into a beacon of light in his later translations (1986).[13] The Catalan Carme Riera imagined a 'Fragment mai no escrit de Safo' ('A fragment never written by Sappho') (1975), while Odysseas Elytis' translation rediscovered the roots of Eros in Lesbos ([1984]1996). Sappho's and Catullus's erotic power resurfaced to kindle the imagination of poets at the end of the century, this time with a fully developed gender consciousness in the poetic translations and rewritings of the British Josephine Balmer, the Canadian Anne Carson and the Italian Rosita Copioli, whose Sapphos and Catulluses performed a critique of patriarchy between the 1990s and the early 2010s.[14] These are just few examples from the realm of poetry. In addition to the various biographical novels on the two poets,[15] artists and musicians made Sappho and Catullus their subjects, too: for instance, Cy Twombly quoted lines of Sappho in his 1959 *Sperlonga drawings* and his series of paintings *Poems to the Sea*, and also called an enormous three-panelled painting *Untitled (Say Goodbye, Catullus, to the Shores of Asia Minor)* (1994); Anselm Kiefer (2002–5)'s *Sappho* sculpted the Lesbian poet's head as an open book; Carl Orff put the Roman poet to Music in 'Catulli Carmina' (1940–43) and used the wedding poems of both Sappho and Catullus for his scenic concert *Trionfo di Afrodite* (1951) (Aphrodite's Triumph)…The list is endless. Mapping all instances of the reception of Sappho and Catullus in twentieth- and twenty-first-century western literary culture would be a colossal task beyond the remits of any single monograph; but even from the limited list above, the magnitude of Sappho's and Catullus's transnational presence is indisputable. Mostly associated as lyric models, they travel together in the cultural imaginary in the same way as other literary duos, such as Homer and Virgil, Virgil and Dante, Pound and Eliot, have, epitomizing the dynamics of literary tradition and exchange.

This book considers for the first time the reception of Sappho and Catullus as a literary pair who transmits poetic culture across the world from the twentieth century to the present. I analyse selected 'sightings' of Sappho and Catullus in two of the most prolific hubs of their reception: North America and Italy. While it is not my intention to trace a complete history of the poetic reception of the two ancient poets, these illustrations reveal the defining role of Sappho and Catullus as catalysts of modern poetic practices across the two national literatures, helping to define ideas of origins, gender, sexuality and national identities. The widespread circulation of the two ancient poets in translation, rewritings and scholarship in various languages establishes a transnational aesthetic and cultural discourse centred on their figures, what David Damrosch would define a 'constellation' across cultures (2003: 281), which I here begin to unpack.

In this introductory chapter I identify some key defining moments in Sappho's and Catullus's reception, which aid understanding their cultural impact in the twentieth and twenty-first centuries. I also set up the theoretical framework of my study: grounded in textual criticism, the analysis employs a combination of translation, reception, gender and sexuality theories as a tool to approach and unpack the multifaceted subject of the reception of Sappho and Catullus, while positioning the two ancient poets within world literature.

The poets and their texts

Sappho Fr. 31

Φαίνεταί μοι κῆνος ἴσος θέοισιν
ἔμμεν' ὤνηρ, ὄττις ἐνάντιός τοι
ἰσδάνει καὶ πλάσιον ἆδυ φωνεί-
   σας ὑπακούει

καὶ γελαίσας ἰμέροεν, τό μ' ἦ μὰν
καρδίαν ἐν στήθεσιν ἐπτόαισεν·
ὡς γὰρ <ἔς> σ' ἴδω βρόχε' ὥς με φώνη-
   σ' οὐδὲν ἔτ' εἴκει,

ἀλλὰ †καμ† μὲν γλῶσσα †ἔαγε†, λέπτον
δ' αὔτικα χρῶι πῦρ ὑπαδεδρόμακεν,
ὀππάτεσσι δ' οὐδὲν ὄρημμ', ἐπιβρό-
   μεισι δ' ἄκουαι,

†έκαδε† μ' ἴδρως κακχέεται, τρόμος δὲ
παῖσαν ἄγρει, χλωροτέρα δὲ ποίας
ἔμμι, τεθνάκην δ' ὀλίγω 'πιδεύης
   φαίνομ' ἔμ' αὔται.

ἀλλὰ πᾶν τόλματον, ἐπεὶ †καὶ πένητα†

Catullus 51

Ille mi par esse deo videtur,
ille, si fas est, superare divos,
qui sedens adversus identidem te
   spectat et audit

dulce ridentem, misero quod omnis
eripit sensus mihi: nam simul te,
Lesbia, aspexi, nihil est super mi
   [vocis in ore]

lingua sed torpet, tenuis sub artus
flamma demanat, sonitu suopte
tintinant aures, gemina teguntur
   lumina nocte.

otium, Catulle, tibi molestum est;
otio exsultas nimiumque gestis;
otium et reges prius et beatas
   perdidit urbes.

(**Sappho fr. 31:** He seems to me to be equal to the gods / that man who sits opposite you / and nearby listens to your / sweet voice / and amorous laughter; truly this / makes my heart flutter in my breast; / for when I look at you for a moment, / I cannot speak anymore / but my tongue breaks, at once / a subtle fire runs under my skin, / I see nothing with my eyes, / my ears roar, / a cold sweat comes over me, trembling / seizes me all, I am greener than grass, / and I seem to me to be little far from death. / But all can be endured, since even a poor man…

Catullus 51: He seems to me to be equal to a god, / that man, if it is possible, seems to surpass the gods, / who sitting opposite you always / looks at you and hears you / sweetly laughing. This rips all senses / from me miserable: / for as soon as I see you, / Lesbia, I have no / voice left in my mouth / but my tongue numbs, a subtle flame / runs down through my limbs, / with a sound of their own / ring my ears, a twofold night covers my eyes. / Idleness, Catullus, is giving you trouble; / in idleness, you revel and yearn too much; / idleness has already destroyed both kings and / happy cities).[16]

Sappho 31 survives thanks to the treaty *On the Sublime*, mistakenly attributed to Longinus, which quotes the ode as one of the highest examples of poetic sublime. As some of the earliest extant lyrics, Sappho's fragments, and fr. 31 in particular, have often been viewed as the original occurrences of an unmediated lyric self,[17] although it is likely that their function was primarily social rather than personal.[18] The original context of fr. 31 is unknown; scholarship has variously identified it as a song sung at a wedding or about a wedding, a farewell poem for one of the girls in Sappho's circle, a manifestation of jealousy or a description of the effects of beauty on the senses.[19]

Catullus's free translation of Sappho's text reflects Roman authors' liberal approaches to their sources.[20] He substitutes the female poetic persona of fr. 31 with his male lyric voice, reconstructing her poem as a declaration of heterosexual love for a woman desired by another man.[21] While Sappho's beloved remains anonymous, Catullus names his poetic addressee, Lesbia, the metrically equivalent namesake for Clodia, the woman critics have identified as Catullus's beloved, wife of Metellus Celer and sister of the radical demagogue P. Clodius Pulcher.[22] By evoking Sappho through the namesake,[23] he redoubles his sense of longing directed both toward the beloved and the lyric tradition represented by Sappho.[24] As a translator, Catullus might also be expressing his 'yearning for a communion with a historically, culturally, and linguistically distant text' (Young 2015: 170). Catullus's poem thus adds a degree of self-reflexivity and meta-literary awareness to Sappho's original,[25] explicitly articulating the tension 'between originality and convention and between new and traditional structures that shape literary memory' (Conte 1986: 91), which defines any work of art. As the earliest translation of Sappho available in modernity, Catullus 51 inevitably sets a standard for generations to come.

Together with (Pseudo-?) Ovid's *Heroides* 15, Catullus 51 is one of the key texts responsible for the masculinization of Sappho's lyric voice and the normalization of her homoerotic poetry. Ovid's epistle, where Sappho wishes to jump off the Leucadian cliffs because of her unrequited love for Phaon, was the most influential mythologization of Sappho's life from the Renaissance to the twentieth century. Although by the beginning of the seventeenth century Sappho had developed her own independent tradition, the masculinization and normalization effected by Catullus and Ovid continued to exert their influence on portrayals of Sappho and of her poetry well into the nineteenth century.[26]

The kind of biographical fictionalizing exemplified in *Heroides* 15 has determined not only Sappho's but also Catullus's reception for centuries. Being attributed exceptional literary value and often canonical status, their works have continued to be passed on. At the same time, the lack of information on Sappho's and Catullus's respective lives has increased the imaginative appeal of the two authors, whose biographies have often become vessels for alternating dominant views. Indeed, Sappho's and Catullus's personas feature as characters in various literary works. Scholarship, too, has, since the Renaissance, customarily censored or emphasized particular aspects of the poets' biographies to suit changing constructions of gender, sexuality and national identity. Until the late nineteenth century both poets' biographies and works were more often than not edited to suit heteronormative values and standards of 'decency', 'chastity' and 'purity'.[27]

We know that Sappho was born on the Greek island of Lesbos between the seventh and sixth century BC, that she had three brothers, got married, had a daughter and was exiled to Sicily. She wrote nine books of poetry, of which fewer than 200 fragments remain, containing expressions of love for both men and women.[28] In the absence of information, throughout the centuries her biographers have made her into a chaste woman, a lustful, ugly prostitute, a heterosexual and a lesbian, a revolutionary and the embodiment of nationhood and, in the most extreme case of conflation between author and text, a fragmented, absent body. Epitomized by the provocative blank page for her entry in Wittig's and Zeig's encyclopaedia of female homosexuality (1986), the history of Sappho's reception reveals a painstaking concern, nearing obsession, with her life in general, and her sexual life in particular, which, with few exceptions, until the late twentieth century was habitually rewritten into a heterosexual plot.[29]

Gaius Valerius Catullus was born around 84 BC in Verona and died, aged only thirty years old, in 54 BC in Rome.[30] One of Rome's first major lyric poets, he was a member of an aristocratic provincial family, who had ties with Julius Caesar.[31] Suetonius narrates that Catullus managed to ruin Caesar's reputation by writing scurrilous poems about his protégé Mamurra, although Caesar, after Catullus's apology, did not hold it against him.[32] Catullus's corpus consists of 116 poems in various metres and on several subjects. The standing collection was probably not published during Catullus's lifetime.[33] He became known as the most prominent member of the 'Neoterics' or 'The New Poets', a derogatory term coined by Cicero (*Att.* 7.2.1). Catullus and his circle, including the poets Licinius Calvus, Cornificius, and Cinna, wrote in Callimachean and Alexandrian style, privileging private and everyday subjects, erudite allusions, especially to Hellenistic poetry, and refined, chiselled versification.[34] Championed by Kenneth Quinn's 1959 study *The Catullan Revolution*, the twentieth century has often depicted them as the promulgators of a new intimate form of poetry, anticipating the introspective mode of modern lyric. But as Martindale notes (1999: xi), Catullus's poetry may be equally framed into a story of continuity with the past and tradition, so that it would be impossible to establish the historicity of one account over another; as is the case for Sappho, any critical narrative inescapably reflects contemporary concerns. Assuming that the Catullan poetic persona corresponds with the author of the lyrics, it is possible to extract some information from Catullus's poems: he was a member of the personal staff of the propraetor C. Memmius in Bithynia, probably between 57 and 56 BC (*c.* 10, 28, 46),[35] he had a brother who died prematurely and was buried in the Troad (*c.* 65, 68 a–b, 101), his family probably owned a villa in Sirmio on Lake Garda (*c.* 31) and an estate between Tibur and the Sabine district (*c.* 44), he was acquainted with various poets and influential political figures in Rome, he loved a woman nicknamed Lesbia and a boy called Juventius. Very little else is known, especially about the later part of Catullus's life.

Besides Sappho 31 and Catullus 51, another set of lyrics reveals the affinities between the Lesbian and the Roman poets – the wedding poems. Sappho's epithalamia fragments (frr. 104a to 117b) and Catullus 61 and 62 are, with Idyll 18 by Theocritus, the earliest wedding poems handed down to us from Graeco-Roman antiquity.[36] As I discuss at length in the book, with various motifs recurring in both the Sapphic and Catullan material, these poems constitute an epithalamic cluster that has repeatedly attracted the attention of modern poets and has contributed to the tradition of Sappho and Catullus and their reception as a literary pair.

World reception/world authors

While humanists and scholars occupied themselves with Sappho and Catullus, the ancient poets remained mostly unknown by the wider public, who did not read Greek or Latin, until the late eighteenth century, when they started being translated in major European languages, including French, English, German, Italian and Spanish. By the first decades of the nineteenth century, translations of Sappho and Catullus were widely available throughout Europe.[37] In the twentieth century, the circulation of ideas and aesthetics through publications, translations, articles and letters became increasingly transnational and globalized, affecting a supra-national aesthetic discourse on the two ancient poets.

Global palimpsests

The development of classical philology into an academic discipline in the nineteenth century represents a turning point for the modern reception of both Sappho and Catullus. In the absence of their original texts, so much of their reception has been in the hands of classical philologists as intermediaries. As Holquist points out, '[p]hilology [...] displays a multiple history, composed of the various attempts to appropriate past meaning through minute study of texts based on expert knowledge of language. It is the history of how a set of technical practices [...] has been employed across the globe and in different ages to establish as close to a past textual meaning as humans reasonably can be expected to achieve' (2011: 154). The global nature of the discipline and the worldwide currency of critical editions of classical texts has enabled the creation of a transnational discourse on Sappho and Catullus. Several poets reimagining Graeco-Roman literature are scholars or studied classics. In this book, for instance, Giovanni Pascoli and Anne Carson taught ancient Greek and Latin at university; Ezra Pound was a specialist in Romance philology; Robert Lowell and Rosita Copioli earned degrees in classics. The philological model as an inquiry into the roots of western culture has informed creative appropriations of Sappho and Catullus, by virtue of their position at the origins of lyric poetry.

No other classical corpus has undergone such dramatic changes as Sappho's oeuvre since the nineteenth century. In 1843, the German philologist Theodor

Bergk published his edition of Sappho including 109 fragments – the largest collection before the advent of papyri. It provided a new text for Sappho 1, which gave definite textual evidence of the homoeroticism of Sappho's lyric. Influenced by the literary fictions on Sappho's life, a corruption in l. 24 (where Sappho asks Aphrodite for help in winning her beloved's attentions) had, since the sixteenth century, been assumed to refer to a male lover, often identified with the Ovidian Phaon. Bergk's new text made explicit that Sappho's beloved in the poem is a woman, producing an unambiguously homoerotic lyric. The conjecture was later confirmed by manuscript evidence and eventually became the standard text of fr. 1.[38] Bergk helped debunk the narrative encouraged by Catullus and Ovid that Sappho's life and poetry were the expressions of a heterosexual female subject. Although attempts to suppress Sappho's homoeroticism did not stop,[39] the formalization of classical philology into a scientific discipline separated Sappho's texts from her biographical fiction and her name began to be associated with the lyric fragment.

In 1880, the first scrap of papyrus was discovered in modern Fayum and published by Friedrich Blass,[40] followed in 1889 by the first Sapphic finding from the treasure trove of Oxyrhynchus. A new Sappho golden age opened, with her corpus rapidly growing and new fragments emerging throughout the century. Most recently, two papyri were found in 2004 and 2014, now known as the 'New Sappho' and the 'Newest Sappho'. The former completed and corrected some assumptions concerning fr. 58 contained in P.Oxy. 1787, in which Sappho laments her old age before recounting the myth of Tithonos; the latter bore two new fragments: in the first, often referred to as the 'Brothers Poem', Sappho speaks of her two brothers Charaxus and Larichos; in the second, the 'Kypris Poem', we find an invocation to the goddess Aphrodite.[41]

Though the twentieth century saw an increasing interest in Sappho the poet, over Sappho the lover, the homoeroticism of her lyrics never stopped attracting the attention of writers and classical scholars alike. In the first decades of the century, Sappho found herself between those who used her name to promote sexual freedom and lesbian identity and those who felt compelled to defend her "reputation".[42] The debate on the homoeroticism of her poems is as yet not altogether over. With the development of classical reception studies since the 1990s, seminal scholarly works on Sappho's reception have been published, mostly focusing on the French and Anglo-American worlds. These works, employing feminist and gender approaches, remain seminal today and I often refer to them throughout my study. In particular, Joan DeJean (1989), *Fictions of Sappho: 1546–1937*, tracing the history of Sappho's reception in France and

Yopie Prins (1999), *Victorian Sappho*, on the reception of Sappho in nineteenth-century Britain have proved fundamental reference works in developing my own study.[43] The extraordinary critical interest in Sappho with a vast variety of approaches has continued into the twenty-first century, as testified by the recent *Cambridge Companion to Sappho* (2021) edited by Patrick Finglass and Adrian Kelly, including a large section on Sappho's world reception, which covers Europe, the United States, India, China, Japan and Hebrew literature.

Similar critical issues concern past and present scholarship on Catullus. In the sixteenth and seventeenth centuries Catullus's poems, especially those of the Lesbia cycle, had enormous influence in Italy and France, and with some delay in the UK.[44] Differently from Sappho, biographical speculation was not the main concern of poets and scholars at the time.[45] It is in the nineteenth century that a new interest in the love affair with Lesbia brought scholarship to attempt a full account of Catullus's life based on the assumption that Lesbia was the historical figure Clodia Metelli. The crucial work was Ludwig Schwabe's *Quaestiones Catullianae* of 1862, which reconstructed a detailed chronological table of Catullus's life by combining a biographical reading of the poems with the information provided by Cicero on Clodia and Caelius Rufus and presenting his biographical reconstruction as historical fact. Schwabe offered a 'coherent and dramatic story of love and jealousy' (Wiseman 1985: 217), which emphasized the importance of Lesbia in the Catullan corpus, and had great impact on later scholarship. For instance, the eminent scholars Emil Baehrens, who produced his edition of Catullus in 1876 and commentary in 1885, and Robinson Ellis, who wrote one of the most extensive commentaries on Catullus to date in 1876, followed Schwabe's theories and were very much concerned with Catullus's biography. Translators and poets felt free to interpret and re-arrange the order of the poems in Catullus's oeuvre according to biographical chronology.[46] The Romantic interest in spontaneous poetry and intimacy fuelled the investigation into Catullus's verse as a sincere expression of intimate feelings. The nineteenth century thus opened the way to the portrayal of Catullus – still current today – as a poet of intense lyricism, with a sincere and intimate voice.

Catullus's homoerotic and sexually explicit poems did not have a better fate than Sappho's lyrics. Since the end of the seventeenth century, the group of poems in which Catullus declares his love and physical attraction for the young Juventius (*c.* 24, 48, 81, 99) were repeatedly omitted from anthologies or normalized by changing the sex of the boy.[47] Until the late nineteenth century, the narrative of Catullus's life constantly depicted him as a heterosexual. Richard

Burton's translation (1894) is the only one to accept Catullus's pederasty (Gaisser 2009: 204). As far as obscenity is concerned, standards of 'decency' often provoked censorship. The 1929 translation by F. W. C. Hiley and Jack Lindsay was one of the first to render the scatological poems honestly, although the vulgarities were considerably toned down in the English (Gaisser 2009: 210).

The influence of poststructuralist approaches to the classics in Anglo-American scholarship has brought about new interpretations. Much has been done to separate the author from his poetic persona. Theories of gender and sexuality have re-evaluated homoeroticism and obscenity in Catullus's corpus, until the mid-twentieth century omitted from anthologies: in Fordyce's renowned commentary of 1961, the critic left out thirty-two lyrics deemed inappropriate for a general audience. At the same time, Wiseman notes that Fordyce was criticized for his exclusions and, since the 1950s, discussions of Catullus's work encompassed the whole corpus of his writings (1985: 242). The influence of Callimachus and Alexandrian writers has been another hotly debated topic, especially in relation to poetic reflexivity. Kenneth Quinn's *The Catullan Revolution* casts Catullus as one of the greatest poets, the precursor of modern lyric, precisely because of his awareness and ability to manipulate lyric subjectivity.

While comparatively less studied than Sappho's reception, Catullus's fortune has been investigated in various major works. Julia H. Gaisser opened the way to the study of Catullan reception. Her book *Catullus and His Renaissance Readers* (1993) remains seminal, in addition to her chapters on the Anglo-American reception of the Roman poet in her 2009 volume. David Wray's study on Catullus's poetics of masculinity opens with some acute insights into many key aspects of Catullan reception in Anglo-American and European literature. Charles Martindale's 1999 introduction to Quinn's *The Catullan Revolution*, by then a classic, assesses the main critical positions holding sway through the twentieth century, emphasizing the influence of Quinn's presentation of Catullus as the first modern poet. Henry Stead's recent volume, *A Cockney Catullus* (2016), has opened a more extended investigation of nineteenth-century Catullus, with a focus on British Romanticism. All these studies offered great guidance as I wrote my book.

Any enquiry into the reception of Sappho and Catullus must account for the history of scholarship on these two poets. Throughout my discussion, I make references to such history in order to highlight the transnational exchange between poets, scholars and intellectuals, which contributed to shape various aspects of Sappho's and Catullus's modern reception.

Poetry is Sappho and Catullus

In the twentieth century, Sappho and Catullus are often framed as the greatest singers of love and eros. They are associated with the intimate subjectivity of the lyric mode and the appeal of the lyric fragment. For instance, Gaisser introduces Catullus saying that 'No ancient poet except Sappho writes of emotions and personal experience with such intensity' (Gaisser 1993: 2). She stresses the emotional quality of Catullus's poetry and reproduces the comparison with Sappho, deeming her his only equal. Gaisser is not alone in describing Sappho and Catullus in these terms: Quinn hails Catullus as the first true modern poet and, most recently, Alessandro Fo has reclaimed the Roman poet from Martindale's sceptical assessment of his literary value (1999: xxiv), to make him 'uno dei più grandi poeti della nostra tradizione [...] per la profondità e la ricchezza della sua vocazione' (one of the greatest poets of our tradition [...] for the depth and richness of his inspiration) (2018: viii). As Miller points out, Snell talks of 'Sappho's deeply emotional confessions' (1953: 52–9) and Bowra of her 'remarkable intimacy and candour' (1961: 178) (quoted in Miller 1994: 79).

Wray has argued that twentieth-century approaches to Catullus as a model of spontaneous lyricism both in scholarship and poetry are a consequence of the lasting influence of the Romantic paradigm, perpetuated in Quinn's model. The short lyric fragment became the predominant way of conceptualizing 'poetry' in the twentieth century, informing definitions taught in schools across Europe and the United States, eventually coming to coincide with 'modern poetry' (Wray 2001: 23). Today, this is by far the most popular and widespread paradigm filtering through the work of poets, scholars and critics, and affecting the reception not only of Catullus, but also Sappho. Presented as the first woman poet writing at the origins of erotic lyric and a heroine enduring or sacrificing herself to the gods of love, in the nineteenth century Sappho stood as a privileged archetype.[48] Since then, her lyric sublime, erotic drive and fragmentation have been echo chambers for constructions of poetic subjectivities, gendered selves and sexual identities.

Twentieth-century poets who engaged creatively with Sappho and Catullus were still drawn to them by virtue of their status of canonical literary models, following the assumption singled out by Casanova that 'the classic incarnates literary legitimacy itself, which is to say what is recognized on constituting *Literature*' (2004: 92). As the century progressed toward postmodernism, poets and scholars reusing Sappho and Catullus became increasingly aware of the loaded dynamics of reception and tradition; yet, the two ancient poets remained habitually associated with the 'dual prestige of priority and perfection' (Casanova 2004: 56) conventionally attributed to canonical works. Twenty years into the twenty-first century, these ideas are in many aspects eroding, as poststructuralist, feminist and postcolonial critiques – among others – of literary value and tradition have taken hold. However, while classical antiquity may have lost its primacy in the cultural world and 'priority' some of its prestige, the uninterrupted curiosity of contemporary poets for Sappho and Catullus reveals the creative allure of the literary pair even today.

The 'translocal stretch'

Enhanced possibilities for transnational exchange in the twentieth century and the increased mobility of modern writers facilitated the circulation of particular interpretative paradigms on Sappho and Catullus beyond national borders. The Anglo-American poets considered in this book led intensely 'transnational lives'.[49] Leaving the United States in their twenties, Ezra Pound and H.D. came to Europe at the turn of the century, establishing themselves in London and Paris. Pound then moved to Italy in 1925; H.D. lived in the UK, France, Switzerland and Austria, where she underwent analysis with Sigmund Freud.[50] Between 1950 and 1953, Lowell travelled around Europe (Hobsbaum 1988: 72–3). Zukofsky was the son of Russian-Jewish immigrants. While the Italian authors I consider did not live lives characterized by the same degree of transnational movement, the 'translocal stretch' (Ramazani 2009: 14) of modern poetry plays a key role in shaping the supranational discourse on Sappho and Catullus. According to this model, all modern poetry, even in its most apparently nationalistic guise, is inherently transnational because it is enmeshed with the development of tropes and genres which are taken from a trans-linguistic tradition that re-uses material from cross-national sources. Therefore, although it may be a valuable starting point, a critical paradigm focusing exclusively on the national aspect of the reception of Sappho and Catullus risks embedding a methodological approach that remains insufficient.

As Ramazani stated, '[b]ecause of the interconnecting cultural traces wound into the DNA of poetic forms and poetic language, poetry's cross-national molecular structure betrays the national imaginary on behalf of which it is sometimes made to speak' (2009: 13). Following an analogous line of thought, Matthew Reynolds pointed at the love sonnet as an inherently transcultural genre since its inception (2016: 56). The same goes for the lyric poetry of Sappho and Catullus. Indeed, as well as circulating transnationally, in the twentieth and twenty-first centuries, Sappho and Catullus are woven into and inform the translocal character of the modern lyric poetry that they came to symbolize.

From Italy to North America and Back

In this book I consider the transnational reception of Sappho and Catullus focusing on Italy and North America, two pivotal centres of their modern reception, where communities of readers and writers have consistently engaged with the two poets from the beginning of the twentieth century to the present day. Studying sightings from both the New World and Europe widens the range of the investigation, especially considering the different linguistic, geographical and educational relationships Italy and North America have with Graeco-Roman antiquity. Despite the significant decentralization of ancient cultures in favour of modern ones in the second half of the twentieth century,[51] Italian cultural identity is still very much negotiated in relation to the classics, whether to invoke, renew or refute them. However much the labels attributed to Greek and Roman cultures may sway between the positive (timeless, beautiful, original), or the negative (old, stale, hegemonic), in Italy the ancient classics continue to hold cultural capital. As Carlo Caruso eloquently put it, 'classical antiquity appears to have retained an uncanny ability to brand itself in a variety of ways without losing the prerogative of being perceived as *one* phenomenon' (2018: 2). Greek, and especially Latin, have been taught in high schools in Italy since 1859 with the Legge Casati, which established a high-school classical strand, whose main subject was Latin, with even more contact hours per week than Italian. In 1923, the reforms of the education system by Giovanni Gentile, the neo-idealist philosopher and Minister of Public Education, gave even more impetus to humanistic education. Until the 1960s, Latin was a required subject in all Italian high schools. Gentile gave prominence to the Liceo Classico and Liceo Scientifico – schools to prepare the Italian elites. Until 1969, Liceo Classico, where both Ancient Greek and Latin were (and still are) required studies, was the only school which granted access to university. The legislation, passed in 1923 while Gentile was Minister of Public Education, still largely informs many aspects of the Italian school system. Selections of Sappho and Catullus, excluding the sexually explicit and scatological poems, have been part of the Liceo Classico's syllabus since its inception.

Italy's geographical and linguistic contiguity with Greek and Roman antiquity has engendered a classically oriented predisposition through which cultural identity is often negotiated. Italianness is often configured as a tendency toward conservation and balance over innovation and rupture, because classical antiquity is mostly perceived as an un-dead presence shaping the Italian landscape, language and literature (Camilletti 2018). A walk around Rome, or indeed the majority of Italian cities, quickly reveals the tangible contiguity between Hellenic and Roman cultures and contemporary Italy. Besides the monuments and ruins dotting the landscape, Latin and Greek still echo in inscriptions, while Graeco-Roman aesthetics reverberate in neoclassical monuments and Fascist appropriations. Various forms of classicism have shaped the conventions of Italian art and literature from the fourteenth century onwards; throughout time, including in many ways in the twentieth century, 'the modern' has been repeatedly defined against the benchmark of classical standards.[52]

In the North American tradition, the history of the relationship with the classics is, of course, much shorter and does not have to negotiate the same geographical contiguity with Graeco-Roman culture. Yet, modelled on European cultural politics, the classics have been associated with cultural capital in the United States since the eighteenth century.[53] Ancient Greek and Latin classics still suggest cultural and social elitism, but they are considerably less popular than in Italy, with very few people today knowing Latin or Greek. While Latin is taught in some high schools, and despite being a relatively popular subject, it is usually an elective, and Greek tuition is virtually absent. According to the Texas Classical Association, as of 2000, only thirteen state schools offered Ancient Greek in the United States.[54] Until the 1960s, Catullus was usually not taught at secondary school (Ancona and Hallett 2007: 483).

Although not immediately evident, there are several points of contact between Italian and North American literary cultures, connecting the Sappho and Catullus constellation across the two countries. Some are evident, others hidden. In the twentieth century, the exchange between the Anglo-American Modernists and Italian literary tradition was profound – Dante Alighieri was the main bridge. The Italian poet was a guide for key Modernists such as Ezra Pound, T. S. Eliot, James Joyce and Samuel Beckett, who turned to him to talk about literary authority, craftmanship and literary psychology (Leland 1992: 965). Pound, whose rewritings of Sappho and Catullus I discuss in Chapter 2, together with the works of H.D., devoted the final chapter of his first book, *The Spirit of Romance* ([1910–29] 2005) to Dante. Dante would become one of Pound's primary inspirations, a reading guide shaping his own personal canon and approach to poetry. Reacting against philology as an exercise in the reconstruction of texts serving the purposes of newly fashioned national ideologies and literary canons, Pound distanced himself from Anglo-American identities and defined himself as a direct descendant of Dante, the medieval troubadours and ancient melic poetry. Through this transnational afflatus, he was drawn to Dante's *De vulgari eloquentia* (On Eloquence in the Vernacular), the work that best expressed analogous views to his own attempt at founding a 'U.S. verse' based on spoken language (Kenner 1985: 43). *The Cantos*, whose title places Pound's work into the tradition of *La Divina Commedia* (*The Divine Comedy*), open as a descent to hell.[55] T. S. Eliot's *Wasteland* (1922) is another modernist *inferno*, while 'Little Gidding' (1942), the last of his *Four Quartets* (1943), evokes Brunetto Latini's episode in *Purgatorio* XV. Their Irish contemporaries took Dante as a model of the poet in exile, with Joyce's *Ulysses* ([1922] 1993) as yet another hellish vision, while Beckett used the *De vulgari eloquentia*'s model to criticize the dominance of English in Ireland, probing the correlations between national and literary languages.[56]

The Modernists' relationship with Italy went beyond the literary. Ezra Pound lived in Rapallo between 1925 and 1945 and returned after his release from St Elizabeth's hospital between 1958 and the year of his death in 1972. James Joyce made Trieste his home from 1904 to 1915. At the time, it was a territory of Austria-Hungary although Italian was the main language spoken. He also spent a year in Rome between 1906 and 1907. They both participated in the intellectual life of Italy. Pound published several of his works there for the first time. As though following in Pound's footsteps, Lowell, in the 1950s, also lived for a time in Italy (Hobsbaum 1988: 72–3). Translation, as 'an active transactional reading practice between cultures' (Caselli and La Penna 2008: 4), represents the main vehicle of exchange between Italian and North American poetry. Italian writing was one of the main strands in translations in English, 'one woven with the succession of trends and debates that have characterized Anglo-American cultures' (Venuti 2000: 467). This engagement is concentrated in the second half of the century, with Ungaretti, Quasimodo and Montale being translated, albeit with some delay, in the 1950s.[57] As discussed in Chapter 4, Lowell, who was a key player in US poetic culture, read and translated several Italian poets, including Leopardi, Ungaretti and Montale in *Imitations* (1961), his anthology of creative translations; the same volume contained some of his rewritings of Sappho. In Italy, American fiction was widely translated from the 1930s and US verse circulated among poets.[58] In contrast with the hegemony of Humanist and Renaissance Italy in the world of letters, twentieth-century Italian literature was peripheral to the dominant power of US and British literary cultures worldwide. Within the poetry scene, translating foreign modern texts was an extremely popular practice, overriding the historical predominance of classical literature. The figure of the poet-translator became central to the literary world, with translation representing a main source of income for poets in the second half of the century.[59] The Anglo-American modernist aesthetic was crucial for many poets in Italy; T. S. Eliot and Pound were translated widely.

The sightings of Sappho and Catullus here analysed are caught within this complex transnational network, which I begin to chart. For instance, Salvatore Quasimodo's Sappho, which he translated in his 1940 anthology *Lirici greci*, landed in the United States via the Poundian school; before sending her translations to Pound, Mary Barnard spoke highly of Quasimodo's anthology, saying that his translations had inspired her own versions of Sappho (1984: 281–2). Barnard's episode is a testament to the complex interrelation between the local and transnational in the modern reception of Sappho and Catullus.

For obvious space limitations, perhaps I have had to leave out far more examples than I could include in this book – Barnard's episode, for one, is described in more depth in Chapter 3, but I do not analyse her translations. I first and foremost selected poets for whom both Sappho and Catullus were fundamental references; secondly, I wanted to present some of the most original or influential takes on Sappho and Catullus since the 1900s. I was particularly interested in exploring how the two ancient poets have dialogued with and informed individual poetics throughout the century, while maintaining a transnational perspective in order to begin recording any elements of the two poets' constellation across cultures. The analysis continuously negotiates the relationship between the translocal and local dimensions of Sappho's and Catullus's modern reception. On the one hand, the two ancient poets are involved in a wider discourse on lyric poetry and poetics; on the other hand, the single Italian and North American poets are rooted within individual national traditions and the respective histories of engagement with Sappho and Catullus and the classics at large.

Who? What? When? And Why?

My analysis considers translations and rewritings of Sappho's and Catullus's poetry and biographies by various influential poets of 'the long twentieth century', starting with the juvenile rewritings of Giovanni Pascoli in the 1880s and finishing in the 2010s with Anne Carson's reinvention of Catullus 101 in *Nox* (2010) and Rosita Copioli's 2016 poem 'Saffo'. Countering Eric Hobsbawm's 'short twentieth century' (1994) beginning with the First World War in 1914 and finishing at the end of the Cold War in 1989, the 'long twentieth century', recently defined by contemporary historians and increasingly used in literary studies and teaching, reflects the need to account for a continuity of trends and ideas between fin-de-siècle and twentieth-century literature as well as the spill overs between late twentieth- and early twenty-first-century literary cultures.[60]

I am concerned with both the overt and the hidden literary reception of Sappho and Catullus in this period. I therefore study not only published translations, creative rewritings and aesthetic prose on the two ancient authors, but also some relevant unpublished documents and private correspondence by modern poets. Considering both published and unpublished documents is fundamental to illuminate and understand the dynamics of the modern reception of Sappho and Catullus, assessing, on the one hand, how the literary pair entered the public literary domain and, on the other hand, how they shaped the poetic laboratories of the writers considered, interacting with the development of key twentieth-century poetics.

The analyses of published and autograph material are carried out through close readings supported by principles of textual criticism and a combined framework employing reception, translation, gender and sexuality theories. The various sources considered are contextualized within contemporary literary cultures and broader transnational trends in the reception of Sappho and Catullus across Italy, the Anglo-American world and Europe. Moreover, throughout the book, a critical closeness to texts is matched and given breadth by forms of comparative 'distant' reading of the kind advocated by Franco Moretti (2000: 56–8). These emphasize the occurrence of shared themes, tropes and devices in order to interrogate the cross-cultural relations occurring in the reception of Sappho and Catullus as world literature authors.

Unless otherwise specified, whenever I refer to 'the reception of Sappho' or 'the reception of Catullus', I mean the general complex of their reception, including the fortune of their works, their critical appraisal and the various fictions about their lives and poetic personas. I also use the term 'translation' in a rather encompassing form. I refer to target texts aiming at semantic equivalence and fidelity to the source such as academic translations, as well as creative or generative target texts, namely, those translations, as defined by Stephen Yao, that serve an 'expressly generative and literary mode of writing, rather than a principally linguistic operation limited in scope simply to reproducing the "meaning" of a foreign text' (2002: 13–14). These types of translations include works such as Ezra Pound's *Homage to Sextus Propertius* (1919) or Louis

Zukofsky's *Catullus* (1969),[61] which should be deemed comparable to and constitutive of other forms of poetry and prose (Yao 2002: 14). Therefore, I am less interested in assessing a translating strategy's success than considering its creative import, the poetic outlook it may carry and what this does to and with modern conceptualizations of Sappho's and Catullus's source texts.

My considerations are based on the premise articulated by Matthew Reynolds that 'there is fundamentally no such thing as "an original": there is only the source text that gives rise to interpretations in collaboration with readers' (2016: 59). Reynolds spells out and brings forward Walter Benjamin's seminal reflection that 'a translation issues from the original – not so much from its life as from its afterlife' ([1923] 1999: 72). This is part of the constitution of Sappho and Catullus, whose original lost texts make any translation into an act of interpretative textual reconstruction. Indeed, Karen Emmerich has noted how, especially in cases where the source is fragmented or consists of several texts, translation defines 'the content and form of an "original" in the act of creating yet another textual manifestation of a literary work in a new language' (2017: 2). This dynamic of realization of the original in its afterlife is particularly relevant for Sappho, who 'is both the active principle "in" translation and the product "of" translation' (Prins 1999: 40), but the same is valid for Catullus. The authorial and cultural positioning of poet-translators toward Sappho and Catullus, and the literary material emerging from their interpretative and creative acts, are the objects of study of this book.

This requires probing translating approaches against not only individual poetics, but also translation history and current translation theories. Indeed, as Lefevere (1975) drawing on Paz (1970) remarked, if we consider it as a function of literature, poetic translation will engage with the tradition that sets the terms of the art (1975: 5). At the same time, the socio-cultural contexts informing various positionings toward Sappho and Catullus are investigated in order to assess how translations and rewritings of the ancient poets bring into play particular constructions of origins, gender, sexuality, authorial and national identities.

While alongside translations I consider creative rewritings of Sappho and Catullus, the study of translating practices has proven fundamental for gauging the transnational dimension of the ancient poets' reception. As Venuti remarks, translation 'enables the international reception of literary texts' and at the same time is 'fundamentally a localizing practice' since the translation process is 'mediated by values, beliefs, and representations in the receiving situation' (2011: 180). Translation is also one of the main vehicles for the creation of literary canons, a matter which is particularly relevant for my analysis given that the circulation of Sappho and Catullus in the twentieth century is, in most cases, granted by their assigned role as lyric models. The analysis of translating practices at translocal and local levels is fundamental to the discussion in this book.

In order to facilitate the dialogue between the two dimensions, this book alternates chapters on Italian and North American contexts. Chapter 1 is on the Italian poet Giovanni Pascoli (1855–1912), a foundational figure for Italian twentieth-century poetry, focusing on his works in Italian and Neo-Latin from the 1880s to the 1910s. I show that Sappho and Catullus were crucial to the creation of Pascoli's literary and symbolic systems. His juvenile poetic laboratory, analysed using a considerable amount of unpublished material I found during archival research, reveals that Sappho's and Catullus's works are behind Pascoli's later use of images of blooming flowers as symbols of eroticism, hymenaic themes and poetic creation. In his mature work, the literary pair is entangled with mythopoeic processes: representations of ritual and mythical patterns linked to natural cycles, such as the alternation of day and night, the motif of eros and thanatos and patterns of death and rebirth. These helped him define his approach to poetry as an enquiry into the origins of humankind and the sources of life, while revealing a tendency toward normalizing sexuality, reflecting contemporary moralizing attitudes toward sexual promiscuity in Italy. Pascoli's poetics of appropriation and mythical rewritings had considerable resonance among later Italian poets, including several discussed in this book; similarly, it is possible to trace a line of continuity between Ezra Pound and several of the North American poets who follow him in the discussion.

Chapter 2 considers Sappho and Catullus in the modernist works of Pound (1885–1972) and H.D. (1886–1961), the latter mostly interested in Sappho. I discuss the ancient poets' role as catalysts for the development of the modernist movement of Imagism founded by the two American poets, their poetics of fragmentation, as well as their works after the Imagist experience. While growing into two very different artists, Pound's and H.D.'s rewritings of Sappho and Catullus in the 1920s and 1930s share with Pascoli an interest in the motifs of eros and thanatos, hymenaic themes and the legend of Sappho and Phaon as a solar myth. These appear to be based on a similar search for the underlying patterns ordering and uniting consciousness and culture. But if Pascoli's and Pound's rewritings uphold heteronormative and male-centred fictions of Sappho and Catullus, H.D.'s works address issues of gender and female sexuality.

Chapter 3 deals with the translations by the 1959 Nobel Prize Winner Salvatore Quasimodo, enveloping Sappho and Catullus into his Hermeticist poetics aimed at the foundation of a new literary humanism. The analysis of some of Quasimodo's unpublished correspondence reveals aspects of the intellectual network that formed around Sappho and Catullus. The discussion enters post-war poetry in Chapter 4 with an analysis of Robert Lowell's take on Sappho in *Imitations* (1961) and how he recast Sappho and Catullus as confessional poets. His rewritings are juxtaposed with the 1969 objectivist take on Catullus by Louis Zukofsky, who, with his wife Celia, attempted a homophonic translation of Catullus's poetry. That year also saw the publication of Guido Ceronetti's own translation of Catullus, an irreverent volume that for the first time in Italy brought the obscenities and vulgarities of Catullus's verse to the page. Together with his gnostic take on Sappho, Ceronetti's Catullus occupies the first part of Chapter 5; the second is dedicated to the highly refined and idiosyncratic Sappho by Rosita Copioli (1948–) and includes excerpts from a rich unpublished interview on the poet's relationship with Sappho, Catullus and poetry at large. Her Sappho, painted in neo-platonic hues and incarnating a divine view of eros, is at the antipodes of Ceronetti's desacralizing Catullus. The book ends with the postmodern take on Sappho and Catullus by the Canadian poet Anne Carson (1950–), whom I also had the pleasure of interviewing a few years ago. Carson's comments on her translating and poetic practices support my analysis.

Within this bubbling diversity there are significant themes and patterns emerging across the Italian and North American receptions of Sappho and Catullus. In addition to the shared imagery among Pascoli, Pound and H.D., I investigate some recurring themes among the various poets' receptions, which also negotiate discourses on individual and collective identities, often based on questions of origins. Most prominent are: first, an interest in eros as a life-giving power driving poetic faculties; second, the identification of Sappho and Catullus as lyric models and a consequent designation of their poetry either as the first mythopoeic expression of a shared human essence, or as a way into forms of mythic revisionism aimed at questioning heteronormative and patriarchal gender structures. These are just some of the elements that I attempt to unpack in what follows. Although it will not be possible to exhaust the discussion of Sappho and Catullus as a transnational literary pair, I hope the dual comparative perspective on their reception will illuminate several uncharted corners of their global constellation, opening new avenues for future scholarship.

1

Mythical Rewritings

As you walk into Giovanni Pascoli's studio, a neat wide room in his home in the Tuscan village of Castelvecchio, three late-nineteenth-century wooden desks of various shapes and sizes soon catch the eye. He notoriously used each of them for a different occupation: one to compose his Italian poetry, another for his Latin verse and a third to pen his Dantean criticism.[1] Pascoli's knowledge and command of ancient languages was remarkable: he wrote as much poetry in Latin as he did in Italian and his few epigrams in classical Greek stand out as refined stylistic exercises.[2] While his volumes on Dante were never received well by the academy, a cause of great distress for Pascoli,[3] his three working desks are reminders of the equal importance of the classical and vernacular traditions in his intellectual life.

With his sister Maria, Pascoli spent the last seventeen years of his life from 1895 to 1912 in this immaculate country home, interrupted only by his teaching commitments.[4] Now a museum and archive of his papers, the house was bought with five of the thirteen golden medals Pascoli had won over the years at the *Certamen poeticum Hoeufftianum*, the prestigious competition of Neo-Latin poetry that took place in Amsterdam between 1845 and 1978.[5] Pascoli would travel to and from Castelvecchio while carrying out his duties as professor of classics at the universities of Bologna, Messina and Pisa, eventually taking over the chair of Italian literature back in Bologna, following in the footsteps of his mentor and fellow poet Giosue Carducci.[6] His poetry of small things and his linguistic experimentalism, found in the lyric fragments of *Myricae* (1892–1903) and the rural world of *Canti di Castelvecchio* (Songs of Castelvecchio) (1903), were very influential for later generations of Italian poets.[7] The mythopoeic project of *Poemi convivali* (Convivial poems) (1904–5) was his most popular collection outside Italy – a series of narrative poems tracing the history of western literature from its origins to early Christianity, characterized by Pascoli's personal rewriting of myth. By the end of his life in 1912, Pascoli had become, with Gabriele d'Annunzio, one of the leading poets in early twentieth-century Italy.

His scholarly and creative endeavours mutually informed each other to shape a type of poetic anthropology. With his ambitious and vast poetic project, Pascoli aimed at recovering the shared origins of humankind, which he found in the archaic myths narrated in Greek and Latin literatures and the biblical and Vedic traditions.[8] Painted as two fundamental poetic archetypes in the history of literature and humanity, Sappho and Catullus inhabit not only Pascoli's Italian poetry, but also his criticism and Latin verse. From the very beginning of his poetic career to maturity, he closely analysed, translated and reused the work of both poets idealizing and rewriting their lives.

Already as a university student in Bologna (1874–80) and then as a young school teacher in Matera (1880–84), Pascoli had spent a lot of time thinking and writing about Sappho and Catullus. Echoes of both ancient poets' verse emerge from his early publications; moreover, a wide unpublished corpus of autographs, notebooks and notes, while mostly intended for personal use, reveal an intense workshop concentrating on the two ancient poets.[9] Heralding his mythologization of Sappho and Catullus in his later work, this literary pair is entangled with young Pascoli's reflection on ancient myth as a paradigm of existence and a primordial linguistic formulation of the relationship between human life and natural cycles.

The second and more mature period of engagement with the two ancient poets covers four intense years, from 1895 to 1899, when Pascoli published the bulk of his creative and critical output on Sappho and Catullus while working as a professor of classics at the universities of Bologna (1895–97) and Messina (1897–1903).

This includes three main works: the opening poem of *Poemi conviviali*, 'Solon', first printed in 1895, which places Sappho at the origins of the western poetic tradition by rewriting the Ovidian legend of her suicide for Phaon into a solar myth on the natural cycle of day and night;[10] the high-school anthology of Latin poetry *Lyra* ([1899] 1915), comprising a selection of Catullus's poems with a commentary and a long prefatory essay entitled 'La poesia lirica in Roma: commentario primo' (Lyric poetry in Rome: first commentary);[11] and, finally, the Latin poem *Catullocalvos* (1897), a Catullan pastiche narrating a poetic game between Catullus and C. Licinius Calvus inspired by *Cat.* 50.[12]

As he was working on Sappho and Catullus between 1895 and 1897, the poet also wrote and published the first version of his essay 'Il fanciullino' (The little child),[13] a long contemplation of the nature of poetry and of poetic inspiration, now widely acknowledged as the kernel of Pascoli's poetics. The essay identifies classical antiquity and ancient myth as foundational sources of humankind's cognitive and psychological structures, shaping archetypal notions of desire, death, sorrow and art.[14] It describes the poetic faculty as an ancient child, who, by virtue of his innocence, can see the world anew:

> Tu sei il fanciullo eterno, che vede tutto con maraviglia, tutto come per la prima volta. [...] Tu sei antichissimo, o fanciullo! E vecchissimo è il mondo che tu vedi nuovamente! E primitivo il ritmo (non questo o quello, ma il ritmo in generale) col quale tu, in certo modo, lo culli o lo danzi! [...] veder nuovo e veder da antico, e dire ciò che non s'è mai detto e dirlo come sempre si è detto e si dirà!
>
> (You are the eternal child, who looks at everything with wonder, everything as for the first time. [...] You are most ancient, oh child! Like the world that you see anew! And the rhythm (not a particular one, but rhythm in general) with which you, in some way, cradle it and dance with it is also primitive! [...] to see anew and to see as an ancient, and to say what has never been said and to say it as it has always been said and will be said!)
>
> Pascoli [1907] 1914: 13–15

Like a child that looks at the world for the first time, in the same way as the unspoilt ancient civilizations at the dawn of time, a poet creates new visions of the present in a universal aesthetic dimension. Indeed, the *fanciullino* is paradoxically defined 'antichissimo' (most ancient), while he is also the main agent of modern, novel myth-making.[15] A direct illustration of these views, Pascoli's vast body of work reaches toward grasping the most primitive cultural manifestations of the poetic faculty to re-enact them in the present, in the firm belief that humanity ought to find its shared defining essence in poetry and myth. An idea Pascoli takes up again in a 1905 address:

> Per vero, io non sono così antiquato da confondere l'idea di antichità con quella di bellezza; ma so quel che tutti sanno, che nelle letterature greca e romana è in alcuni scrittori o almeno in alcuni scritti ciò che si può chiamare l'eterno, che è sempre nuovo.
>
> (Truly, I am not as old-fashioned as to confound the idea of antiquity with that of beauty; but I know what everybody else knows: that in Greek and Roman literatures there is, in some writers or at least in some writings, what may be called the eternal, that is always new.)
>
> Pascoli [1907] 1914: 268

The ancient writings of Sappho and Catullus are repositories of a universal poetic sentiment, the 'eternal that is always new', which became the primary object of Pascoli's artistic and academic enquiry. At the same time, Pascoli's *fanciullino*, lost in the age of disenchanted modernity (Pascoli [1907] 1914: 45–6), takes the poet beyond a neoclassical interpretation of antiquity as a beautiful perfection to imitate ('I am not as old-fashioned as to confound the idea of antiquity with that of beauty');[16] we are presented with a post-Romantic idealization of the primitive and spontaneity, which uses classical works as repositories of lyric and dramatic motifs to be appropriated and reclaimed.

In this chapter I discuss how Sappho and Catullus are called upon by Pascoli to explore the poetic origins of humankind and re-enact them in the present through his mythologizing rewritings and domesticating translations. It emerges that his appropriative approach to the two ancient poets is consistent with late-nineteenth-century scholarly interests in their biographies, while his process of recreation reflects gender constructions and normalizing attitudes toward homosexuality in fin-de-siècle Italy.

Sappho and Catullus at the origins: Pascoli's poetic laboratory (1877–84)

Sappho

The autograph material I found in the maze of the Castelvecchio archive shows that Pascoli studied contemporary scholarship on Sappho, translated the larger part of the extant Sapphic canon and used it as a starting point for his own poetry from his early twenties, giving us an insight into the relationship between his ancient sources and his creative processes.[17] A notebook entitled 'Studi di traduzione dal Greco' (Studies of translation from Greek) dating to 1881–82 contains thirty-nine draft translations of Sappho's fragments, including some early versions of frr. 1 and 31.[18] The autographs of fr. 1, the only poem to be translated twice in the notebook, reveal the seeds of his later re-elaborations in 'Preghiera a Afrodite' (Prayer to Aphrodite), an 1899 translation of fr. 1 included in *Lyra*,[19] which reflects Pascoli's reinvention of the legend of Sappho's love for Phaon into a solar myth (I discuss this text in the next section).

In fr. 1, an unrequited lover named Sappho invokes Aphrodite to win the attention of her beloved. Historically, because of an ambiguity in the Greek text, fr. 1 was often interpreted as a heterosexual poem; in Pascoli's time, though, this interpretation, which was based on the Ovidian tradition, had already been debunked by Theodor Bergk, whose 1843 edition provided textual evidence confirming Sappho's beloved in fr. 1 to be a woman.[20] Pascoli was well aware of this; indeed, he used Bergk's third edition of *Poetae Melici* (1867) as his source text for these translations of Sappho.[21] However, he deliberately translated the end of fr. 1 in such a way as to keep the gender of Sappho's beloved ambiguous.

In his initial revision of his first draft, Pascoli excises all references to the gender of the beloved from the penultimate stanza, in which Aphrodite reassures Sappho that, by virtue of love's justice, the beloved who now makes her suffer will soon undergo the same experience.[22] Below I provide the text of the penultimate stanza of fr. 1 edition and a diplomatic transcription of Pascoli's translation draft:

καὶ γὰρ αἰ φεύγει, ταχέως διώξει,
αἰ δὲ δῶρα μὴ δέκετ', ἀλλὰ δώσει,
αἰ δὲ μὴ φίλει, ταχέως φιλήσει
κωὐκ ἐθέλοισα.

ll. 21–4, Bergk 1867: 86

     se   ti
Poiché ~~quella che~~ fugge, presto inseguirà
     se
e ~~quella che~~ non riceve di doni, invece li darà
    se
E ~~quella~~ che non ama, presto amerà
        anche se non voglia.[23]

(Because ~~that woman who~~ if she/he runs away, she/he will soon chase, / and ~~that woman who~~ if she/he does not receive gifts, she/he will give them instead, / and ~~that woman who~~ if she/he does not love, she/he will soon love, / even if he/she did not want to.)

MS LXXIV, 3, fol. 161 / G.74.3.1 = Piantanida 2013: 187

All feminine demonstrative subject pronouns 'quella' (that woman) disappear. There are certainly poetic and metrical reasons behind Pascoli's decision: aiming toward a hendecasyllable, the two-syllable formula 'se ti' is smoother and more economical than the clunky three syllables of 'quella che'. Indeed, the second re-drafting, in which these edits are maintained, reveals a progressive refining of the poetic solutions to fit a rigorous metrical pattern of Italian Sapphic stanzas. However, the work of *labor limae*, leaving the gender of Sappho's beloved open to interpretation, affects a partial normalization of the homoerotic desire expressed in the original Greek, which, as we shall see, also conveniently supports Pascoli's use of the Ovidian legend of Sappho's love for Phaon in his later writings. I give here the text of the second draft according to my 2013 edition:

chè s'or ti schifa, ti verrà **poi** dietro;

E se i regali |**or**| ti rimanda, presto
ne farà; t'amerà, via, **se** non t'ama
Voglia o non voglia[24]

(If she/he now despises you, she/he will then go after you; / and if she/he sends back your gifts, soon / she/he will give some; she/he will love, then, if she/he does not love you, / whether she/he wants it or not)

MS LXXIV, 3, fol. 168 / G.74.3.1 = Piantanida 2013: 193

Pascoli adds direct objects ('ti', 'you') after verbs detailing the consequences for Sappho's lover ('ti schifa' (despises you), 'ti verrà poi dietro' (will go after you), 't'amerà' (will love you)). Although many readers have assumed 'you' to be the most natural supplement, direct objects are absent in the original, which suggests that these lines are primarily concerned with the general context of love's universal rules rather than Sappho's individual situation.[25] The translation brings the stanza into Sappho's private sphere, evoking a more conventional lyric scenario of unrequited love.[26]

Pascoli's reticence in expressing Sappho's homoeroticism was consistent with some of the leading critical theories at the time. In a notebook of personal notes from the early 1880s, he recorded the interpretations of the German scholar J. Welcker and the Italian Domenico Comparetti; both scholars, while acknowledging that Sappho loved women, argued that the feelings articulated in her lyrics were the poetic expression of a form of ideal love – chaste, pure and never sensual.[27] Comparetti was a central figure in the Italian academy at the end of the nineteenth century (Nava 1984: 511). While still partly challenging Sappho's homoeroeticism, in two important 1876 articles he firmly argued for the need to distinguish Sappho the author from her poetic persona and the Ovidian character. Meditating on the impossibility of determining who she really was, Comparetti cast her into a figure of modernity: 'Saffo non è il nome di una poetessa: è un personaggio poetico dei moderni, ed inevitabilmente nell'animo dell'uomo odierno (e della donna), per poco còlto ch'egli sia, il di lei nome si associa con idee sentimentali, romantiche e poetiche' (Sappho is not the name of a poet: she is a modern poetic character, and inevitably her name is associated, in the mind of today's man (and woman), even if little educated, with sentimental, romantic and poetic ideas) (Comparetti 1876: 253). Such iconic value as a lyric archetype and her active presence in modern consciousness fuelled Pascoli's deep investment in Sappho's works, too. In yet another notebook containing notes toward a critical project on Lesbian lyric, he commented:[28]

> Uscendo dalle fredde regioni della critica, ritempriamo l'anima nella contemplazione della vera Saffo, nella eternamente attraente realtà sua, lieti di poter tutt'ora ripetere [...] che vivono tuttavia, [...] i poetici affettuosi ardori sfogati in carmi divini dall'anima bella della donna di Lesbo. [...]
>
> Saffo è la lirica nel più stretto senso della parola, e l'amore non corrisposto sa esprimere vivamente con un lirismo infuocato che dipinge intiero lo stato dell'anima sua delirante...

(Going beyond the cold regions of criticism, let us comfort our soul by contemplating the true Sappho, in her eternally attractive reality, glad to be able to say even now that her poetic and affectionate ardour, released in divine poems by the beautiful soul of the woman from Lesbos, is alive. [...]

Sappho is lyric poetry in the strictest sense of the word, and she can express unrequited love vividly and with an inflamed lyricism that depicts the status of her delirious soul.)

MS LXXXI, 3, fol. 10/G.81.3

These notes reveal the intersections between international classical philology and Pascoli's creativity; they also show that Pascoli valued the idealized portrayal of Sappho painted by the literary tradition more than the Sappho of scholarship, which was perceived as an empty and cold vessel. The symbolic function of Sappho and her burning lyricism inflamed by eros would be fully exploited by the poet later in his career in his mythical rewritings of the 1890s.

Sappho emerges as one of the sources of Pascoli's earliest reflections on the nature of poetry and artistic creation in another fundamental autograph, MS LXX, 9, fol. 8^{r-v}/ G.70.9.1, which contains a draft translation of fr. 3Bergk (34Voigt) with an accompanying prose,[29] followed by a series of rewritings of fr. 109Bergk (114Voigt). The prose stresses Sappho's archetypal function in Pascoli's literary imagination:

> Non è codesto un graziosissimo idillio mitico nella
> sua indeterminatezza?
> [...]
> Questo non è mito: non fa appello a nessuna tradizione:

a nessuna favola: a nessuna rappresentazione plastica
o pittorica: è proprio naturalmente sbocciato nella mente
    di Saffo.

(Isn't this, in its indeterminacy, an extremely pretty mythical idyll? [...] This is not myth: it is not drawing from any tradition or fable, or any plastic or figurative representation: it is truly naturally bloomed in Sappho's mind.)

MS LXX, 9, fol. 8^r/ G.70.9.1 = Piantanida 2013: 203-5[30]

The metaphor of blooming as renewal, rebirth and creative power is taken up by Pascoli over and over again in his poetry. The rest of the autograph shows that this pattern has a Sapphic origin.

After the prose, the attention focuses onto epithalamic poetry, with a literal translation of fr. 109Bergk. The Greek source text accompanies the translation on the recto:

Παρθενία, Παρθενία, ποῖ με λιποισ' οἴχῃ;
Οὐκέτι ἥξω προς σέ, οὐκέτι ἥξω

MS LXX, 9, fol. 8^r/ G.70.9.1 = Piantanida 2013: 204

Verginità, verginità dove m'andasti che non sei quà:
Non tornerò verso te più, non tornerò, non mai, non più

(Virginity, virginity, where did you go, you are not here:
I will not return to you, I will not return, not ever, not any more)

MSLXX, 9, fol. 8^v/ G.70.9.1 = Piantanida 2013: 204

This translation is then modified and incorporated into various poetic fragments through a series of word substitutions. The invocation to 'Παρθενία' (Virginity) here translated with the vocative 'Verginità' (Virginity) is then exchanged with the phrase 'Botton di rosa' (rose button), creating a rich poetic analogy:

Botton di rosa, botton di rosa.
Dove m'andasti, dove sei tu?
S'è aperto il fiore, sbocciò la rosa,
cadran le foglie, |la gioventù| non torna più.
    bocciuol di rosa non torni più.

(Rose button, rose button. / Where did you go? Where are you now? / The flower has opened, the rose bloomed, / the leaves will fall, youth will never return / rose bud you will never return.)

MS LXX, 9, fol. 8^v/ G.70.9.1 = Piantanida 2013: 204

The substitutions establish a direct link between virginity and the image of blooming flowers, a recurring pattern in Sappho's epithalamia, where the bride is often given floral attributes (e.g. frr. 93 and 94).

Tellingly, more than ten years later, Pascoli would use the phrase 'Botton di rosa' again in one of his own poems from the cycle 'Nelle nozze di Ida' (For Ida's Wedding) (1895), written for the wedding of his sister:

> Ricordi? la siepe ... ricordi? ...
> di rose era tutto un bottone;
> e larghi s'aprivano i fior di
>   passione!

(Remember? The hedge ... remember? / all covered in rose buttons; / and opening wide the flowers / of passion!)

ll. 1–4 = M. Pascoli [1933] 1943: 49

As in the Sapphic rewritings, the image of rose buds is employed metaphorically to refer to the moment of the discovery of eros in the rite of passage of the wedding. The use of the word 'bottone' (button) – otherwise quite rare in Pascoli's oeuvre – in both 'Nelle nozze di Ida' and the autograph rewritings connects the phytomorphic representation of virginity with the lament for the loss of maidenhood described in Sappho 109Bergk. This is made explicit in the final lines of Pascoli's poem, ending on a virgin's song: 'Cantava una vergine: fior di / passione!' (A virgin sang: flowers of / passion!) (ll. 7–8).

Meeting a fin-de-siècle taste, this Sapphic framework informs Pascoli's frequent use of blooming as a poetic symbol of eroticism, defloration and poetic creation in his wider oeuvre.[31] In *Primi poemetti* ([1904] 1997), especially in the well-known texts 'Digitale purpurea' (Purple foxglove) and 'Il vischio' (The mistletoe), Pascoli employs the same images he used in his early autographs, of a flower opening, falling on the ground and fading, to evoke erotic desire, while the symbol of the woman-flower acquires the strongest sexual connotations (15–76).[32]

These analogic structures are also loci in which Pascoli constructs his poetic syncretism. The fourth poetic rewriting shows how Pascoli fits the phytomorphic representations into a contemporary popular context. On the one hand, he continues to refer to the previous hymenaic setting; on the other, he inserts the hymenaic theme within a traditional backdrop of Easter festivities:

> viole e rose, rose e viole
> non fanno gioia che solo a Pasqua
> sono sbocciate per appassir.

(violets and roses, roses and violets / they do not bring joy but at Easter / they have bloomed to fade.)

MS LXX, 9, fol. 8ᵛ/ G.70.9.1 = Piantanida 2013: 205

The *doppi quinari*'s (double five-syllable lines) rhythm recalls that of the popular ballads employed by Pascoli in *Canti di Castelvecchio*; the violets, roses and seeds drag the fragment into a rural farming landscape, while the reference to Easter connotes both festive and religious contexts. Ending the series, the last rewritings compare the woman to a seed. This metaphor is rich, bringing the spheres of love, sex and marriage in contact with that of the natural cycles: 'Cadean le foglie, restava un seme, / Sei tu quel seme e un altro egli è.' (The leaves were falling, a seed remained, / you are that seed and another one is he.) (LXX, 9, fol. 8ᵛ/ G.70.9.1 = Piantanida 2013: 205.)

This series of poetic reworkings uses a progressive sequence of images – a flower blooming, then fading and bearing seeds – mirroring the different stages of a nineteenth-century woman's life, seen through a male gaze: from virginity, to marriage, to motherhood. References to Easter transpose the Sapphic hymenaic context into a ritual Christian setting, enriching the images of coming of age and eros, with multiple analogic associations. Most prominently, the pattern of death and rebirth essential to natural cycles is mirrored in the ritual commemoration of the death and resurrection of Christ at Easter.[33]

But in the autograph prose accompanying the nocturne of fr. 3 Bergk in the same folio, the images of blooming are also linked to poetic creation. Pascoli says the fragment 'naturally bloomed in Sappho's mind'. Modelled on Sappho, the metaphor of lyric poetry as the blooming of a poet's mind returns in the 'Preface' to *Canti di Castelvecchio*: 'Mettono queste poesie i loro rosei calicetti (che l'inverno poi inaridisce senza farli cadere).' (These poems grow their little pink chalices that winter then hardens without making them fall). (Pascoli [1903] 1907: viii = Vicinelli 1968: 709) In Pascoli's poetic system, the Sapphic flower, blooming, opening, being culled, or fading recalls hymenaic wedding rituals celebrated in ancient epithalamia; at the same time, it evokes contemporary rural culture and, ultimately, poetic creation as blooming:

Solo però quando l'epos cessò di fiorire, quando fu mietuta quella messe e portato via quel raccolto la lirica germinò, per così dire, nella maggese di quello.

(Only however when epic stopped blooming, when that harvest was reaped and brought away, lyric germinated, so to speak, in that fallow land.)

Pascoli [1899] 1915: xiv)

Establishing a link between ancient literature and the natural proceeding of human experience, Pascoli's Sapphic framework develops through a generative linear progression: Sapphic eroticism => phytomorphic analogy => poetic creation.

Catullus

Catullus is not as prominent as Sappho in Pascoli's early writings; however, his interest in rituals and eroticism led Pascoli to experiment with Catullan themes at around the same time as he was working on the Lesbian poet. One of the first examples of Pascoli's interaction with Catullus is the poem 'Qual serenata – zunnene zunnene –' (What a serenade – zunnene zunnene) (1877). The poem envisages the triumphal return of the pagan deity Dionysos in a modern Christian setting. In the city of Bologna, a cohort of monks assist and stare in disbelief at a ritual procession of frenzied Maenads, following Ariadne and Dionysos: 'Lieo procede bianco tra i pampani, / E tuffa la man ne' capelli / D'oro della Minoide Arianna.' (White Lieo procedes among the vine leaves, / And he plunges his hand in the golden / hair of the Minoan Ariadne) (Garboli 2002: I 333–49).[34] These lines echo aspects of Catullus 64, a long account of the mythical wedding of Peleus and Thetis: the Bacchanal scene recalls Ariadne's vision in *Cat.* 64.252–65, where she is also said to have 'capelli d'oro' (golden hair).[35] Pascoli would return to the same section of *Cat.* 64 in a later translation entitled 'Baccanale' (Bacchanal) (*Cat.* 64.252–65), one of three excerpts from Catullus 64 together with 'La statua' (The Statue) (*Cat.* 64.60–7), and 'Ariadna' (Ariadne) (*Cat.* 64.86–104).[36] 'Qual serenata''s eroticism and sensuality also evoke the Aeolic themed lyrics Pascoli produced in the same period, including 'Lesbo', 'Ὦ τὸν Ἄδωνιν' (1881), and 'Epitalamio Lesbio' (Lesbian Epithalamion) (1882).[37]

Pascoli's interest in Catullus 64 confirms that he was fascinated by ancient epithalamia, probably because these poems included some of the earliest literary representations of eroticism and sexual desire within a ritualized social setting. Another undated draft translation of *Cat.* 64 (MS G. 81.3.7, fols 104–8) and a detailed commentary of the poem (MS G.81.4.7, fols 187–211), which was probably preparatory material for one of Pascoli's university lessons, are kept in the Archive of Castelvecchio. The commentary summarizes the subject of Catullus's poem as 'la glorificazione delle nozze e del buono amore portata epicamente nei tempi eroici' (the glorification of marriage and honest love epically brought to heroic times) (MS G.81.4.7, fol. 187). Whether or not Catullus

64 hides Catullus's personal narrative of tormented love is a matter that has been hotly debated by criticism (Fo 2018: 791); Pascoli's comment reflects the aspect of Catullus's poem that most chimed with his own interests at the time – the matter of fidelity in love, or 'honest love'.

In *Traduzioni e riduzioni* ([1913] 1923) (Translations and reductions), the posthumous volume collecting Pascoli's translations edited by his sister Maria, there are several other Catullan versions, but the majority were first published after Pascoli's death.[38] These translations with the accompanying metrical notes were left in draft form by Pascoli, who had originally written them to accompany his essay 'Regole di metrica neoclassica' (1901) (Rules of Neoclassical Metrics), where he outlined a new metrical system to render Graeco-Roman verse into Italian.[39]

Pascoli translated Catullus 22, with the title 'Suffeno' (Suffenus), the three extracts from Catullus 64 mentioned above, 'La statua', 'Ariadna' and 'Baccanale'; an excerpt from poem 65 with the title 'Catullo non oblia' (Catullus does not forget); one of poem 70 entitled 'Giuramenti' (Oaths); poem 72 called 'Contradizione' (Contradiction); poem 75, 'L'inestricabile' (The inextricable); poem 85, 'Odio e Amore' (Hate and love) and poem 101, epigraphed 'Alla tomba del fratello' (At the brother's tomb).[40] The same themes at the basis of Pascoli's fascination with Sappho come into play in his translations of Catullus: erotic love, death, and wedding rituals are at the forefront.

In his choice of texts to translate, Pascoli seems to be guided by his interest in the intersection of poetic imagery, hymenaic contexts and rituals. This clearly emerges from the three sketches of Ariadne's myth he extracted from Catullus 64. 'La statua' describes the naked body of Ariadne who has been abandoned on the shore by her beloved Theseus.[41] 'Ariadna' and 'Baccanale' focus on the Dionysian ritual, showing Ariadne taking part in an orgiastic rite in honour of Dionysos, chanting the ritual invocation to the god with other Maenads. 'Ariadna' shows a particular concern with the same literary archetypes that inform Pascoli's reuse of Sappho:

> Lui non appena fissò curiosa con gli occhi la pura
> figlia del re, cui vedeva sbocciare la sua cameretta
> piena di soavità, tra le blande carezze materne:
> come un arbusto di mirto cui nutre con l'onde l'Eurota,
> come i colori che suscita e sparge la brezza d'aprile:
> ecco non prima di lui declinava l'ardore degli occhi,
> che la trascorse una fiamma per tutta la bella persona
> dentro, e sentì che pungea le midolle dell'essere il fuoco.
>
> M. Pascoli [1913] 1923: 118[42]

These lines translate Catullus 64.86–93:

> Hunc simulac cupido conspexit lumine uirgo
> Regia, quam suauis expirans castus odores
> Lectulus in molli complexu matris alebat,
> Quales Eurotae progignunt flumina myrtos
> Auraue distinctos educit uerna colores,
> Non prius ex illo flagrantia declinauit
> Lumina quam cuncto concepit pectore flammam
> Funditus atque imis exarsit tota medullis.[43]

As Ariadna falls in love with Theseus, the eroticism of the scene and her sexual attraction to him is conveyed with metaphors of blooming. '[C]ameretta' (small bedroom) translates the diminutive 'lectulus' (small bed) (*Cat.* 64.88) with Petrarchan echoes ('O cameretta che già fosti un porto' [Oh little bedroom, you were already a harbour], *RVF* 234.1).[44] As soon as Ariadna sees Theseus, the room fills with a scent of blooming flowers. Exploiting analogic connections between the arousal of erotic desire and the natural awakening in spring, Pascoli freely translates 'suauis expirans castus odores / lectulus' (the chaste little bed breathing out suave scents) (87–8) with 'vedeva sbocciare la sua cameretta' (she saw her little room bloom). Picking up the reference to spring in the following lines, Pascoli translates 'suauis odores' with 'sbocciare', producing a synaesthetic effect by which the image of blooming flowers is associated to a suave scent. The picture is completed with 'come i colori che suscita e sparge la brezza d'aprile' (as colours that the April breeze excites and spreads), translating 'aurave distinctos educit verna colores' (or flowers of every hue the air brings out in spring) (90), with 'colori' (colours) metonymically recalling the previous image of blooming.

These translations and rewritings of Sappho and Catullus strike one as an exploration of eros not only as sexual desire, but also as a ruling force of nature and human life as well as a divine manifestation. In Pascoli's oeuvre, however, this vitality is always counterbalanced by a sense of loss; the joy of love and desire socially celebrated in wedding rituals entails the loss of virginity and youth, leading to adulthood. These refrains are embryonic inspirations for the re-elaborations of the dialectic of eros and thanatos in the second phase of Pascoli's reflection on ancient lyric, paving the way to the development of a formalized approach to the ancient sources.

Modern myths: 1895–99

Sappho and the blooming flowers of dusk

In the prefatory essay to his anthology *Lyra*, 'La poesia lirica in Roma', a collage of prose translations of Sappho – frr. 29, 62, 68, 4, 54, 53, 52, 39, 88, 90, 85, 38, 42, 93–5, 68b Bergk[45] – Pascoli gives a pitcuresque description of Lesbian poetry and society ([1899] 1915: xxiv–xxvi). The art of 'Sappho la bella' (Sappho the beautiful) (xxiv), as Plato called her,[46] is placed into a romanticized setting, populated by lovers, girls, boys and brides singing in ritual processions. The allure of the fragments kindles Pascoli's imagination, 'La fantasia compie il frammento che sorride intero, per un istante, come un'apparizione, e poi vanisce lasciandoci della grazia nel cuore' (Fantasy completes the fragment that smiles in its entirety, for an instant, like an apparition, and then vanishes leaving grace in our heart) (xxv). The momentary poetic epiphany stimulated by the corrupted state of Sappho's work actualizes the theory that 'La poesia consiste nella visione d'un particolare inavvertito, fuori e dentro di noi' (Poetry consists in the vision of an unnoticed particular, in and out of us) (Pascoli [1907] 1914: 41). A similar idealistic take on Sappho shapes 'Solon', as Giacomo Debenedetti remarked (1979: 233). Both *Lyra* and 'Solon' were first published in 1895;[47] this was a crucial year in Pascoli's creative life, during which his poetic investment in Sappho's and Catullus's poetry became more explicit. Pascoli's reuse and mythologization of the Ovidian legend of Sappho's tragic love for Phaon is at the centre of his engagement with the Lesbian poet in this period.

'Solon' is occasioned on Aelian's anecdote that the Athenian legislator Solon wanted to learn a song of Sappho before dying;[48] it contains two Sapphic odes, one on love and one on death, constructed with translations and rewritings of the Lesbian poet's fragments.[49] An unnamed woman from Eresso, one of the ancient cities that claimed to be Sappho's birth-place, sings them. The first recounts Sappho's suicide for the love of Phaon:

> Dileguare! e altro non voglio: voglio
> farmi chiarità che da lui si effonda.
> Scoglio estremo della gran luce, scoglio
>   su la grande onda,
>
> dolce è da te scendere dove è pace:
> scende il sole nell'infinito mare;
> trema e scende la chiarità seguace
>   crepuscolare.

(To fade away ... that's all I want: I want
to become the glow that is diffused from him.
Outermost rock, where rest the final rays of the sun,
rock poised over the wave,

sweet the descent from you to where is peace.
The sun descends into the infinite sea;
the afterglow of the twilight glimmers,
follows the sun's descent.)

'Solon', ll. 53–60 = Pascoli [1904–5] 2008);
Transl. Lunardi and Nugent 1979: I 4, 6

Pascoli describes Sappho's leap using an extended analogy: she longs to disappear, jumping down the Leucadian rock to follow her sun, Phaon, and shine with him as the evening twilight. In a letter to his editor Adolfo De Bosis, Pascoli explains:[50]

> Si fonda in vero su un'idea che credo tutta mia che o Sappho fosse persona mitica significando la chiarità crepuscolare (Cαπφώ = clara) o la poetessa così nomata scherzasse in certo modo sul suo nome. Certo Faone significa Sole e probabilmente Sole Occidente. Con quel canto io spiegherei come nelle poesie di Sappho potesse trovarsi l'accenno al salto di Leucade (Rupe Leucade è per me l'orizzonte, la linea che passa il sole tramontando, seguìto dalla sua amante, la Sappho, la chiarità crepuscolare).[51]

> (It is based on an idea, which I believe to be entirely my own, that either Sappho was a mythical figure representing the glimmer of twilight (Cαπφώ = bright) or the poet called Sappho in some way played with her own name. Certainly Faone means Sun and probably Western Sun. With that song, I would explain how one could find the mention of the Leucadian Leap in Sappho's poems (According to me, the Leucadian Rock is the horizon, the line crossed by the sun as it sets, followed by his lover, Sappho, the glimmer of twilight).

'Letter to Adolfo De Bosis, 24 April 1895' = Ghelli 2007: 48

Driven by his archaeological interest in retracing the origins of humankind, Pascoli turns Sappho's legend into an aetiological myth of the alternation of day and night powered by the vital forces of eros and thanatos. This theory was inspired by Max Müller's comparative linguistic studies.[52] *The Science of Language* (1861) and *The Science of Religion* (1870) by Müller were indeed both present in Pascoli's library in French translation.[53] Using the etymological roots of patronymics for ancient divinities, Müller identified sunlight as the original element of every myth and religion:[54]

The highest god had received the same name in the ancient mythology of India, Greece, Italy and Germany [...]. These are not mere names: they are historical facts. [...] These words are not mere words, but they bring before us, with all the vividness of an event which we witnessed ourselves but yesterday, the ancestors of the whole Aryan race, thousands of years it may be before Homer and the Beda, worshipping an unseen Being, under the selfsame name, the best, the most exalted name, they could find in their vocabulary under the name of Light and Sky.

Müller 1870: 34

Anchoring Sappho's name to the root of σαφής (*LSJ*: clear, plain, distinct) and Phaon's name to the root of the Greek φάος, the word primarily denoting the light of the sun,[55] Pascoli's myth strove to give the archetypal lyric poet a foundational role in western civilization, a role for which, as Welcker and his tradition had amply argued, a feminine heterosexual persona appeared much more suitable.[56]

Pascoli's poem makes love and death complementary natural forces. As he states, love is 'fratello della morte' ([1899] 1915: xx). Just like 'Solon', his translations of Sappho 1 and 31, 'Preghiera a Afrodite' and 'Dolor d'Amore', contribute to this dialectic between eros and thanatos and sanction Pascoli's mythical rewriting of Sappho's life.

Fr. 1 Bergk
Ποικιλόθρον', ἀθάνατ' Ἀφρόδιτα,
παῖ Δίος, δολόπλοκε, λίσσομαί σε,
μή μ' ἄσαισι μήτ' ὀνίαισι δάμνα,
    πότνια, θῦμον·

ἀλλὰ τυῖδ' ἔλθ', αἴ ποτα κἀτέρωτα
τὰς ἔμας αὔδως ἀΐοισα πήλυι
ἔκλυες, πάτρος δὲ δόμον λίποισα
    χρύσιον ἦλθες

ἄρμ' ὑπαζεύξαισα· κάλοι δέ σ' ἆγον
ὤκεες στροῦθοι περὶ γᾶς μελαίνας
πύκνα δινεῦντες πτέρ' ἀπ' ὠράνω αἴθε-
    ρος διὰ μέσσω

αἶψα δ' ἐξίκοντο· τὺ δ', ὦ μάκαιρα,
μειδιάσαισ' ἀθανάτῳ προσώπῳ,
ἤρε', ὄττι δηὖτε πέπονθα κὤττι

Preghiera a Afrodite
Afrodite, figlia di Giove, eterna,
trono adorno, piena di vie: ti prego!
non domar con pene e con crucci, o grande
    nume, il mio cuore.

Anzi vieni qua, s'altra volta ancora,
quella voce mia di lontano udendo,
l'ascoltavi: dalla paterna casa
    subito uscisti;

aggiogasti al carro tuo d'oro i belli
tuoi veloci passeri: sulla nera
terra, tra l'azzurro del cielo, con un
    battere d'ale

rapido, eccoli! ecco che tu, beata
con un riso dell'immortal tuo viso
mi chiedevi cosa mai fosse, cosa

δηὖτε κάλημμι,	mai ti chiamassi,
κὤττι μοι μάλιστα θέλω γένεσθαι μαινόλᾳ θύμῳ· τίνα δηὖτε Πείθω μαῖς ἄγην ἐς σὰν φιλότατα, τίς σ', ὦ Ψάπφ', ἀδικήει;	cosa voglio mai per il folle cuore mio. Chi vuoi che Dolce-parola ancora tra codeste braccia conduca? chi, o Clara, t'offende?
καὶ γὰρ αἰ φεύγει, ταχέως διώξει, αἰ δὲ δῶρα μὴ δέκετ', ἀλλὰ δώσει, αἰ δὲ μὴ φίλει, ταχέως φιλήσει κωὐκ ἐθέλοισα.	Ché se fugge, poi ti vorrà seguire, se ricusa i doni, vorrà donarne, se non t'ama, poi t'amerà se anche tu non lo voglia.
ἔλθε μοι καὶ νῦν, χαλεπᾶν δὲ λῦσον ἐκ μεριμνᾶν, ὄσσα δέ μοι τέλεσσαι θῦμος ἰμέρρει, τέλεσον· σὺ δ' αὔτα σύμμαχος ἔσσο.	Vieni anche ora e scioglimi dalle dure pene e tutto ciò che il mio cuore brama che s'adempia, adempimi tu: tu vieni meco alla guerra.
Bergk 1882: 84–7[57]	[1899] 1915: xxv–xxvi

The eccentric rendition of the names in fr. 1 reveals Pascoli's etymological approach to translation,[58] which, replicating Müller's theories, upholds his mythopoeic discourse. The name of the goddess Πείθω (literally: 'persuasion') is translated with 'Dolce-parola' (Sweet-word), an epithet constructed on the etymological Latin roots of the Italian verb 'persuadere' (persuade).[59] The Latin *per-suadere*, does indeed retain the meaning 'dolce' in its *suadus*.[60] Similarly, the name of Sappho, 'Ψάπφ' is translated with 'Clara', establishing a connection with Pascoli's understanding of Sappho as a mythological figure of twilight, once again perpetuating the heterosexual legend of her love for Phaon.

While in other European countries homoerotic fictions of Sappho began to consolidate at the same time as Pascoli's 'solar' mythologization, in late nineteenth-century Italy Sappho remained firmly heterosexual.[61] Exemplary is A. Cipollini' *Saffo* (1890), a study of the Greek poet and her fortune including translations of the extant fragments, aiming at revitalizing classical studies as 'la più valida forza meccanica per lo sviluppo intellettuale dei popoli' (the most effective mechanic power for the intellectual development of peoples) (15). Cipollini made Sappho into a nationalistic model of femininity and motherhood: 'giovinetta casta, amabile, bellissima, adorabile; madre affettuosa, tenera e soave: matrona dai costumi onorati, (mascula, come la chiamò Orazio), forte, amante dell'arte e della patria' (chaste girl, lovable, most beautiful, adorable; affectionate mother, tender and suave: matron of honoured customs (*mascula*, as Horace called her), strong, lover of art and her fatherland) (263). In a nutshell, a patriarchal account of the ideal Italian woman: a feminine chaste mother, upholding the value of art and her nation.

Pascoli's translation maintains an elevated register throughout the seven stanzas. Aphrodite appears ineffable, addressing 'Clara' from the upper spheres: she is eternal ('eterna'), omnipotent ('piena di vie', 'nume') and regal (she sits on a throne, 'trono adorno'). Emphasizing the distance between the goddess and the speaker with its tone and diction, the Italian poem arguably overlooks one of the most peculiar characteristics of Sappho's ode, identified by Gentili in the friendly and human portrayal of Aphrodite, quite different from the aloof goddess of epic (1966: 58). Calling the goddess of eros 'eterna' (eternal), a relatively free translation of 'ἀθάνατ[α]' (immortal), Pascoli completely removes Aphrodite from the human sphere.

This may be justified by metrical constrictions, as the translations of Sappho are written in a re-elaborated form of Pascoli's *systema sapphicum*, the metrical pattern he devised to translate Greek and Latin sapphics into Italian. He renders the Greek Sapphic stanza with five *endecasillabi saffici* and a *quinario*.[62] The hendecasyllabic lines are structured as five-foot lines built with two trochees at the beginning and end of the line and a dactyl in the middle, eliminating the caesura and putting the main stress on the fifth syllable ([1899] 1915: xcix–c). 'Eterna' is a three-syllable word ending with a trochee, while the Italian 'immortale' with its extra syllable would not fit metrically; at the same time, the word 'eterna' connects Aphrodite to Pascoli's poetic system. 'Eterno' is a key word of his poetics: ancient literatures defined 'l'eterno, che è sempre nuovo' (the eternal that is always new) (Pascoli [1907] 1914: 268), the same quality of the 'fanciullo eterno' (eternal child) (13–15). Using this word in his translation of Sappho's poem, he attributes to the Lesbian poet and the erotic drive found in her lyric an archetypal value for his own poetic discourse.

This is confirmed by the syncretism of the translation. The source text exploits the structures and literary conventions of the 'kletic hymn' – a prayer to a divinity.[63] With the title 'Preghiera a Afrodite' Pascoli frames the ode within the same genre. However, in the Italian context, 'preghiera' is immediately associated with the Christian-Catholic tradition. His interest in tracing the anthropological roots of the lyric in wedding rites and epithalamia may have played a role in his decision to stress the prayer-like quality of fr. 1; his oeuvre is also dappled with references to Christian-Catholic festivities.[64]

An analogous attention to literary tradition as in 'Solon' and 'Preghiera' characterizes Pascoli's translation of fragment 2Bergk (31Voigt):

Fr. 2Bergk
Φαίνεταί μοι κῆνος ἴσος θέοισιν
ἔμμεν ὤνηρ, ὄστις ἐναντίος τοι
ἰζάνει, καὶ πλασίον ἆδυ φωνεύ-
    σας ὑπακούει

καὶ γελαίσας ἰμερόεν, τό μοι μάν
καρδίαν ἐν στήθεσιν ἐπτόασεν·
ὡς γὰρ εὔιδον βροχέως σε, φώνας
    οὐδὲν ἔτ' εἴκει·

ἀλλὰ καμ μὲν γλῶσσα ἔαγε, λέπτον δ'
αὔτικα χρῷ πῦρ ὑπαδεδρόμακεν,
ὀππατέσσι δ' οὐδὲν ὄρημ', ἐπιρρόμ-
    βεισι δ' ἄκουαι.

ἀ δὲ μίδρως κακχέεται, τρόμος δὲ
παῖσαν ἄγρει, χλωροτέρα δὲ ποίας
ἔμμι, τεθνάκην δ' ὀλίγω 'πιδεύες
    φαίνομαι (ἄλλα).

ἀλλὰ πὰν τόλματον, [ἐπεὶ καὶ πένητα].
    Bergk 1882: 88–90

Dolor d'amore
A me pare simile a Dio quell'uomo,
quale e' sia, che in faccia ti siede,
e fiso
tutto in te, da presso t'ascolta, dolce-
    mente parlare,
e d'amore ridere un riso; e questo
fa tremare a me dentro il petto il cuore;
ch'al vederti subito a me di voce
filo non viene,

e la lingua mi s'è spezzata, un fuoco
per la pelle via che sottile è corso, già
non hanno vista più gli occhi, romba
    fanno gli orecchi,

e il sudore sgocciola, e tutta sono
da tremore presa, e più verde sono
d'erba, e poco già dal morir lontana,
simile a folle.
    [1899] 1915: xxvi

Sappho's text is again interpreted through her *Nachleben*. For instance, 'ἆδυ φωνεύσας' (sweet speaking) and 'γελαίσας ἰμερόεν' (amorous laughter) are translated with two infinitive clauses 'dolcemente parlare' and 'd'amore ridere un riso' respectively, reverberating the parallel structure in Horace's ode to Lalage (*Carmina* 1.22): 'dulce ridentem Lalagen amabo, / dulce loquentem' (1.23–4), itself echoing Catullus 51's 'dulce ridentem'. Pascoli notes this intertextuality in his commentary to Catullus 51 ([1899] 1915: 42); the reference seems to emerge also in Petrarch's famous *RVF* 159.14 ('et come dolce parla / et dolce ride') (and how she sweetly speaks and sweetly laughs) another fundamental love lyric model.[65] With intra-textual references to 'Solon"s 'il mio non sembra / che un tremore' (ll. 46-7) (mine does not seem but a tremor) in Pascoli's translation the speaking voice is pervaded by a 'tremore' (tremor) while in the frenzy of love. The irrationality of love that brings to death makes her 'folle' (mad), a rendition which may seem far-fetched since there is no reference to folly in Bergk's text. In fact, Pascoli seems to follow the textual notes to line 16, 'ἄλλα, i.e. ἠλεή *(demens) adieci*', where it is suggested that ἄλλα has the meaning of 'out one's mind'.[66] This is a fine example of Pascoli's habit of digging into the critical apparatus for alternative solutions to the set text to suit his own interpretation. His translations were led more by aesthetic than scholarly purposes, in the same way as his etymological digging was justified by his archeological interests and mythopoeic drive.

Catullus and the perpetual ritual of lyric

As glimpsed from 'Dolor d'amore', Pascoli's appropriations of Sapphic and Catullan poetry between 1895 and 1899 dialogue closely. In 'La poesia lirica', he places Roman lyric and all subsequent poetry in a direct line of descent from an original nucleus found in archaic Greece: 'maestra di Roma e di tutti' ([1899] 1915: xiii). *Lyra* is a testament to Pascoli's belief in the archetypal function of classical literatures for modern consciousness and its pedagogical potential for Italian high-school students. It is an important document of the reception of Sappho and Catullus in fin-de-siècle Italy, not least because it became hugely popular among school teachers, who adopted the manual throughout the country.[67] As the Italian nation state was consolidating, *Lyra* addressed the need for a new anthology of Latin literature compiled by an Italian for Italians, which would replace Loescher's German textbooks circulating in translation. Pascoli's publisher remarked in a letter that the German anthologies were 'pure e semplici compilazioni di cose tedesche ed hanno un valore didattico assolutamente negativo' (pure and simple compilations of German things and have an absolutely negative didactic value), inviting the poet to include in the anthology 'tutto quel che crede di poesia amorosa. Io credo che nessun giovane sia mai stato né possa essere corrotto da Orazio e da Catullo' (all love poetry that you deem necessary. I believe that no youth has ever been or can be corrupted by Horace and Catullus) (Pistelli to Pascoli (1892) = Pecci (1958: 160)). If Catullus's love poetry may have been perceived by some as inappropriate for high-school students, its cultural capital for the education of young Italians transcended such limitations. Pascoli did include several Lesbia poems in the anthology, but it would have been impossible to incorporate an openly sexual poem. He also keeps Juventius out of the picture. The only exception is poem 11, with that 'ilia rumpens' (breaking the groins) (l.20), whose interpretation, however, Pascoli delegates to Achilles Statius, whose commentary suggested to him the tame and school-friendly translation of 'spezzando il cuore' (breaking the heart) (Pascoli [1899] 1915: 72).

For Pascoli, Roman lyric poetry stretched the rules that defined ancient poetic genres, while still preserving the 'primitive' quality necessary for great poetry. Indeed, Catullus's originality resided precisely in his ability to mix different poetic genres, mirroring the coexistence of happiness and sorrow in life: 'questa mistura e confusione di generi è ciò per cui piacque e piace, per cui sembrò e sembra originale il poeta Veronese. La sua poesia è "vita" descritta, e la vita ha vicino il sorriso alla lagrima, il sogghigno al dolore.' (this mixture and confusion of genres is the reason why the Veronese poet was liked and he is liked, the reason why he seemed and seems original. His poetry is "life" described, and life keeps smile and tear, sneer and sorrow close) ([1899] 1915: li). With his 'sincere' poetic persona, Pascoli's Catullus upholds the same romantic values that characterize his reception as the founder of modern lyric poetry in the second half of the twentieth century.

To illustrate Catullus's cross-genre contamination of erotic and elegiac elements, Pascoli chooses poem 5, which describes the love between Catullus and his lover through a solar metaphor based on the pattern of eros and thanatos: 'I soli possono tramontare e ritornare: noi, appena tramontato questo breve dì, una notte dobbiamo dormire, infinita, senz'alba ... Dammi mille baci, poi cento, poi altri mille, poi altri cento ...' (The suns may set and return: we, as soon as this brief day has set, must sleep for a long night, infinite, without dawn ... Give me a thousand kisses, then a hundred, then another thousand, then a hundred ...' ([1899] 1915: xviii) Adding the phrase 'senz'alba' (without dawn) to the Latin 'nobis, cum semel occidit brevis lux / nox est perpetua una dormienda' (for us, when that brief light has set once / we must sleep one eternal night) (*Cat.* 5.4–5.5) reinforces the image of the infinite night. Pascoli's translation creates an inverse aubade context, in which the lovers never see dawn, but are bound by their shared destiny of eternal night, conjuring images similar to Sappho's crepuscular leap to follow Phaon beyond the horizon in 'Solon'. Sappho and Catullus are thus indirectly made closer by Pascoli's poetic hermeneutics.

The two ancient poets are also discussed together as a literary pair. Catullus 51 provides the occasion to dramatize Catullus's poetic inspiration as the first translator of Sappho 31:

> Egli tradusse per esprimere il sentimento nuovo, che l'invadeva tutto, un'ode di Sappho [...]. La ignota di Sappho siede di contro a un uomo, parla soave e canta amabile. [...] Catullo tralascia l'ultima strofa della Lesbia e conclude di suo, volgendosi a sè stesso, chiamandosi a nome con un triste presentimento. *Lesbia* egli chiama la donna amata, come a dire *Sappho*, perché bella, perché appassionata, perché partecipe delle rose Pierie.
>
> (He translated an ode of Sappho to express the new feeling that was invading him. Sappho's unidentified girl sits opposite a man, she speaks suavely and sings amiably. [...] Catullus leaves out the last stanza of the Lesbian poet and concludes

with his own, addressing himself, calling himself with sad foreboding. He calls his beloved woman *Lesbia*, as if to say *Sappho*, because she is beautiful, passionate and sharing in the rose of Pieria.)

[1899] 1915: xliii

In the moment of the highest poetic inspiration, Catullus expresses his 'new feeling', just as Pascoli's *fanciullino* creates poetry by unifying old and new. Going against contemporary scholarship that believed the last lines of Catullus's poem to be spurious, Pascoli assumes them to be authentic (Perugi 1984: 2270).[68] Sappho is confirmed the highest poetic and feminine model, although the doubts surrounding her conduct surreptitiously re-emerge in a footnote:

> Mi sono domandato qualche volta se Catullo nel dare a Clodia il nome di Lesbia ricordasse e non curasse, o non sapesse o non credesse ciò che di Sappho avevano detto i comici attici e poteva malignamente interpretare ogni lettore. Questa ode stessa... ma io credo che egli, avendola forse senza l'ultima strofa, la riputasse soggettiva bensì ma, per così dire, in persona d'altri, dell'uomo.

> (I asked myself a few times if Catullus in giving Clodia the name of Lesbia remembered and did not care, or did not know or did not believe what Attic comedians had said of Sappho and any reader could infer. This very same ode... but I believe that he, having it perhaps without the last stanza, considered it to be subjective but, so to speak, in another's persona, that of the man.)

[1899] 1915: xliii, n. 3

Did Catullus not know that by associating Clodia with Sappho he would also have evoked the Lesbian poet's problematic reputation? Could he possibly have condoned Sappho's homoerotic tendencies? Pascoli, it seems, did not – retreating into a safer interpretation, he suggests that the only explanation must be that Catullus could read the first three stanzas and assumed them to be spoken by the man in the poem.

Lyra reveals Pascoli's deep investment in Catullus's life as a model for his own. He follows closely contemporary biographical interpretations: Baehrens (1876–85) was Pascoli's reference text for the anthology ([1899] 1915: xi) and he often references Ellis' commentary (1876), together with Schwabe (1862), Lachmann (1874), Reise (1884) and Mueller (1892). Following in the footsteps of Schwabe's biographical school, Pascoli narrated Catullus's life in 'La poesia lirica' ([1899] 1915: xxxviii–lv) using information from the Latin poet's lyrics. He also arranged the selection of Catullus's poems in the anthology according to a supposed diaristic order of composition based on the Roman poet's life, completely altering the manuscript sequence. In order to map the key events of Catullus's life he gives each lyric a title and assigns them to a series of subsections focusing on: the Roman poet's early friendships ('Amici e conoscenti dei primi anni', 30) (Friends and acquaintances of the early years), his love for Lesbia ('L'ammaliatrice', 42) (The enchantress), the death of his brother ('Intermezzo doloroso', 50) (Painful intermission), the high and lows of Catullus's relationship with Lesbia ('Nuvolo e sereno', 57) (Cloudy and sunny), the end of Catullus's relationship with her ('Il tramonto dell'amore', 63) (Love's sunset), and a final section on his stay in Bithynia ('Il viaggio in Bithynia', 72) (The journey in Bithynia). The emphasis is on two main aspects of Catullus's life, his love for Lesbia and the death of his brother, narrated as counterbalancing forces. This mirrors the alternation of love and death which informs much of Pascoli's relationship with ancient literatures.

In Pascoli's narrative, the brother's death occurs at the peak of Catullus's attraction for Lesbia. As Perugi (1981: II 2268) pointed out, some of the themes dear to Pascoli echo in his appropriations of Catullus, not only in the macrostructure of eros and thanatos, but also in the narrative of familial loss. Like Catullus, Pascoli had lost several of his siblings, including an older brother, and related personally to the pain of mourning: 'Catullo volò a Verona e si abbandonò al suo dolore, tenero e acre, quasi capriccioso, come di fanciullo.' (Catullo flew to Verona and abandoned himself to his pain, tender and sharp, almost capricious, as that of a child) ([1899] 1915: xliv). As Traina remarked (1968: x–xii), with his sincere tone the Roman *fanciullino* writes life into verse, synthesizing the opposition between dark and vital forces, hate and love, that, according to Pascoli, characterizes the mystery of human existence: 'Catullo fu un giovane [...] sincerissimo e pronto perciò sì all'amore e sì all'odio.' (Catullus was the sincerest youth, ready therefore for both love and hate) ([1899] 1915: l) Pascoli's moral tale moderately chastises Catullus's capricious penchant for hatred and anger. The Roman poet is eventually forgiven for his impulsiveness because Pascoli shares with him similar sorrows and a tendency to commiseration and elegiac tones. This reaches the peak in 'Nozze di Ida', in which the poet feels bereaved after his sister's marriage: 'E intervenuto l'Amore, cosa gentile e terribile, che uccide e crea: che agli uomini dà la gioia presente, unico, e, unico, conserva agli uomini il dolore per il profondo avvenire' (And Love intervened, a thing kind and terrible that kills and creates: the only one that gives men joy in the present, and the only one that protects men from sorrow in the future) ([1933] 1943: 47).

Pascoli's appropriations of Sappho and Catullus seem to be the only moments of reckoning with love and with the possibility that poetry may encompass romantic love. They represent an exception to the rule stated in 'Il fanciullino' that 'Non sono gli amori, non sono le donne, pur belle e dee che siano, che premono ai fanciulli' (No love, no woman, even if a beautiful goddess, is important for children) ([1907] 1914: 4). Raised to the realm of myth and thus turned into universal narratives of the experience of nature and poetry, or of 'l'amore come presenza cosmica' (love as a cosmic presence) (Traina 1969: xiii), the works and lives of Sappho and Catullus allow Pascoli to reflect on the otherwise impossible theme of desire.

Catullocalvos (1897)

Pascoli's most extended reflection on Catullus in *Catullocalvos* intersects a crucial moment in the development of his poetics: published in 1897, the *satura* saw the light at the same time as an early version of 'Il fanciullino' and only two years after the first editions of 'Solon' and *Lyra*.[69] Finding its occasion in Catullus 50, *Catullocalvos* is a 328-line poem in Latin, which narrates a poetic contest between Catullus and his friend Calvus. A comment in *Lyra* reveals Pascoli's inspiration for his poem: 'Di tutto il crocchio Catullo amò subito Calvo, più giovane di lui di cinque anni. La loro amicizia divampò, per così dire, in un grazioso duello poetico' ([1899] 1915: xxxix). (Of the whole group, Catullus immediately loved Calvus, five years younger than him. Their friendship blazed, so to speak, during a delicate poetic duel.) Catullus's blazing fire of emotions, as described by Pascoli, fuels the fictional account of the poetic *agon* in *Catullocalvos*, adding elements to the picture painted in Catullus 50 (Traina 1969: ix). After an introductory section setting the scene, Calvus and Catullus take turns in composing poems on various themes, forming a miscellaneous verse collection encompassing all Catullan metres in an amoebaean structure.

Undeniably, *Catullocalvos* represents an exercise in virtuosity, revealing Pascoli's mastery of Latin.[70] In a sort of self-fulfilling process, this Catullan recreation helped Pascoli refine and establish his own aesthetic grounds. The poems pronounced by the character of Catullus frequently explore particular aspects of Pascoli's poetics or his theories on the creative process, while his interest in the relationship between ancient literatures and solar myths, as well as hymenaic and Sapphic themes, resurfaces through intertextual allusions and explicit references.

Catullus's character becomes an exemplary *fanciullino*, with implications for the reception of the Roman poet's texts and life. In the poem 'Silenus', pronounced by Catullus in section IV (Valgimigli 1960: 12), the poet speaks with the statue of the rustic god of wine-making and foster-father of Dionysos, which emerges from white marble as is carved by its sculptor (ll. 136–43). The poet-child is able to see a form in the marble, to have a vision of the potential work of art by looking at the world with new eyes, to find the poetic in his own experience. In the same way as a sculptor sees a statue in a block of marble, so a poet is able to find poetry in reality and express it through language. This idea, which echoes the Platonic conception of art as an ideal form implicit in matter (Nava in Pascoli [1904–5] 2008: 242) is the occasion of a homonymous *poema conviviale*, 'Sileno' (1899), confirming the close-knit relationship between the Italian collection, Pascoli's aesthetic musings, and his appropriations and translations of Sappho and Catullus in *Lyra* and *Catullocalvos*. Although 'Silenus' contains some intertextual references to Catullus's own poetry,[71] in the Roman poet's works there is no trace of these views of art. The Catullan persona voices Pascoli's poetics of the object which, anticipating Anglo-Modernist depersonalization, upheld that poetry ought to deal with objects of reality rather than subjective musings, a concept synthetized in Pascoli's aphoristic proclamation that poetry 'si scopre, non s'inventa' (is discovered, not invented) ([1907] 1914: 55).[72] Pascoli thus assigns the Catullan persona the role of *vates*, turning him into a symbol of poetry and the poetic life.

Aiming to produce new visions of reality, Pascoli's poetics called for a freer approach to the ancient sources than nineteenth-century imitation. Reflecting on the alternating fortune of Catullus throughout the centuries, Pascoli imputed Catullus' fall into oblivion after the end of the Roman empire to the negative effects of imitation:

> Dopo il secolo d'Augusto la fama di lui crebbe [...]. Fu anzi tanto imitato e contraffatto, che venne a noia. Così è: un'opera d'arte buona e bella, ha nella sua bontà e bellezza la ragione del suo dissolvimento; poiché quella eccellenza la fa amare, l'amore la fa imitare, l'imitazione la rode, la consuma, l'annulla.

> (After the century of Augustus his fame grew. He was so imitated and forged that he became stale. So, a good and beautiful work of art has within its goodness and beauty the reason for its own dissolution; because that excellence invites love, love invites imitation, imitation erodes it, consumes it and annihilates it.)
> [1899] 1915: li–lii

Inevitably, Catullus's self-positioning toward literary tradition as an innovator was appealing for Pascoli, who lingered on Catullan rewritings of Sappho. Intertextual references to Catullus 51 are scattered throughout *Catullocalvos*. The first poem recited by Calvo, 'Eidolon Helenae', opens: 'Otium, Valeri, tibi molestum est' (Idelness, Valerius, is troublesome) (Valgimigli 1960: 8), substituting the vocative of the *cognomen*, 'Catulle' of the Catullan rewriting (*Cat*. 51.13) of Sappho 31, with the more formal use of the *nomen* 'Valerius'

(Traina 1969: 6). Similarly, in the second poem recited by Catullus's character, 'Alaudae', we find 'tintinant aures' (ears ring) (*Cat.* 51.11).

Pascoli's engagement with the intertextual relationship between Sappho and Catullus emerges most evidently in 'Hesperus'. The poem's nucleus is found in Catullus 62 in which, with clear echoes of Sapphic hymenaic poetry, the evening star Hesperus is identified with its morning counterpart, Lucifer, which is also the star of the wedding night (*Cat.* 62.34–5). Pascoli's poem brings his own themes to dialogue with these motifs:

Ne, puer, maledixeris	
Liquens Lucifero domum	
Cum patris grege, cum pedo,	
Quod tu, Lucifer ut iubet,	
Peram sumis abisque;	215
Unus et peragras agros	
Tu quidem, unus et emicat	
Caelo Lucifer, atque alau-	
Dae superne canunt, sonant	
Tintinnabula terris.	220
Perge, ne maledic, puer,	
Namque vespere te domum	
Sidus et referet. Domi	
Ligna sunt, puer, in foco	
Mater est, bona puls est.	225
Unus et peragras humi	
Tu quidem, unus et emicat	
Sublime Hesperus: abstulit	
Lucifer, referet novo	
Nomine Hesperus idem.	230
Nupta, tu quoque ne nimis	
Criminare, quod Hesperus	
Tardus haereat (hoc quidem	
Tu tecum, bona sed palam	
Carpis advenientem):	235
Uxor in thalamo viri	
Mane cras eadem nimis	
Criminabere, quod nimis	
Lucifer properet, novo	
Nomine Hesperus idem.	240

(No, child, do not curse / Lucifer when you leave your home / with your father's flock and crook / because you, as Lucifer commands, / must take up the pouch and go forth; / and alone you wander through the fields / as Lucifer shines alone / in the sky; and above the skylarks / sing, on the earth / the cow bells ring. / Go on, do not curse, child, / and in the evening the star / will bring you home. At home, / oh child, there is wood in the fire, / your mother is there, child, and a good meal. / Alone you wander on the earth, / indeed, and alone Hesperus / shines sublime: / Lucifer has brought you away, with a new name, / but the same star, Hesperus, will bring you back. / Bride, you too, do not excessively / recriminate, because Hesperus / lingers late (this at least / you think to yourself, modest in public, / you blame him when he arrives): / as a wife, in the bed of your husband, / tomorrow morning you will reproach because / Lucifer, who is the same Hesperus with a new name, / came too quickly.)

Catullocalvos, ll. 211–40 = Valgimigli 1960: 18, 20

The lyric opens with a reference to a child, 'puer', the poetic enactment of the *fanciullino*, representing the poetic faculty, who is guided by the natural movements of Hesperus. The destiny of the wandering child-poet is analogous to that of a bride, as both are shaped by the natural order. As in his solar myths on Sappho, Pascoli superimposes human experience, poetry and cosmic rhythms (Traina 1968: 38). The image of Hesperus bringing the child back to his mother (ll. 222-4) reuses a Sapphic motif, drawn from fr. 95Bergk (104aV), one of the epithalamia Pascoli translated in 'La poesia lirica': 'Espero, tu porti quanto disperse l'aurora, porti l'agnella, porti la capra, riporti alla madre il suo ragazzo' (Hesperus, you bring what dawn dispersed back, you bring the lamb, you bring the goat, you bring the boy back to his mother) (Pascoli [1899] 1915: xxv). Moreover, like Hesperus, the bride is both the same and a different person after her first wedding night, echoing the lament for the loss of virginity in Sappho 109Bergk, which Pascoli had explored in his juvenile autographs. As he voices Pascoli's views on poetry, Catullus's character becomes a symbol of the poetic life.

The theme of looking at existence from the privileged if solipsistic standpoint of the poet returns in his final lyric on love, 'Amor, 2', another recreation of *Cat.* 62:

Ut flos in clausis humilis viget hesperis hortis
inter odoratas violas et lilia, nullo
in pretio, quippe ex se nullum exspiret odorem: 305
praeteriens luci despectat iure viator:
ast idem redeat multa vel nocte viator:
nocte olet et secum vigil aurea sidera mulcet:

sic amor: ut luci despectent, ut male volgo
audiat; ut tranquilla quies advenit et umbra   310
ille animum quodam secretum ture vaporat.

(As in closed gardens the humble flower of the night violet grows / among scented violets and lilies, with no / value, because it does not emanate any scent: / the wanderer in the day passing by justly overlooks it: / but may the wanderer return when the night is deep: / at night it has a scent and as in a vigil it delights the golden stars: / so is love: in the day, let everybody disrespect it, let it be publicly / slandered; when the calm quietness and the shadows arrive, / it envelops the soul in its secret, as if frankincense.)

Catullocalvos, ll. 303–11 = Valgimigli 1960: 26

Responding to a chastising Calvus who denigrates the futility of love, the Catullan persona defends the inebriating power of the most mysterious, nocturnal aspects of desire, which for Pascoli drove not only human life and natural cycles, but also poetry. Looking at a humble flower with new eyes, the one who searches for truth – the wanderer, the poet – may discern the essence of reality and wonder. Identifying himself with Catullus, Pascoli thus assigned to the Catullan poetic persona his own aesthetic views.

Putting himself in a direct line of descent from Catullus and, via his Latin verse, Sappho, Pascoli models his poem on Catullus 62.39–45, where the image of a flower in an enclosed garden, 'Ut flos in saeptis secretus nascitur hortis, / [...] quem mulcent aurae' (39–41) (As a flower in enclosed secret gardens germinates, / [...] which the winds lightly touch), is compared to a bride, 'sic virgo' (45) – the Sapphic hymenaic motif with which Pascoli had engaged in his juvenile rewritings of Sappho. In 'Amore, 2', Pascoli rewrites the Catullan simile, using the phytomorphic analogies to describe love and poetic creation, while anchoring his poem to *Cat.* 62 through lexical borrowings, such as the verb 'mulcent' (stir lightly) (*Cat.* 62.40) reused in 'aurea sidera mulcet' (l. 308). *Catullocalvos* confirms Pascoli's investment in Sappho and Catullus as endless repositories of poetic knowledge and inexhaustible creative models.

This Sapphic/Catullan floral symbology emerges in the subtle intertextuality of *Canti di Castelvecchio*, too. In one of Pascoli's most famous epithalamia, written in the same year as *Catullocalvos*, 'Il Gelsomino notturno' (1897), the inebriating smell of jasmine flowers preludes to the first night of love of a newly-wed couple: 'E s'aprono i fiori notturni / [...] Per tutta la notte s'esala / l'odore che passa col vento.' (ll. 1, 17–18) (And so night flowers open / [...] all night their scent exhales / carried by the wind). Another example is the poem 'La nonna', built on a line taken from

Catullus 61, as Pascoli reveals: 'confesso che è di Catullo il canto "La nonna": *Cana... anilitas Omnia omnibus annuit*' (I confess that the poem "The grandmother" is from Catullus: *Cana... anilitas Omnia omnibus annuit*) (Vicinelli 1968: 710). Catullus 61 describes a Roman wedding ritual, developing the hymenaic theme through floral imagery which, with clear Sapphic echoes, connects the bride and groom to vegetation (Fedeli 1972: 13). Catullus's lines 'usque dum tremulum movens / cana tempus anilitas / omnia omnibus annuit' (until white-haired old age, / shaking a trembling head, / nods assent to all for all) (61.154–6) are assimilated in the first stanza and throughout the poem. Extracting this cursory reference to the passing of time and old age, Pascoli constructs a re-enactment of an old woman's surrender to death in 'La nonna'. '[T]remule / a / o' (trembling), translation of 'tremulum', recurs in lines 8, 19 and 25 and 'capo d'argento' (silver head), for 'cana', is employed in line 3.

Pascoli's intertextual references to *Cat*. 61 create various interpretative layers. Both Italian and Latin poems address a group of boys: 'Tollite, o pueri, faces' (Lift, boys, the torches) (l. 114) in the Catullan carmen, and 'bimbi' (kids) (4) in Pascoli's poem. The reiterative 'sì' pronounced by the grandmother resounds as the word of a spouse in a Christian wedding. At the same time, in Pascoli's juvenile autographs and 'Nelle nozze di Ida' marriage is explicitly connected with the loss of the bride's maidenhood at the ritual level and to the disintegration of the family's nucleus at the personal level. Similarly, in 'La nonna', dissolution, represented by the grandmother's surrender to death, is linked with the hymenaic context of Catullan / Sapphic origins, providing another variation of the poetic trope of eros and thanatos.

The sightings of Sappho and Catullus presented in this chapter reveal Pascoli's regular engagement with the ancient literary pair throughout his work. The poetry, lives and traditions of Sappho and Catullus inform Pascoli's investigation of human origins. Through Sapphic and Catullan imagery, Pascoli anchors his poetic symbolic system in ancient lyric, which is conceived as an archetypal poetic expression, repository of essential knowledge and enactment of the existential pattern of eros and thanatos. In a rich web of references spanning over twenty years of his career, Pascoli's rewrites Sappho's and Catullus's lives and works to represent the transcendent connections of human experience with natural phenomena and poetry. Sappho and Catullus are thus turned into modern symbols of the poetic life, enabling Pascoli's meta-literary reflection on poetic creation.

2

Modernist Rites

In 1897 Bernard Grenfell and Arthur Hunt started their work at Oxyrhynchus, beginning to excavate and collect masses of papyri. Several new Sappho fragments were found among these in the first decades of the new century. The novelty of these early discoveries had an enormous impact on the way readers thought of Sappho, whose name evoked lyric fragments and the eroticism of absence. Catullus was being rediscovered not only as her first translator, but also as a poetic model in his own right: 'the Greeks might be hard put to it to find a better poet among themselves than is their disciple Catullus. Is not Sappho, in comparison, just a little Swinburnian?' Ezra Pound (1885–1968) asked provokingly in a 1917 essay (1954: 240). Pound's revaluation of Catullus, whom he deemed to be even superior to Sappho, carried the Roman poet into modernity.

In the early decades of the twentieth century, Anglo-American Modernists Pound and H.D., the pen-name of Hilda Doolittle (1886–1961), brought Sappho and Catullus to the centre of the avant-garde discourse on poetry, first with the experience of Imagism (1913–17) and its aesthetic of the fragment, then with their mythopoeic approach to poetry. The two ancient poets acquired transnational resonance through Europe and the United States as a literary network of poets and intellectuals, often orbiting around Pound, became increasingly interested in antiquity as a site of western cultural origins, where myth and rituals first articulated those archetypal psychological structures considered foundational to the human mind. Associated with the earliest expressions of lyric subjectivity in the Greek and Roman traditions, Sappho and Catullus came to represent the contiguity between past and present sought after by modern poets.

Boasting that '[a]ll ages are contemporaneous' (Pound [1910–29] 2005: 7), Pound endeavoured to define the synchronic quality of literary tradition from his earliest work, *The Spirit of Romance*, his study of medieval poetry published in 1910 directly after his travels in Provence.[1] In this volume and his later essays, Pound made clear that:

> The two great lyric traditions which most concern us are that of the Melic poets and that of Provence. From the first arose practically all the poetry of the 'ancient world', from the second practically that of the modern.
>
> Pound 1954: 91

In Graeco-Roman lyric and medieval poetry Pound found those archetypal psychological structures which for their 'germinal consciousness' were closest to the 'vital universe', the erotic drive defining reality and poetry: 'their thoughts are in them as the thought of the tree is in the seed, or in the grass, or the grain, or the blossom' (Pound [1910–29] 2005: 92–3). His outmost 'maestro' was Dante, who admired Arnaut Daniel and Guido Cavalcanti, and led Pound to them.[2] Pound's associative and universalizing mind thus used Sappho and Catullus not only as literary but also psychological models in constant dialogue with later traditions. In a cursory remark on Dante's sonnet 11 in the *Vita Nova*, for instance, he underlines the resemblance between the line 'Whence is he blest, who first doth look on her' (translating 'ond'è laudato chi prima la vide', l. 11), and the first line of Sappho 31, translated quite literally in Catullus 51. Pound concluded: '[it] is perhaps mere accident; but the sequent similarity of thoughts is interesting' ([1910–29] 2005: 110). Dante never read either Sappho or Catullus, but the point here for Pound is the consonance of thought processes, the contiguity of poetic images expressing a mood across traditions, the mythic quality of the lyric structures of Sappho, Catullus and Dante.

Such a psychologizing of poetry and mythic structures was also characteristic of Pascoli's poetry. Indeed, as Pascoli defined poetry the 'blooming of a poet's mind', Pound's views of poetic faculty as germination established a direct link between poetry and natural phenomena. These forms of universalizing primitivism were encouraged by the development of anthropology as a discipline, which enforced the idea that humans are inescapably mythopoeic animals (Bell 2010: 365). In Chapter 1, I discussed Pascoli's use of Müller's theories on solar myths; twenty years later, Anglo-American Modernists were irremediably attracted by comparative anthropological studies of mysticism, folkloric rituals and seasonal myths of death and rebirth. The Cambridge ritualists and James Frazer's *The Golden Bough* (1880 [1981]), particularly its third edition published between 1911 and 1915, generated a lot of interest among intellectuals.[3] As Pascoli in Italy had reused Sappho and Catullus to create a new literary mythology for modernity based on the pattern of eros and thanatos, a generation later, the Anglo-American Sappho and Catullus catalysed a reconceptualization of poetry as a form of erotic spiritualism that took myth as its main aesthetic and psychic structure. Drawing on the idea of humans' mythopoeic nature, the modernist 'mythic method', so defined by T. S. Eliot ([1923] 1975), did 'not so much return to the archaic myth as create an ostentatiously modern equivalent through overtly aesthetic means' (Bell 2010: 366). This free and synchronic approach to rewriting literary tradition and works of the past was succinctly and notoriously summarized in the Poundian slogan *Make it New* (1935).

The universalizing mythopoeia of Pascoli and Pound, though, did not give much space to more nuanced approaches to matters of gender and sexual difference. While desire, longing and eroticism were integral themes in their receptions of Sappho and Catullus, the representation of the often-homoerotic drive of the ancient poets' love lyrics seemed a minor concern. Sappho's love for women and Catullus's lyrics for Juventius were entirely left out by Pascoli and Pound.

In the meantime, in the hands of female Modernists in France and the United Kingdom, during the first twenty years of the century, Sappho was developing into the female poetic model and homosexual icon still current today.[4] Intellectuals such as Natalie Barney, Renée Vivien and Colette formed the 'Sapho 1900' group, attempting to recreate a lesbian society at Barney's literary salon in Paris, regularly visited by the contemporary modernist elite, including writers of the calibre of Rainer Maria Rilke, who was highly invested in Sappho's fragmented eroticism.[5] Some Imagist women writers, too, including H.D. and Amy Lowell, who knew and read the work of lesbian writers like Colette and Virginia Woolf, were drawn to the complex sexuality of Sappho's lyrics, contributing to develop a kind of 'Sapphic modernism'. Although female homosexuality was perceived as problematic – Radcyliffe Hall's *Well of Loneliness* was still considered offensive in 1929 – Sappho and her lyrics were enabling a discourse on non-normative sexualities, which is now recognized to have been central for modernist aesthetics.[6] As Collecott noted, '"Saph" was slang for lesbian among H.D.'s correspondents' and 'Virginia Woolf referred in private to writing about "Sapphism" but feared being "hinted at for a Sapphist" by the world at large' (1999: 3).

Sappho remained a sort of poetic double throughout H.D.'s life. The poetic status achieved by the Lesbian poet and the rich eroticism of her lyrics directed at both women and men was ever attractive for H.D. – a bisexual poet who entertained a life-long relationship with the English heiress Winifred Ellerman (Bryher), married her fellow-Imagist Richard Aldington, had a daughter in 1915 as a result of her affair with Cecil Gray, and between 1933 and 1934 underwent psychoanalysis with Freud to solve her writer's block.[7] While sharing many of

Pound's concerns with the redefinition of poetry and myth in her appropriations of Sappho and Catullus, her approach is radically different in focus, addressing issues of gender and female sexuality.

In this chapter I investigate the presence of Sappho and Catullus in the poetry and aesthetic writings of Ezra Pound and H.D., first during Imagism and then in their later works, including Pound's *Cantos*, the unpublished opera *Collis O Heliconii* (1932–34), and H.D.'s collections *Hymen* (1921) and *Heliodora* (1924).[8] Like Pascoli, both poets engage with contemporary developments in mythology and comparative anthropology, and especially with studies on ancient ritualism. Pound matures his reception of the ancient literary pair in three interconnected phases in which the Sapphic and Catullan masks develop in opposition to each other. H.D. engages with Sappho and Catullus as a literary pair to negotiate her critical stance on patriarchal gender structures.

Sappho and Catullus *Imagistes*

Pound's musings on the lyric tradition were the first anticipations of the nascent Imagist movement. Within two years of the first publication of the *Spirit of Romance*, the poet was submitting the typescript of *Ripostes* to the London publisher Stephen Swift and Co; the book was published in October 1912.[9] Pound was not working alone. In the same period, he would regularly meet H.D. and Richard Aldington at the British Museum to study the newly found fragments of Sappho. After reading John Maxwell Edmonds' articles commenting on the discoveries of the Berlin parchments of 1880 and 1902 in the *Classical Review*,[10] Aldington was the first to take an interest, but he was too young to access the reading room, so H.D. would copy the fragments and bring them to the tea room of the museum so that they could discuss them together. In her memoir on Pound, H.D. narrates that, on one of these occasions, she showed her Sappho-inspired poems 'Priapus' and 'Hermes of the Ways' to him, who, jubilant, 'slashed with his creative pencil' a few lines and signed them 'H.D. Imagiste', sealing both the birth of a poet and of the Imagist movement (1979: 40).[11]

Soon after, Pound sent H.D.'s Sapphic poems across the Atlantic to Harriet Monroe, the editor of the American magazine *Poetry*, where they were published in January 1913. In the March volume of the journal, Pound then announced his manifesto 'A Few Don'ts by an Imagiste'.[12] The programme focused on the poetic image as an 'intellectual and emotional complex' and invited the 'direct treatment' of the poetic object, using economy of words and paying attention to the music of rhythm (Pound 1954: 4). Sappho and Catullus are signalled as Imagist models, the only ancient authors in a list of exemplary authors: 'If you want the gist of the matter go to Sappho, Catullus, Villon, Heine when he is in the vein, Gautier when he is not too frigid; or, if you have not the tongues, seek out the leisurely Chaucer' (Pound 1954: 7). The directness of Sappho's fragments and Catullus's poetry anticipated his Imagist poetics.

In this period Pound repeatedly returned to Sappho and Catullus as examples of poetic achievement. Advising the young poet Iris Barry in 1916, Pound compiled a personal reading list of ancient Greek and Latin literature, stating that 'Wharton's Sappho is the classic achievement' and that 'Catullus, Propertius, Horace and Ovid are the people that matter. Catullus most. Martial somewhat ... Catullus has the intensity' (Letter to Iris Barry, London, [?20] July, in Paige 1950: 87).[13]

Mentioned by Pound as 'the classic achievement', Henry Thornton Wharton published his influential edition of Sappho's fragments in 1885, starting Sappho's popularization in Victorian England. Entitled *Sappho: Memoir, Text, Selected Renderings, and a Literal Translation*, it was meant to 'familiarize English readers, whether they understand Greek or not, with every word of Sappho, by translating all the one hundred and seventy fragments that her latest German editor thinks may be ascribed to her' (Wharton 1908: xvi). The anthology was extremely successful and went through four editions.[14] Wharton's source text was Theodor Bergk's 1882 edition of Sappho's fragments, the same reference text employed by Pascoli and, indeed, the vulgate text at the time; the Greek was accompanied by Wharton's prose translations and an anthology of some of the most influential poetic renditions of the fragments. Prins notes that 'Wharton's book simultaneously composes a portrait of the woman poet and presents her as a decomposing text' (1999: 4); it is precisely this double connotation that became key for Sappho's reception in English – before Wharton her popular circulation was mostly mediated by Ovid's *Heroides* 15 (Prins 1999: 17).

Wharton resisted the openly erotic Sappho of the French versions and instead followed Welcker, presenting her as a pure woman and an incomparable female poetic model: 'Sappho [...] was something wonderful: at no period within memory has any woman been known who in any, even the least degree, could be compared to her for poetry' (1908: 11). Wharton's idealizing volume is the main source of Anglo-American modernist Sappho. H.D. owned the volume, too, and repeatedly quoted Wharton's translations in her own works; Eileen Gregory even argued that she absorbed Wharton's Sappho at 'the pre-verbal level' (1997: 154).

By the beginning of the twentieth century, translations of Catullus into English comprised all poems, although the obscenities were usually toned down. Richard Burton's *The Carmina of Caius Valerius Catullus* (1894) was the only one to openly accept Catullus's pederasty. As Gaisser points out, it represents a rebellious, anti-bourgeois attitude, resisting Victorian morality (2009: 208). The same attitude emerges from Arthur Symons' translations of Catullus in *Knave of Hearts: 1894–1908* (1913). Pound admired the work and professed it the best available translation at the time (1979–80: 57);[15] conversely, he detested romanticizing Victorian Catulluses, as emerges in his peer-review of Ruth S. Dement's *The Lesbiad of Catullus and Pervigilium Veneris (Mood transcriptions) and Songs of a Wayfarer* (1915) for Harriet Monroe's magazine:

> LESBIAD. NO. HELL NO.
>
> I began reading it carefully, pleased that someone should try the impossible, knowing the immense difficulty ... Even Landor turned back from an attempt to translate Catullus. I have failed forty times myself so I do know the matter. *But* there are *decent* and *dignified* ways of failing, and this female has not failed in any respectable way. The most hard-edged and intense of the Latin poets should not be cluttered with wedding-cake cupids and clichés like 'dregs of pain', etc. etc. ad inf. Pink blue baby ribbon.
>
> Letter to Harriet Monroe, Coleman's Hatch,
[February] (1916) = Paige 1950: 116

From Pound's derogatory terms verging on sexism, it is clear that, for him, Catullus was not the enamoured poet of the Lesbia cycle; he was the poet of directness and intensity, a 'hard-edged' lyricist associated with masculinity and poetic prowess; in other words, Pound's poetic alter-ego. This take on Catullus is behind *Lustra* (1917), one of Pound's most experimental collections in which both Sappho's and Catullus's works and poetic personas are reused to develop his Imagist poetry.[16]

Angels and drabs in Pound's *Lustra* (1917)

Ezra Pound only ever made two creative translations of Sappho. They were both included in *Lustra*. The first, entitled 'Papyrus' is a version of the extremely corrupted lines 2 to 4 of the Edmonds' edition of fr. 95, in which the speaking voice overwhelmed by desire wishes to die:

του
ἦρ' ἀ
δῆρα το
Γογγύλα τ

Edmonds 1909b: 156

'Papyrus'
Spring...
Too long...
Gongula...

Sieburth 2003: 289

The second translates ll. 16–18 of Edmonds' edition of fr. 96, in which the speaking voice laments the absence of a woman who left for Lydia and is imagined remembering Atthis from afar. I provide the fragment's extract and Edmonds' translation:

πόλλα δὲ ζαφοίταισ' ἀγόνας ἐπι-
μνάσθεισ' Ἀτθιδος, ἰμέρω
λέπταν ϝοι φρένα κῆρ ἄσαι βόρηται.

And oftentime when our beloved, wandering abroad, calls to mind her gentle Atthis, the heart devours her tender breast with the pain of longing.

Edmonds 1909a: 102

'Ἰμέρρω'
Thy soul
Grown delicate with satieties,
Atthis.

O Atthis,
I long for thy lips.
I long for thy narrow breasts,
Thou restless, ungathered.

Sieburth 2003: 290[17]

Although in *Lustra* 'Papyrus' precedes "Ἰμέρρω', the latter was published earlier, in 1916. Pound had been made aware of Edmonds' fragments in 1912 by Aldington's translation in 'To Atthis (After the Manuscript of Sappho Now in Berlin)', which he had recommended to Harriet Monroe for publication in her new magazine *Poetry*. After she refused to print Aldington's text because Paul Shorey, the head of the Department of Greek at the University of Chicago, had rejected the translation on the ground of its inaccuracies, Pound was not put off and later included Aldington's poem in his anthology *Des Imagistes* (1914: 19) (Kenner 1991: 55, 56–8).

Indeed, Pound's own version of fr. 96 is indebted to Aldington's linguistic choices. In Sappho's fragment, the poetic persona speaks of a Lydian woman, who often thinks with longing of her beloved distant Atthis. Like Aldington, Pound makes Atthis the direct addressee of his translation, while the source text speaks of Atthis in the third person. His choice of 'satieties' (l. 2) recalls Aldington's last lines 'I yearn to behold thy delicate soul / To satiate my desire', rewriting of 'ἱμέρῳ / λέπταν οἱ φρένα κῆρ ἄσαι βόρηται' (translated by Edmonds: 'the heart devours her tender breast with the pain of longing'). Pound alters the source text completely, maintaining the sense of longing with a coda, 'thou restless, ungathered', which increases the sense of distance and unreachability of the beloved Atthis, while also conveying sexual desire explicitly.

With 'Papyrus', Pound continued his Sapphic investigations. The translation follows Edmond's edition only formally. The source text is so corrupted that it is impossible to decipher the Greek with any certainty, so the translation stretches the language of the fragment to fit Pound's agenda. He appears to read the Greek phonically, translating the source text by means of homophonic associations with other Greek words. Although the first word of the fragment may not even be a noun, 'ἦρ''' is translated as the contracted form of ἔαρ (ἦρ), 'spring'; similarly, he takes 'δῆρα' for δηρός, 'too long'.[18] The English translation conveys the syllabic increase in the three Greek lines, which present two syllables in l. 2, three in l. 3 and three and a half (if the 'τ' is counted) in l. 4. The progression from the one-syllable 'Spring', to the two-syllable phrase 'too long' and the three-syllable name Gongula matches the Greek structure.

The poem fits into Pound's interest in poetic fragments and their 'hard-edged' directness; the reference to desire in spring upholds his view of Eros as a vital force of life and poetry, sustaining the 'germinal consciousness' of the poets and the seasonal cycle of natural rebirth: 'when we do get into contemplation of the flowing we find sex, or some correspondence to it, "positive and negative", "North and South", "sun and moon", or whatever terms of whatever cult or science you prefer to substitute' (Pound [1910–29] 2005: 93). The flowing force of Eros – the mythical equivalent of sexual desire – runs between polarized ends, which visually grow into archetypal pairs of opposites, positive and negative, north and south, sun and moon. As an electric current established between opposite charges, desire appears to be the drive of nature, of life with its rituals, and poetry, allowing their co-existence and intercommunication at all levels.[19] In 'Papyrus', Pound plays on this concept of eros, too.

By means of verbal and formal allusion, 'Papyrus' exploits the notion of desire as a force propelled by distance and absence – in this particular case, the absence of Gongula, the girl addressee of the poem. The corrupted text's lacunae, which are deliberately reproduced in the poem with ellipses, represent a material lack. The elliptical language increases the allusiveness of the poem, as in a veiled courtship. The mask of the Poundian poem addresses Gongula and seems to state that spring, separating the *persona loquens* from the girl, is too long to be endured. The use of 'too long' as a temporal expression also contributes to create the overall suggestive tone of the poem, given that 'too long' is homophonic to the equivalent English verb of longing and desire. The verb 'to long' is also the direct translation of the title Ἱμέρρω, a quotation from Sappho 96 (l. 17), anaphorically repeated in translation in the body of the poem: 'I long for thy lips / I long for thy narrow breasts'. The elegiac tone of the two poems idealizes the absent lyric addressees, emphasizing the dynamics of eros as lack.[20] Although the intense sensuality of Ἱμέρρω and 'Papyrus' suggest that the Poundian Sappho was not as chaste as Welcker posited, the two translations still silence the homoerotic tension of the originals, since Sappho is never acknowledged as a source and the gender of the poetic persona is left neutral. As Buck notes, 'typically, the assumption that the subject is neutral actually locates it as masculine, in the sense that where the subject is posed as "generic" then a feminine difference is effaced' (1991: 22).

In the rest of this section, I discuss how in *Lustra* Sapphic eros becomes the signifier of a form of idealized love stirred by absence, which is to be read and contrasted with the worldly desire of the Catullan appropriations. Indeed, the Sapphic and Catullan masks in *Lustra* appear to be constructed on reciprocal opposition; this contrastive dynamic characterizes the first phase of the Sappho/Catullus polarity in the American poet's work.

Although there is a clear Sapphic presence, *Lustra* is inherently a Catullan collection.[21] The debt to the Latin poet is acknowledged by Pound in his epigraph: 'Vail de Lencour / Cui dono lepidum novum libellum' (To Vail de Lencour / I give my new delightful little book) (Sieburth 2003: 261). Vail del Lencour is the pseudonym of Brigit Patmore (1882–1905), English writer and literary hostess; the Latin sentence is a direct quotation from the first line of the opening poem of Catullus's *liber*, itself a dedicatory text and a statement of poetics.[22] In typical Poundian fashion, the English and Latin realms intermingle anticipating the mood of the collection.

After developing the idealized Sapphic mask in 'Papyrus' and "Ἱμέρρω", Pound presents a series of poems engaging with literary representations of women as objects of desire. In 'Shop Girl', the poetic persona compares a girl in a shop with various literary characters, who are dismissed as inferior – the poem seems to suggest – because they are fictional, while the girl in the shop is real (Kenner 1968: 220), thus adhering to Pound's Imagist tenet that 'the natural object is always the *adequate* symbol' (Pound 1913: 201). Set in chronological order, these include Guido Cavalcanti's shepherdess in *Ballata* 9.221.23-222.18,[23] Baudelaire's prostitutes and also the various women of Swinburne's verse.[24] The poetic series ends with a final representation of an unremarkable woman in 'To Formianus' Young Lady Friend', a bitter and sarcastic translation of Catullus 41. The voice of the poem laments the praises received by Formianus' lover, whose beauty is a product of her skills in cosmetics and deceit (ll. 7–10). This cycle of poems meta-poetically enacts Pound's Imagist poetics and his idea that literature is defined by recurring archetypal patterns remerging in new forms, tracing a progressive decline from the original Sapphic archetype of desire to the more ordinary variations of later lyrics. As Kenner remarks: 'Pound has fitted Sappho [...] into an historical process, complicating the ancient tradition of poetic *aemulatio* with his own concern for cultural gradations' (1968: 221).

Within the poetic of loss typical of Pound's recreations of the fragments of Sappho, the lyric addressees are idealized and absent, ancient counterparts to the women-angels of medieval lyric, as expounded in the *Spirit of Romance*. Conversely, in Pound's appropriations of Catullus, the inflated masculinity of the Catullan poetic mask drags female addressees to the contingent, and by virtue of this 'fall', women are liable to ridicule and are degraded. The representation of women either as angels or prostitutes stands out as an objectifying act that replicates stereotypical hegemonic representations of masculinity and femininity, reinforced, according to Buck, by Imagism's rejection of a 'model of language as social and conventional in favour of a universal and "natural" model of language' (1991: 22).

A mixture of lyricism and satire breeds *Lustra*'s Catullan atmosphere, as exemplified in 'Ladies', a Catullan collage in four parts: the epigrams 'Agathas', 'Young Lady', 'Lesbia Illa' and 'Passing'.[25] Modelling the contents and appositive structure of Catullus 58, a poignant invective against Lesbia and Roman society, Pound's 'Ladies' is a variation on the theme of betrayed love and ironic reversal. The collage hinges on the adverb 'now', translating the Latin 'nunc' (*Cat.* 58.4). In three out of four epigrams ('Agathas', 'Your Lady', 'Lesbia Illa'), the adverb is used to contrast past and present situations, to bolster the attack. Let's take, for example, 'Lesbia Illa':

> Memnon, Memnon that lady
> Who used to walk about amongst us
> Is now wedded
> To a British householder.
> *Lugete, Venere! Lugete, Cupidinesque!*
>
> Sieburth 2003: 281

As Fordyce remarks, in the last line of Catullus 58, 'glubit magnanimos Remi nepotes' (takes the skin off the great descendants of Remus), the irony of the 'quasi-epic grandiose phrase [...] is enhanced by the contrast with the offensive verb: the heirs of Rome's greatness are the associates of Lesbia's degradation' (1961: 231-2). Pound plays on this same theme by translating the reference to Roman society with: 'is now wedded / to a British householder', toning down the obscenity of the original line. The exact meaning of the Latin 'glubit' is uncertain, but we know that it was an agricultural word literally meaning 'to strip the bark', most likely used by Catullus with obscene connotations. The vast bibliography on the topic suggests various solutions from 'fleeces (of their money)' and 'strips (of their clothes)' to meanings related to masturbation and fellatio (Fitzgerald 1995: 77). The final line, '*Lugete, Venere! Lugete, Cupidinesque!*' is a variation on *Cat.* 3.1: 'Lugete, o Veneres Cupidinesque!' (Mourn, o Venuses and Cupids!) The poem mourns the loss of Lesbia's pet sparrow, using disproportionally formal invocations to the divinities for the relatively minute subject of the lament, downplaying her sorrow. Pound's poem uses the same deflating effect, increased by the reference to Catullus.

The poetic persona changes in each of the four epigrams in 'Ladies', conveying a bustling atmosphere in which voices overlap in various layers of communication. The voices contribute to create the overall conversational buzz of the collection as in the busy *fora*. With its sarcastic title, the Catullan banter infiltrates 'Ladies' from the very beginning, anticipating its series of invectives against women. The different interactions of the male voice with the women in the four epigrams may be read as versions of the same emotional pattern. This emotional motif is extended to the whole collection by the repeated use of a handful of poems in the Sapphic and Catullan corpus. For instance, both poems 58 and 3, together with extracts of translations from Catullus 31, 51, 72, 80 are taken up again in the second of 'Three Cantos of a Poem of Some length', now often referred to as Ur-Cantos, establishing an internal pattern to the collection.

In the first of 'Three Cantos', references to Catullus 31 are inserted within a discussion on lyric poetry. The ghosts ('ghosts move about me patched with histories') of Browning (referenced via 'Sordello'), Arnaut and Dante are invoked in a Provençal environment intertwined with images of *Cat.* 31's *locus amoenus* of Sirmio on Lake Garda: '"Home to sweet rest, and to the waves deep laughter"' (Sieburth 2003: 319).[26] The light of dawn gives new life to the landscape. Catullan and Sapphic references are explicitly placed within Pound's wider reflection on Eros and sexual drive as a vivifying source of artistic inspiration. The second section of Canto II opens in medias res with a reference to Catullus 3's sparrow:

> Society, her sparrow, Venus' sparrows. [**See Catullus 2–3**]
> Catullus hung on the phrase (played with it as Mallarmé
> Played for a fan: 'Rêveuse pour que je plonge.');
> Wrote out his crib from Sappho:
> God's peer, yea and the very gods are under him [**See Catullus 51**]
> Facing thee, near thee; and my tongue is heavy,
> And along my veins the fire; and the night is
> Thrust down upon me.
> That was one way of love, *flamma demanat*,
> And in a year: 'I love her as a father,' [**See Catullus 72**]
> And scarce a year, 'Your words are written in water,' [**See Catullus 70**]
> And in ten moons: 'O Caelius, Lesbia illa,
> Caelius, Lesbia, our Lesbia, that Lesbia
> Whom Catullus once loved more
> Than his own soul and all his friends,
> Is now the drab of every lousy Roman'; [**See Catullus 58**]
> So much for him who puts his trust in woman.
>
> Sieburth 2003: 323

Immediately presenting Catullus's sparrows within Venus' sphere of influence of love and desire, as in Sappho fr. 1 and in the invocation of Catullus 3.1, Pound plays with the long-established interpretation of Lesbia's sparrow (in poems 2 and 3) hopping around his lady and lying in her lap as a phallic symbol (*Cat.* 3.8–10).[27] The appositive relationship between 'society' and 'her sparrow' implies a rather large group of wooing sparrows in the beloved's entourage. Pound fictionalizes Catullus's poetic persona using his poems as a biographical lattice. As if in the hope of relieving himself from a case of writers' block ('hung on the phrase'), Pound's Catullus turns to translating Sappho 31. Indeed, he believed that translation stimulated creativity.

Via Catullus's translation of Sappho, the ancient literary pair is used to speak about the effects of love and eros. Love, a fire flowing in the veins of the lover and symbolizing the erotic flow of artistic creativity, pinpointed by Catullus's phrase 'flamma demanat', is not as absolute as one might think: 'that was one way of love'. No form of love is pronounced superior to the other, no way of writing poetry. As Thomas argues, Pound's 'Catullan translations isolate Lesbia as an image either of divine love or of base desire; in this dual role she represents Pound's personal ambivalence about his own poetic program to resuscitate the past' (1983: 21). The depersonalization of Catullus's poem into a universal aesthetic paradigm is made stronger as Pound opts to remove the direct reference to Lesbia ('God's peer [...] upon me'). In an earlier version of the poem of 1917, she was still mentioned, together with several other explanatory passages, such as the translation of *flamma demanat*, 'the slow fire', probably eliminated at Eliot's suggestion in order to make the text more elliptical and 'impersonalise' it.[28] The rest of the excerpt shows a deterioration of the Catullan persona's feelings of love toward Lesbia, going from the idealized portrayal of *Cat.* 51 to distrust and offensive accusations: 'is now the drab of every lousy Roman'. This mirrors the corrosion of love and his critical approach to tradition in the earlier Sapphic and Catullan clusters.

A translation of Catullus 58 closes the cycle, although in a much more accurate version than in 'Lesbia Illa'. The translation of the final lines maintains the opposition between the Catullan poetic persona and Remus' ancestors, who are now Lesbia's lovers. The contrast is enhanced by the use of 'drab', a rare word of obscure etymology, connected with Gaelic and German, meaning a dirty and untidy woman or a prostitute;[29] the use of the Germanic linguistic group enhances the juxtaposition between a supposedly Anglo-Saxon poetic persona and the 'lousy Roman', perhaps hinting at Catullus's origins in Verona. The Catullan pastiche ends with the *sententia* 'So much for him who puts his trust in woman'. The delusion of love and the ensuing disillusionment fuel the poetic drive, while exerting the poetic persona's masculinity over the female gender, castoff as untrustworthy.

The appropriations of Sappho and Catullus in *Lustra* exemplify Pound's re-conceptualization of tradition, which envisioned past and present literatures on a horizontal plane and invited his contemporaries to make the old new again, to hold on to poetry's 'luminous details', the original qualities of a work of art that is also 'the permanent basis of psychology and metaphysics' (Pound 1973: 23). The instrumental role of translation in this comparative endeavour was relentlessly stressed by the poet.[30] He was certain that '[a] great age of literature is a great age of translations' (Pound 1954: 232). For Pound, translation was a creative act, marking a fundamental shift in the approach to source and target texts. As Matthew Reynolds suggests, after Pound it became necessary to elide the hierarchical division between original poetry and translation as a secondary practice, and rather start thinking in terms of the 'poetry of translation' (2011: 266–7). As early as 1911 one of Pound's early reviewers had denounced how his work blurred the boundaries between original and translated poetry, lamenting that 'the bulk of the work in [*Canzoni* (1911)] is not ostensibly translated, but it reads as though it were' (Flint 1912: 28). Flint had grasped one of the most original and enduring elements of Pound's writing; one echoed in the 'stile da traduzione' (translative style) that Franco Fortini identified as one of the main traits of Italian poetry in the second half of the twentieth century (1976: 390).

H.D.'s Sappho in the Imagist period

Sappho is a constant presence in H.D.'s work; her deep relationship with the Lesbian poet is articulated through a complex web of allusions to both Sappho's writings and the 'imaginative construct' evoked by her name (Collecott 1999: 2). This Sapphic intertext has been studied and mapped thoroughly,[31] revealing that H.D.'s 'creative dialogue' (Collecott 1999: 3) with Sappho is predicated on an inner emotional consonance between the ancient and the modern poets, empowering H.D. to reclaim a leading female and homoerotic poetic tradition. In her 1919 essay 'The Wise Sappho', she describes the Lesbian poet: 'Not roses, but an island, a country, a continent, a planet, a world of emotion, differing entirely from any present day imaginable world of emotion' (H.D. [1919] 1982: 58). Despite the cultural differences engendering unique emotional realms, H.D. is drawn to the vividness and rich variety of sentiment in Sappho's lyrics, which redefine themselves (an island, a country, a continent, a planet) as they continue to inform poetic imagery: 'So Sappho must live, roses, but many roses, for tradition has set flower upon flower about her name and would continue to do so though her last line were lost' ([1919] 1982: 68).

In her first collection, the Imagist *Sea Garden* (1916), H.D. pulls Sappho into her poetic landscape, dotting her poems with repeated Sapphic images of roses, hyacinths and myrtle. Through a series of poetic rewritings that proceed analogically as those by Pascoli, floral images are frequently employed to conjure eroticism and symbolize poetic creation, resurfacing also in scenes of marriage rituals. The recurring image of the rose is the most poignant case in point. In 'Garden', for instance, the Sapphic rose is used as a symbol of poetry and beauty:

> You are clear
> O rose, cut in rock,

> hard as the descent of hail.
> [...]
> If I could break you
> I could break a tree.
>
> ll. 1–3, 7–8 in Martz 1986: 24

A stone rose, or a rose that grows in rock crevices, carries an oxymoronic quality – the ephemeral lightness of the petals made heavy, hard and sharp as they emerge cut in the rock becomes a metaphor for the effort of poetic creation, the chiselling of a poetic image. As Cassandra Laity points out, H.D.'s Imagist flowers in *Sea Garden* are indebted to the roses and blossoms that dot the poetry of Baudelaire, Pater and Swinburne (Laity 1996: 49–50), in the same way as forms of decadent aestheticism stirred the atmosphere of Pascoli's juvenile experiments. At the same time, H.D.'s flowers retain a 'cutting edge' quality just like Sappho (Collecott 2012: 103), whom she described with analogous images: 'she is indeed rocks set in a blue sea' (H.D. [1919] 1982: 67). In this poem, therefore, the 'rose cut in rock' is both the poetic image signifying itself, and the strenuous, almost impossible, task of poetic creation, requiring the same strength as needed to chop down a tree.[32]

The immediacy and hardness of H.D.'s Sapphic fragments were praised by Pound, who sent Harriet Monroe some of her lyrics: 'This is the sort of American stuff that I can show here and in Paris without its being ridiculed. Objective – no slither; direct – no excessive use of adjectives, no metaphors that won't permit examination. It's straight talk, straight as the Greek!' (Monroe 1938: 264, quoted in Mackay 2012: 55). The perceived directness of Sappho's lyric fragments was a fundamental aesthetic model for the Imagist poetry of Pound and H.D., which was conceived as an 'evocation and re-enactment of the experienced power of the image' (Gregory 1986: 545):

> O wind, rend open the heat,
> cut apart the heat,
> rend it to tatters.
>
> 'Garden', ll. 12–14, in Martz 1986: 25

It is indeed a 'Muse in Tatters', to use Hugh Kenner's definition (1968). In H.D.'s essay 'The Wise Sappho', the image of heat, the fiery energy of powerful yet painful poetic creation, is linked to Sappho's burning lyrics, her bittersweet eros:

> [I]t is not warmth we look for in these poems, [...] but another element [...]: white, unhuman element, containing fire and light and warmth [...].

> I think of the words of Sappho as these colours, or states rather, transcending colour yet containing (as great heat the compass of the spectrum) all colour. [...] [Re]ading deeper we are inclined to visualize these broken sentences and unfinished rhythms as rocks – perfect rock shelves and layers of rock between which flowers by some chance may grow but which endure when the staunch blossoms have perished.
>
> [1919] 1982: 58

With strong similarities to Pound's conception of the vital power of eros, H.D. locates the substance of poetic creation in the heat of Sapphic desire. As she identifies herself as a modern Sappho (Gregory 1986: 535), she aims to write poetry as imperishable as the Lesbian poet's fragments:

> True, Sappho has become for us a name, an abstraction as well as a pseudonym for poignant human feeling, she is indeed rocks set in a blue sea, she is the sea itself, breaking and tortured and torturing, but never broken. She is the island of artistic perfection where the lover of ancient beauty (shipwrecked in the modern world) may yet find foothold and take breath and gain courage for new adventures and dream of yet unexplored continents and realms of future artistic achievement. She is the wise Sappho.
>
> H.D. [1919] 1982: 67

Sappho and her works enable the modern poet to envisage the creation of poetry that is new and lasts, that resonates throughout time and space, moulding an imperfect modernity into artistic achievement.

As an empty name filled with different meanings at various points of her reception, Sappho inhabits H.D.'s oeuvre both as a lyric model and a 'latent mythic presence' (Gregory 1986: 529). In *Sea Garden*, H.D.'s appropriation of Sappho as a female poetic archetype intersects with her take on the Ovidian legend. The intermingling of the heterosexual and homosexual versions of Sappho's life and poetry appear to fit within the collection's overall interest in bisexual desire, as the gender of the poetic voice, often left unspecified, emerges as 'hermaphroditic, collective and atemporal' (Gregory: 1986: 537). In 'The Cliff Temple', H.D. rewrites the motif of Sappho's jump from the Leucadian rock into a solar myth, in a comparable way to Pascoli's rewritings in 'Solon'. A suppliant overtaken by erotic desire for a god longs to be reunited with him:

> III
> Shall I hurl myself from here,
> shall I leap and be nearer you?
> Shall I drop, beloved, beloved,

ankle against ankle?
Would you pity me, O white breast?

If I woke, would you pity me,
would our eyes meet?

Have you heard,
do you know how I climbed this rock?
My breath caught, I lurched forward –
I stumbled in the ground-myrtle.

Have you heard, O god seated on the cliff,
how far toward the ledges of your house,
how far I had to walk?

IV
Over me the wind swirls.
I have stood on your portal
and I know –
you are further than this
still further on another cliff.

Martz 1986: 27–8

Wanting to jump from the cliff to be reunited with the god, the suppliant conjures a solar myth based on the motif of Sappho's suicide for Phaon. The god 'seated on the cliff' is to be identified with Apollo conflated with the Sun god Helios: 'you lift, you are the world-edge / pillar for the sky-arch' (1.10–11, Martz 1986: 26).[33] Strabo (10.2.9) reports that Apollo had a temple and an ancestral cult practice on the Leucadian cliffs,[34] which according to myth (e.g. *Odyssey*, 24.1–14) were also identified with the Gates of the Sun. They also represented the threshold to the underworld (Nagy 1973: 140). In H.D.'s appropriation of Sappho's Leucadian cliffs, the jump driven by eros becomes a spiritual experience of union with the divine, which brings annihilation as it perpetuates life, in the same way as the natural cycle repeats itself. H.D.'s cosmological version of Sappho's leap underlines the closeness of erotic and death drives, reproducing the pattern of eros and thanatos.

As for Pascoli's work, contemporary anthropological studies on Greek cults may be behind some of the imagery in 'The Cliff Temple'. Frazer mentions the Leucadian sacrificial practices as well as the temple of Apollo set on the Rock

([1880] 1994: 600) and Jane Ellen Harrison's *Prolegomena to the Study of Greek Religion* (1903) discusses Apollo/Helios.[35] The psychologizing of myth typical of late-nineteenth-century scholarship and literature is found in H.D.'s poem, too, as the jump from Leucas marks the psychological threshold of erotic and creative desires. As Gregory points out, 'as a psychic event, then, the dive from Leukas suggests an entrance through desire into an unconscious emotional element, where the soul is vulnerable to the *eidola* of fantasy [...]. The cosmological dimension of the myth amplifies this psychic meaning' (1988: 117). The boundary between inner and outer is repeatedly underlined with liminal images: portals, rock-edge, the world-edge and crevices.[36]

The speaker's love frenzy corresponds to the struggle of a poet creating new verse. The storm of bitter-sweet eros beats the poet, while enabling her poetic vision. The suppliant's grasping after the god seems to enact an inverted version of the myth of Apollo and Daphne:

> for ever and for ever, must I follow you
> through the stones?
> I catch at you – you lurch:
> you are quicker than my hand-grasp.
>
> 'The Cliff Temple', 2.2–5, in Martz 1986: 27

The suppliant pursues Apollo, the god of love and poetry forever escaping. As H.D. remarked in her 'Notes on Thought and Vision', '[t]here is no great art period without great lovers' ([1919] 1982: 21) and 'we must be in love before we understand the mystery of vision' (22). Giving access to the spiritual vision of the poetic image, eros made the poet into a seer: 'I have stood on your portal / and I know' ('The Cliff Temple', 4.2–3). But desire is unquenchable: eros, god and poetry are always further away from her, on another cliff.

Sappho and Catullus beyond Imagism

Erotic ritualism: H.D.'s *Hymen* (1921) and *Heliodora* (1924)

H.D.'s engagement with Sappho reached a peak in the early 1920s. As she was formalizing her views in 'The Wise Sappho' (1919) and exploring the role of sexuality in creativity, the poet was also compiling her second collection *Hymen*, eventually published in 1921. The volume saw the light only two years after H.D. began her relationship with Bryher and kick-started H.D.'s revisionist approach to ancient myth, aimed at giving voice to female desire against the silencing act of heteropatriarchy. Strongly criticized by Pound for moving away from the objectivist criteria of the Imagists to privilege an exploration of the feminine lyric 'I',[37] H.D. embarked on her new poetic project to explore themes of women's creativity, subjectivity, sexuality and gender through a series of long dramatic monologues using the personas of female mythical figures. In *Hymen*, and in the following 1924 collection *Heliodora*, Sappho remains the original female poetic model. In her fragments, H.D. found the earliest literary representations of those types of relationships between women – friendship, love and maternal bonds – that she was so invested in bringing forward in her own poetry.

Explicit references to the Lesbian poet, however, surfaced only in time. *Hymen*'s title poem stages an ancient wedding ritual, as described in Sappho's epithalamia and Catullus 61 and 62. The intertext is rich, but the Sapphic and Catullan presences remain hidden in allusion. Sappho is mentioned explicitly only in six poems: 'Fragment 113' in *Hymen*; 'Fragment 36', 'Fragment 40', 'Fragment 41', 'Fragment 68' in *Heliodora*; 'Calliope' in *Red Roses for Bronze* (1931). Each 'fragment poem' is subtitled with a quotation from Wharton's translation of the Sapphic fragments. In this chapter, I mostly focus on 'Hymen' since, on the one hand, it is in this poem that the recreation of a Sapphic fiction first develops into a catalyst for the development of H.D.'s new aesthetic; on the other, 'Hymen' is a rare yet key text where H.D. explores Sappho and Catullus as a literary pair, serving her discussion of gendered power structures. Moreover, 'Hymen' has received comparatively less attention than the 'fragment poems', which I discuss briefly at the end of this section.

'Hymen' (1921)

'Hymen', originally published in *Poetry* in 1919, is a poetic masque set in a Hellenic context representing a wedding ritual between a bride and the allegorical character Love. The composition is divided in ten parts corresponding to various phases of the ceremony, which appears to model the wedding rituals described in the epithalamia of Sappho and Catullus.[38] Recent scholarship has established that each of Sappho's epithalamia fragments may be linked back to a particular step of the nuptial ceremony 'according to a synchronization of song and ritual in which the former is almost a function or made of the latter' (Ferrari 2010: 120). In a wedding ritual sung by Sappho, the bride would travel from her own house to that of the groom, where the marriage would be consumed, finalizing the bride's passage into mature life with a new family (Ferrari 2010: 119–20). These structures are reflected in Catullus's wedding poems, even though they functioned primarily as literary texts.[39]

Wharton's *Sappho* continued to be a main reference point for H.D. The anthology followed the Alexandrian organization of Sappho's fragments, with several epithalamia grouped under the same heading. Wharton provided a description of wedding rites by the fourth-century writer Himerius:

> Aphrodite's orgies we leave to Sappho of Lesbos, to sing to the lyre and make the bride-chamber her theme. She enters the chamber after the games, makes the room, spreads Homer's bed, assembles the maidens, leads them into the apartment with Aphrodite in the Graces' car and a band of Loves for playmates. Binding her tresses with hyacinth, except what is parted to fringe her forehead, she lets the rest wave to the wind if it chance to strike them. Their wings and curls she decks with gold, and drives them in procession before the car as they shake the torch on high.
>
> Wharton 1908: 133

H.D.'s description of the ritual follows an analogous structure. Following a procession of various groups of girls singing chants and bearing gifts of flowers to the bride, a group of 'older serene young women' (Martz 1986: 107) attend to the preparation of the bridal bed, after which the bride enters the room to be possessed by Love and the union is celebrated by a procession of boys holding torches. Via Wharton's translations,[40] Sappho's fragments are integrated into the masque, informing its narrative structure and thematic focus, while offering a juncture to reflect on the bride's own experience of the ritual.

The Sapphic intertext is complemented by various references to Catullus's epithalamia 61 and 62, although the chiefly Sapphic context establishes a hierarchical relationship ruled by Sappho. On Catullus 51 she comments:

> Catullus, impassioned lyrist, left off recounting the imperfections of his Lesbia to enter a fair paradisal world, to forge silver Latin from imperishable Greek, to marvel at the praises of this perfect lover who needed no interim of hatred to repossess the loved one.
>
> H.D. [1919] 1982: 69

H.D. dismisses Catullus's work and obliquely inserts the Roman poet into gender politics: the inferior Catullus is only redeemed by his devotion to Sappho. Sappho is idealized into the figure of the generous 'perfect lover', who does not need Catullus's petty hatred 'to repossess the loved one' – from the perspective of H.D.'s aesthetic eroticism, Sappho represents the perfect poet, too. Overturning Pound's ranking, H.D. indirectly rebutted his Catullan mask, which perpetrated precisely the hetero-patriarchal gender stereotypes that her work attempted to deconstruct. But since H.D. identified herself with Sappho and Pound with

Catullus, the reversal also put her at the top of the poetic hierarchy, reclaiming her place in the literary tradition.

Catullus 61 provided an additional source for the particulars of the marriage rituals in 'Hymen': the bride's 'snow-white foot' and 'yellow shoe' were drawn from Catullus:

> flammeum cape, laetus huc
> huc veni, niveo gerens
> luteum pede soccum;
>
> (put on the bridal veil happily here, / here come, wearing on your snow-white / foot the yellow shoe)
>
> *Cat.* 61.8–10

In H.D.'s poem, the bride wears a veil and a 'saffron shoe'; the image returns in a second description:

> We fastened the veil,
> And over the white foot
> Drew on the painted shoe
> Steeped in Illyrian crocus.
>
> Martz 1986: 105; 106

Throughout the poem, ritual clothing, headdress and colour, carefully employed with strong symbolic connotations, are repeatedly mentioned. Yellow and white are associated with the bride and her retinue, while various shades of purple and red refer to Love, male desire and (forced) marriage union.[41]

A crescendo of reds and crimsons signals the arrival of Love, winged and burning:

> The figure itself is a flame, an exaggerated symbol; the hair a flame; the wings, deep red or purple, stand out against the curtains in a contrasting or almost clashing shade of purple. The tunic, again a rich purple or crimson, falls almost to the knees. The knees are bare; the sandals elaborately strapped over and over. The curtain seems a rich purple cloud, the figure, still brighter, like a flamboyant bird, half emerged in the sunset.
>
> Love pauses just outside the bride's door with his gift, a tuft of black-purple cyclamen.
>
> Martz 1986: 108

This imagery originated from the works of Catullus and Sappho. Catullus 61 provided the association between the groom's desire and fire:

> illi non minus ac tibi
> pectore urit in intimo
> flamma, sed penite magis.
>
> (in his most intimate heart / no less than in yours / burns the flame, / but deeper inside)
>
> Cat. 61.169–71

Catullus 62.20–3 also presented the light of Hesperus, the star harbinger of wedding nights, as fire, with the groom as a *iuvenis ardens* (burning youth). The reds and purples of Sappho's epithalamia, variously translated in Wharton's anthology, also resurfaced in H.D.'s passage. The rich tunic of Love in her poem is similar to the description in Wharton's translation of fr. 64Bergk (54Voigt), 'Coming from heaven wearing a purple mantle' (Wharton 1908: 111); J.A. Symonds' version of the same fragment, 'the red chlamys burned like a flame' included in Wharton's anthology (1908: 111) is also evoked in the symbolic flame of Love. The Catullan intertext unequivocally re-emerges in the violent sexual union ending the rite of passage. In the consummation scene, for instance, 'the crimson cover of her bed' (Martz 1986: 108) echoes the purple couch on which the groom eagerly awaits the bride in Catullus 61.164–6. If, as I discuss below, Sappho's fragments sustained H.D.'s fiction of an ancient community of women living and writing for each other, partly validated by contemporary scholarship on Sappho's *thiasos* modelled after Welcker's theories,[42] Catullus's epithalamia, in which virginity is meaningful only in relation to male penetration and the social needs of procreation (Gregory 1997: 156–7),[43] provided H.D. with buttresses to recreate a sense of the patriarchal masculine order.

Overall, the masque focuses mostly on the female perspective, as the performance is almost entirely carried out by groups of young women and the groom is assimilated into the symbolic figure of 'Love'. From its very title, 'Hymen' draws attention to the bodily aspect of the rite of passage, casting marriage as a moment of irreparable loss for the woman: a forced renunciation of virginity and the bonds of love and friendship with other women, and a silencing of female desire. Suggesting that women could never commend the completion of the patriarchal rite, the only group of young boys featuring in the masque enters to sing the last song after Love has violently possessed the bride (109–10). Indeed, before the beginning of the procession, four girls in the bride's circle lament the loss of their friend, who, as a wife, can never re-join them:

> Never more will the wind
> Cherish you again,

Never more will the rain
[…]
The snow is melted,
The snow is gone,
And you are flown:

Like a bird out of our hand
Like a light out of our heart,
You are gone.
Martz 1986: 103

As Pascoli reused Sappho's invocation to virginity in fr. 109Bergk (114Voigt) to lament the loss of his sister Ida who left the family nest to marry, so H.D. rewrites the same fragment to underline the sense of loss left by marriage. In another comparable move to Pascoli's, H.D. connects rites of mating with the seasonal cycle: as the snow thawed, the flower/bride has blossomed to be culled by the god of Love. As Gregory notes, the association between the wedding ritual and death is heightened in 'Hymen's song 'From citron-bower be her bed', in which the bridal bed transforms into a coffin (1997: 159):

That all the wood in blossoming,
May calm her heart and cool her blood
For losing of her maidenhood.
Martz 1986: 108

Laments on the caducity of life also characterize Pascoli's appropriations of Sappho's epithalamia. Both the Italian and the American poets layer their rewritings with references to marriage and funerary rites. The former connects the wedding rite to the loss of the family nucleus, the latter to the loss of a community of women. Significantly, while 'Hymen' is recounted from a feminine perspective, the bride is never given a voice, as a representation of the silencing of female desire by heteropatriarchy.

The poem's pivotal moment is reached in the violent marital union. In a series of explicit images, the god of Love in the form of a bee violates ('a plunderer', 109) the bride-flower ('slips / between the purple flower-lips', 109), who recalcitrantly, yet silently, bears the violent passion of the god ('stern the petals drawing back'; 'her shoulders drawing back!', 109). H.D. repeatedly exploits myths of violent possession of women by a male god or a violent husband in *Hymen*, for instance in 'Leda' and 'Thetis'. While this strikes as the beginning of H.D.'s revisionist approach to patriarchal myths, it also reveals her interest in eroticism as a form of divine possession, which she posited as the basis of creativity. As Gregory showed (1997: 121; 160), the figure of the *Hieros gamos* is likely to have informed representations of sexual union as divine possession in H.D.'s oeuvre as in, for instance, 'The Cliff Temple', where the female lyric 'I' seeks to be possessed by Apollo/Helios; similar divine epiphanies are found also in the last song of 'Hymen':

> Where love is come
> (Ah love is come indeed!)
> Our limbs are numb
> Before his fiery need;
>
> Martz 1986: 110

A 'sense of daimonic eros' (Gregory 1997: 160), emerges from this stanza, in which echoes of the 'limbs-numbing eros' of Sappho's fr. 40Bergk (130Voigt) and the surging of the subtle fire of desire of fr. 2Bergk (31Voigt) imply divine possession. In this way, H.D. anchors Sappho's fragments to a metaphysical conception of eros as divine incarnation found also in Plato and Dante, bringing together the Greek and medieval traditions, in perfect modernist fashion.

H.D.'s Sapphic fragments

As the first explicit mentions of Sappho in H.D.'s work, critics have variously interpreted the fragment poems as H.D.'s admission of her lesbian sexuality (Du Plessis 1986: 24), as representations of a struggle to inscribe herself into a female tradition originating in Sappho's work (Gubar 1984: 56–7) and as an attempt at modelling a lesbian poetics (Collecott 1999: 15–39). Yet, as Gregory notes, the fragment poems are also 'clearly implicated within a male-identified erotic discourse' (1997: 153), which maintains a sense of bisexual eros in the collection. The 'fragment poems' of the 1920s and 1930s encompass heterosexual and homosexual desires, while favouring Sapphic eros as the first incarnation of the spiritual, daimonic form of eroticism that informs H.D.'s poetics.

With the exception of brief quotations of Sappho's poetry as subtitles, the 'fragment poems' show little direct textual engagement with the originals. The name 'Sappho', cited beside the quotations, radiates as a prism the countless meanings attributed to the life and work of the Lesbian poet over the centuries: the first female poet, the legendary literary figure of the Ovidian tradition, the original literary source of homoerotic desire between two women, the fragment completed by imagination, and finally, in H.D.'s words, 'the island of artistic perfection' ([1919] 1982: 67), a signifier of poetry itself. Below I discuss 'Fragment 113' and one of the four 'fragment poems' included in *Heliodora*, 'Fragment 36', in which the relationship between Sapphic eros and H.D.'s views on poetry emerges most strongly.

Wharton's translation of fr. 113Bergk (146Voigt) becomes a structuring refrain in 'Fragment 113: "Neither honey nor bee for me." – Sappho'. The repeated use of negations reinforces the struggle of the poetic 'I', who abandons 'old' sensual desire for the aesthetic rapture that fuels poetic vision. Both heterosexual and lesbian desires are negated:

> Not honey,
> not the plunder of the bee
> [...]
> not honey, not the south;
> ah flower of purple iris,
> flower of white,
> or of the iris, withering the grass –
> [...]
> Not this, nor any flower
>
> Martz 1986: 131

The 'plunder of the bee', the same image she used in 'Hymen' in her description of sexual union with the husband, has become impossible, just as desire for women, which is often symbolized in H.D.'s poetry by flowers and the colour white, 'purple iris, / flower of white', is left behind. In 'The Wise Sappho' ([1919] 1982: 58), images of whiteness are associated with the particular kind of homoerotic desire that, according to H.D., fuelled Sappho's poetic drive. The use of this symbolism allowed her to allude to homoeroticism without openly speaking about lesbianism.[44] Bisexuality and, indeed, an interest in desire beyond the gender and sex of its object characterize H.D.'s poetry, as the speaking voice of her poems hardly ever emerges as female or male. The Freudian idea that the bisexuality of an individual never disappears completely after childhood was liberating for H.D.,[45] whose representations of desire as an unbound force allowed her to inscribe her poetry into a non-heteronormative literary tradition, originating in Sappho and mediated by another of her poetic models, Algernon Charles Swinburne, who argued that 'great poets are bisexual' (Collecott 1999: 25). Lesbianism, still a taboo at the time, is never mentioned explicitly, but it may be inferred from her language (Collecott 1999: 28). H.D.'s reuse of Sappho points at the idea that both Sapphic and sapphic traditions rest on fragments, which become symbols, in Wittig's words, of the 'female ruptured by entry into language' (quoted in Collecott 1999: 28) and the impossibility of articulating homoerotic desire within the patriarchal symbolic order.[46]

Despite being enraptured by sensual desire so strong that impairs the senses, similarly to Sappho 31, the speaker of 'Fragment 113' chooses to channel her longing into a form of aesthetic eroticism that may give life to new poetry:

> but if you turn again,
> seek strength of arm and throat,
> touch as the god;
> neglect the lyre-note;
> knowing that you shall feel,
> about the frame,
> but heat, more passionate
> of bone and the white shell
> and fiery tempered steel.
>
> Martz 1986: 131–2

This new poetry privileges the poetic intensity and terseness of 'heat', 'bone', 'white shell' and 'tempered steel', which are found in Sappho's fragments, over the softer notes of other lyric poetry. Heat, already employed in 'Garden' with similar connotations, returns in this recreation of Sappho's 133Bergk to define H.D.'s aesthetics.

'Fragment 36: "I know not what to do: / my mind is divided." – Sappho', first published in *Poetry* in 1921 and later included in *Heliodora* (1924) expresses the same tension between erotic and poetical passions through a free adaptation of Sappho's fr. 36Bergk (51Voigt).[47] The speaker, whose gender remains ambiguous, asks if she should prefer love's or poetry's gifts, wondering whether or not to wake his/her lover asleep at night. If we assume a female poetic persona as in Sappho's fragment, as suggested by the use of white imagery ('O I am eager for you! / As the Pleiads shake / white light in whiter water', 166), the speaker's dilemma is whether to abandon herself to a homoerotic relationship or to opt for aesthetic passion. She is, however, unable to decide, as choosing involves a fragmentation of self, language, as well as poetic form. The poem, with its pounding refrain 'I know not what to do', drawn from Sappho's 'Οὐκ οἶδ' ὅττι θέω', emphasizes the strife of the self, threatened by rapture. Putting art over life would entail an endeavour to position herself in language and tradition, to illuminate glimpses of knowledge through the 'scattered light' (167) of words. This existential paradox is fundamental to H.D.'s work overall, as she defined her poems as 'finished fragments': 'Finished fragments? Yes, I suppose they are that, stylistic slashings, definitely self-conscious, though, as I say, impelled by some inner conflict' ('Letter to Norman Pearson (1937)' in 1988: 73).[48] Taking ambivalence and strife via fr.36Bergk to the centre of her creative process, H.D. reiterates her debt to Sappho, shaping her own authorial identity in a matrilineal succession from the Lesbian poet.[49]

The second phase in Pound's reception: The two masks of Eros

Alongside Sappho 95 and 96, excerpts from frr. 105b, 109 and Catullus 61 and 62 are repeatedly inserted or rewritten in the *Cantos*, where Pound's myth-making finds its wider expression. Sappho and Catullus as a literary pair form a lyric cluster that portrays them as the original lyric models in the history of literature, while articulating mythic and anthropological configurations of erotic desire as a vital force.[50] Like Pascoli and H.D., Pound is attracted to the ritualistic aspect of ancient epithalamia. This approach characterizes the second phase of the Sappho/Catullus polarity in the American poet's work.

References to Catullus's wedding song 61 are everywhere in Pound's work: it appears in his criticism, letters, in Cantos 2, 4, 5, 20, 28, and in his unfinished opera libretto *Collis O Heliconii*.[51] The presence of the *carmen* is particularly felt in Canto 4:

> Torches melt in the glare
>   set flame of the corner cook-stall,
> Blue agate casing the sky (as the Gourdon that time)
>   the sputter of resin,
> Saffron sandal so petals the narrow foot: Ὑμήν,
> 'Ὑμέναι ὦ, Aurunculeia! Ὑμήν, Ὑμέναι ὦ, [**See Catullus 61**]
> One scarlet flower is cast on the blanch-white stone. [**See Sappho 105b**]
>   Pound [1986] 1996: 15

Canto 4 holds many similarities with Ur-cantos I-II, although most of the early translations and explicit references to the texts are excised, creating an elliptical aesthetic reflection on lyric poetry as an expression of the mythical and psychological structures of eros. To this end, Pound focuses on the hymenaic aspects of Catullus 61. Drawn, as H.D. in 'Hymen', to the delicate image of the bride's foot clad in yellow, his Imagistic translation exploits the metaphor of the bride as flower; her sandal 'petals' her foot, before culminating in the invocation to Hymen. In a 1950 letter to his friend James Laughlin, founder of the publishing house New Directions, Pound explains why, for the second edition, he decided to transliterate the invocation into Greek alphabet:

The other chance is in p / 15 yr / edtn / Canto IV. Takin the Catullus back to HarryStopHerKnees, whaar Cat / mebbe got it any.

Anyhow the greek shows the real way Cat/ wd / hv tookd it fer graunted the Epithalamium wd / be sung.

'EP to JL, n.d. St. Elizabeth's Hospital' = Gordon 1994: 206

According to Pound, the Greek better conveys how the original wedding song would be sung and how Catullus must have thought about it, confirming his investment in the ritualistic aspect of his poetry. The letter illuminates another intertextual element behind the invocation to Hymen: Aristophanes' ('HarryStopHerKnees') comedy *Pax*, which includes a choral epithalamion.[52] The Catullan quotation is accompanied by echoes of Sappho's hymenaic poetry in fr. 105b ('χάμαι δέ τε πόρφυρον ἄνθος', l. 2) (the purple flowers lie) in 'one scarlet flower is cast on the blanch-white stone'. Commenting on the 'scarlet flower' in this line, Terrell notes that '[t]his image of the virgin's loss of maidenhood on her wedding night is paralleled by the much used topos of Provençal and other medieval poetry of the knight being reminded of his beloved by blood drops in the snow' (1980: 14). The Canto declines the hymenaic theme recalling images from various points of the literary traditions and the Sappho / Catullus cluster is made to interact with archaic, medieval and modern lyric traditions, sanctioning Pound's theories as first expounded in *The Spirit of Romance*, *Lustra* and 'Three Cantos'.

Canto 5 brings Catullus 61 back, within a much stronger Sapphic presence than before:

The fire? always, and the vision always,
Ear dull, perhaps, with the vision, flitting
And fading at will. Weaving with points of gold,
Gold-yellow, saffron... The roman show, Aurunculeia's
And come shuffling feet, and cries 'Da nuces!
'Nuces' praise, and Hymenaeus 'brings the girl to her man' **[See Catullus 61]**
Or 'here Sextus had seen her'.
Titter of sound about me, always.
    and from 'Hesperus...' **[See Sappho 104 / Catullus 62]**
Hush of the older song: 'Fades light from sea-crest,
'And in Lydia walks with pair'd women
'Peerless among the pairs, that once in Sardis
'In satieties...   **[See Pound's 'Ἱμέρρω' (l.2) / Sappho 96]**
    Fades the light from the sea, and many things
Are set abroad and brought to mind of thee,' **[See Sappho 95]**

And the vinestocks lie untended, new leaves come to the shoots,
North wind nips on the bough, and seas in heart
Toss up chill crests,
    And the vine stocks lie untended
So many things are set abroad and brought to mind
Of thee, Atthis, unfruitful. [**See Sappho 96**]

Pound [1986] 1996: 17–18

The Canto represents the Roman wedding of Aurunculeia, the bride of Catullus 61, including the ritual details of the throwing of nuts ('Da nuces pueris', l. 124) (Give the nuts to the boys) heralding fertility.[53] The reader is then taken to a Sapphic context via Catullus 62 ('Vesper adest', l. 1) (Hesperus appears), evoked by the reference to Hesperus, followed by rewritings of Sappho 95 and 96 – the same fragments translated in *Lustra*.[54] The importance of the Sappho/Catullus lyric cluster is, as Kenner remarks, emphasized by the omission of the main Homeric simile in fr. 96: '[He] denied himself even the splendid word *brododaktylos*, apparently because it bespoke Homer too insistently to be usable. Catullus and Sappho were his terms of reference, and later privations and troubadours, but nothing epic' (Kenner 1991: 65). The two ancient poets are raised to exemplary lyric pair foundational to modern poetry and culture: 'So many things are set abroad and brought to mind / Of thee'. The natural, social and mythical structures of eros, which Pound found in the verses of Sappho and Catullus, are brought to new life in his poem, and stand as examples of the modernist 'mythic method'.

The third phase in Pound's reception: Private and public poetry

Collis O Heliconii, the third and unfinished opera written by Pound between 1932 and 1934 after *The Testament* and *Cavalcanti,* was meant 'to be the final composition of a trilogy on sacred, ideal and profane love' but never saw the light of day (Fisher 2005: xvi). Ever concerned with reproducing the ancient rhythms of Greek and Latin poetry in a new and contemporary form, and frustrated by what he thought was the unsuitability of English to convey the cadence of the ancient languages (particularly Greek),[55] with *Collis* Pound originally wanted to create a musical module that translated the Sapphic and Catullan metres into music (Fisher 2005: viii; 4). But of course, 'Pound's musical experiments were a by-product of his studies in poetic versification' (Taruskin 2003). Having decided to employ the Latin text of Catullus 61, which also provides the title line for the composition, and the Greek of Sappho 1, Pound was facing the challenge of respecting quantitative metre and caesuras, as well as the 'pitch or stress accent against the recurring ictus of the metrical rhythm' (Fisher 2005: viii). After few months, finding it too complicated, Pound abandoned the project. Nevertheless, *Collis*, with *The Testament* and *Cavalcanti*, remains one of his most visionary works.

The manuscript material for the opera includes a libretto (with a scenario for Catullus's poem), three instrumental works, and two arias – one entitled *Collis O Heliconii* for a bass singer, based on Catullus 61, and the second *Poikilothron*, for mezzo-soprano, based on Sappho 1.[56] Pound never translated either Catullus's or Sappho's texts in full and these musical experiments remain in embryonic form. Yet Margaret Fisher, in her edition of the unpublished opera's manuscripts, has argued that *Collis* should be considered Pound's attempt at criticism by music.

Catullus 61 and Sappho fr. 1 are employed as librettos one after the other. According to Fisher, *Collis*' engagement with Catullus's hymenaic song in juxtaposition with the Sapphic ode reflects Pound's conviction of 'the necessity of Latin to salvage the Greek heritage for an English audience'. It finally displays the syncretism of the Catullan ode, pointing at 'the role of the gods in the ritual of the marriage bed, and the anthologizing reach across centuries and cultures to forge in music a love poetry that aspires to restore a love cult' (Fisher 2005: 7). Pound also plays with the elements of the Sapphic and Catullan masks developed in his earlier poetry, taking the relationship between the two a step forward.

As the finale of Pound's operatic love trilogy, *Collis* stands as another literary enactment of eros as a vital spirit. The appropriations of Sappho and Catullus this time focus on the private and public aspects of love and sexual union. They also confirm Pound's interest in ritual. Pound polarizes his discourse by juxtaposing Sappho's intimate address to Aphrodite and the public performance of Catullus's epithalamion. The stage directions of the opera confirm this division. Fisher points out that 'A libretto mentions two groups, possibly girls and boys' choruses' (Fisher 2005: xvii), mirroring the dialogic structure of Catullus 61. The performative aspect of the ritual subsumed in Catullus's poem is thus implemented by the insertion of the lyric into the performative context of the opera, but also in the prefiguration of an actual dramatization in the theatre, as a manuscript scenario for the staging of Catullus 61 shows.[57] Pound, thus, meta-poetically, draws attention to Sappho's intimate subjectivity through the contrast with the official poetry of the Catullan poem. The two poets stand in the opera as equals and paradigms of two different kinds of lyricism.

Focusing on the complementary aspects of Sappho and Catullus as a lyric pair, Pound often envisioned them as binary counterparts, representing ideal and real spheres or private and public realms. He juxtaposes the Sapphic and

Catullan masks in *Lustra* as well as in *The Cantos* and his opera, *Collis O Heliconii* to explore the various ways in which poetry expresses the erotic structure of reality. At the same time, the continuous presence of Sappho and Catullus throughout Pound's oeuvre confirms the importance of the ancient literary pair within his aesthetic operation of renewal of modern poetry. In the next chapters, it emerges that Pound's take on Sappho's and Catullus's lyricisms, on the one hand casting them as lyric archetypes for modernity, on the other, appropriating their poetic personas to develop his own ironic and meta-literary approach to lyric poetry, became one of the main paradigms of Sappho's and Catullus's reception in twentieth-century US literature. Similarly, H.D.'s reception of Sappho and Catullus confirms the key role of the two ancient poets in shaping first her Imagist poetics, then her mythic revisionism, bringing to light another crucial aspect of their reception in the twentieth century: the questioning of patriarchal constructions of gender and sexuality.

3

Classical Hermeticism

When the Sicilian poet and Nobel Prize winner Salvatore Quasimodo (1902–68) published *Lirici greci* (Greek lyrics) in 1940 – to this day the most famous anthology of archaic Greek lyric on the market in Italy – he was at the apex of the Hermeticist stage of his career.[1] With affinities to the French symbolism of Verlaine and Mallarmé, in the interwar period Hermeticism had developed into one of the most prominent literary movements in Fascist Italy. By the outbreak of the Second World War, poets including Giuseppe Ungaretti, Eugenio Montale, Mario Luzi and Quasimodo himself, working alongside *critici militanti* (militant critics) such as Carlo Bo, Oreste Macrì and Luciano Anceschi, were discussing and actively promoting Hermeticist poetics. Their speculations were based on the notion of 'letteratura come vita' (literature as life) and aimed to achieve 'poesia pura' (pure poetry).[2] The debate cautiously remained in the aesthetic realm, avoiding explicit political discourse – an attitude which enabled Hermeticism to elude fascist censorship, but which was strongly criticized for its lack of *impegno* (political commitment) in the immediate aftermath of the war.[3] Positing the impossibility of engaging with the external reality plagued by fascist propaganda and the war, Hermeticist poetry retreated into the inner subjective dimension of the self, voicing the song of isolated poets. Advocating the autonomy and self-sufficiency of art, poetry was conceived as a series of lyric fragments, revelations of a metaphysical absolute that took priority over the everyday, however troubled reality may have been. Quasimodo's investment in archaic Greek lyric, especially Sappho, emerged from this cultural environment and Hermeticist definitions of pure poetry as monodic lyric song.[4]

Until the early 1940s, Quasimodo's work displayed a tension between its lyric poetic persona and its self-referential language, which, giving prominence to signifier over signified, pulled poetry toward non-representational expression. His verse showed a concern with the pre-eminence of the word as a self-contained poetic element and a manifestation of an unreachable metaphysical absolute, labelled by the Hermeticist critic Oreste Macrì as 'poetica della parola' (poetics of the word).[5] In its most daring experiments, this emphasis on the expressive power of individual words created syntactic displacement and produced an intensely analogic discourse pointing beyond sensory reality. The origins of this kind of non-representational and non-narrative poetry may be traced back to nineteenth-century works by Hölderlin, Poe, Baudelaire and Leopardi, and found contemporary consonances in Paul Valéry's writings on 'pure poetry'.[6] Only after the end of Hermeticism and the Second World War did Quasimodo begin to write socially engaged and anti-Fascist poetry with *Giorno dopo giorno* (1947) (Day after day), moving toward mimetic language.

Regardless of these stylistic fluctuations, throughout his career ancient Greek and Latin literature remained central to Quasimodo's poetry. Beginning with his first collection *Acque e terre* (Waters and lands) (1930), echoes of Sappho, Alcaeus, Homer, Catullus, Virgil and Ovid began to emerge and progressively become stronger in *Oboe sommerso* (Submerged oboe) (1932) and *Erato e Apollion* (1936). With the release of *Lirici greci* in 1940, Quasimodo revealed his programmatic investment in the classics. Being the first of a long series of book-length translations of ancient and modern literatures into several languages signed by the poet, *Lirici greci* represented a turning point in Quasimodo's poetic career.[7] After *Lirici*, translation, both as a form of art and a bridging process between different cultural systems, constituted the backbone of Quasimodo's aesthetic research.

His translation anthologies outnumber his collections of poetry. His main workshop took place in the 1940s, during which the poet forged his relationship with forms of creative translation. The compendium of ancient Greek lyric was immediately followed by an anthology of Ovid's *Georgics* in 1942 and one of Catullus's poetry, entitled *Catullus Veronensis Carmina* (The poems of Catullus of Verona), in 1945, re-issued in the expanded and revised edition of 1955 as *Canti di Catullo* (Catullus's songs). Between 1938 and 1945, Quasimodo established a translating practice that would last to the end of his career and formalized his Hermeticist poetics in dialogue with ancient Greek and Latin poetry and, above all, Sappho and Catullus.

Quasimodo's experience as a translator began with Sappho and Catullus – the first translations published by the poet between 1938 and 1939 were of Sappho 31 and Catullus 31 and 65. First and foremost poetic models, the ancient literary pair epitomized the poetic process itself, as if, after the physical and psychological destruction brought about by Fascism and the Second World War, translating Sappho and Catullus enabled Quasimodo to write again, using their voices.[8]

Sappho's fr. 31 was the very first translation published by Quasimodo in 1938 and was included in the collection *Poesie* (Poems) under the title 'Dal Greco di Saffo' (From the Greek of Sappho). This was followed in April 1939 by his translations of Catullus 31 and 65 published in the journal *Corrente*.[9] In the former, entitled by Quasimodo 'A Sirmio' (To Sirmio), Catullus expresses his joy in returning home after his travels in Bythinia, and in the latter, given the Italian title 'A Quinto Ortensio Ortalo' (To Quintus Hortensius Hortalus), a letter in verse is sent to a friend to accompany Catullus's translation of Callimachus' *Lock of Berenice* (*Aitia* fr. 110 translated in Catullus 66). As Giuseppe Savoca notes (1986), this embryonic stage of Quasimodo's reflection on poetic translation and literary tradition took shape through his relationship with Catullus as Ur-poet-translator of Sappho and Callimachus, enabling him to project himself into the contemporary literary landscape as a modern poet-translator following in the ancient's footsteps. As he sent a draft translation of Sappho 31 to his partner Maria Cumani, Quasimodo dismissed previous eminent poetic translations, at the same time putting himself on a par with the greats of Italian literature:

> Ma, se ti capita, confronta la traduzione tentata dal Foscolo della stessa ode e vedrai quanto il *melodramma* abbia reso ridicola quella purissima poesia. E quella di Pascoli?

> (But if you have the chance, compare the translation of the same ode attempted by Foscolo and you will see how its *melodrama* makes the purest of poems sound ridiculous. And the one by Pascoli?)
> 'Letter of 10:VII:XV' = A. Quasimodo 1985: 75

The romantic 'melodrama' emerging from the translations by Ugo Foscolo and Pascoli is rejected for a style that would come closer to the purity of Sappho's lyric.[10] Yet, Foscolo and Pascoli, as poet-translators of both Sappho and Catullus, also represented illustrious models, which Quasimodo set out to outdo. In this way, he replicates the seventeenth-century dynamics of appropriation of Sappho 31, which saw established, typically male, poets emulate Catullus, while competing for the best translation.[11]

The contemporary discourse on the role and function of translation and literary tradition certainly impacted on Quasimodo's reception of Sappho and Catullus. A self-taught classicist, he neither had the command of Greek and Latin achieved by his predecessors Foscolo, Leopardi, Carducci and Pascoli, nor the analytical sophistication of academic scholars.[12] Distancing his translations from historicist methods that posited the pre-eminence of the source over the target text, he nurtured creative approaches to translating practices.[13] His translations collided with the academicism of poet philologists, such as Carducci and Pascoli, whose experiments with neoclassical metrics still targeted a degree of formal and semantic equivalence.[14] In the 'Chiarimento e note alla traduzioni' (Clarification and notes to the translations) of *Lirici*, Quasimodo explains:

> Quella terminologia classicheggiante [...] che pretese di costituirsi a linguaggio aromatico, adatto soprattutto alle traduzioni dei testi greci e latini, [...] è morta nello spirito delle generazioni nuove.

> (The classicizing terminology that demanded to establish itself as an 'aromatic language', especially suitable for the translation of Greek and Latin texts, is dead in the spirit of new generations.)
>
> [1940] 2004: 207

Dismissing the linguistic ornaments of academic neoclassicism, with *Lirici greci* he wanted to restore the ancient texts' musicality, which, he thought, had been lost in 'the verse attempts of illustrious Greek scholars' (Quasimodo [1940] 2004: 208), such as the classicizing stiff translations by Giuseppe Fraccaroli (1910–13).

As Anglo-American Modernists of the previous generation, Quasimodo aimed to remove classical texts from a static conception of the literary tradition as a monument to the past. Looking back on *Lirici* after two decades, the militant critic and philosopher Luciano Anceschi, a close collaborator in the compilation of the anthology, made a connection between Quasimodo's translation and the 'idea del tradurre' (the concept of translation) characterizing the modernist experiments. He found a shared anti-academic approach to translation in both Quasimodo's work and the ideas emerging from Eliot's excoriating reviews of Gilbert Murray's translation of Euripides and Pound's letters to Dr Rouse on translating the *Odyssey* ([1951] 2004: 333, [1978] 2004: 337).[15] Despite the introduction of censorship (*bonifica libraria*) by the Fascist regime in 1938, American writing had been circulating in Italy since the 1920s, aided by a boom in the publication of foreign translations between 1929 and 1938,[16] and disseminated by poetry journals such as *Solaria* and *Circoli*.[17] Gathering similar critiques to those imputed to Pound's *Homage to Sextus Propertius* (1919), Quasimodo's *Lirici* was not unanimously applauded by Italian classicists, who found several inaccuracies in the text, imputing them to the author's scant knowledge of Greek.[18] However, some also recognized the translations' poetic value as self-standing texts.[19]

This reception dynamic reflected the contemporary debate on translation, which was posed within wider discussions on theories of language and mind and divided between historicist and idealist positions.[20] On the one hand, classicists such as Giorgio Pasquali carried out a staunch defence of philological accuracy and linguistic approximation informed by historical knowledge of the sources.[21] On the other hand, idealist philosophers had a metaphysical approach to inquiries into translation, which led to claims of autonomy of the target text and to the development of aesthetic approaches to translating practices. The leading idealist philosopher, Benedetto Croce, argued that poetic texts were fundamentally untranslatable, resulting in translations that are 'Brutte fedeli o belle infedeli' (faithfully ugly or unfaithfully beautiful) ([1902]1990: 87), freeing poet-translators from the requirement of accuracy.[22] In 1920, moving beyond issues of (un)translatability, Giovanni Gentile, co-founder with Croce of the journal *La Critica*, further argued that translation was a cognitive process inherent in all reading practices – including reading one's own native idiom – and even all thought expressed through language.[23] Quasimodo's *Lirici* arises from this idealist milieu, which fostered his creative approach to translation as a poetic process.

In a revised version of Eliot's 'simultaneous order' of past and present works (1920: 60), Quasimodo's aesthetics aimed at 'inaugur[are] un neo-umanesimo; [...] un segno indistruttibile della nostra presenza nel mondo' (to inaugurate a neo-humanism; [...] an indestructible sign of our presence in the world) (Letter to Susini (4 May 1939) = Musolino 2003: 58). This form of 'neo-humanism' finds another parallel in the contemporary theorizations of Werner Jaeger in Germany with *Paideia: The Ideals of Greek Culture* (1939–45). Jaeger's was a celebration of Hellenism in the history of education and a re-evaluation of the model of *Bildung* (self-cultivation) which formed the basis of the Prussian university system in the nineteenth century, claiming that ancient Greek culture was the foundation and model for modernity.[24] Both Quasimodo and Jaeger were writing at a time of domination by Fascists and Nazis – both authors held, at least on the surface, a purportedly apolitical approach to the classics, but distanced themselves and their writing from the culture of appropriations of *Romanitas*.

In this chapter I show that, through his process of creative and appropriative translation, Quasimodo pushed forward his own aesthetic view of the world, tracing its origins back to the ancient lyric of Sappho and the elegiac poetry of her first translator, Catullus. Sappho and Catullus became the lenses through which Quasimodo envisaged a form of classical Hermeticism.

Tradition and translation towards a lyric absolute

The first edition of *Lirici greci*, with a programmatic 'Introduction' by Anceschi, was published in 1940 by Edizioni di Corrente. The success of the anthology among the wider public produced four new editions: *Lirici greci* (Mondadori, 1944), with Anceschi's 'Introduction' partially modified; *Lirici greci* (Mondadori, 1951) with a new 'Introduction' also by Anceschi; *Lirici greci* (Mondadori,1958, reproducing the 1951 'Introduction'), which is considered the definitive text, and, finally, *Lirici greci*, 'Opera Omnia' (Mondadori,1965). Its influence endures today as the anthology continues to be reprinted.[25]

The selection of fragments reveals a concern with monodic lyric, occupying over half of the anthology. Of a total of seventy-three fragments, forty-two are monodic lyrics. Sappho is the most prominent poet, with nineteen translations, almost as many as all fragments by Alcaeus (ten), Erinna (three) and Anacreon (ten) put together. There are only thirteen choral lyric fragments – four by Alcman, one by Stesichoros, six by Ibycus and two by Simonides.[26] Most striking is the absence of the two choral poets Pindar and Bacchylides. While Quasimodo's source text, Ernest Diehl's *Anthologia Lyrica Graeca*, in the second edition of 1936,[27] also excludes the two poets, it does so on the grounds of their relevance in the history of Greek literature. As T. Hudson-Williams remarked in his review of Diehl's first edition, after the discoveries in Egypt, both Pindar and Bacchylides deserved a dedicated volume (1925: 182–3). Soon condemned by several contemporary classicists,[28] Quasimodo's poetic alignment with monodic lyricism and brevity sprang from a deliberate shunning of dialogic genres, including epic. Born from an active collaboration with the militant critical action of Anceschi and his Hermeticist aesthetic agenda, the aims of the anthology were clearly stated in the 1940 introduction:

> Entro i limiti di una pura (attuale e antica) idea della poesia perciò fu osservata la scelta dei testi [...]. Naturalmente è ben definito il senso anche delle esclusioni di poeti disposti a mettere a servizio della 'celebrazione' la magnificenza di uno stile espertissimo, come Pindaro: o, come Bacchilide, abile e colto in una dolcezza di analisi descrittive. E, sempre, poi, un rigore senza concessioni ha voluto la esclusione, o almeno, la limitazione nella presenza di poeti 'semilirici' (giambici o elegiaci, gnomici o politici) troppo disposti alla *sentenza*, all'*esortazione* o alla *narrazione*: a indubbie condizioni di prosa.

> (The choice of texts was made within the limits of the idea of pure (contemporary and ancient) poetry [...]. Naturally, the reasons for the exclusions of poets like

Pindar, who are willing to use their expert and magnificent style for 'celebration' purposes, or Bacchylides, skilful and learned in his sweet, descriptive analyses, emerge clearly. And again, our rigour without concessions has excluded or at least has limited the presence of 'semi-lyric' poets (iambic or elegiac, gnomic or political), too prone to maxims, exhortations or narration, and with undeniable propensities for prose.)

Anceschi [1940] 2004: 315

Too celebrative or narrative for the Hermeticist agenda, choral, epigrammatic and elegiac poetry was excluded, as Quasimodo set out to translate monodic lyric poetry with the clear intention of following a conception of 'pure poetry'.

Criteria of semantic and metrical equivalence were displaced by measures of 'poetic voice' and 'ricerca equilirica' ('equilyric research') (Quasimodo [1940] 2004: 208). Moving from Hermeticist interpretations of ancient lyric and poetry at large, his translations aimed to recreate the lyric 'purity' of the originals, through a language privileging the rendition of 'voce poetica' (poetic voice), also defined as 'canto del poeta' (the poet's song), preferred to semantic equivalence (Quasimodo [1940] 2004: 208). In this creative process, linguistic and metrical approximations became secondary standards of translation, favouring the rendition of '[la] vera quantità d'ogni parola (nella piega della voce che la pronuncia)' (the real quantity of each word (unfolding in the voice of the one pronouncing it)) (Quasimodo [1940] 2004: 208). Searching for target texts that would match the expressive lyric power of individual words freed the poet from the constraints of accuracy.

This approach is analogous to creative translating practices of Anglo-American Modernists, who, as Stephen Yao points out, while coveting the authority of the ancient classics, also use translation as 'a strategy by which to underwrite their own cultural ambitions and advance their own aesthetic and ideological ends' (2002: 10). Overall, Quasimodo never maintains the metrical form of the originals, favouring renditions in free verse. He liberally excises lines of the source and adds new ones, regularly expanding or reducing the original and blurring the boundaries between poetic experience and translating practice.[29] For instance, Elena Salibra (1985: 35–45, 66–75) underlined that a specific group of words from *Lirici* populates Quasimodo's poems: the semantic chains bee-honey and moon-horse, the adjectives 'cupo, celeste, profondo' (dark, sky-blue/celestial, profound); the pair 'fanciulli-conchiglie' (children-shells); the colour red. Lorenzini (2004: 261–4) also drew attention to the intertextual connection of *Nuove poesie* (New poems) (1942) with *Lirici*, establishing a two-way exchange between Sappho's and Quasimodo's poetry.

Quasimodo's 'equilyric research' reverberates in the poetic ideals programmatically laid out by Anceschi in his first introduction to *Lirici greci*. According to the critic, mid-twentieth-century poets lived in a time of spiritual correspondences between antiquity and the present ('amabili concordanze della contemporanea spiritualità', [1940] 2004: 309), which allowed them to identify and highlight '*una poetica della purezza lirica*' (*a poetics of lyric purity*) (312).[30] For Anceschi, the translation of ancient lyric represented an operation of recovery of the metaphysical lyric essence of poetry, conceived as a self-standing unity transcending space and time. For its brevity and terseness, Greek monodic lyric was identified as the purest form: 'i "melici": qui è la lirica più pura' (the melics, here is the purest lyric) (Anceschi [1940] 2004: 315). This is emphasized in the anthology by the layout, with only one fragment per page, the facing Greek text, and a lot of surrounding blank space. Rejecting the possibility of a satisfactory philological interpretation of the individual poetic utterances, as well as the mythopoeic approach that characterized Pascoli's account of ancient lyric (see Chapter 1), the translations in *Lirici*, aimed at creating a new lyricism modelled on Sappho and the other melic poets, which would encapsulate the 'storia del cuore dell'uomo' (history of the heart of man) and an 'assoluta condizione di canto' (absolute state of song) (Anceschi [1940] 2004: 310). Sappho's poems are put forward as abstract, metaphysical epiphanies of poetry itself. Ancient and modern texts are thought to belong to the same aesthetic plane, envisioned as different moments in which poetry, as a universal self-standing entity, manifests and progressively takes consciousness of itself. In this way, Hermeticism de-historicizes Sappho's poetry in order to better connect it to the present.[31]

Following the papyri rediscoveries in the early twentieth century, biographical reconstructions springing from the Ovidian version of Sappho's life were not as common as in the past and derogatory stances toward her sexuality had mostly been overcome. In a 1953 essay, Quasimodo remarks: 'La "mascula" Saffo non sopporta biografie ideali, che svaniscono nella fragile persuasione delle notizie degli antichi scrittori. Alzandole intorno ripari, può apparirci un mostro o un angelo, sospeso nel cielo dei boschi sacri.'[32] ("Mascula" Sappho won't endure ideal biographies that vanish in the fragile opinions found in ancient writers' testimonies. As we build shelters around her, she may appear to us either as a monster or an angel, suspended in the sky of the sacred woods) (Quasimodo 1960: 99). While he is aware of the processes that affected her reception, variously making her a depraved to shun or a model to follow, Quasimodo's words contribute to her idealizing representation in the present. With references to the sacred grove of fr. 2 and some Eliotian echoes, 'floating in the sacred woods' Sappho herself becomes a semi-divine appearance to be written into poetry.

The connections between Anceschi's and Quasimodo's views on the classical legacy, lyric and the poetics of the fragment suggest that the writing and compilation of *Lirici greci* was a collaborative project. The critic and the poet exchanged several letters in the years leading to the publication of *Lirici*. Quasimodo would send Anceschi the drafts of his translations, asking for advice and for help. A 1938 unpublished letter from Quasimodo to Anceschi runs:

> Ti ringrazio della traduzione del-
> l'Ode ad Afrodite; per ora la metto insieme ad altre due
> che già posseggo e al mio primo tentativo di risolvere
> poeticamente questo testo, invero assai duro nel suo nume-
> ro geometrico.
>   Fui quasi tentato di aggiungere questa tradu-
> zione nel mio libro; ma quel senso di legittimo rigore
> che è stato norma costante di moralità e di costume lette-
> rario me lo impedì.
>   […]
>   Attendo da te altre traduzioni, da Saffo, da
> Alceo (quella dell'Estate per esempio). Di Saffo deside-
> rerei che ti procurassi il testo dell'ode che comincia al-
> l'incirca così: "bello è vedere un campo con armati….
> ma più bello è l'amore della donna, ecc.". Questa poesia
> è poco nota e, credo, non tradotta in versi italiani.³³

> (Thank you for your translation of
> the Ode to Aphrodite; for now, I'll add it to two others
> that I already have and to my first attempt at unravelling
> poetically this text, indeed quite hard in its
> geometric rhythm.
>   I was almost tempted to add this translation
> to my book; but that sense of rightful rigour
> that has always led my moral and literary practice
> stopped me.
> […]
>
> I expect other translations from you, of Sappho, of
> Alcaeus (the one on Summer for instance). I would
> like you to get the text of the ode by Sappho that begins
> more or less like this: 'it is beautiful to look at a field with armed men…

but more beautiful is the love of the woman, etc.'. This poem is little known and, I believe, was never translated in Italian verse.)

As this letter shows, Anceschi actively contributed not only to the theoretical framing of the anthology, but also to the drafting of the translations. A comment by Anceschi in an unpublished 1937 postcard to Enrico Falqui confirms that he guided Quasimodo's initiative: 'Con Quasimodo stiamo traducendo Saffo: anzi Quasimodo traduce Saffo, ed io lo aiuto'[34] (With Quasimodo we are translating Sappho: actually, Quasimodo translates Sappho, and I help him out). Anceschi's 1940 programmatic introduction to the volume was an integral part of the collaborative project of *Lirici*, testifying to the crucial role of Hermeticist critics in Italian literary culture of the first half of the twentieth century. Their critical work was seen as a creative enterprise with equal status to the poetry it promoted. In this sense, *Lirici*, with the introduction by Anceschi, is inherently a Hermeticist collection.

Carlo Bo's 1938 essay 'Letteratura come vita' (Literature as life) posits Hermeticism as a way of life. This further explains Hermeticist tendencies towards all-encompassing ideological interpretations and evaluations of literature, in which we should include Quasimodo's appropriation of Sappho and his negative value judgment of 'discursive', non-lyric genres. *Lirici* stands as an attempt to define a classical lyric canon, in the same way as the anthology *Lirici nuovi* (New lyricists), edited by Anceschi and published in 1943, aims at associating new lyric poetry with Hermeticism.[35] Significantly, in the introduction to *Lirici nuovi*, Anceschi employs the same exact words of his 1940 introduction to *Lirici greci*:

> **Per noi, la lirica è ancora, certamente, 'storia del cuore dell'uomo'**. [...] [E] **neppure ha da essere risolta in diario o in narrazione**: nella lirica, la parola fruisce di una franca **condizione di canto** in cui il suo senso logico giunge quasi al limite dell'annullamento.
>
> (For us, lyric is still, certainly, 'the history of the heart of man' [...] [And] it should not be resolved into a diary or a narration: in lyric, the word enjoys a frank state of song in which its logical sense almost reaches the limit of annihilation.)
>
> 1943: 10, my emphasis

Key phrases such as 'the history of the heart of man' and a 'state of song' return. *Lirici* was published at a crucial moment of the heated cultural debate around Hermeticism led by the literary journal *Primato* in its investigations 'Parliamo dell'ermetismo' (Let's speak about Hermeticism) and 'L'ermetismo e gli ermetici' (Hermeticism and Hermeticists). Between June and July 1940, the journal gathered fifteen contributions over three issues by Hermeticist and non-Hermeticist poets and critics, with the intention to define the terms of the developing poetics and its 'confessione metafisica' (metaphysical beliefs) (Pavolini 1940: 8). In one of the articles in *Primato*, Cesare Angelini noted that Quasimodo's and Anceschi's reframing of Sappho's and Alcaeus' lyric as 'pure song' was intentionally equivocal:

> Anche la grande lirica greca tendeva al mito. Che è essenzialmente narrativo. [...] I cosidetti frammenti che, secondo gli ermetici rappresenterebbero la massima conquista nella purezza lirica, sono arrivati a noi come frantumi; nativamente eran parti di liriche costruite. E di Saffo ci restan due liriche intere.

> (Even great lyric tended toward myth, which is essentially narrative. [...] The so called fragments that, according to the Hermeticists would represent the highest achievement in lyric purity, have come to us as debris; originally they were parts of constructed poems. And we only have two entire poems by Sappho.)
> Angelini 1940: 8

Angelini raises a valid point: Quasimodo's and Anceschi's ahistorical and decontextualized interpretations, which typically do not account for the fragment's original context, their history or their tradition, deduce from the archaic fragments a supposed overcoming of Homeric epic and its narrative tone toward lyric purity (Anceschi [1940] 2004: 313). However, as Angelini points out, the poetry of Sappho and Alcaeus not only continued to engage intertextually with Homer, but also considerably employed Homeric myth as its subject.[36]

In order to maintain Sappho and Alcaeus as poets of brevity and lyric density, the larger fragments with either an epic or a political theme were excluded from the anthology; important and representative odes by Sappho engaging with myth, such as frr. 27a and 27bDiehl (16Voigt) using the figure of Helen of Troy, and frr. 55a and 55bDiehl (44Voigt) on the myth of Hector and Andromache, are also omitted. The entire corpus of fragments by Alcaeus on politics, the fragments written against the dictator Pittacus (frr. G1, D14) are absent, too. Beside the aesthetic criteria, the anthology's disengagement with any form of political discourse may reflect the deliberate disassociation of the Hermeticist group from any form of political activism during the Fascist regime. Controversially received by its contemporaries,[37] the alternating fortune of Hermeticism inevitably determined the future reception of Sappho and ancient Greek lyric, which, as I discuss in the last section on *Lirici greci*'s reception, was, for a long time, associated with Quasimodo's classical Hermeticism.

The notes to the translation of Sappho 96Diehl (94Voigt), in which the lyric 'I' remembers with longing the time she spent with a beloved girl before she left, and entitled 'Vorrei veramente esser morta' (I truly wish to be dead), are particularly revealing of Quasimodo's translating method and his Hermeticist interpretative categories:

> Ho preferito perciò che la poesia continuasse l'eco di un 'suono' che i secoli avevano interrotto sulle scritture degli amanuensi. [...] Qui la parola della poetessa, oltre la consueta potenza evocativa, acquista valori drammatici e visivi: siamo quasi al 'discorso' ma non al discorso parlato che sarà l'errore, nei periodi della decadenza, degli elegiaci (in parte) e degli gnomici. [...] Il dolore per la lontananza della fanciulla amatissima è immutato, ha la stessa intensità del momento storico. L'occasione del sentimento' che invita Saffo a parlare con voce non ripetibile, con linguaggio ignoto agli imitatori dell'epica, ci rivela i moti della sua vita più segreta e con essi i costumi d'un mondo scomparso.

> (I wished therefore that the poem continued to propagate the echo of a 'sound' that centuries had interrupted on the scribes' writings. [...] Here the poet's word, besides its usual evocative power, acquires dramatic and visual qualities: we have almost reached 'discourse', but not the spoken discourse that is the mistake of the elegists (partly) and the gnomic in times of decline. [...] The sorrow for the beloved girl's distance is unchanged [today], it has the same intensity as in its historical moment. The 'occasion for the feeling' that inspires Sappho to speak with unrepeatable voice, with a language unknown to the imitators of epic, reveals the impulses of her most secret life and with them the customs of a bygone world.)
>
> Quasimodo [1940] 2004: 211–12

Quasimodo aims to convey Sappho's sonorities ('l'eco di un "suono"'). Her poem is considered a perfect example of pure lyric: it is evocative ('consueta potenza evocativa'), monologic, the fragmentary expression of an inner feeling ('siamo qui al "discorso", ma non al discorso parlato'), absolute ('voce non ripetibile'), and ultimately the revelation of a mysterious hidden dimension ('ci rivela i moti della sua vita più segreta'). His translation reflects his Hermeticist interpretation:

καὶ στρώμν[αν ἐ]πὶ μολθάκαν	e i molli letti
ἀπάλαν παρ[·]α, [·]ονων	dove alle tenere fanciulle joniche
ἐξίης πόθο[ν αἰ νε]ανίδων,	nasceva amore della tua bellezza.

κωὖτε τις [χόρος οὔ]τε τι
ἶρον οὐδ᾽ὐ[μέναιος εἶς]
ἔπλετ᾽, ὄππ[οθεν ἄμ]μες ἀπέσκομεν·
    Fr. 96Diehl, ll. 21–6
    = Quasimodo [1940] 2004: 36

Non un canto di coro,
né sacro, né inno nuziale
si levava senza le nostre voci;
    'Vorrei veramente esser morta', ll.
    21–6, Quasimodo [1940] 2004: 37

Supplementing two key Hermeticist concepts 'canto' (song, l. 24) and 'voci' (voices, l. 26), both absent from the source text, Quasimodo shapes his Hermeticist Sappho. If he partly tones down the sexual desire expressed in 'πόθο[ν' with 'nasceva amore' (love was born, l. 23), his translation freely acknowledges the homoeroticism of Sappho and the girls in her circle, explaining in his notes to the text that Sappho reveals the 'customs of a bygone world'. While literary representations of homoeroticism in classical texts were tolerated during fascism, representations of homosexuality in contemporary literature were not. The first positive representations of lesbianism appeared in the 1920s, but by the 1930s female homosexuality was being denounced as a sign of decadence.[38] In a post-war essay, eventually making his position explicit, Quasimodo completely distances himself from any censoring interpretation of Sappho's poetry: 'I talismani morali per Saffo sono stati incisi su una pietra tenera e il tempo li ha cancellati' (Moral talismans for Sappho were engraved into a soft stone and time has erased them) (1960: 99).

Sappho as a lyric abstraction:
Poetic voice in *Lirici greci*

Lirici greci is characterized by the recurring themes of absence and solitude and a unitary poetic voice.[39] As the essence of poetry and reality is located in a distant beyond, in Hermeticist poetry the theme of absence takes various forms, among which the absence of the lyric addressee, the absence of linguistic referents, and the absence of a viable empirical reality with which to identify at the time of fascism and the war. Memory, as a process that makes present and is strictly linked to consciousness, enables Quasimodo's neo-humanism by establishing a connection with the purest forms of poetry – that of Sappho and ancient Greek lyrics – and, as in a moment of self-remembering, with poetry as the 'history of the heart of man'. As Bo states, memory is 'memoria [dello spirito]' (memory of the spirit) and 'coscienza di noi stessi ripresa ad ogni momento' (consciousness of ourselves at every moment) ([1938] 1978: 161).[40]

The role of memory in Quasimodo's poetry is oppositional to its bleak present;[41] his interest in memory and 'rimembranze' (remembrances) that fuel poetic drive is Leopardian in character, and so is Quasimodo's view of the poet as a lonely creature resisting the dissolution of present reality and making an ethical stance in society through his poetry.[42] Since the time of *Oboe sommerso* (1932) days are like ruins, 'i giorni una maceria' ('Oboe sommerso', l. 13 = Finzi 1996: 39), and joy can only be remembered through someone else's experience, 'gioia di foglie perenni, / non mie' (joy of perennial leaves, not mine) ('Oboe sommerso', ll. 5–6 = Finzi 1996: 39). Emblematic of an ultimate act of existential resistance, poetic fragments, including Sappho's, stand as last debris of memory, illustrative of life-affirming lyric purity.[43] Despite the fragmentary nature of the poems, the unitary poetics of *Lirici* resists potential dissolution and, through memory, affirms the possibility of a survival of the lyric voice over the destruction brought about by history.

Underlining, as Anceschi suggests, the spiritual correspondences between antiquity and the present ([1940] 2004: 309), Quasimodo merges different fragments into a single poem, removes or adds lines, freely interpreting the Greek to suit his aesthetic operation. In the poem 'Tramontata è la luna', a collage of various fragments by Sappho, he combines frr. 94; 50; 137; 52 and 20Diehl (168b, 47, 130, 146, 36Voigt). It opens with a translation of fr. 94Diehl (168bVoigt):

Δέδυκε μὲν ἀ σελάννα
καὶ Πληιάδες μέσαι δέ
νύκτες, παρὰ δ'ἔρχετ'ὤρα·
ἐγὼ δὲ μόνα κατεύδω.

fr. 94Diehl, ll. 1–4 = Quasimodo [1940] 2004: 24

Tramontata è la luna
e le Pleiadi a mezzo della notte;
anche giovinezza già dilegua,
e ora nel mio letto resto sola.

ll. 1-4, Quasimodo [1940] 2004: 25

In his notes to the text Quasimodo explains his translation of 'ὤρα', usually translated with 'time' or 'hour', with 'giovinezza' (youth) citing Bruno Lavagnini's interpretation in the popular school-anthology of ancient Greek Lyric *Aglaia* (1937) as his source of his rendition; he underlines that according to Lavagnini, ὤρα gained its astronomical meaning only after the fourth century BC (Lavagnini 1936: 146; Quasimodo [1940] 2004: 211–12). This is not exactly accurate, since, as Franco Ferrari pointed out, in this fragment ὤρα holds the meaning of time not in absolute terms, but relative to a particular action (that of sleeping) ([1987] 1994: 233). Indeed, as Nicola Gardini has shown, Quasimodo's translation appears to take after Leopardi's 'Il tramonto della luna' (Gardini 2000: 61–2). The choice of 'giovinezza' and the verb 'dileguare' in 'anche giovinezza già dilegua' (also youth already vanishes) are clear echoes of Leopardi's simile describing the setting moon:

> Tal si dilegua, e tale
> Lascia l'età mortale
> La giovinezza.'
> 'Il tramonto della luna', ll. 20–2, Leopardi [1837] 1984: 247.

Another poem by Leopardi, 'L'ultimo canto di Saffo', contributes to enrich the intertext of Quasimodo's translation.[44] In Leopardi's lyric, the solitude of Sappho is shown as a consequence of the poet's ugliness and lost youth. Because of her physical appearance, Sappho is rejected by Phaon and is ignored by Mother Nature; her destiny is to suffer.[45] These same themes are present in Quasimodo's 'Tramontata è la luna' where the poet brings together the theme of solitude, unrequited love and absence of referents by combining his translations of various Sapphic fragments. In fr. 94Diehl (168bVoigt) the speaking voice is neglected by the rest of the world: 'resto sola' (I am left alone) (l. 4); in fr. 50Diehl (47Voigt) she is overtaken by love: 'Scuote l'anima mia Eros' (Eros shakes my soul) (l.5); in frr. 52Diehl (146Voigt) and 20Diehl (36Voigt), forming the last two lines of Quasimodo's collage, she defines herself by subtraction – by what she does not have and cannot do:

> Fr. 52Diehl
> μήτ'ἔμοι μέλι μήτε μέλισσα
> Fr. 20Diehl
> Καὶ ποθήω καὶ μάομαι
> Quasimodo [1940] 2004: 24

> Ma a me, non ape, non miele;
> e soffro e desidero.
> 'Tramontata è la luna', ll. 10–11, Quasimodo [1940] 2004: 25

The Leopardian theme of solitude is heightened by the use of a self-referential lyric 'I', expressing a split lyric subject, who only dialogues with herself or with an absent addressee. By literally translating the possessive dative 'ἔμοι' with 'a me' (to me), instead of *non ho* (I do not have), and letting the line's tonic stress fall on 'me', Quasimodo emphasizes the self-referentiality of the poem, whose addressee is never made known. The choice to maintain the source text's ellipsis of the verb 'to be' accentuates the already awkward use of the complement 'a me' (to me), conveying a sense of estrangement and foreignness. Carefully placing the word 'ape' (bee) before 'miele' (honey) and thus inverting the word order of the Greek 'μήτ' ἔμοι μέλι μήτε μέλισσα' (but for me neither honey nor bee) the poet traces a regular rhythmic and sound pattern within the first part of the line before the *caesura*. Moving the word 'miele' (honey) from the middle of the line to the end maintains the alliterative pattern of the nasal ('m') throughout the verse, reproducing a similar effect to the alliterating 'μ' in the Greek text. The 'a' and 'e' of 'a me' are replicated in the 'a' and 'e' of 'ape' (bee) producing an internal assonance, like those in the Greek text, where every word begins with a syllable containing a nasal and an 'e' sound: μή-, ἔμ-, or μέ-. Sappho's sonorities are thus brought by Quasimodo into the present.

Leopardi is evoked also in Anceschi's introduction to *Lirici*, where he presents the Hermeticist search for lyric purity as a continuation of Leopardi's own poetic investigations ([1940] 2004: 310). In the *Zibaldone*, Leopardi's famous collection of thoughts on life and literature, the lyric is identified as the most poetic of all genres:

> Il lirico, [genere] primogenito di tutti; [...] più nobile e più *poetico* d'ogni altro; vera e pura poesia in tutta la sua estensione; proprio d'ogni uomo anche incolto, che cerca di ricrearsi o di consolarsi col canto.
>
> (The lyric, the first of all genres; [...] most noble and most *poetic* of any other; true and pure poetry in all its extent; belonging to any man even uneducated, who tries to reinvigorate himself and console himself with song.)
> Leopardi 1840 (4234, 15 Dicembre 1826) = Flora 1967: II 1063

Validating the Hermeticist interpretation of ancient lyric by tracing it back to Leopardi, Anceschi also puts Quasimodo in a direct line of descent from the poet of Recanati.[46] But we ought to remember that Leopardi spent the final years of his life working on the *Paralipomeni della Batracomiomachia* (1842), a satiric narrative poem that moved beyond the lyricism of his *Canti*. Anceschi's and Quasimodo's accounts of both Sappho's and Leopardi's work were constructed to sustain their own Hermeticist revaluation of the lyric.

The theme of solitude binds Sappho, Leopardi and Quasimodo throughout *Lirici*, as solitude is the main characteristic of Sappho's poetic persona in the anthology. In a 1953 essay this underlining connection is made explicit: 'la luna non risplende per Saffo (e per Leopardi)' (1960: 103) (the moon does not shine for Sappho and Leopardi). If the notions of loneliness, solitude and lack of a present referent stem from the compendium's general theme of absence, the word 'solitudine' (solitude) and its derivatives appear only in Sappho's section.[47] In the translation of fr. 94Diehl (168bVoigt) the Italian translation 'sola' (alone) sticks closely to the Greek 'μόνα'. But in another fragment entitled 'Ad Ermes' (To

Hermes), which is part of his translation of the very lacunose fragment 97Diehl (95Voigt), Quasimodo adds the noun 'solitudine' (solitude):

> ... ["Ερ]
> μας γ' ἔσηλθ'ἐπα[...]
> εἶπον· ὦ δέσποτα, ἐπ[...]
> ο]ὐ μὰ γὰρ μάκαιραν [...]
>
> fr. 97Diehl, ll. 1–4 = Quasimodo [1940] 2004: 38

Ermes, io lungamente ti ho invocato.
In me è solitudine: tu aiutami,
despota, ché morte da sé non viene;

(Hermes, for a long time I invoked you. / Solitude is in me: help me / despot, because death does not come of her own accord)

ll. 1–3, Quasimodo [1940] 2004: 39

A literal translation of these lines of the Diehl fragment would be: 'Hermes came in [/ and I said: "O Master, no for the blessed [/ I do not enjoy being too excited"'. These deviations from the original text accentuate the loneliness of Sappho's poetic persona, while making the lyric 'I' the mouthpiece of the tradition set by Leopardi.[48] Sappho as a paradigm of absence and existential loneliness remained a referent of Quasimodo's poetics beyond the openly Hermeticist experimentations. In the 1950s, he continues to speak of her poetry as the purest of all, and once again the two poets find an affinity in their shared loneliness: '[t]utto è già stato in questa poesia: [...] il tempo perduto si ripete nella solitudine' (everything has already been in this poetry: [...] lost time repeats itself in solitude) (Quasimodo 1960: 99–100).

The theme of lost youth informs also the translation of fr. 131Diehl (114Voigt), entitled 'Fanciullezza' (Youth). As discussed in Chapter 1, the same epithalamion was translated by Pascoli in one of his juvenile autographs. While Pascoli constructs a symbolic analogy of defloration substituting the word 'virginity' with the image of a fading rose bud, Quasimodo emphasizes the supposed innocence of the poetic voice by translating 'παρθενία' (literally: 'virginity') with the toned down 'fanciullezza' (childhood / youth), attenuating the sexual connotation of the word: 'Fanciullezza, fanciullezza, mi lasci, dove vai?' (Childhood, childhood, you are leaving me, where are you going?) (l. 1, Quasimodo [1940] 2004: 53). However, the reference to the epithalamion setting is maintained through the association with the word 'fanciulla', which in the first half of the twentieth century also denoted an unmarried woman.[49] At the same time, employing the abstract noun 'fanciullezza', the poet develops a self-reflection on the passing of time. These lexical choices avoid any direct reference to the heterosexual union celebrated in the epithalamia, which one of Quasimodo's later comments illuminates: 'L'uomo è assente dalla lirica amorosa di Saffo: è nemico che porta delirio e confusione e le toglie ora Anattoria ora Attide, è la violenza e l'offesa alla purezza' (Man is absent from Sappho's love lyric: he is the enemy who brings frenzy and confusion and takes away at times Anactoria at times Atthis, he is violence, an insult to purity) (1960: 101).

The emphasis on time, absence and solitude effects also the representation of desire in Quasimodo's translations. Sappho's homoeroticism is openly acknowledged, but through the Hermeticist lens becomes more abstract. If we compare Quasimodo's translation of fr. 98Diehl (96Voigt) in 'Ad Attide' with Pound's rendition of the same fragment in 'Ἰμέρρω' this is even more evident:

πόλλα δὲ ζαφοίταισ᾽ ἀγάνας ἐπι-
μνάσθεισ᾽ Ἄτθιδος ἰμέρωι
λέπταν ποι φρένα, κῆρ <δ᾽> ἄσα βόρηται.
ll. 15–17, Fr.98 Diehl = Quasimodo [1930] 2004: 42

Solitaria vagando, esita
a volte se pensa ad Attide:
di desiderio l'anima trasale,
e il cuore è aspro.
ll. 15–18, Quasimodo [1940] 2004: 43

Atthis is not directly invoked by the *persona loquens* as in Pound's fragment ('O Atthis', l. 3); remaining closer to the original, Quasimodo's Atthis can only be remembered in a distant past. The sense of solitude and loneliness in Quasimodo's poem is heightened by the adjective 'solitaria' at the beginning of the line, which, as in 'Ad Ermes' Quasimodo deliberately adds to the more laconic source text, contributing to the Hermeticist operation toward the absolutizing of the lyric form.[50]

Quasimodo's elegiac Catullus

First published in 1945, *Catullus Veronensis Carmina* is the only other translation of non-narrative poetry by Quasimodo after *Lirici*. Reissued in an expanded and revised edition of 1955 entitled *Canti di Catullo*, which included nine new texts (from thirty-two to forty-one), the anthology from Catullus's *liber* sanctioned Quasimodo's investment in creative forms of translation. In his 1945 essay 'Traduzioni dai classici' (Translations from the classics), Quasimodo reflected on his experience of translating Greek and Latin poetry, saying that he was drawn to monodic lyric for its 'contenuti eterni' (eternal contents) and to Catullus because in his elegies 'la sua pena d'uomo raggiunge l'accento più eterno' (his human suffering reaches the most eternal inflection) (1960: 76). He thus built a narrative of his translating experience as an exploration of the consonance between the past and the present, found in the 'eternal' matter of poetry, using an essentialist rhetoric similar to that upholding *Lirici*.

Quasimodo's use of the word 'eterno' dialogues with Pascoli's aesthetics. As seen in Chapter 1, the concept of 'the eternal' was key for Pascoli, who singled it out as the essential attribute of all true poetry, emerging most clearly in the works of the ancients. Moreover, Pascoli's anthology of Latin poetry, *Lyra* (1895), which Quasimodo probably read in the 1934 Giusti edition, appears to have been one of his reference texts for his translation of Catullus. He also extensively consulted Massimo Lenchantin de Gubernatis' *Il libro di Catullo veronese* (1938), from which he extracted the Latin text for his own volume, and the 1932 French edition with a translation by Goerges Lafaye.[51] In Quasimodo's 1945 *Catullus*, twenty-seven out of thirty-two texts correspond with Pascoli's choices in *Lyra*; in the 1955 edition, this is twenty-nine out of forty-one. As Pascoli selected and isolated extracts from the longer poems of Catullus for his anthology, so Quasimodo did not refrain from editing the source texts. He cut the last five lines of poem 68a and the last two of 107 in both the Latin and the Italian.[52] A similar free approach to the source texts was used in *Lirici*. Following Meschonnic, Savoca has described this practice as a way of producing what he defines a 'translation-text', namely, a translation that also presents a new source text by modifying it (1986: 117). Quasimodo never discusses his excisions in the volume, which has no paratextual material, or anywhere else, and he only signals the cuts with ellipses. The excision of the lines in Catullus 68a produces a clear-cut ending focusing on the themes of home and time passing:

Quod Romae vivimus: illa domus, [me,
illa mihi sedes, illic mea carpitur aetas
. . .

Cat. 68a.34–5 = Quasimodo 1955: 128

Perché vivo a Roma: quella la mia patria,
quella la mia casa, là il mio tempo si consuma
. . .

Quasimodo 1955: 129

As a Sicilian poet self-exiled in Milan, these lines must have resonated with Quasimodo. The intensity of poem 107 is also heightened by the removal of the last two lines, which present Catullus's own self-reflexive intellectualization of feelings, leaving space to the spontaneous expression of happiness of the preceding verse.

Several other translations of Catullus were available at the time, many produced in the 1940s and 1950s and others reprinted from earlier editions, confirming the popularity of Catullus in twentieth-century Italian culture. Some of these texts reached a wide audience and went through various reprints, such as Carlo Saggio's 1928 edition, revised in 1949, which had wide circulation because it was part of BUR's classical collection, or Ugo Fleres's 1929 volume, which was reprinted for decades (Pontani 1977: 637; 631). As well as Quasimodo's Catullus, 1945 saw the publication of a translation by Vincenzo Errante, *La poesia di Catullo*, whose intent was to update existing poetic versions, but avoiding 'trasformare Catullo in un lirico italiano del Novecento, magari stracittadino o ermetico' (to transform Catullus in an Italian twentieth-century lyricist, perhaps extra-urban or Hermeticist); Errante rather aimed to translate according to a poetic and linguistic sensibility 'coltivata in severi studi umanistici' (cultivated in rigorous humanistic studies) (quoted in Pontani 1977: 633). The vast majority of translations of Catullus published in the following years had similar intents, proposing themselves as rigorous academic texts; very few had the ambition of a creative poetic rendering. An exception is the translation by the Latinist and poet Enzio Cetrangolo, *Poesie di Catullo*, published in 1950 by Feltrinelli, an anthology of forty-three poems translated in *endecasillabi sciolti* and aimed at the wider public (Pontani 1977: 638). Within this context, Quasimodo's work is ground-breaking in bringing to Italy creative approaches to translation. As in the case of Sappho, in *Lirici*, his translations of Catullus remained the most influential throughout the first half of the twentieth century, until Guido Ceronetti's 1969 versions, which I discuss in Chapter 5.

Expressing his aesthetics, Quasimodo's anthology of Catullus once again strikes one as a programmatic poetic operation. Despite Quasimodo having distanced himself from biographical interferences, which had characterized the reception of Catullus since its inception, the volume gave a personal portrayal of the Roman poet. Quasimodo defined Catullus's *liber* as a 'diario elegiaco' (elegiac diary) (1960: 63) and indeed he favoured the elegiac poems over the epithalamia and the epigrams.[53] He briefly explained his selection and translating criteria in 'Traduzione dai classici', where he set his work apart from the wide-spread portrayals of Catullus as an *enfant terrible* that were based on biographical interpretations of his epigrams. The essay laments an excessive attention to the Catullus of the invectives and the scatological poems, which Quasimodo considers unpoetic: 'quella sorta di licenza [...] così lontana dalla poesia quanto lo può essere un grido da un canto' (that sort of licence [...] as far from poetry as a scream can be from song) (Quasimodo 1960: 76). Quasimodo fails to find in Catullus's more violent invectives the song-like quality that was so crucial to his conception of poetry; therefore he focuses on the elegies as the loci 'là dove la sua pena d'uomo raggiunge l'accento più eterno, là dove non più Callimaco lo tocca ma la sua natura di latino, la sua umana disperazione di giovane già destinato alla morte' (where his human suffering reaches the most eternal inflection, where Callimachus no longer influences him and his Latin nature emerges, the human desperation of a youth already destined to die) (1960: 76). I agree with Morelli (2015: 154) that this view of Catullus as the melancholy youth destined to a poetic life is equally stereotyped and often employed in modern Catullan criticism. It reflects Quasimodo's fascination with Catullus's originality, with his ability to assimilate and overcome the Hellenistic influences to find his own voice as a Roman poet (Morelli 2015: 155), as if Quasimodo's himself was aspiring to do the same in the Italian context.

The first edition of the anthology excluded the epithalamia and the hymns, and had very few epigrammatic poems: *Cat.* 49, an epigram directed at Cicero, *Cat.* 58 on Lesbia, *Cat.* 93 dedicated to Caesar, *Cat.* 108 on Cominius's old age, and *Cat.* 116 to Gellius. What is more, any overtly sexual or scatological elements were toned down considerably. For instance, Quasimodo translates the last lines of poem 58 with 'ora, nei vicoli e i quadrivi, tira / via la pelle a quei gran figli di Remo.' (now in the alleys and crossroads, pulls / the skin off those great sons of Remus) (1955: 103). Quasimodo's 'tira via la pelle' (literally: pulls the skin off) which in Italian, especially in the form 'levare la pelle', means to scold or mortify someone, mostly eliminates the double-entendre of the famous 'glubit', diminishing the rhetorical effect of the whole poem.[54]

This approach attracted the criticism of some of his contemporaries, including Carlo Emilio Gadda, who complained that the selection left out some of the most significant lyrics of the *liber*, and blamed Quasimodo for his 'filtro alquanto circospetto e attrattivo, una emendazione purificatrice [che] tempera e smorza le note più crude' (rather circumspect and attractive filter, a purifying emendation [that] tempers and muffle the crudest notes) (Quoted in Savoca 1986: 105). This judgement is informed by exactly the same idealizing rhetoric on Catullus's biography that Quasimodo wanted to avoid, as he dismissed 'Catullus *enfant terrible* di una società indemoniata e terribile' (Catullus *enfant terrible* of a demonic and terrible society) (Quasimodo 1960: 76). In other respects, though, Gadda has a point. As well as the epigrams, Quasimodo excludes some of the most famous Catullan poems, including the epithalamion of Peleus and Thetis in 64 and the famous Catullus 51. The latter omission is most puzzling. Quasimodo was fascinated by Catullus as a poet-translator: one of his earliest translations was of poem 65, Catullus's letter accompanying his own translation into Latin of Callimachus fr. 101 in poem 66; indeed, this Catullan translation is included in Quasimodo's anthology. It is safe to assume therefore that Quasimodo was not against making a translation of a translation. Why excluding poem 51? Perhaps, having translated Sappho's ode himself, he wanted to avoid any interference, to circumvent any references to his previous work, or, more likely, the poem did not fit his idea of the elegiac Catullus.

Partly to address critiques like Gadda's, the 1955 expanded edition added nine translations, almost all of which are epigrams.[55] Overall, the lexis of the anthology, while adding some cruder vocabulary, remains connected to Quasimodo's poetic and translating language. A telling instance is the word 'cuore', used by Quasimodo in the collection *Giorno dopo giorno* (1947), especially in 'Forse il cuore' (Maybe the heart), and in the famous 'Alle fronde dei salici' (Before the willows' branches): 'E come potevamo noi cantare / con il piede straniero sopra il cuore' (And how could we sing / with the foreign foot on hour heart) (ll. 1–2). Anceschi also used the word several times in his aesthetic writings to describe lyric as 'the history of the heart of man' (Anceschi [1940] 2004: 310; 1943: 10). As Morelli noted, in Quasimodo's *Catullus*, 'cuore' is consistently used to translate *medulla, animus, pectoris*, and *mens* (2015: 158).[56] For instance, the substitution of mind for heart adds intensity to the feelings of trepidation and anxiety in 46.7, 'iam mens praetrepidans avet vagari' (now my mind fluttering in anticipation yearns to wander) translated 'Già freme il cuore in ansia di vagare', and in 68a.8, 'cum mens anxia pervigilat' (while the concerned mind remains awake), translated 'poi che veglia in ansia il cuore'. This fits within the elegiac view of Catullus's work, which, together with Sappho, functions as a catalyst for Quasimodo's Hermeticist poetics.

While sharing the same aesthetic premises, Quasimodo's anthologies of Sappho and Catullus position the poet-translator within an evolving Italian literary landscape. Moving away from the free verse of *Lirici*, Quasimodo translated the majority of the poems included in the Catullan anthology using a tight set of Italian hendecasyllables, losing the metrical specificity of the Latin.[57] The only exception is the use of *doppi-settenari* (double seven-syllable lines) to translate iambic trimeters (e.g. poem 8). Arrigoni rightly notes that in *Canti* 'l'endecasillabo è apparso come lo strumento più idoneo per descrivere il sentimento della solitudine del poeta veronese' (the hendecasyllable appears as the most suitable instrument to describe the feeling of solitude of the Veronese poet) (2010: 385). Catullus, like Sappho, is considered a paradigmatic example of the lyric poet's solitude. Quasimodo's selections of texts and translations aim to emphasize a supposed shared spirituality between ancients and moderns based on existential loneliness, thus inserting Catullus within modern sensibility (Della Corte 1989: 166). However, with these Catullan versions in *endecasillabi*, Quasimodo's translations also partly break with the Hermeticist operation of *Lirici* and settle into a more narrative type of lyricism, which dialogues with the Italian literary tradition of Dante, Petrarch and Leopardi. From this perspective, his translation of Catullus is much more domesticating than the fragmented free verse of *Lirici*. It reveals the intent to enter more directly into a dialogue with the history of literature and translation and uses Catullus to stand with the great voices of Italian poetry. Moreover, while the elegiac lyric voice of Quasimodo's translations is clearly defined, the inclination toward abstraction of the Hermeticist translations characteristic of *Lirici* is substituted by more subtle lexical appropriations and a strict adherence to the original.

In tune with this evolution, his style, lexis and poetic voice after 1945 abandoned Hermeticism for a more representational and accessible kind of poetry, which accounted for the experience of the Resistance and the cultural, political and social changes brought about by the end of the Second World War. Quasimodo's critical statements after the war were often contradictory, distancing himself from 'poesia pura' to accommodate the social and political turn advocated by the emerging intellectual current of Neo-Realism;[58] nevertheless, his approach to poetry and translation as expressions of the heart of man did not change. In many ways, the two nuclei of Quasimodo's work before and after 1945 may be seen as complementary parts of the same aesthetic undertaking, which puts lyric poetry in its various forms at the centre of an evolving neo-humanist project.[59] Mitigating the Hermeticist stance, in the 1950s, his views of poetry as an ethical mission emphasize a purposeful idea of art and trust in the figure of the poet as a social agent. Indeed, while the shift in style and language was evident after the Neo-Realist experiences, Quasimodo's poetry invariably employed a unitary lyric voice and consistently engaged with the classical tradition – the latter made especially prominent in *La terra impareggiabile* (The incomparable earth) (1958). Yet, as I discuss in the following section, notwithstanding all his efforts to move beyond Hermeticism, critics of the second half of the twentieth century continued to associate Quasimodo almost exclusively with *Lirici greci* and a notion of Hermeticist and solipsistic lyricism.[60]

Lirici greci's reception

There are two reasons why I focused more extensively on Quasimodo's reception of Sappho over Catullus: the incredible success of *Lirici greci* with the wider public and its complex critical reception in the second half of the twentieth century. *Lirici* was the first of a long string of translations produced by Quasimodo between the 1940s and the 1960s. Of these, more than half are of either Greek or Latin authors: Ovid (1942), Catullus (1945), Homer (1945), St John (1946), Sophocles (1946, 1954), Aeschylus (1949), Ovid (1959), Euripides (1966), Greek Anthology (1958);[61] yet between the 1940s and the 1970s the critical attention mainly focused on *Lirici*, at times more extensively than on Quasimodo's own poetry.[62] Despite the fact that *Lirici* had attracted some criticism in the immediate aftermaths of its publication, as discussed in the previous sections, later criticism was mostly favourable to the translation. Literary scholars today generally acknowledge the anthology as one of the most emblematic documents and successful experiments of Hermeticism, Quasimodo's greatest achievement and his most influential work. This is the result of a process of canonization of *Lirici greci* started by leading Hermeticist critics in the 1940s, first and foremost Anceschi, and then perpetuated by later criticism well into the 1980s, which Quasimodo's own attempts at decentralizing his poetry from the Hermeticist discourse could not buffer. Between the 1940s and the 1970s, Quasimodo and his anthology were subjected to a continuous process of critical re-appraisal,[63] which also complicates the reception of archaic Greek lyric, and especially Sappho.[64]

Lirici and Quasimodo's oeuvre overall were entangled in a critical discourse that used Quasimodo's poetry up to *Ed è subito sera* (And soon it is evening) (1942) as a receptacle of exempla of Hermeticist poetic formulas; this critical narrative described the history of Italian literature before and after the Second World War as divided between Hermeticist and anti-Hermeticist movements, apolitical and engagé poetry.[65] Moreover, despite the international recognition, a negative Italian reception of Quasimodo's poetry after *Ed è subito sera*, which reached its highest peak in the 1960s,[66] did not allow the poet to become a reference figure for the following generations. It is true that, as Alberto Frattini notes, after the Nobel in 1959 the attention to Quasimodo's oeuvre increased; Gianfranco Contini included a chapter on Quasimodo in *Letteratura dell'Italia Unita* (1968) (Literature of United Italy) and the prestigious Meridiani edition of Quasimodo's collected works was published in 1974 (Frattini 2002: 1001–8). However, the overall critical acclaim focused mostly on his engagement with

Hermeticism, which, already by the 1950s, the leading Italian intelligentsia considered to be a phenomenon of the past.

Between the 1950s and the 1970s, Anceschi continued to support the trend in Quasimodo's criticism that emphasized the affiliation of his translations of the Greek lyrics with Hermeticism and *poesia pura*, in this way contributing to propagate his own conceptualization of poetry as an autonomous entity. In his 1978 introduction to a reprint of *Lirici*, almost forty years after its first publication, Anceschi reiterates the canonical status of Quasimodo's translations:

> Si tratta veramente di un molto discusso libro canonico proprio di un movimento della poesia italiana del novecento [...]. [L]'opera [...] più [...] sorprendente, e, per certi aspetti, fortunata di un segreto faber della seconda generazione poetica di un lungo momento della letteratura che continuiamo a dire ermetismo.

> (It is truly a much discussed canonical book, belonging to a movement of twentieth-century Italian poetry [...] [T]he work most surprising, and, under certain aspects, most successful of a secret *faber* of the second poetic generation of a long literary moment that we still call Hermeticism.)
>
> 1978: 335–6

As Lorenzini notes, while *Lirici* continued to be acclaimed, Quasimodo's poetic production and the rest of his translations after the war were mainly disregarded by the stars of Italian criticism in the 1970s and 1980s: Pier Vincenzo Mengaldo, Romano Luperini, Franco Fortini and Edoardo Sanguineti (2004: 243). These critics decentralized the figure of Quasimodo from the history of Italian literature, dismissing his value as a poet and stressing his value as a translator. Albeit from different perspectives, they sustained the dialectic started by Anceschi and brought *Lirici greci* to the status of a canonical work belonging to a bygone period of Italian literature. Emblematic of this phenomenon is Edoardo Sanguineti's choice to include thirteen translations from *Lirici* and only a couple of poems from Quasimodo's corpus in his 1969 anthology *Poesia italiana del Novecento* (Italian poetry of the twentieth century).[67] Mengaldo and Luperini, in their respective accounts of the history of Italian literature, point to *Lirici* as Quasimodo's most exemplary work, disregarding completely every other translation that came after the anthology and deeming Quasimodo's own poetry a mediocre achievement.[68]

Whether or not *Lirici greci* is Quasimodo's masterpiece, his established fame as Ur-translator of the Greek melic poets in the Italian twentieth century has bound Sappho to a Hermeticist idea of poetry as absolute lyric, to political disengagement and to solipsism. The post-war reaction to Hermeticism, with the socio-political turn of the cultural environment and the Marxist activism of the 1970s, rejected absolute lyricism as an obsolete form of poetry. This emerges also from the numerous *Quaderni di traduzione* (Translation notebooks) signed by various lyric poets, customary practice in the 1950s and the 1960s, which did not include any translations of ancient lyric. In fact, Quasimodo's anthology is an isolated phenomenon in the Italian literary panorama of the second half of the twentieth century.

The fortune of Sappho and Catullus is entangled with its complex reception, the history and development of the different poetics in the aftermath of the Second World War up to the 1980s, and the critical debate around poetry and engagement in Italy in the second half of the twentieth century.

The resonance of *Lirici* was so powerful to cross national boundaries, even before Quasimodo achieved international fame by winning the Nobel. Quasimodo's volume was the inspiration for Mary Barnard's *Sappho: A New Translation* (1958), widely read for decades in the Anglo-American world. In her autobiography, *Assault on Mount Helicon* (1984) she recounts that while she was convalescing from a severe illness in 1951, she received from the Paiges, who were in Rapallo, a copy of Quasimodo's volume (281):

> This little book removed one of the chief obstacles to translation, so far as I was concerned, by showing me how to use a third language as a bridge.
>
> In addition, I found the Italian translations very beautiful and wanted to match them, if I could, in my own language. Most important of all, however, I found here in Sappho's Greek, as revealed to me now through the medium of the Italian, the style I had been groping toward, or perhaps merely hungering for, when I ceased to write poetry a number of years before. It was spare but musical, and had, besides, the sound of the speaking voice making a simple but emotionally loaded statement.
>
> 1984: 281–2

After reading *Lirici*, Barnard started translating Sappho and sent her first drafts to Pound, her life-long mentor, whose positive comments encouraged her to continue (1984: 282). As Ramazani points out, 'poetry [...] travels because poems travel' (2009: 52). The twentieth-century reception of Sappho is remarkably entangled in these physical and intellectual journeys. Barnard's words point at another fundamental aspect of Sappho's modern reception: it is transnational not only because her poetry travels in translation across nations, but also because her translators often establish a relationship with the difficult Aeolic dialect of her verse through another language, be it Catullus's Latin,

Wharton's English or Quasimodo's Italian. As translators 'use a third language as a bridge', to quote Barnard, to access Sappho's poetry, the target texts are inevitably a step removed from the source. Yet this bridging dynamic, triangulating Sappho, her old translators and her new ones, establishes a collaborative, if distant, relationship among those who have engaged with her poetry and the languages they have used, granting Sappho's survival in modernity.

4

The Self and the Object

In his famous 1961 interview with Robert Lowell (1917–77) for the *Paris Review*, Frederick Seidel gives his impressions of the poet's study (Seidel 1961 = Giroux 1987: 235); two large portraits stood out: one of Ezra Pound, Lowell's ideal poetic mentor, the other of James Russell Lowell, Robert's great-great-uncle, a renowned Harvard professor, poet and diplomat.[1] Tokens of his chosen literary and family lineage, the pictures open a way into Lowell's self-fashioning as America's post-war poet. While his life in a family of Boston Brahmins is central to his autobiographical work, Lowell's care for form, tradition and the ancient classics emanates from his esteem of High-Modernists like Pound, Eliot and William Carlos Williams. His approbation was nurtured by the particular formalist brand of modernism devised by his teachers Allen Tate and John Crowe Ransom.[2] Lowell admired Pound because he thought that 'by courage [he] let the heart break through the iron rib ... more heart than any poet since Hardy' (Giroux 1987: 274).[3] In particular, the mixture of Imagist juxtapositions and autobiographical details of Pound's *Pisan Cantos* represented an exciting model. As much an expression of reverence as a form of self-validation of his own interest in poetic sincerity, Lowell's comment reveals his allegiance to the modernist tradition, proposing himself as its innovator through his heart-on-my-sleeve 'confessional' style which consecrated him to the Gotha of American poetry. In conversation with Stanley Kunitz in 1964, he remarked:

> The kind of poet I am was largely determined by the fact that I grew up in the heyday of the New Criticism, with Eliot's magical scrutiny of the text as a critical example. From the beginning I was preoccupied with technique, fascinated by the past and tempted by other languages. It is hard for me (now) to imagine a poet not interested in the classics. The task is to get something new into old forms, even at the risk of breaking them.
>
> Kunitz 1964: 35

The same interest in tradition and in 'Mak[ing] it New' informs Lowell's approach to poetry and the classics, including Sappho and Catullus.

Lowell studied Latin and Greek at school and then at university, first at Harvard and then at Kenyon, where he earned a degree in Classics.[4] He was particularly well-versed in Latin literature, with some (although not outstanding) knowledge of Greek.[5] From the outset Lowell's poetry is saturated in the classics, which for him appeared to be as alive as modern and contemporary poetry.[6] The genealogical relationship between Latin and English, together with his attraction to Rome as the site of the Catholic Church, to which he converted in his twenties,[7] justified his engagement with Latin literature. In the period that led to the publication of his ground-breaking *Life Studies* in 1959, Lowell lived for over three years in Europe (between 1950 and 1953), including extended periods of time in Florence and Rome. The latter is a spiritual and political symbol at the centre of the opening poem 'Beyond the Alps'.[8] From a literary point of view, Lowell was attracted to what he perceived as the 'frankness' of Graeco-Roman authors:

> You take almost any really good Roman poet – Juvenal, or Vergil, or Propertius, Catullus – he's much more raw and direct than anything in English, and yet he has a block-like formality. The Roman frankness interests me. Until recently our literature hasn't been as raw as the Roman, translations had to have stars. And their history has a terrible human frankness that isn't customary with us – corrosive attacks on the Establishment, comments on politics and the decay of morals, all felt terribly strongly, by poets as well as historians.
>
> Seidel 1961 = Giroux 1987: 253

This interest in the forthrightness of the Roman poets chimes with his poetic pursuit for a semblance of authenticity and his consequent move toward autobiographic writing in the late 1950s, which was notoriously labelled as the 'confessional' style.[9] With *Life Studies*, Lowell brought some of the most private details of his personal life to American poetry, including his psychological distress, hospitalizations and the failure of his marriage, in order to carry out a broader critique of contemporary society. More often than not, the poetic persona of Lowell's works coincides with the author himself, acquiring an air of 'personal confidences' (Rosenthal [1959] 1999: 64) – yet a very crafty type of confession, as Lowell notes on his autobiographical poems:

> They are not always factually true. [...] I've invented facts and changed things, and the whole balance of the poem was something invented. So there's a lot of artistry, I hope, in the poems. Yet there's this thing: if a poem is autobiographical – and this is true of any kind of autobiographical writing and of historical writing – you want the reader to say, This is true. [...] And so there was always that

standard of truth which you wouldn't ordinarily have in poetry – the reader was to believe he was getting the *real* Robert Lowell.

Giroux 1987: 246–7

With its selective system and crafted poetic voice Lowell's poetry is not entirely an authentic confession as Rosenthal argues; it rather falls into Lionel Trilling's definition of sincerity as a poetic intention toward truth.[10]

Even though Catullus and Sappho may not be as noticeable as other classical authors in Lowell's oeuvre, they are at the kernel of his reflection on poetry. The first and arguably most creative moment for Lowell's appropriations of the two ancient poets is in the late 1950s and early 1960s with the publication of *Life Studies* and *Imitations* (1961), his collection of creative translations of classical and modern European poetry. In comparison to the other poets I consider in this book, Lowell's engagement with Catullus seems to be rather discreet. A reader sifting through the hefty volume of Lowell's *Collected Poems* (2003) looking for Catullan reminiscences, at a first reading, would not find much worthy of note except passing references; there is only a free translation of Catullus 5, which was published posthumously and is now relegated to the Appendix (986). Yet Lowell made sure to disclose that 'To Speak of Woe That is in Marriage', one of the key lyrics in *Life Studies*, started as a translation of Catullus 76: 'I don't know what traces are left, but it couldn't have been written without Catullus' (Seidel 1961= Giroux 1987: 254). This makes the absence of explicit Catullan references in his work rather conspicuous. Solving a conundrum with which critics have been at a loss for decades, Talbot (2006) has demonstrated that, when one looks at previous versions of the poem, Catullus is indeed behind Lowell's initial inspiration. As Talbot justly noted, although never enquired, this reveals a much more profound, if subterranean, connection between Catullus and Lowell than has been previously acknowledged. This relationship is particularly interesting because the Catullan references in Lowell's oeuvre are concentrated at a turning point for the development of Lowell's confessionalism. His first translations of Sappho are of the same period and were published in *Imitations* (1961). While the range of fragments he employs is limited, rewritings of Sappho resurface throughout his oeuvre, including in *Notebook* (1967–68; 1970) and *History* (1973).

'A Statement for Poetry' (1950) by Louis Zukofsky (1904–78) appears to share the same premises as Lowell's *Life Studies*: 'Poetry is derived obviously from everyday existence (real or ideal)' (Zukofsky [1981] 2000: 19). The two poets were writing more-or-less at the same time and were both concerned with the problem of the sincerity of the lyric self. Yet their poetry could not be more different. Zukofsky's highly experimental and philosophical poetry exemplified best in his long poem 'A' (1928–68) is a world away from the autobiographical verse of Lowell. But both poets were direct inheritors and indefatigable disciples of Pound's modernist intellectual tradition, which made objects of reality the kernel of the poetic imagination. Like Lowell, Zukofsky developed his interest in Catullus from Pound. With his wife Celia, he published a translation of the whole Catullan *liber* in 1969, a highly experimental work that stretched the boundaries of creative translation to its limits.[11]

Lowell and Zukofsky came from different backgrounds and did not have the same success. The first, from one of the wealthiest families of the Bostonian upper class, attended Harvard and Kenyon, married twice and had several mistresses. By the time of *Life Studies*, Lowell had become the most prominent American poet of post-war America; he was widely published, gave readings all over the country and became an established public intellectual who could even dare to turn down an invitation to read at the White House.[12] The second was born and lived all his life in New York; the son of Russian-Jewish immigrants, he grew up bilingual in Yiddish and English and learned Hebrew. He attended Columbia University, earned his living as a teacher and editor and his wife, the violinist Celia Zukofsky, was his life-long companion. He became associated with 'Objectivist' poetry, a term coined by Zukofsky in the 1931 special issue he edited for *Poetry*. Objectivism was very much indebted to Pound's Imagism, gathering several poets with a loose shared interest not only in poetic objects, but also in poems as self-referential aesthetic objects. According to Zukofsky, poetic creation had to account for the two concepts of 'sincerity' and 'objectification'. The former concerns itself with the way 'of seeing, of thinking with the things as they exist', the latter is the process by which, starting from sincere apperception, the mind supplies the missing elements to achieve a 'rested totality' and create a poem as an object (Zukofsky 1931: 273–4 = Zukofsky [1981] 2000: 194). The idea never quite took off. While he is now recognized as an important American poet, Zukofsky certainly did not achieve the success he thought he deserved and always struggled to publish his work. However, he continued his passionate poetic research based on objectivist principles; his poetic reflection is imbued with his version of Catullus.[13]

In this chapter, I study how Lowell's and Zukofsky's rewritings of Sappho and Catullus became springboards for their respective poetics of sincerity, effecting a social commentary of power structures, gender dynamics and sexuality in contemporary United States.

Rewriting the self with Catullus: Lowell's *Life Studies*

In a 1969 letter to Richard Tillinghast, Robert Lowell recognized the impact of translating classical and foreign literature on his creative laboratory:[14]

> I began 'Skunk Hour' as a loose rendering of Hölderlin's 'Brot' [sic], and heaping on Maine scenery. I think no Hölderlin is left. Then (roughly, I was working on five or six things at once) 'Commander Lowell', drawn from Rimbaud's 'Poètes des Sept Ans'...'Crane' revised...'To Speak' (from a late bitter poem of Catullus, but maybe nothing's left of that).
>
> Hamilton 2005: 522

By the end of 1960 Lowell had written fifty 'free translations' produced over three years.[15] Reading and translating Catullus determined the development of two important poems in *Life Studies*. The text of Catullus 11 as well as its Catullan persona serve as scaffolding and intertext in 'Words for Hart Crane', while Catullus's 'late bitter poem' 76 lies behind 'To Speak of Woe That Is in Marriage'.

'Words for Hart Crane' is the climactic poem of a cycle of four on modern poets with whom Lowell felt some sort of affinity.[16] The poem is made of fourteen iambic pentameter lines – Lowell's version of a sonnet and his privileged form after *Life Studies*. They give voice to a dramatic monologue spoken by Hart Crane's persona. Crane, who died at sea at a very young age and greatly suffered for the lack of critical recognition during his life, was considered by Lowell to be one of the best contemporary poets of his generation. His poetic alter ego defines himself as '*Catullus redivivus*':[17]

> When the Pulitzers showered on some dope
> or screw who flushed our dry mouths out with soap,
> few people would consider why I took
> to stalking sailors, and scattered Uncle Sam's
> phoney gold-plated laurels to the birds.
> Because I knew my Whitman like a book,
> stranger in America, tell my country: I,
> *Catullus redivivus*, once the rage
> of the Village and Paris, used to play my role
> of homosexual, wolfing the stray lambs
> who hungered by the Place de la Concorde.
> My profit was a pocket with a hole.
> Who asks for me, the Shelley of my age,

must lay his heart out for my bed and board.

Bidart and Gewanter 2003: 159

The identification between Crane's and Catullus's poetic personas takes place on several levels. In poem 11, Catullus repudiates his mistress Lesbia and asks his friends Furius and Aurelius to inform her that he no longer wants anything to do with her. As Catullus casts off Lesbia, who has betrayed his love, Crane snubs the American literary establishment which never recognized his value as a poet. Identifying with a *Catullus redivivus*, Crane pleads for a stranger to speak for him, echoing Catullus's entreaty to his friends 'pauca nutiate meae puellae / non bona dicta' (tell my girl these few nasty words) (*Cat.* 11.15) (Talbot 2006: 273).

Appropriated into Crane's persona, Catullus is recast as a progressive yet misunderstood poet. The idea that Catullus and the noetoeric were revolutionary promoters of a subversive kind of poetry, which resisted traditional forms of 'public' and 'institutional' verse, was taking root in mid-twentieth-century scholarship.[18] Kenneth Quinn's 1959 *The Catullan Revolution* used exactly the same New Critical paradigms in which Lowell was steeped to carry out a re-evaluation of Catullus as the precursor of modern lyricism. Catullus's ability to 'Make it New' while speaking of his everyday life must have resonated with Lowell in a creative period in which, as he states, 'I wanted to see how much of my personal story and memories I could get into poetry' (Kunitz 1964: 35). As Marjorie Perloff noted, fusing an element of 'the projection of the romantic lyrical "I"' with realistic conventions typical of the novel, which stress detail and locale, Lowell's confessional style effects a careful poetic mythologization of his own private life (1970: 487). In his recreations Lowell seems to find a consonance with Catullus as one of the most mythologized and self-mythologizing poets in the history of western literature. A similar sort of attraction characterizes Lowell's engagement with Sappho. Precisely because very little was known of their respective biographies, Catullus and Sappho function like empty vessels for Lowell's own poetic-projections and self-narratives in both his original poems and his translations.

'Words for Hart Crane' emphasizes the shared performativity of Crane's and Catullus's poetic personas as *enfants terribles* of the literary establishment. Flaunted promiscuity is the element connecting the two personas: 'I, / *Catullus redivivus* [...] / [...] used to play my role / of homosexual' (ll. 10–11). This is reinforced by the reference to Whitman, the most canonical of American poets, who also penned openly homoerotic images. The process of constructing literary identity and poetic affirmation is made explicit and questioned, with Crane's persona rejecting the false morality and prudishness of the establishment that chastised poets such as Catullus and himself for their writings. In the final lines, Lowell, via Crane via Catullus, states his poetic dictum: poetry lies in heart-felt frankness. As Crane demands that his interlocutor 'lay his heart out' (l. 14), we are taken back to Lowell's verdict on Pound, someone who had 'more heart than any poet since Hardy' (Giroux 1987: 274). The illusion of truth must be upheld by the constructed sincerity of the performative lyric self. This is the core of Lowell's interest in Catullus, whose staged sincerity stood at the origins of modern poetry's intimacy.[19]

Typical of Lowell's practice of continuous redrafting, there is an earlier version of 'Words for Hart Crane', entitled 'Epitaph of a Fallen Poet' published in 1953 in *Partisan Review* (Bidart and Gewanter 2003: 1037). There are no references to Crane, the invective is against England and *Catullus redivivus* rules Rome instead of New York's Village, together with Paris. The identification of Catullus as the writer of scandalous poetry is much more explicit, as the poetic persona laments the attention given to the one 'who scrubs Catullus' tongue with soap' (l. 2). In the second version of the poem, Lowell substitutes references to 'England' (l. 1), 'Rome' (l. 9), 'the classics' (l. 6) and 'Catullus' tongue' (l. 2) with American analogies like 'the Pulitzers' (l. 1), 'Whitman' (l. 6), 'The Village' (l. 9) and 'our dry mouths' (l. 2). As Simon Van Schalkwyk notes, this process of 'translational domestication', while silencing foreign and potentially un-American influences, adds an aspect of social critique to Lowell's poem, locating forms of resistance towards the 'containment culture' of the McCarthy era (2017: 3–4). In 'Words for Hart Crane' the censoring and marginalization of Catullus/Crane 'play[ing] the role of homosexual' reflect the persecution of homosexuality in McCarthyist America, a form of 'sexual paranoia linking "perversion" to national weakness' (Tyler May quoted in Van Schalkwyk 2017: 4).[20] Lowell's narrative of the self, constructed through the poetic persona of Catullus/Crane becomes, by metonymic substitution, the narrative of post-war America.[21]

Although increasingly popularized,[22] between the 1950s and the early 1970s Catullus's poetry was generally absent from the high-school curriculum in the United States; the majority of classics students encountered his work only at university.[23] Catullus was difficult and posed a problem because of his sexually explicit content, as Gilbert Highet, one of the most prominent American classicists at the time, remarked in 1957:

> Even in ancient times, he was not universally studied and revered as a 'classic' … [He] was not exactly suitable to be taught in colleges and schools. He is still unsuitable. It is extraordinarily difficult to read and discuss one of Catullus'

poems of passionate love in any classroom; and still more difficult if, two or three pages away, the readers can see another poem which begins and ends with a revolting obscenity.

quoted in Ancona and Hallett 2007: 483

A conservative attitude toward Catullus's corpus was still in place in 1961 when one of the standard editions, with commentary by J.C. Fordyce, was published with a warning: 'a few poems which do not lend themselves to comment have been omitted' (v). Obviously the difficulties of teaching openly sexual and violent material are not to be underestimated; however, it is evident that this kind of censorious attitude towards Catullus inevitably led to a misrepresentation of the poet's corpus, which influenced its reception. Early twentieth-century imaginative constructions of the poet's work and his biography often exploited the popularity of the Lesbia plot and, as Pound would say, the cluttering of Catullus 'with wedding-cake cupids' (Paige 1951: 116). It is precisely to this bowdlerizing that Lowell seems to be reacting in 'Words for Hart Crane', denouncing the problematic puritanical attitude of the establishment toward non-heteronormative sexuality and explicit writing.

Lowell's appropriations of Catullus in *Life Studies* are geared to his overall critique of the 'tranquillized *Fifties*' ('Memories of West Street and Lepke', Bidart and Gewanter 2003: 187). 'To Speak of Woe that Is in Marriage' uses Catullus to take on the matter of institutional love relationships. As in Catullus 11, in poem 76 the relationship between Catullus and Lesbia is over and his betrayed persona struggles to distance himself from her, fed up with and drawn into toxic love. On the surface, Catullus 76 and 'To Speak of Woe' seem to be linked only by the theme of abusive love relationships. Overlaid with Lowell's fictionalized memories of his own problematic marriage with Elizabeth Hardwick, Catullus's text seems to have almost completely dissolved in 'To Speak of Woe'. Chaucer's prologue to 'The Wife of Bath' (l. 3) and Schopenhauer's *The World as Will and Idea* ([1818–44] 1909: 342) are much more prominent, providing title and epigraph, respectively.[24] Yet Talbot (2006: 268–9) has revealed echoes of Catullus 76 in an earlier draft of this poem, 'Holy Matrimony' (Bidart and Gewanter 2003: 1044–5). He finds traces of 'nam quaecumque homines bene cuiquam aut dicere possunt / aut facere' (And actually what good a man can say or do to anyone) (ll. 7–8) in the line 'But *What can I do for you*? What can I do for you' (Bidart and Gewanter 2003: 1045). Similarly, he interprets the speaker's plea to 'Have pity' (1045) as a rewriting of the Catullan invocation to the gods, 'o di, si vestrum est misereri' (Oh gods, if you take pity) (l. 18), while 'Why prolong our excruciation?' (1045) would translate Catullus's 'quare cur tete iam amplius excrucies?' (So why do you continue tormenting yourself?) (l.10). And, Talbot remarks, the rarity of the noun 'excruciation' in English would suggest a calculated allusion to Catullus's 'excrucies' (you torment), echoing also the famous carmen 85, which ends on the verb *excrucior* (l. 2). This seems to me very plausible, considering that both Latin poems display similar conflicting sentiments of love and hate as those articulated in Lowell's dramatic monologue.

Rejection, frustrated expectations and a fundamental inability to communicate represent for Lowell the most poignant elements of Catullus 11 and 76. In 'To Speak of Woe', he lingers on the adulterous relationship between Catullus and Lesbia, a union in open conflict with Roman morality, for which *foedus*, a form of social alliance, which also regulated a union between a man and a woman, was inviolable.[25] Critics have pointed out the foundational role of *Cat.* 76, whose poetic persona for the first time in the history of ancient literature stands in contradiction to traditional mores. Despite being in an adulterous relationship, Catullus characterizes his love for Lesbia according to the values of *foedus* (pact / alliance), *fides* (trust) and *pietas* (duty / piety), thus claiming the validity of his individual feelings against traditional morality.[26] In his poem Lowell taps into similar conflicts. Adjusting the love relationship to his own biographical situation, he reverses the gender of the speaking voice, associating himself with the betraying Lesbia and the female speaking voice with Catullus (Talbot 2006: 269); yet of course, since he is the author, he also gives voice to the wife/Catullus's dramatic monologue. He thus transposes the Catullan situation into stereotypical gender roles of masculinity and femininity common in the 'tranquillised fifties'. A complex co-dependent relationship characterizes the bond of love and sexual attraction between betrayed wife and betraying husband, despite all its exploitative and violent traits. The stifling atmosphere is made more cumbersome by references to the mental illness of both husband and wife. Indeed, the poem is part of the final section of *Life Studies*, culminating in the hellish vision of 'Skunk Hour'.[27]

Lowell's critique of social norms in 'Words for Hart Crane' and 'To Speak of Woe' is enabled by literary figures of the past, who have entered the tradition as revolutionaries of one kind or another. His Hart Crane evokes Catullus and Whitman to corroborate his 'sincere' approach to art and life; in 'To Speak of Woe', a poem about painful, abusive and violent love, the Catullan lattice is supplemented by the references to Chaucer and Schopenhauer, exhibiting the literariness of Lowell's chosen theme. The boundaries between representations of facts and literary fiction are constantly blurred, in a 'study' of life that is not only personal but ultimately aesthetic and analytical. His poems are both life sketches and studies in composition and technique. The illusion of truth is what holds their realism together; at the same time, the literary tradition provides the filter for Lowell's understanding of life and self-mythologization. This process of literary consecration involved not only Catullus's poetry and his modern reception, but also many other classical personas, including Agrippina, Caligula and, as I discuss below, Sappho.[28]

Sappho through a prism

Lowell's preface to *Imitations* underscores his creative approach to translation:

> This book is partly self-sufficient and separate from its sources, and should be first read as a sequence, one voice running through many personalities, contrasts and repetitions. I have hoped somehow for a whole, to make a single volume, a small anthology of European poetry. The dark and against the grain stand out, but there are other modifying strands. I have tried to keep something equivalent to the fire and finish of my originals. This has forced me to do considerable re-writing.
>
> Bidart and Gewanter 2003: 195

Explaining that the translations in the collection should be considered self-sufficient poems, Lowell unashamedly admits his appropriative tendencies that reduce his sources to one voice, his own, following the modernist approach to generative translation (Yao 2002: 209-10). He 'tried to write alive English and to do what [his] authors might have done if they were writing their poems now and in America' (195), placing himself in the tradition of John Dryden who, in his 1697 translation of the *Aeneid*, wished 'to make Virgil speak such English as he would himself have spoken if he had been born in England, and in this Present Age' (Kingsley 1958: III 1055). For its free approach, the collection was at first received negatively, but then went on to win the 1962 Bollingen Poetry Translation Prize.

Homer and Sappho are the only ancient authors translated in the collection. They open the volume, followed by poems of the German, French and Italian traditions from the Middle Ages to Lowell's contemporaries, arranged chronologically, as if tracing a history of European literature. This makes Homer and Sappho the chosen progenitors of Lowell's very own literary tradition. Latin literature is completely ignored, which is rather striking considering the importance of authors like Catullus, Virgil, Propertius and Horace for the poet, as well as the fact that he intended the anthology as a compendium of European poetry.[29] An image of Ovid's *Metamorphoses* is used, however, as an illustration of the 1961 edition and, upon a closer look, Latin poetry emerges in intertextual references filtering through the works of the modern poets he selected. Two key Italian poets feature among those who were steeped in classical culture: Giacomo Leopardi, with 'The infinite' ('L'infinito'), 'Saturday Night in the Village' ('Il sabato del Villaggio') and 'To Sylvia' ('A Silvia') and the twentieth-century poet Giuseppe Ungaretti with 'You Knocked Yourself Out' ('Tu ti spezzasti').[30] Two other twentieth-century poets are included: Umberto Saba and, in particular, Eugenio Montale, whose poems occur ten times in the collection, signalling Lowell's deep exchange with Italian contemporary writers.

In his preface Lowell lingers on his imitations of Sappho, admitting that they should be considered 'new poems based on hers' (Bidart and Gewanter 2003: 195–6). They are collected under the title 'Three Letters to Anaktoria' (2003: 199–200) and mostly engage with three Sapphic fragments: the notorious fr. 31, on the psychological and bodily effects of love; fr. 16, one of two poems in Sappho's corpus in which the speaker declares her love for the girl Anaktoria; and fr. 168b, in which the poetic persona muses on her loneliness while contemplating the night sky. Lowell's imitation emphasizes the deadly fleetingness of love and the passing of time, which brings to a night that seems eternal, '[a] dead whiteness spreads over / my body' (ll.13–14 = Bidart and Gewanter 2003: 199); this culminates in the final letter, rewriting fr. 168b:

> III.
> The moon slides west,
> it is midnight,
> the time is gone –
> I lie alone!
> 'Three Letters to Anaktoria', ll. 42–5 = Bidart and Gewanter 2003: 200

In Lowell's loose chronological arrangement of the poems in his anthology, the imitation of Sappho comes immediately after 'The Killing of Lykaon', a rewriting of extracts from *Iliad* 1 and 21. The intimate and more pessimistic tone of the Sappho imitation contrasts with the epic theme of the Homeric poem, positioning Sappho at the origins of lyric poetry, while also showing the metamorphic potential of the translator's poetic persona speaking through the various voices of his sources. As Yenser remarks, *Imitations* is not only a history of literature but may also be seen as a poetic exploration of a poet's life, 'because the poet, be he Homer or Ovid or Lowell, undergoes in the course of his work those changes of personality which Lowell insists are at the heart of this book' (1975: 169). Lowell's use of lexical repetitions across several poems confer unity to his collection, deliberately giving the impression of 'one voice running through many personalities'.

The collection can also be read thematically, with corresponding poems at the two opposite poles of the volume, which frame the poet's voyage (Yenser 1975: 169–70). The sister poem to 'Three Letters to Anaktoria' is 'Hamlet in Russia, A Soliloquy', a collage of poems by Pasternak, which concludes with an echo of the lonely lyric self, gazing at the stars of Sappho 168b:

> The last bow is in the cards, or the stars –
> but I am alone, and there is none …
>
> Bidart and Gewanter 2003: 314–15

The repetition of themes has the effect of linking the poems to Lowell's overarching poetic persona and points at the dynamics of poetic tradition, while revealing a neo-humanistic approach to literature and a modernist interest in the presence of the past.

In 'Three Letters to Anaktoria', Lowell reimagines the love relationships in Sappho 31 and 16 as a heterosexual love triangle: 'The man or hero loves Anaktoria, later Sappho; in the end, he withdraws or dies' (Bidart and Gewanter 2003: 199). Sappho's persona speaks in three private conversations with Anaktoria, but it is the man of fr. 31 who takes centre stage as the object of Sappho's love. In the first letter, Sappho pines after the man who is in love with Anaktoria; in the second, the man is in love with Sappho:

> For some the fairest thing on the dark earth is Thermopylae
> and the Spartan phalanx lowering lanced to die –
> Salamis and the half-moon of Athenian triremes
> sprinting to pin down the Persian fleet;
> nothing is as fair as my beloved.
>
> ll. 17–21 = Bidart and Gewanter 2003: 199

In order to emphasize Sappho's adoration for the man, Lowell exploits the rhetorical effect of fr. 16's priamel – the figure of speech in which a series of items, culminating in the preferred one, are listed for comparison:

> O]ἰ μὲν ἰππήων στρότον, οἰ δὲ πέσδων,
> οἰ δὲ νάων φαῖσ᾽ ἐπ[ὶ] γᾶν μέλαι[ν]αν

ἔ]μμεναι κάλλιστον, ἔγω δὲ κῆν' ὄτ-
    τω τις ἔραται·
(Some say an army of horsemen, others of foot soldiers, / Others of ships is the most beautiful thing / on the black earth, I say / it is what one loves)

fr. 16.1–4

In his poem, Lowell rewrites this opening and adds an anachronistic reference to the gruesome battle of the Thermopylae following the Persian invasion of Greece, perhaps as a commentary on the war in Vietnam, to which he was fiercely opposed.

In the third letter, Sappho plays the role of the abandoned woman. While Sappho's poetry was mostly meant for social consumption,[31] Lowell makes it into a private communication between Sappho and Anaktoria. His choice reflects the common view developed between the 1940s and 1960s and propagated by Bruno Snell's 1946 study, *Die Entdeckung des Geistes. Studien zur Entstehung des europäischen Denkens bei den Griechen*, translated into English in 1953 as *The Discovery of the Mind: The Greek Origins of European Thought*, that Greek lyric represented the defining moment of the first discovery of subjectivity.[32] The practice of translating Sappho 31 as if it was directed to a man was long gone by the 1960s.[33] The Ovidian version of Sappho's character seems to intrude into these imitations, however, as the title 'Letters' evokes the epistles of *Heroides*. Dryden, Lowell's declared model, also translated Ovid's *Heroides* 15 and his translation may contribute to the intertext of the Sapphic imitation. Catullus 51 could also be a mediator of Lowell's heterosexual Sappho, especially considering that Lowell was rewriting Catullus roughly at the same time. All these poetic male voices may be interacting with Lowell's rewritings of Sappho, which show a concern with her text as much as with her literary tradition. Lipking notes that Lowell's normalizing move, showing an overbearing masculinity and heteronormativity, is consonant with the poet's tendency to speak through female personas abandoned by a man (1988: 118) as he does in 'To Speak of Woe That is in Marriage' through the prism of Catullus. As in his Catullan poems, Lowell's imitation of Sappho overlays the source text with references to the literary tradition and with his autobiographical and aesthetic concerns. The poetic persona of Sappho in *Imitations* is emblematic of the process of Lowell's self-inscription into literary tradition.

Lowell returned to Sappho six years later in *Notebook 1967–68* (1969), with a poem entitled 'April – 12. Sappho', also included in the expanded 1970 edition of the collection. In this poem, 'Three Letters to Anaktoria' is compressed into fourteen lines of unrhymed blank-verse:

April – 12. Sappho

'I set this man above the gods and heroes –   1
all day he sits before me face to face,
like a cardplayer. My elbow brushes his elbow,
if I should speak, he hears. The touched heart stirs,
the laughter is water hurrying over pebbles. . . .   5
He is the fairest thing on this dark earth;
I hear him, a hollowness is in my ears,
his footstep. I cannot speak, I cannot see.
A dead whiteness trickles pinpricks of sweat. . . .
I am greener than the greenest green grass;   10
I can easily make you understand this –
a woman seldom comes to what is best:
her child, her slaves, her daily household ache –
the moon slides west; time gone; I sleep alone.'

Lowell 1970: 156–7

This sonnet-like poem underlines Sappho's dramatic monologue using quotation marks, while the date links the poem to the diaristic nature of the collection. The three Sapphic fragments – 31, 16 and 168b – correspond in the sonnet to lines 1–5, 7–10; 6, 12–13; and 14, respectively. In the transition from 'Three Letters' to 'April – 12. Sappho', the second woman, Anaktoria, is eliminated. Sappho sits alone next to her beloved man. With the exception of 'he is the fairest thing on this dark earth' from fr. 16.2–3, the rewriting of fr. 31 occupies the first ten lines of the sonnet. Removing both the homoerotic aspect and the triangulation of Sappho 31, Lowell neutralizes the multifaceted desire dynamic of the source, which is reduced to a predictable plot of unrequited love. As she idealizes the man, whose mere proximity causes her love rapture, Sappho sounds conventional and melodramatic (Lipking 1988: 119).

While Lowell's appropriation of the Sapphic persona points at his sense of masculine entitlement, his operation is complicated by the addition of excerpts from frr. 16 and 168b as a coda, which shifts the overall mood of the poem in the last four lines from melodramatic to a down-to-earth recognition of the truth: women's entrapment into a life not chosen. Lines 11 to 13 are a free rendition of the second and third stanzas of fr. 16:

πά]γχυ δ᾽ εὔμαρες σύνετον πόησαι
π]άντι τοῦτ᾽, ἀ γὰρ πόλυ περσκέθοισα
κάλλος [ἀνθ]ρώπων Ἐλένα [τὸ]ν ἄνδρα
    τὸν [αρ]ιστον

καλλ[ίποι]ς᾿ ἔβα ᾿ς Τροίαν πλέοι[σα]
κωὐδ[ὲ παῖδος οὐδὲ φίλων το[κ]ήων
πά[μπαν] ἐμνάσθ<η>, ἀλλὰ παράγαγ᾿ αὔταν
         ]σαν

(It is easy to make this understood / by all, because she who surpassed / in beauty any human being, Helen, having left the best of husbands behind / crossed the sea to Troy / and not for her child or beloved parents / did she have a thought, but . . . led her astray)

Lowell removes any references to myth and makes Helen's deserting of her family to chase after Paris into a paradigmatic reaction to the condition of women, trapped in the banality of domestic chores: 'a woman seldom comes to what is best: / her child, her slaves, her daily household ache –'. Sappho's over-the-top infatuation arises as the inevitable consequence of the domestic boredom suffered by mid-twentieth-century American women, rather than from genuine feelings. The role of Romantic Sappho as the extraordinary poet of love and personal emotions is thus demystified, reduced to the average.[34] Turning the first woman poet –the ideal of eroticism, lyricism and the sublime, who has inspired writers, including the high-modernist Pound and Eliot, since antiquity – into a frustrated housewife is a powerful rhetorical stunt. On the one hand, it appears to be a rather violent and unjustified appropriation of a female voice and her homoerotic desire into a masculine and heteronormative setting. Commenting on an analogous normalizing strategy of fr. 31 by John Hall, who also gave a very prominent role to the man, Prins notes that Sappho 'is made to speak as "woman poet", but only by dying' (1999: 44). Lowell's Sappho is also stripped of her agency, since without her man she feels 'a dead whiteness' inside her and is destined to sleep alone. On the other hand, demystifying the model by projecting onto Sappho the demands of society on women's lives since antiquity, Lowell's poem suggests the impossibility for any woman, regardless of her status, to escape from the patriarchal structure of human affairs. The narrative of a woman's frustrated love-relationship with a man who ignores her, along with the trap of social convention and gender roles in 1960s America informs a social critique similar to Sylvia Plath's in her poem 'Lesbos' (1962), which presents the birthplace of Sappho as an unreachable ideal, the counterpart to the reality of contemporary women's lives. Ironically, Lowell's normalized rewriting, turning a powerful female voice and her homoerotic desire into a housewife's lament, ends up perpetuating the crime it seeks to denounce.

Matter-of-fact honesty is the trademark of Lowell's Sappho and she becomes a metaphor for 'women' as well as for 'poetry'. As Sappho and Helen of Troy are made into ordinary women in 'April – 12. Sappho', so romantic lyricism is dissected and presented as a form of escapism, highlighting the inauthenticity of the lyric persona. The poem's deflating views of the lyric tradition embodied by Sappho are in line with Lowell's deconstructing approach to American lyric, aiming at refocusing poetry's tone and subject matter on true-to-life representations. He thus contributes to the poetics of sincerity started with *Life Studies*, underlining the interaction between life and art. In his 'Afterthought' to *Notebook* (1970) he wrote:

> As my title intends, the poems in this book are written as one poem, intuitive in arrangement, but not a pile or sequence of related material. It is less an almanac than the story of my life. Many events turn up, many others of equal or greater personal reality do not. This is not my private lash, or confession, or a puritan's too literal pornographic honesty, glad to share secret embarrassment and triumph. The time is a summer, an autumn, a winter, a spring, another summer. I began working sometime in June 1967 and finished in June 1970.
>
> 1970: 262

The collection of sonnets is envisaged as one poem, grounded in his personal experience, but refuting the label of 'confessionalism' as a mere regurgitation of one's own personal life on the page. While it is safe to assume that the overarching poetic persona in *Notebook* is 'Robert Lowell', Lowell takes great care in displaying the textuality of the poetic self, its constructedness – a form of mediation that validates any poetic act and draws a line between the man and the poet. As Carruths remarks, '[w]e cannot read Lowell's autobiographical writing [...] without seeing that we are in touch with a writer who is making his life as he goes along' (1969, quoted in Yenser 1975: 269). Sappho is included in the section of *Notebook* entitled 'April', whose poems are all loosely connected around the theme of eros and sexual attraction. In 'April' and *Notebook* at large, Lowell appears to reiterate a tension between the flux of experience and a modernist narrative of the cyclical return of the seasons and patterns of death and rebirth. Lowell's Sappho is placed at the centre of this narrative, stressing her archetypal role in linking the mythopoeic drive of eros and thanatos to representations of individual subjectivity.

A revised version of 'April – 12. Sappho' is included in *History* (1973). The title and addressee of the poem are changed again, this time to reflect the source texts of frr. 31 and 16, restoring the original triangulation between Sappho, her beloved girl and a man. The speaking voice, Sappho, addresses a girl:

Sappho to a Girl

I set this man before the gods and heroes –
he sits all day before you face to face,
like a cardplayer. Your elbow brushes his elbow;
when you speak he hears you and your laughter
is water hurrying over the clear stones . . .
If I see you a moment it's hollowness;
you are the fairest thing on this dark earth.
I cannot speak, I cannot see –
A dead whiteness trickling pinpricks of sweat.
I am greener than the greenest green grass –
I die. I can easily make you understand me –
a woman is seldom enslaved by what is best;
her servants, her children, the daily household ache –
the moon slides west, the Pleiades; I sleep alone.

Bidart and Gewanter 2003: 435

Lowell maintains the overall structure of the dramatic monologue, but the numerous variants alter the dynamic of the poem considerably. Reflecting the general practice of revision from *Notebook* to *History*, he makes punctual changes focusing mostly on deictic markers, pronouns and demonstratives, rather than lexis. Calder has noted that the changes unsettle the primary poetic subject, generally identified with 'Robert Lowell' in *Notebook*, by undercutting the cues that pointed the reader to this unitary lyric voice speaking through various personas (1999: 134). The variants in 'Sappho to a Girl' have the same effect.

Softening his interventions on the source text by switching the personal pronouns from the first to the second person, he grants Sappho her homoeroticism. The social critique is maintained; the sense of stifling entrapment is heightened and more explicit in comparison to the previous poem. '[A] woman is seldom enslaved by what is best' features in place of 'a woman seldom comes to what is best', 'enslaved' pointing at the complete lack of agency of women. This is epitomized by Sappho's condition who, despite loving a woman, is oppressed by a marriage that she does not want. In the second version, Sappho's death-drive intensifies in 'if I see you a moment it's hollowness', becoming explicit in 'I die', while her speech is more personal: the generalizing 'I can easily make you understand this' becomes 'I can easily make you understand me', drawing attention to the speaking voice's subjectivity and making the poem look inward. Moreover, the last line, 'The moon slides west, the Pleiades, I sleep alone', is a closer translation of fr. 168b, 'Δέδυκε μὲν ἀ σελάννα / καὶ Πληϊάδες [. . .] / [. . .]

ἔγω δὲ μόνα κατεύδω' (ll. 1–2; 4) (The moon has set / and the Pleiades [...] / [...] I lie alone). This is the first time that Lowell inserts the Pleiades detail into his rewritings. These specificities contribute to free Sappho's voice from some of Lowell's interferences, without diminishing the social critique. The running commentary on 1960s America is sustained and made more direct by the removal of references to the past: the 'slaves' of the previous version are here 'servants'.

Lowell revised his poems 'endlessly' (Giroux 1987: 248) and considered all versions valid (Bidart 2003: xii). From this point of view, the various revisions of his translations of Sappho between 1961 (with *Imitations*) and 1973 (with *History*) may enact a 'prismatic' approach to translating. Matthew Reynolds has recently drawn attention to these kinds of 'plural translation practices' (2020: 3), underscoring the need to think of translation as a prism that 'open[s] up the plural signifying potential of the source text and spread[s] it into multiple versions, each continuous with the source though different from it, and related to the other versions though different from all of them too' (2020: 3).[35] Lowell's multiple translations of Sappho create an analogous multidimensional effect, which emphasizes the plurality of Sappho's text and its interpretations. At the same time, together with Catullus, Sappho becomes a vehicle for Lowell's creativity, enabling the development of his poetic realism. By virtue of the lacunose historical knowledge of their biography, as well as the fragmentary nature of their works, Lowell can fill the gaps with his own autobiographical projections and validate his own poetic self. Sappho and Catullus as mutually influencing poetic models and protean literary figures become paradigms of the poet's life.

Objectivist Catullus: The Zukofskys' translations

In 1969, Louis and Celia Zukofsky published *Catullus: (Gai Valeri Catulli Veronensis Liber)*, their translation of the entire corpus of Catullus's poems, including the fragments. The uniqueness of the Zukofskys' Catullus lies in their translation method. The versions are concerned with reproducing the phonemic structures of the Latin, with finding those English words, or combination of words that, when read out loud, may replicate the sound of the original. Semantic equivalence is a secondary concern. The Zukofskys do follow in the footsteps of modernist creative translations exemplified in Pound's work. Nevertheless, Pound did not use much phonetic, or, as they are often called, 'homophonic' translations, except for sporadic attempts in 'Papyrus' and *The Seafarer* (1911).[36] Their approach to Catullus was new and it remains one of the most original.

Presented with facing Latin text, a practice usually reserved for academic editions, the Zukofskys' *Catullus* gave prominence to the source as an integral part of the work. However, the translation is hardly an academic one. In fact, for its wildly experimental character it was initially received extremely negatively by critics across the spectrum, especially Latinists.[37] This was symptomatic of the lasting historicist methodology still widespread in the 1960s and 1970s in academic circles, which treated generative approaches to translation with sharp scepticism, particularly those such as *Catullus*'s that sacrificed transparency and foreignized language, thus tending towards opacity.[38] A few years earlier, Lowell's *Imitations* had also attracted criticism from many of his academic readers; but while his book later went on to receive the Bollingen Prize, the Zukofskys' translation remained a marginalized text.

Zukofsky started his acquaintance with Catullus in the 1930s with a translation of poem 8, included in *Anew* (1946), which was much more concerned with fidelity.[39] His only other major translation was another 'homophonic' version of Plautus' *Rudens*, which forms movement 21 of *'A'*. Phonetic transliteration is a technique that he often used in his later work, using texts in Greek, Hebrew, Latin, Ojibway and Welsh among other languages, revealing the poet's life-long investment in formal constraints and non-referential forms of language.[40] The translators' preface to *Catullus* reads:

This translation of Catullus follows
the sound, rhythm, and syntax of his
Latin – tries, as is said, to breathe
the 'literal' meaning with him.[41]

Giving prominence to sound, rhythm and syntax, the Zukofskys aimed to reproduce the 'literal' meaning of the Latin as 'breathed' by Catullus. What this means in practice is that they imitate in English the sound of Catullus's Latin (Wray 2004: 71). But the intention goes further. The word 'literal' does not have the usual sense of 'close to the meaning of the original' but, as Burton Hatlen remarked, 'rather reminds us that the letter, is an aural and visual shape, not a "meaning"' (1979: 348). The Zukofskys wanted to use words as sequences of syllables, stressing their sensory, material quality as utterances.

The attention to words as physiological objects is very much in line with Louis Zukofsky's broader views on language, that 'the human world is a world of language' and that language 'constitutes the only reality human beings can know' (Scroggin 1998: 332). Zukofsky posited a fundamental relationship between sensory perceptions and poetic language which became fundamental to his translation of Catullus:

> Because of the eyes' movement, something is imparted to or through the physical movement of your body and you express yourself as a voice. [...] The eye concerns the poet; the ear concerns the poet because he hears noises [...] and he's affected. [...] The eye is a function of the ear and the ear of the eye [...]. So much of the word is a physiological thing. I know all of the linguists will say I'm crazy. In fact I think there's a close relationship between families of languages, in this physiological sense. Something must have led the Greeks to say *hudor* and for us to say *water*.
>
> But the word is so much of a physiological thing that its articulation, as against that of other words, will make an 'object'.
>
> Zukofsky [1981] 2000: 231

Language depends on perception and, especially for the poet, words are direct vocal articulations of what he sees and hears. As embodied expressions, words become tangible objects, as Scroggins explained: 'a tangible shaping of air and sound by an embodied person' (1998: 36). Indeed, for Zukofsky the physiological aspect of words emerging in poetry establishes a common ground among different languages. Poetry could, therefore, be conceived as a supranational and translinguistic form of literature, with the potential to communicate across cultures. In a 'Statement for Poetry' (1950) he argued:

> It is this musical horizon of poetry (which incidentally poems perhaps never reach) that permits anybody who does not know Greek to listen and get something out of the poetry of Homer: To 'tune in' to the human tradition, to its voice which has developed among the sounds of natural things, and thus escape the confines of a time and place, as one hardly ever escapes them in studying Homer's grammar. In this sense poetry is international.
>
> [1981] 2000: 20

The 'musical horizon of poetry', which reproduces the sound of the 'human tradition', would supersede semantic understanding and allow communication among people speaking different languages. By virtue of Zukofsky's theories on embodied language, reading the poetry of Homer and experiencing its sound in the original would mean to connect with Homer's reality. From this point of view, the Zukofskys' *Catullus*, with its emphasis on translating the sound and structure of Catullus's poetry, represents an analogous attempt to 'tune in' to 'the human tradition' expressed in the Roman poets' work, eluding 'the confines of a time and place'.

In his 1929 essay on 'Ezra Pound', Zukofsky already singled out speech as the only truth-bearing aspect of language, therefore the only one worth carrying over in translation:

> What construction can be considered truth about the past? [...] Only speech
> transforms whatever skeleton remains of the past and conveys judgments of it to
> the intelligence.
>
> [1981] 2000: 73

On the one hand, *Catullus* realizes Zukofsky's poetics of language, based on a physiological conception of the word as an embodied expression of human perception, overcoming linguistic specificities – a superstructure that nods at Walter Benjamin's pure language.[42] This is most evident in the way the translations aim to close the gap between the historical Gaius Valerius Catullus and the present by creating poems that 'shape sound and air as closely as possible to the ways in which he shaped them in his poetry some nineteen hundred years ago' (Scroggins 1999: 36–7). For this reason, *Catullus*'s foreignizing translations draw attention to the interconnections and interdependence between Latin and English.[43] For Catullus to live again in the present, Zukofsky must evoke the sound of Latin through his English in a manner that 'enacts the process of poetic memory and demands that we undergo that same process' (Hooley 1988: 68). To this end the translation must necessarily stretch the limits of the English language to show its link with the Latin. On the other hand, the Zukofskys' *Catullus* re-elaborates the modernist, horizontal, synchronic view of tradition that also characterized Lowell's classicism. The focus is shifted to language, defining humanity's cognitive horizon and to translation as the most effective vehicle to foreground the intrinsic relationship between various languages of the past and the present. The Zukofskys' approach debunks principles of semantic equivalence and clarity championed by the establishment to emphasize what they thought to be the truth about language and reality.

Catullus's Latin is translated syllable by syllable, with the English lines aiming to maintain roughly the same length of the source.[44] Focusing primarily on rendering the original sound of Latin phonemic sequences over meaning, the Zukofskys allowed themselves freedom from semantic closeness to the original.[45] As the book progresses, the language of the translations is increasingly concerned with approximating the sound of Latin signifiers over meaning, in its most extreme instances producing a semantically independent text. As if gradually taking the reader through the various stages of the eccentric translation, in the Zukofskys' generative versions, as Yao argued, 'process, [...] as well as sound, constitutes one of the crucial dimensions of signification' (2002: 231). The metaliterary attention to process emerges in Lowell's self-aware Catullan personas and his constant revisions of his Sappho imitations, too. The latter have the ultimate effect of drawing attention to the constructedness of Sappho's lyric voice and the process of self-inscription that characterizes his rewritings in *Imitations*, *Notebook* and *History*. *Notebook*, with its diary-like form, may be considered an extended process poem in itself.[46]

Celia and Louis worked on the translation of Catullus over a period of more than eight years from 1958 to 1966, with a pause of about two years between spring 1958 and May 1960.[47] In conversation with Burton Hatlen, Celia described the process of their collaboration and the extent of her involvement:

> I did the spade work. I wrote out the Latin line and over it, indicated the quantity of every vowel and every syllable, that is long or short; then indicated the accented syllable. Below the Latin line I wrote the literal meaning or meanings of every word indicating gender, number, case and the order or sentence structure. I used Lewis and Short Latin Dictionary (Oxford Un. Press) and Allen & Greenough Latin Grammar (Ginn & Co.). Louis then used my material to write poetry – good poetry. I could never do that! I never questioned any of his lines, just copied his handwritten manuscript to facilitate the typing.
>
> Hatlen 1979: 347

This process of collaboration was central to the work and it is displayed openly in the cover of the 1969 edition, which reproduces some of the autograph pages of the translation of Catullus 85, containing both their work. Louis was extremely methodical, dealing with one poem at a time and translating it systematically from beginning to end, as he writes to the poet Cid Corman in a letter: 'dogged as ever, I'm doing 'em in order' (24 April 1958, Zukofsky Collection, quoted in Horáček 2014: 111). The only exception was Catullus 64, which Zukofsky approached last (C. Zukofsky 1979: 391). Remarkably, Louis did not know any Latin and Celia's command of the language was rudimentary. Collaborative translations became common practice among early and late modernist poets (e.g. see Pound's Chinese translations in *Cathay* (1915), which reworked Ernest Fenollosa's versions).[48] In his translations of Pasternak, Lowell also used cribs of the Russian source text to write his own imitations. Although lamented by the poet, Louis' ignorance of Latin was arguably useful to his homophonic experimentation because it allowed him freedom from meaning.[49]

Calques and interlingual puns are the main techniques deployed to achieve the phonemic translation in a gesture that aligns the Zukofskys' translation with Joyce's linguistic experiments in *Finnegans Wake* ([1939] 2002);[50] approximation to the meaning of the original is often only hinted at obliquely or metaphorically. For example, the opening of Catullus 51 is translated:

> He'll hie me, par *is* he? The God divide her,
> He'll hie, see fastest, superior deity
>
> ll.1–2

Corresponding to the Latin:

> Ille mi par esse deo videtur
> ille, si fas est, superare divos,
>
> 51.1–2

A literal translation of these lines would be '[he] seems to me to be equal to a god, / that man, if it is possible, seems to surpass the gods'. The Zukofskys' phonemic translation stretches the limits of the English language lexically and syntactically, introducing archaisms such as 'hie', an Elizabethan word meaning 'to hurry', to render the second syllable of 'ille', or the Latinism 'par' directly lifted from Catullus; the verb 'divide' approximates the sound of 'videtur'. The meaning is opaque and made more obscure by confused syntax. For the most part, the English departs completely from the Latin, such as in the translation of 'si fas est' (lit: if it is possible) with 'see fastest', or 'superior deity' for 'superare divos' (lit: surpass the gods), which deliberately misconstrues the grammar through a linguistic calque translating the infinitive 'superare' with the adjective 'superior' and the accusative plural 'divos', in the Latin functioning as the direct object of the verb, as an apposition of the subject.

At the same time, one could argue with Venuti that in *Catullus* 'the opacity of the language is due, however, not to the absence of meaning, but to the release of multiple meanings specific to English' (Venuti 1995: 216). In poem 51, the multiplicity of meanings achieved through word play establishes a continuity between the source and the target texts. The translation maintains the comparison between a speaking voice and another godlike man ('par *is* he?', 'The God', 'superior deity'), but the similarity is constructed on words of speed and hurrying, which, despite having no semantic correspondence with the source, serve the purpose of phonemic equivalence. By extending the limits of the English language to approximate the sound of Latin, the Zukofskys' foreignizing versions make the reader aware they are reading a translation, while underlining certain shared elements between source and target texts.[51]

The facing Latin source text plays a fundamental part in the reader's experience of the work, reminding one of the contiguity of sound between the Latin and English texts and 'completing the English sense' (Hooley 1988: 68). As Yao noted, Zukofsky's notion of translation is predicated upon the principle of metonymy:

Carrying forward the Modernist revolution in translation to its logical extreme, then, Zukofsky's greatest accomplishment lies in actualising a metonymic sense of translation as a mode of literary production in which the source-text stands as at once the originary cause and contiguous fulfilment of the translation itself.

2002: 233

By foregrounding the presence of Latin in the English language, the translations highlight the process of cross-cultural exchange between Catullus and the Zukofskys.[52] From this point of view, the Zukofskys' *Catullus* is effectively a multilingual work. This is hardly surprising from a polyglot such as Zukofsky, whose bilingualism in Yiddish and English meant that he was constantly undergoing a process of self-translation in either language and for the same reason was also probably acutely aware of the various aspects of inter-lingualism.

His poetic language in *Catullus* may be seen as a way of Americanizing Latin or Latinizing American English. The hybridization of language in these translations has the effect of 'recovering marginal cultural forms to challenge the dominant' (Venuti 1995: 217) and through language manipulation activating forms of cultural renewal. Venuti isolates such 'discursive heterogeneity' as a modernist practice which uses a 'range of Englishes, dialects and discourses that issued from the foreign roots of English (Greek, Latin, Anglo-Saxon, French) and from different moments in the history of English-language culture' (1995: 216–17) in order to propose alternative cultural models. I have discussed Zukofsky's use of Renaissance English and Latin calque in Catullus 51; the translation of poem 81 is a successful example of his use of foreign languages and contemporary American colloquialisms:[53]

> Nemone in tanto potuit populo esse, Iuventi,
>   bellus homo, quem tu diligere inciperes
> praeterquam iste tuus moribunda ab sede Pisauri
>   ospes inaurata pallidior statua
>
> (Isn't there no one in such a large population, oh Iuventius,
> no handsome man, whom you might begin to love
> besides that guest of yours, from the settlements of the dying Pesaro,
> paler than a gilded statue)

Cat. 81.1–4

> Not many enchant you (put to it) popular is he, Juventi,
>   Belle who's *homo*, can't your diligence keep open your eyes
> Pry there qualm instead of this moribund bad seed of Pisauri
>   Hospice an aureate pallid decor of statue

81.1–4, C. and L. Zukofsky 1969

With 'Belle who's *homo*' he extends the nominal construction 'bellus homo' into a full sentence, rendering 'bellus' with the French word '*belle*', close in sound and meaning; 'homo' (man) is translated with the conveniently homophonic and short form for 'homosexual': the derogatory *homo*. *Homo* may be both directed to Juventius and to his lover, otherwise defined 'moribund bad seed' and 'aureate pallid decor'; it also fits with the poem's insulting tone toward Juventius's guest and Catullus's wider use of invectives in his *liber*. As well as a degree of phonic equivalence, the poem puts forward some key concepts expressed in the original: the dismay of Catullus's poetic persona at Juventius's choice of a different partner than him and a disparaging attitude towards his lover. The Zukofskys' translation is rather progressive as one of the first to openly portray the homoeroticism, promiscuity and scatological tendencies of Catullus's poetry.

One of the most interesting effects of Zukofsky's linguistic–objectivist approach to Catullus is that it places Catullan obscenity at the centre of the translation. The tension between Catullus's love poetry and his obscene verse is at the kernel of Catullus's problematic reception even in the 1960s and 1970s. For Horáček, Catullan obscenity is central for the Zukofskys' procedure, constituting a formal and thematic layer of the text, suffusing the entire work and showcasing the playfulness and performativity of the original (2014: 109; 130). This attention to obscenity and open sexual innuendo, involving both heterosexual and homosexual jokes treated with playfulness, shifts the paradigm of Catullus's reception to allow various aspects of Catullan poetry to emerge.

By the mid-twentieth century, studies of Catullus's poetic skill had supplemented the biographical focus of the nineteenth century. Yet Catullus was still seen as 'an intensely personal maker of a meaning' (Wray 2004: 34). In an unprecedented way *Catullus* went beyond the intimacy attributed to the Catullan persona and the emphasis on the Lesbia cycle to encompass the linguistic, thematic and formal virtuosity of the *liber*.[54] Some of the Zukofskys' most successful and less obscure translations carry over both the allusive charge and the liveliness of Catullus, reproducing the range of the original, from its most learned pedantry to its crudest jokes.[55] In the Zukofskys' hands, Catullus becomes an experimental poet of language.[56]

Catullus's mixing of popular and academic cultures, archaic and current vocabulary, literary and technical expressions, had, according to Venuti, a subversive character in the history of translation, since as it 'calls attention to the social conditions of its own English language effects, it interrogates the unified appearance that English is given in fluent versions' (Venuti 1995: 219). Indeed, the Zukofskys' approach to translation was, for many, impossible to reconcile with the established values of fluency and transparency. It is no surprise that *Catullus* was repeatedly reviewed and commented upon by various classicists in highly negative terms and at times dismissed as nonsense. Considering the impenetrability of some of the poems in the collection, these negative responses are understandable. Yet they fail to comprehend the Zukofskys' translation as a creative work, whose merits emerge in Davenport's lapidary judgement: 'the only other modern Catullus is Carl Orff's' ([1973] 1979: 369).

Zukofsky never elaborated on why he chose to translate Catullus. The Roman poet and his American translator have several things in common. They were both urban intellectuals who wrote from a position of partial estrangement from their own chosen city. Indeed, the idea that Catullus's Latin was the language spoken in Augustan Rome and, therefore, a progenitor of the English spoken in New York may be one of the reasons behind Zukofsky's investment in Catullus's works. Besides the actual linguistic relationship between Latin and English, both the ancient and modern metropolises were characterized by a wildly diverse citizenry and a mixture of tongues, which intersected and coexisted; the English and Latin spoken in New York and Rome would have been shaped by such rich cultural encounters.[57] The emphasis on the interlingual aspect of translation and on discursive heterogeneity may also be a way of addressing the fact that, just as Zukofsky himself, Catullus was writing in a borrowed language – the Latin spoken in Verona was very likely different from the language of Augustan Rome. But Catullus's poetry must have also represented a model of sincerity and objectivity. Hatlen (1979: 354–5) and Wray (2004: 77–9) convincingly argued that an epistemological view of love is the key aspect driving Zukofsky's interest in Catullus. Catullus's poetic world is coloured by his ethical view of love and marriage through which he understands his romantic relationships and his friendships; for Zukofsky, humans knew and perceived through love: 'No one really knows us who does not love us, / Time does not move us, we are and love' ("A"-9.110). As poetry is based on truthful perception and truthful perception is based on love, Catullus's poetry would then represent a sincere expression of the human tradition that informed Zukofsky's poetics.

Post-war Sappho and Catullus, in both Italy and North America, are entangled in the discourse on lyric subjectivity and its authenticity. The Sapphic and Catullan poetic personas of Lowell and Zukofsky are meta-poetically aware and deliberately draw attention to poetry as the vehicle of narratives of the self. Lowell's self-mythologizing realism and Zukofsky's objectivism are still based on the universalizing modernist principle that human identity is realized through the mythopoeic function of literature. Although they developed extremely different types of poetics, Lowell, Zukofsky and Quasimodo all share a belief in the power of poetic language to shape reality: Lowell traced heartfelt frankness back through literary history; Zukofsky's sincerity and objectification enabled poets to '"tune in" to the human tradition'; Quasimodo's neo-humanism expressed 'the history of the heart of man'. In this way, they all locate Sappho and Catullus at the origins of their outlook on poetry and tradition.

5

Body vs Soul

Partly as a reaction to fascist appropriations and partly as a consequence of a gradual opening up to modern foreign literature, by the end of the Second World War in Italy the classics were beginning to lose some of their cultural prestige, becoming more peripheral to the literary discourse.[1] In the second half of the twentieth century, the majority of poets earned their living translating and writing critical pieces for leading newspapers and magazines. Among the internationally renowned poets who worked as translators and critics were Salvatore Quasimodo, Maria Luisa Spaziani, Eugenio Montale and Pier Paolo Pasolini. The interest in foreign culture was also a symptom of the loss of the centrality of Italian literature in the European literary system, so Italian poets turned abroad for inspiration, especially to French and German symbolism.[2]

This spurred the development of the so-called *quaderni di traduzioni* (translation notebooks), anthologies of foreign language poetry translated by leading poets. It was Montale's *Quaderno di traduzioni* of 1948 that formalized the practice through which translation came to be considered a literary genre in its own right and the *quaderni* its direct expression, or meta-genre.[3] If Lowell's *Imitations* constitutes a rather original move within the post-war American landscape where literary translations of foreign language works were very few, in Italy 'about 60 per cent of twentieth- and twenty-first-century poets translated at least one volume' (Blakesely 2014: 8). In fact, it would not be surprising if Lowell modelled his anthology on the *quaderni* by Ungaretti and Montale.

Remarkably, almost none of these *quaderni* contained translations of Ancient Greek and Latin.[4] The classics, however, never disappeared completely from the Italian cultural landscape; since the second half of the twentieth century, dynamics of classical reception and translation have been entangled with a fast-changing publishing market and an increasingly globalized literary world.[5] With the move away from Hermeticist poetics towards a type of socially engaged poetry that reflected on the horrors of fascism and the war, publications on the classics in the 1950s and 1960s preferred to engage with dialogic genres such as drama, novel and epic. Once a boon for Italian poets, Ancient Greek and Latin lyric was soon pushed to the margins.[6]

After Pier Paolo Pasolini's translations of four fragments in Friulian dialect (1945-1947) and Cesare Pavese' fictionalization of Sappho in one of his *Dialoghi con Leucò* (1947), Sappho seemed to have fallen out of the poetic spectrum – minus Quasimodo's *Lirici greci* reprints – with no new major creative translation of her works. One notable exception was Emilio Villa's *Saffo* (1982), a volume of selected fragments illustrated by the artist Alberto Burri who, between 1973 and 1982, created ten lithographs to accompany Villa's translations. Yet the work had a very limited circulation: only 105 copies were published. Sappho, nevertheless, continued to circulate, mostly in paperback editions and academic texts, epitomized by the successful 1969 anthology of Greek lyric translated by Filippo Maria Pontani. Since the 1970s, statistics have registered a growing editorial interest in ancient Greek and Latin texts in translation, often published in paperback editions for a large non-academic audience, which set a new translation standard, superseding the artistic poetic versions of the previous decades.[7] The demand reflects a decrease in knowledge of ancient languages, corresponding with an increase in the level of education of the general public.[8] Even these 'traduzioni di massa' (mass translations) had an openly anti-Hermeticist agenda.[9]

Sappho resurfaced in poetry and fiction in the 1980s, although never again with the intensity of the Hermeticist discourse. Sappho's homoeroticism was by then openly affirmed. In his introductory essay to Franco Ferrari's 1987 edition and Italian translation of Sappho, Vincenzo di Benedetto, one of the leading classical philologists at the time, included an entire section on 'Sappho's homosexual experiences' (11-5), in which he invited the reader to avoid unnecessary purging: 'Se Saffo usa il verbo «amare» (*philei ... philēsei*) senza ulteriori limitazioni, non ce le deve mettere di suo il lettore moderno' (If Sappho uses the verb 'to love' (*philei ... philēsei*) without additional limitations, the modern reader must not impose them himself) (12). The development of feminist and gender study approaches in Anglo-American scholarship, which problematized normalizations of Sappho's homoeroticism in critical and creative discourses, although variously received by historicists and philologists, have filtered through the Italian academic world since the 1990s. Late twentieth-century Italian translations and rewritings of Sappho were fully conscious of the problematic history of her reception, and the ancient poet finally became the well-known icon of liberated eroticism, albeit with a considerable delay over the rest of Europe.[10] For instance, Grytzko Mascioni's biographical novel *Saffo* (1982) portrays her freely expressing her love for other women. The poet Alda Merini, in collaboration with the artist Enrico Baj, created the book-object *L'uovo di*

Body vs Soul 143

Fig. 5.1 Merini, A. and E. Baj (1999–2000), *L'uovo di Saffo*, Belluno: Colophonarte.

Saffo (1999–2000) (Sappho's egg). In a wooden container-object sculpted by the artist, there are five rewritings of Sappho's fragments by Merini; the eroticism of Sappho's poetry emphasized in Merini's poems is amplified by direct references to female sexuality on Baj's box, displaying an egg and a vagina-shaped decoration.[11]

Publishing history shows Sappho's remarkable editorial success in the twenty-first century. To my knowledge, between 2000 and 2020 at least sixteen new editions of Italian translations of Sappho have been published, among which the poetic versions in Rosita Copioli's *Saffo. Più oro dell'oro* (2006) (Sappho. Golder than gold) analysed below.[12] This body of work adds to the several running reprints of existing editions and does not include texts published in anthologies.[13] Revealing a general cultural re-evaluation of the ancient poet, new interest in Sappho's work by academics and poets alike has been stimulated by the recent discoveries of new fragments in 2004 and 2014, now known as the 'New Sappho' and the 'Newest Sappho'.[14]

Such interest chronologically coincides with the first public recognitions of homosexual rights in Italy. On 8 July 2000, 20,000 LGBTQ men and women marched in Rome in celebration of World Pride 2000. As Gary Cestaro notes:

> World Pride in Rome continues to be seen as a historically significant event by Italian gays and lesbians, an important turning point in the history of the Italian

gay rights movement that for the first time garnered serious national – indeed international – attention. [...] World Pride 2000 and the controversy surrounding it reflect the difficult positioning of Italian culture and Italian literature between the classical and the Catholic, between ancient organisations of human sexual activity that left some space for same-sex desire and Christian efforts to redefine and delimit.

2004: 1–2

The law granting the right for same-sex couples to enter into a civil partnership was only passed in 2016. Such tensions between classical models and Christian morality still characterize the discourse on homosexuality in Italy. While classical same-sex desire has been recognized and studied by scholars for decades, the differing interpretations of the classical model of eros mirror the ongoing public debate on eroticism and sexuality.

Catullus's post-war reception follows a trend similar to that of Sappho, with over forty translations published between 1977 and 2000 – an average of more than one a year.[15] This trend continued in the first two decades of the twenty-first century.[16] The most popular was Mandruzzato's paperback translation for BUR, first published in 1982 and reprinted until 2004. Most recently, in 2018, Alessandro Fo published an important translation with a long and detailed commentary for the prestigious series Nuova Universale Einaudi with a grand total of 1,322 pages. The heftiness of the notes apparatus makes Fo's a work for students and specialists of Catullus although, as a poet, Fo also aims at a poetic rendering of the quantitative metres of Catullan verse by matching them to Italian syllabic tonic metres. He developed his own version of *metrica barbara*, as other famous poet-academics such as Carducci and Pascoli had done in the past. As in the case of Sappho, creative poetic translations of Catullus are fewer in comparison to paperback and academic texts. After Quasimodo, the most salient of unabridged translations are those by Enzo Mazza (1962), but especially Guido Ceronetti's 1969 *Catullo*, which I discuss below.[17] They were followed by Mario Ramous's versions of 1975, and by Edoardo Sanguineti's *Omaggio a Catullo* (Homage to Catullus) (1986), a series of seven parodic rewritings of some of Catullus's most famous poems, mocking stereotypical portrayals of Catullan lyricism.[18] More recently, in 2014, Nicola Gardini published a sophisticated verse translation of the whole *liber*, rendering Catullan poetry into various Italian metres.

In this chapter I discuss two of the most salient poetic translations of the entire oeuvre of Sappho and Catullus published in post-war Italy. The 1969 Catullus by Guido Ceronetti (1927–2018) and the 2006 Sappho by Rosita Copioli (1948–).

Ceronetti was an Italian poet, translator, dramatist and public intellectual who wrote for various national newspapers, including *Il corriere della sera* and *La stampa*. The majority of his poetic production, mostly short lyric fragments, is today collected in *La distanza. Poesie 1946–96* (*The Distance: Poetry 1946–96*), published in 1996 by BUR. His last collection *Ballate dell'angelo ferito* (*Ballads of the Wounded Angel*) was published in 2008. In 1970, with his wife Erica Tedeschi, he created Il Teatro dei Sensibili, a private puppet theatre in their flat where they staged dramas written by Ceronetti for an audience of intellectuals such as Eugenio Montale, Natalia Ginzburg, Federico Fellini and Louis Buñuel. In 1985, Il Teatro dei Sensibili moved out of Ceronetti's apartment, becoming an itinerant project travelling around Italy. While he often lamented his exclusion from the literary establishment, he was a prominent, if provocative, figure of post-war literary culture in Italy. Openly anti-communist he never completely fitted into the intellectual circles of Marxist tendencies that dominated the publishing industry between the 1950s and the 1970s. Nevertheless, thanks to his anti-conformist style and brilliant writing skills, in the 1960s he was signed by Einaudi, the leading highbrow publishing house of post-war Italy, with whom he published the majority of his poetry and translations. Ceronetti's poetic and dramatic productions were interspersed with assiduous translation work, from which he made a living.[19] He translated mostly from ancient languages, especially Latin, Hebrew and some Greek, but also modern languages, including English, French, Spanish, German, Arabic and Greek. In *Come un talismano* (Like a talisman) (1986), an anthology of translated poetry including works by ancient and modern authors, he included two translations of Sappho.

    A similar combination of poetry, translation and criticism characterizes the work of Copioli. Born in 1948, a generation younger than Ceronetti, Copioli was a student of Luciano Anceschi, who was her undergraduate supervisor. Yet, as a young poet, she deliberately remained outside the poetic Neo-Avant Garde of the 1960s and 1970s. In 1979 she won the prestigious Viareggio Prize for her first poetry collection, *Splendida lumina solis* (1979, Furore editions). At this time, she was briefly involved with an aestheticizing group of poets, including Giuseppe Conte, Mario Baudino, Tomaso Kémeny, Roberto Mussapi and the philosopher Stefano Zecchi, whose aim was to bring beauty and myth to the centre of the poetic discourse. Although she soon dissociated herself from the group, which later formalized into the movement of Mitomodernismo, she has remained interested in exploring ideas of beauty and myth in her work. Her poetic collections have been published with major houses such as Mondadori and Guanda, and have been translated into English and French. She has published her own translations of Sappho, W.B. Yeats, J.W. Goethe, and G. Flaubert. She was founder and director of the literary journal *L'altro versante* (1979–89), gathering contributions by leading Italian poets and critics on matters of translation, tradition and aesthetics. A prolific non-fiction writer, she has also written several volumes of essays gathering her ideas on literature, art and religion, which inform her poetics and her approach to translation. An interest in myth, spirituality, beauty and the intersections among desire, divine love and creative inspiration in the history of western thought and civilizations characterize her essays and her work overall.[20]

I first discuss Ceronetti's poetic translations of Sappho and Catullus, focusing especially on his pioneering work on the Latin poet, published by Einaudi in 1969 as *Catullo. Le poesie*. Ceronetti's *Catullo* was ground-breaking yet, for many, was a highly controversial translation. For Filippo Maria Pontani, who wrote a survey article on translations of Catullus published from the late nineteenth century to 1977, it was '[l]a più estrosa fra le recenti versioni e fra tutte le versioni catulliane [...]. È la più spregiudicata, cerca gli anacronismi stridenti e civettoni. Un esempio di Kitsch per i continui ammiccamenti, parodici o no, con una tradizione letteraria' (The most inspired of the recent translations and of all Catullan versions. [...] It is the most unscrupulous, it looks for strident and flirty anachronisms. An example of Kitsch for its continuous innuendos, parodic or not, to the literary tradition)' (640). As well as modernizing the source text in several places through various anachronisms, the translation is the first to emphasize the scatological language and ludic aspects of the Catullan collection by accentuating the more corporeal aspects of the Latin poet's work. Quotidian and scurrilous language is deliberately mixed with high-register and poetically sophisticated passages, often with a desacralizing and parodic effect. The translation provoked and continues to elicit mixed critical reactions.[21] Yet Ceronetti's operation, intentionally breaking with the philological tradition and resisting the pruderies that characterized the Catullan reception, was not only highly original but, with all its excesses and tendencies towards rewriting, for the first-time in Italy, also gave voice to several neglected aspects of Catullus's work, debunking its romanticized portrayals. From this point of view Ceronetti's operation is similar to the Zukofskys' experimental *Catullus*. Sappho is much less prominent in Ceronetti's work; yet her name resurfaces in his essays. Most significantly, in the preface to the 1980 edition of his *Catullo*, the Lesbian poet and her first Latin translator are employed to exemplify Ceronetti's views on translation and tradition.

As a way of comparison, the second part of the chapter focuses on Rosita Copioli's recent translation of the entire corpus of Sappho in *Saffo. Più oro dell'oro*

(2006). Copioli adopts an original approach to the source text, which is informed by her wider poetics, enacting a form of mythic revisionism, based on a syncretic view of culture, echoing late-nineteenth-century mythical rewritings. Approaching Sappho's poems through a neo-platonic lens, Copioli's translation considerably tones down the eroticism of the fragments. Both these approaches to the classics as exemplified in their translations reflect the complexity of the contemporary discourse around ancient lyric models. At the same time, the Italian reception of Catullus and Sappho emerges as a vehicle of current debates on gender and sexuality.

Ceronetti's anti-establishment Catullus

Ceronetti's *Catullo. Le poesie* (1969) included the facing Latin text, a few scattered explicatory notes and a long commentary essay entitled 'Dei e imenei, ladri e matrone' (Gods, hymeneals, thieves and matrons) containing his thoughts on Catullus's poetry. The translation was first published in the prestigious luxury hardback series 'I Millenni', which was launched by Einaudi in 1945 as a collection of classics 'to be read forever' – books considered essential to any 'respectable' library.[22] It comprised a vast selection of works of world literature, the majority of which were in translation[23] and were aimed at an educated middle-class audience, who would be willing to buy luxury editions. Ceronetti proposed a highly idiosyncratic translation, which, with a free approach to the source text, emphasized the 'prohibited' traits of Catullus's *liber* through over-the-top lewd language. In the midst of the left-wing 1968 movement attacking traditionalist Italian society, the translation functioned as a call for anti-conformism. By constructing an irreverent and sordid Catullan persona, much more inflammatory than in the Latin, Ceronetti gave his translation a clear political import, which, as Andreotti (2012) notes, was meant to '*épater le bourgeois*' (shock the bourgeoisie), who were used to a school-friendly, polite Catullus.

Ceronetti's translation is a complex poetic exercise. Its language is lively and entertaining; the verse combines funny and crude passages with peaks of high lyricism.[24] It completely broke with the previous tradition, either characterized by a stale nineteenth-century tone or, when directed towards modernity as Quasimodo's *Canti*, emphasizing the elegiac and elegant tones of Catullus to the detriment of the scatological poems. He aimed to give new life to Catullus's Latin beyond the philological approach of contemporary 'ipertrofiche università di morte' (hypertrophic universities of death) (Ceronetti [1969] 1991: vi).

Ceronetti's disinterest in philological accuracy is confirmed in a brief note in the 1969 edition, where he explains that he used Cornish's Latin text simply because he could not get hold of Kroll's Teubner edition.[25] Inevitably, as almost every single one of the creative translations discussed in this book, Ceronetti's *Catullo* was and still is criticized by the academic establishment for its lack of fidelity, anachronisms and excessive tone.[26] The market passed a different judgement, as the volume was rather successful commercially. The translation was reissued with revisions in 1972, 1980, 1983 and 1991 in Einaudi's more popular Struzzi series, which was founded in 1970 to publish cheaper reprints of successful books for a wider market. The final 1991 revised edition set out the final text and contained Ceronetti's prefaces to his 1980, 1983 and 1991 editions. The volume continues to be reprinted, most recently in 2019 by Adelphi.

In 'Dei e imenei' he further elaborates on the idea that philological knowledge is not sufficient to translate ancient poetry because it does not compensate for 'l'ignoranza degli Dei essenziale' (the essential ignorance of the Gods) ([1969] 1991: 337–8). With Leopardian overtones, Ceronetti finds a rift between the ancients, who located poetry in a divine metaphysical realm, and the disillusioned moderns, who view it as a creative impulse springing from a writer's interiority. Lamenting the latter, he vindicates poetry's metaphysical afflatus: 'La certezza che niente è mandato dal di fuori […] toglierebbe alla vita il suo unico lievito' (337) (The certainty that nothing is sent from outside […] would deprive life of its only leaven). However, facing the impossibility of overcoming the ideological distance between ancient and moderns, a translation remains a violent act on the source text:

> Quando un poeta moderno converte nel proprio linguaggio un poeta antico, se l'operazione gli riesce, avrà compiuto un assassinio degno di essere messo tra i *beux arts*. Nessun midollo semantico, nessun fondo lordamente umano, nessun gioco di superficie, resisterà all'attrazione del dio ignoto, presente nell'altro linguaggio: cadrà nella trappola e risusciterà diverso.

> (When modern poets convert an ancient poet into their own language, if the operation is successful, they will have executed a murder worthy of being listed among the fine arts. No semantic marrow, no spurious human core, no superficial game will resist the attraction of the unknown god present in the other language: it will fall into the trap and will revive as something different.)

[1969] 1991: 338

It follows that Catullus must die by Ceronetti's hands to live again as a new text ('will revive as something different') in his words. The metaphor of translation as a form of renewal, which underlines the modernist 'Make it New' and Quasimodo's neo-humanism, resurfaces once again in Ceronetti's Catullus. A fundamental element of untranslatability allows a degree of poetic freedom denied by the historicist approach, maintaining a Renaissance rhetoric of *aemulatio* of the source. If the notion of the sacrality of the source text is overcome, the cultural authority associated with the classical text as a point of origin is the necessary validation to the appropriative act of the modern translator.

Some adherence must be maintained, '[al] testo di regola bisogna aderire, perché muoia bene' (as a rule it is necessary to adhere to the text, in order for it to die well) (Ceronetti [1969] 1991: 338). Yet this adherence is not strictly semantic. In a contemporary essay on translation, Ceronetti argues that the illusion of dictionary equivalence must be abandoned to generate corresponding 'energies': 'bisogna pensare alla quantità di energia potenziale dei due vocaboli' (one must think about the quantity of potential energy of the two words) (Ceronetti 1969: 93). That is to say, a good translation needs to reproduce the intensities of the original, the effect the source text may have had on readers: 'se sviluppano un'energia uguale si corrispondono' (if they develop an equal energy they correspond to each other) (93).[27] The sought after equivalence is an aesthetic one. This approach produced a decadent Catullus, in which the obscene is emphasized in the most unexpected places, eliciting either humour or scandal, depending on the reader.

There is an overall de-sacralization of language throughout the volume. For instance, in poem 34, the hymn to Diana, '[...] notho es / dicta lumine Luna' (ll. 15–16), literally meaning 'for your reflected / false light you are called "Luna"', is translated with 'Sei la bastarda luna' (you are the bastard moon) (16.16, Ceronetti [1969] 1991: 45). *Nothus* is a high register word of Greek origins denoting falsity. In the context of *Cat.* 34, it probably refers to the ancient theory that the moon shines with reflected light. Quintilian (3.6.97) also explains that the Greeks used *nothus* to refer to an illegitimate child (Fo 2018: 557). Ceronetti's translation plays on these meanings.

Similarly, in poem 70, Lesbia's love declaration is trivialized. The first two lines, 'Nulli se dicit mulier mea nubere malle / quam mihi [...]' (My woman says that she would not marry anybody other than me) (70.1-2), are rendered with 'Solo con te dice la donna mia / solo con te io chiaverei' (70.1-2, Ceronetti [1969] 1991: 231). *Nubere*, the word referring to marriage union, literally meaning 'to marry' is translated with 'chiavare' (to fuck). In love poetry the verb *nubere* is often employed to connote a general union with one's beloved, without the meaning of a legal bond (Lenchantin 1952: 228 cited in Fo 2018: 1048). Ceronetti forces the meaning of the verb even further. It is as if the epigrammatic voice of

Martial, himself an admirer of Catullus, had filtered through Ceronetti's Catullan translation. Notably, Ceronetti had published a translation of the epigrams of Martial a few years earlier in 1964.

The scatological poems are rendered with even stronger tones. For instance, the second part of poem 37:

> puella nam mi, quae meo sinu fugit,
> amata tantum quantum amabitur nulla,
> pro qua mihi sunt magna bella pugnata,
> consedit istic. hanc boni beatique
> omnes amatis
>
> Cat. 37.11–14 = Ceronetti [1969] 1991: 82

> Dalle mie braccia volata via
> Anche la donna mia
> Lei, amata come nessuna,
> Per la quale ho combattuto
> Una guerra forsennata,
> Si fa inculare lì,
> Come foste degni di lei
> Tutti ve la chiavate
>
> 37.14–21, Ceronetti [1969] 1991: 83

The language employed to speak of sex and Lesbia's sexual mores is deliberately lower in register than in the original. The over-the-top translation of 'consedit', which literally means 'she sits there with you', with 'si fa inculare' (lets you stick it up her ass) is startling and deliberately provocative. The same emphasis on sex is reiterated in the translation of *amare* with the verb *chiavare*. The canzonetta's rhythm and rhymes, and the frivolous tone heighten the contrast with the subject matter, with grotesque and comic effects.

The lexis gives Lesbia a loud and transgressive sexuality, free of blame, yet more vulgar. Throughout the translation the corporeal is emphasized in the love relationship between Catullus and Lesbia, deliberately questioning the established portraits of the Catullan persona:

> Cercavo disperatamente, al di là del poeta Catullo contemporaneo di Cesare e suo intrepido nemico, il suo mito [...] e di staccarlo un poco dalla gogna biografica e filologica che lo stringe proclamando invariabilmente l'amante neoterico, il giambico deluso, l'alessandrino trapiantato, il provinciale di Verona caduto nei metri di una setta raffinata e nella rete mortale di una scostumata dama.

> (I was desperately searching for his myth, beyond Catullus the poet contemporary with Caesar and his fearless enemy, [...] and to separate him a little from the biographical stocks that tie him, invariably proclaiming the neoteric lover, the deluded iambist, the transplanted Alexandrian, the provincial of Verona fallen in the metres of a refined sect and in the mortal web of a licentious dame)
>
> Ceronetti [1969] 1991: 4

As in the translations and rewritings of Lowell and Zukofsky, Ceronetti's *Catullo* is a text starkly aware of its reception. The type of myth that Ceronetti wants to recreate in his own translation is the demonic, decadent Catullus, playing with another critical and literary trope associated with the Roman poet, that of the *enfant terrible* above morality. This resonates with Lowell's Catullan voice in 'Words for Hart Crane', criticizing the establishment's censoring attitude along with Zukofsky's translations, which are particularly attentive to the explicit aspects of Catullus's language. By the end of the 1960s, both in Italy and North America, Catullus's sexuality stops being censored and becomes a symbol of the anti-establishment.

Ceronetti's corporeal and decadent Catullus finds a detailed (although at times opaque) explanation in his commentary essay. He takes Baudelaire's scathing judgement of Catullus as a poet *purement épidermique* (purely superficial) as guidance:

> La collera di Baudelaire contro Catullo è giusta, da parte di un poeta dei sottosuoli: non è da discutere, è verità. Catullo è un poeta dell'interiorità, ma la sua interiorità appare levigata come una superficie.
>
> (Baudelaire's rage against Catullus is right, from the point of view of a poet of the underground: it is not debatable, it is true. Catullus is a poet of interiority, but his interiority appears to be smooth as a surface.)
>
> [1969] 1991: 340

Ceronetti blames Catullus for giving in to a sense of moral restraint and a chastising attitude towards Lesbia – a critique certainly directed at the sense of middle-class decorum and propriety that he wants to undermine. Taking Baudelaire as his poetic model, he argues that the French poet manages to turn his mistress, Jeanne Duval, into a poetic symbol, an archetype of demonic eroticism, while Catullus's Clodia, in her poetic figuration of Lesbia, fails to make '[i]l salto dall'epidermico al metafisico' (the leap from superficial to metaphysical) (343). Catullus 37.11–14 is compared to the end of Baudelaire's 'Beatrice', showing the apotheosis of Jeanne/Beatrice among a swarm of devils (ll. 26–30), the demonic reversal of the Dantean Beatrice of the *Commedia*. Jeanne/Beatrice owns her sexuality and, with the pose of a cruel divinity, defiantly caresses ('sale caresse', lewd caresse, l. 30) the adoring devils. But Catullus, Ceronetti argues, keeps Clodia in the realm of the ordinary: 'il mondo di Clodia non ha un rovescio celeste' (Clodia's world does not have a celestial counterpart) (344) preventing her to enter the realm of the symbolic (344–5). In the light of these considerations, Ceronetti's translations appear as an attempt to emphasize Lesbia's potential to become an archetype of liberated female sexuality, which he exasperatingly calls an 'archetipo di puttanità infinita' (an archetype of infinite whoredom), as the readers are supposed to accept it as a positive archetype notwithstanding his chauvinistic choice of words.

The commentary indeed laments Catullus's affirmation of his own masculinity by showing a moralistic attitude that wants to contain Lesbia's and, more generally, women's free affirmation of sexuality: 'per la debolezza sentimentale del suo amante, che in quello che spianta la miseria e la misura comune dell'amore vede la propria indelebile *iniuria* e toglie la stima (l'approvazione della città ideale)' (for the sentimental weakness of her lover, who sees, in the acts uprooting the common misery and measure of love, his own indelible injury, and thus withdraws respect (the approval of the city)) ([1969] 1991: 345). Ceronetti denigrates Latin literature's tendency to suffocate 'libertà erotica femminile' (female erotic freedom) perceived as dangerous for the social and political patriarchal order, as it 'accerchia con la sua enormità il *vir*' (surrounds with its enormity the man) (342). These are rather progressive views for 1969 Italy, evoking feminist deconstructions of gender and sexual politics. Striking a blow against the Italian middle-class, Ceronetti defends the right of women to have a sexual life beyond the patriarchal structures of marriage and procreation – in 1969 Italy had yet to legalize divorce, whose regulatory law was passed in 1970 (Fortuna-Baslini Law); abortion was legalized only in 1978.

Nevertheless, Ceronetti's Lesbia reproduces the dynamics of symbolic objectification that have traditionally reduced women to either angels or prostitutes, in the same way as Pound pulled Lesbia down from the pedestal of tradition, only to make her into a 'drab'. This is even more problematic when put in the context of Ceronetti's anti-politically correct attitude, especially considering that poetry by women hardly features in his translation anthologies. Emily Brontë and Sappho are the only two women included in *Come un talismano*; with the exception of Sappho 74Diehl (168bVoigt), his last compendium, *Trafitture di tenerezza* (Wounds of tenderness) (2008), only features poems by men. Contemporary translation anthologies in Italy have a lamentable lack of female representation – the vast majority of *quaderni di traduzioni* include only sporadic texts by women. This is not an exclusively Italian phenomenon: Sappho is the only woman translated in Lowell's *Imitations*.

Ceronetti commented on Sappho's '*charme* unico' (unique charm) (Ceronetti [1969] 1991: 3), expressing, however, reservations about her style, which was perceived as too clear and simple. In the following section I discuss how his reflections on Sappho support a wider discourse on language, translation and the poetic tradition. Ceronetti's Sappho is negotiated through the experience of two of her past translators, Catullus and Leopardi. In particular, Catullus's translation of Sappho in poem 51 stands out as a paradigmatic model of the relationship translator and translated text.

The brightness of Sappho and Catullus

In the 1980 preface to the third edition of *Catullo*, Ceronetti reflects on his experience as a translator and evokes Sappho. Sappho and Catullus are presented as the archetypal poets of love and passion. This would not be a particularly original take, except that, for Ceronetti, their exemplarity does not suffice to grant them the unreserved admiration that usually draws poet-translators to their works. Echoing his 1969 observations, Catullus remains a superficial poet, lacking depth of thought and vision. Sappho does not strike a better chord:

> Molto simile a Catullo, ancora più nuda di pensiero, è Saffo che infatti Catullo sente, traduce, parafrasa benissimo, specchiandosi nella stessa infanzia, che in Saffo però vestiva il mistero sacerdotale. E neppure Saffo è tra i miei poeti, nonostante il suo *charme* unico. Le acque di profondità assenti; nella sua lucentezza c'è tuttavia come il tremolare di un tempio demolito, che nasconde un segreto pietrificato.

> (Sappho is very similar to Catullus, with even more naked thought. Indeed, he feels, translates and paraphrases her very well, looking at himself mirrored in the same childhood, which in Sappho was clothed in sacred mystery. And not even Sappho is among my poets, despite her unique charm. Deep waters are absent; in her radiance there is however something like the trembling of a ruined temple that hides a petrified secret.)

[1969] 1991: 3

Ceronetti refutes the idea of Sappho and Catullus as poetic models due to their apparent lack of depth of metaphysical thought. For the Italian poet, Sappho's charm relies on the sacred relationship she develops with her god, eros, and in the way her fragmentary poetry kindles the imagination. Yet her 'lucentezza', the clear brightness that emanates from the simplicity of her lines, is lost in the present.

Ceronetti's outlook on ancient poetry is informed by his tragic vision of reality, in which modern man has lost any sense of the divine and is subject to a descent to hell.[28] *Classicità*, the classical outlook on life, existed only 'nelle aurore umanistiche e nei crepuscoli cristiani' (in humanistic dawns and Christian twilights) ([1969] 1991: 339–40) – it is not part of modernity, but only a received idea. Sappho's poetry, therefore, hides a secret that can never be uncovered, remaining 'petrified' in time. Interpreting history as a progressive descent into darkness,[29] he traces a linear degeneration from the brightness of Sappho's Greek, already tinged with darker hues in Catullus's Latin, to modern Italian as a crepuscular language ([1969] 1991: 3-4).

Thinking back on his translation of Catullus, he admits to 'aver sovente caricato d'ombre il nitore catulliano' (having often charged the Catullan gleam with shadows) (1969] 1991: 3). Rendering Catullus's neat, bright Latin in the more crepuscular Italian language, Ceronetti's translation adds darker tones to the Latin text: 'serotizzare un autore significa nello stesso tempo demonizzarlo' (adding nightly qualities to an author means at the same time to make it demonic). And he justifies this decision when he states: 'Se c'è molta sera c'è molto italiano, il mio scopo era di spostare Catullo fino alla nostra peculiarità sonora' (If there is a lot of evening there is a lot of Italian, my purpose was to transpose Catullus into our own peculiar sonority) ([1969] 1991: 4). He also draws an analogy between his own chiaroscuro translation and Catullus's version of Sappho 31, arguing that Catullus himself adds dark overtones to Sappho's original, especially in 'gemina teguntur / lumina nocte' (my twin lights are covered by night) (4). In this way he finds a further external justification for his own creative choices – integrating the example of Catullus 51 into his own views on language history, Ceronetti implies that it is inevitable to modernize an ancient text when translating it into a younger language; he explicitly inscribes himself into a tradition based on the Sappho/Catullus pair as an archetype of the relationship between source text and translator.

Tapping into the long tradition of mythologizations of Sappho's life, the image of Sappho as a quasi-divine solar manifestation, as an expression of the dawn of poetry, is presented by Ceronetti in another essay 'Leopardi e il Gallo Cosmico' (Leopardi and the Cosmic Rooster):

> Ma la vera, l'amabile compositrice sacra che ebbe nome Saffo è solare come il gallo cosmico tradizionale, amorosa come il gallo della simbologia erotica (di questo gallo tratta Jung come simbolo della libido).

(But the true, lovely sacred composer called Sappho is solar like the traditional cosmic rooster, amorous like the rooster of erotic symbology (Jung speaks of this rooster as a symbol of libido)).

Ceronetti [1988] 2015

The archetypal sacred value of Sappho and her poetry are made explicit by reference to the image of the cosmic rooster, the representation of an angel and the symbol of light in the esoteric Jewish tradition. At the same time, she symbolizes erotic pleasure.

Sappho and Catullus are expressions of Ceronetti's dualistic conception of reality, springing from a wider interest in Gnosticism. He juxtaposes the classical, associated with attributes of light, divinity, antiquity, raw passion and poetic transparency, with the modern, linked to darkness, secularism, modernity, rationality and obscurity. While this Manichean view also transforms into an opposition between corresponding forms of good and evil,[30] Ceronetti implies that to make poetry in the modern world is to make sense of civilization's tragic descent into hell. Poetry gives the only respite from this tragic view: 'Dove passa la poesia c'è un po' meno dolore, un po' più coraggio a morire' (Where poetry treads there is a bit less grief, a little more courage to die) (1996: 7).

The same opposition between light and darkness characterizes *Come un talismano*, the 1986 anthology gathering poems translated during the previous twenty years, which he describes as a '[m]anual[e] di difesa mentale dall'invasione e dalla guerra incessante delle Tenebre' (A manual for mental defence against the invasion and the incessant war with Darkness) ('Poesia e solitudine', Ceronetti [1986] 2015). Sappho is represented in the collection with frr. 94Diehl (168bVoigt) and 50Diehl (47Voigt). By the 1980s, Diehl's source text was quite dated, confirming Ceronetti's relative disinterest in matters of textual criticism. Showing a lonely Sappho at night, fr. 94Diehl (168bVoigt) is one of the most translated fragments. This is Ceronetti's translation:

> O Luna sei già sparita! E voi, le Pleiadi,
> Vi siete fatte smorte.
> Più che mezza la notte è ormai trascorsa,
> Quante ore partite. E io restata
> sola a dormire, a dormire sola

[1986] 2015[31]

Expanding the source text, a stylistic trait of all his translations, Ceronetti emphasizes the loneliness of Sappho in the chiastic structure of the last line, with 'restata / sola' (left alone) adding a sense of abandonment. In line 2 he uses the adjective 'smorte', another supplement, to describe the Pleiades, a compound of the Italian noun 'morte' (death), meaning 'pale as death'. The personification overlays the nocturne with deathly omens. Ceronetti described his own poetry as a series of fragments.[32] The majority of the other translations in the anthology are also fragments of longer poems selected by Ceronetti for their evocative power: 'è il frammento a fare la compiutezza, a fare nel momento intravedere la totalità del tempo, ad annullarla' (it is the fragment that makes wholeness, reveals the totality of time, and erases it in the momentary) ([1988] 2015). Sappho's poetry is once again – as seen in Pascoli, H.D. and Quasimodo – portrayed as a vehicle to access knowledge, a manifestation of esoteric truth.

Copioli's spiritual eroticism

Rosita Copioli's oeuvre stands out as a lifelong artistic reflection on myth, beauty and eros as expressions of a spiritual, metaphysical dimension. Beauty and the life-giving power of the erotic impulse are construed as the driving force of nature, human life and, ultimately, poetry leading to cosmic contemplation. Positing poetry as an epistemological tool, Copioli's essentialist positions based on a solid faith in the representative power of poetic language are openly set against contemporary postmodern critiques of historical grand narratives, to rediscover a metaphysical, unifying approach to myth and literature rooted in antiquity.

Already in her 1983 essay 'Il flauto magico dei classici' (The classics' magic flute) she associates a disposition toward cosmic meditation with the ancient classics, which became the blueprint for her own work. A syncretic attitude allows this kind of metaphysical knowledge about the world to arise:

> La loro attività sincretica dovette essere di complessa natura, simile proprio al lavoro della traduzione, dato che essi [...] non fecero che cogliere dai loro progenitori o dai popoli che li avevano preceduti sulle terre in cui dimoravano, o dalle genti straniere, un [...] concetto del mondo.

> (The syncretic activity of the ancients must have been complex in nature – indeed, similar to the work of a translator, because they did nothing else than taking from their progenitors, or from the populations that preceded them in the lands where they resided, or from foreign peoples, a [...] concept of the world.)

> Copioli 1983: 184

Copioli's writing engaging with myth strikes one as a search for human archetypes realized in symbols. In her poetic exploration of the aesthetic and mythical aspects of existence, W. B. Yeats is Copioli's beacon. As she revealed to me in our interview in July 2019, the Irish poet's aestheticism and mythical writings were foundational to her outlook on literature:

> Io ho avuto veramente una specie di folgorazione con Yeats. Tu mi hai chiesto dei classici: sentivo che restava sempre fuori una base nostra che non sapevo spiegare: apparteneva alle nostre genti che erano prima dei latini: e quindi, quando ho trovato i suoi saggi critici, mi sono messa a tradurli. È stato nei primi anni 80. Prendo questa antologia appena uscita, in una libreria di Londra. Ecco vi trovo una bellezza di pensiero, una capacità di stare sulle cose della poesia, [...] con una fede di rinnovamento delle genti - che sentivo mi assomigliava nel profondo. [...] Poi, non secondo, veniva tutto il mondo celtico: il *mondo immaginale*, secondo l'espressione coniata da Henry Corbin: questa comunione dei morti e dei vivi, che per noi in Romagna era stata fondamentale. Come in tutte le tradizioni, forse: però è chiaro che qui aveva una sua forma intensificata, alla quale Pascoli aveva dato una voce inconfondibile, unica.

> (With Yeats it was really like being struck by a bolt. You asked me about the classics ... but I felt there was a foundation that was ours that remained always out of the picture, and which I could not explain: it belonged to the people before the Latin: and so, when I found his critical essays, I started translating them. It was in the early '80s. I got this newly published book in a London bookshop. I found a beauty of thought, an ability to reflect on poetic matters, with a faith in the renewal of the peoples, which was profoundly like me. And then came the Celtic world: the *imaginal world*, in Henry Corbin's words: this communion of dead and living that for us in Romagna had been fundamental. As in all traditions, perhaps, but it is clear that here it had its own intensified form, which Pascoli had given a distinctive voice, unique.)

In 1987 she published *Il crepuscolo celtico*, her translation of Yeats' *Celtic Twilight* and in 1988 an edited collection of Yeats' essays entitled *Anima Mundi: Studies on Myth and Literature* in her Italian translation. Sharing with Yeats a faith in 'the renewal of the peoples' and an interest in the symbolic imagination that unites them, Copioli launched her investigation of the origins of literary and cultural archetypes before Graeco-Roman antiquity. Dwelling on Yeats' contemporary musings on the Celtic origins of Ireland, Copioli's interest in primordial matter is indebted, first and foremost, to Pascoli's primitivism based in the folkloric and rural culture of Romagna, their shared birthplace. American literature was never a favourite, although some of the recurring images in her works are similar to those expounded by Anglo-American Modernists. Yeats is probably the main bridge connecting the shared imaginative horizon of Copioli, Pound and H.D.

Her engagement with the Graeco-Roman classics, especially Sappho, Catullus, Virgil and Lucretius, is part of her aesthetic pursuit, which she carried out through a meticulous reclaiming of the western literary tradition. While Sappho is rather prominent in her work, Catullus is a hidden presence. She revealed to me in our interview that Catullus was among her most beloved Roman poets: '[F]are Catullo, essere Catullo non è facile. Anche ai suoi tempi io penso che fosse difficile, perché è unico. [...] C'è una gamma amplissima' (To replicate Catullus, to be Catullus is not easy. Even at his time it must have been difficult, because he is unique. [...] His range is vast). Copioli's poetic appraisal of Catullus in part reflects the twentieth-century critical re-evaluation of the Roman poet as a unique virtuoso, a genius whose poetic and emotional range stood above his contemporaries. A renewed attention to poetic technique and Catullus's re-use of Callimachean models is central to scholarship on the poet even today and so is the attention to Catullus as a great lyricist of personal emotions, an aspect appealing not only to scholarship but also to the wider public, as the innumerable anthologies of Catullus's love poetry published in the last twenty years in Italy show. Copioli's appreciation of Catullus, however, is coloured by a much more ambitious and intellectually refined aestheticism. As emerges in this section, an inquiry into the erotic aspect of life and poetry, whose undifferentiated origins are located in Sappho's phenomenology of eros, drives Copioli's enquiry into the classical tradition and myth.

Just like Sappho before him, for Copioli, Catullus grasped the erotic dimension of existence. For this reason, his poem 51 remains for her the most beautiful translation of Sappho 31 ever written. She explained:

> Credo che una delle cose più riuscite sia la capacità di Catullo di essere erotico. L'eros che lui mantiene. [...] Viene una fascinazione completamente nuova, la sconvolge moltissimo, però l'effetto è di attrazione, d'incanto, di sospensione del momento, che è quell'aspetto di sacro, che lui traduce nel sacro e profano, che va benissimo perché è eros puro lo stesso.

> (I believe that one of the most successful aspects [of the translation] is Catullus's ability to be erotic. He keeps the eros. [...] The result is a completely different appeal. He disrupts her [text] very much, but the effect is one of attraction, enchantment, suspended moment, which is that sacral aspect that he translates mixing sacred and profane [...]. [I]t is still pure eros.)
>
> R. Copioli in conversation with the author, 29 July 2019

Catullus's betrayals of Sappho's text are justified in the name of a shared understanding between source and target text concerning the all-encompassing power of eros. Like many other poets discussed in this book, Copioli sets a practice model which privileges aesthetic equivalence over semantic and formal correspondence. She sees affinities between 'the syncretic activity of the ancients' and the process of translation aiming at the union or reconciliation of the diverse beliefs, practices and interpretative traditions characterizing the source and target cultures.

Copioli considers Novalis's 'mythic model' of translation to be the best and, in one of her essays, she reflects on this quotation: 'Le traduzioni mitiche: "rappresentano il puro, compiuto carattere dell'opera d'arte individuale. Non ci danno l'opera d'arte reale, bensì il suo stesso ideale" (Da Novalis, Frammento 1036)' (Mythic translations: 'represent the individual makeup of a work of art in its pure and complete form. They do not translate the real work of art, but rather give us its ideal.' From Novalis, Fragment 1036) (1983: 184–5). When I asked her to elucidate the meaning of Novalis' 'ideal', she explained it using Catullus:

> Forse con realizzazione mitica intende una interpretazione e rifondazione di pensiero e cultura: una appropriazione e trasfusione. Forse la traduzione di Catullo che rifà un'altra cosa sua può sembrare una forma di traduzione mitica perché ridiventa lui stesso Saffo.
>
> (Maybe with mythic translation he means an interpretation and re-foundation of thought and culture: an appropriation and a transfusion. Perhaps Catullus's translation that recreates something else may seem a form of mythic translation because he himself becomes Sappho.)
> R. Copioli in conversation with the author, 29 July 2019

As a poet-translator, Catullus clearly represents a model for Copioli, partly for his poetic prowess, partly because in his poetry she reads a mythical understanding of life and poetry that is central to her own aesthetic realms. She is not bothered by Catullus's masculinization of Sappho's text, because she finds in the beauty of Catullan eros a true interpretation of Sappho's love:

> 'È lo scrittore vero che da innamorato riesce a dare una bellezza tale a Lesbia, riesce ad essere un interprete vero dell'amata; sta dalla parte di lei, in panni femminei è l'amore che arriva a trapassare i confini, e quindi Catullo è anche femmina.'
>
> (It is the true author who, as a lover, manages to give such an all-encompassing beauty to Lesbia that he succeeds in being the true interpreter of his beloved; he

is on her [Lesbia's] side, in its feminine form love overcomes any boundary, and so Catullus is also female.)

R. Copioli in conversation with the author, 29 July 2019

This universalizing view rests on the assumption that the eroticism of both Catullus and Sappho emerged from a shared human nature. This fails to acknowledge Catullus's problematic appropriation of Sappho's subjectivity into an undifferentiated universal male subject. Charles Martindale has already spotted the problem with these essentialist views in modern scholarship, while recognizing that this approach does have the merit of showing why the poetry of Sappho and Catullus might matter to us (1999: xx–xi). However, in order to grasp the full meaning of Copioli's comment, her judgement must be contextualized within the import of her views on eros and Sappho for her wider oeuvre.

Copioli's syncretic approach to poetry and translation is indeed based on essentialist principles; her work on myth also intersects with contemporary feminist discourses on the necessity of deconstructing the patriarchal structure of myth and philosophy – most notably, in Italy, the work of the Diotima group founded by Adriana Cavarero, a key political philosopher of sexual difference, and the feminist metaphysics of Luisa Muraro, both in close dialogue with Luce Irigaray.[33] Copioli was never actively involved with their work, but she agrees with their outlook, almost naturally absorbed into her view of the world: 'Loro rivendicavano mentre io mettevo l'*essere*' (They vindicated while I added *being*).[34] Her poetry destabilizes patriarchal structures through a form of mythic revisionism based on female figures as alternative ideals of femininity. Such attempts also inform Copioli's reception of Sappho.

In *Saffo. Più oro dell'oro,* an erudite and passionate book, Copioli's translations stand on the cusp of semantic and aesthetic equivalence. On the one hand, she is adamant that she wanted to be accurate: 'Tengo al rispetto dell'originale. Se amo i poeti, non voglio permettermi di fargli del male.' (I care about respecting the original. If I love a poet I do not want to let myself hurt them.) Using the exact opposite metaphor of Ceronetti's 'murder', she invokes a considerate approach to the original, assuming a traditional deferential position. On the other hand, her belief in the inevitability of 'betrayal' ('li tradisco inevitabilmente' (I am bound to betray them), appears to give her the freedom to experiment with formal and aesthetic equivalence:

> Quello che avevo cercato di fare, era di imitare con le mie traduzioni il suono, la forza, e possibilmente il tono e il ritmo - non dico la metrica perché noi non la possiamo più fare in italiano.

(What I tried to do [...] with my translations of Sappho was to imitate the sound, the power and, possibly, the tone and rhythm – I am not talking about metrics, because we cannot reproduce it in Italian.)

R. Copioli in conversation with the author, 29 July 2019

In order to reproduce the 'power' of Sappho's works Copioli allows herself some licence. A closer analysis of linguistic choices reveals subtle deviations that convey the 'mythic ideal' of Sappho's poetry, or its 'erotic essence'. In her detailed commentary accompanying the translations, she carries out a mythical appreciation of Sappho and her poetry, ultimately portrayed as the archaic prefiguration of a platonic form of eros.

The title of *Saffo. Più oro dell'oro*, a translation from Sappho 156 ('χρύσω χρυσοτέρα', l. 2), hints at the brilliance of Sappho and her songs and lures the reader into her world. The book comprises translations of all Sappho's fragments included in Voigt 1971 plus the 'New Sappho' of 2004 (in Di Benedetto's 2005 edition) with the facing Greek text, a preface by the poet Giuseppe Conte, extensive commentary notes on both Sappho's texts and Copioli's translations, and a final essay on Sappho entitled 'Le acque gelide della Memoria' (The icy waters of Memory) by Copioli. The book overall offers an original exploration of the mythical aspects of Sappho's poetry and its eroticism, and was positively received.[35]

Lucia Re (1998) was the first to note that Copioli's work tends toward mythic revisionism, echoing contemporary Italian feminist discourses by re-appropriating female mythical figures, such as the Great Mother, or Mater Matuta and Helen of Troy, in order to trace a new feminine genealogy and a new feminine metaphysics.[36] In Sappho, a woman writing about other women, Copioli locates the most truthful interpretation of the myth of Helen of Troy, the most salient figure of her mythopoeia:[37]

> Intorno a Elena, la bellezza, alla sua prima forma di aurora, come emerge dai miti vedici che vedevo trasparire sull'Adriatico nella figura di Mater Matuta e di Maria stilla maris, che sperimentavo nelle reali immagini femminili anche materne, ho intessuto una trama non conclusa. Per me Elena ha sempre significato, secondo la visione di Saffo, bellezza di rigenerazione ed eros, ma soprattutto androginia, libertà e determinazione di scelta.

> (Around Helen, who is Beauty, around her first auroral form – as emerges in the Vedic myths that I saw shining through the Adriatic Sea in the figure of Mater Matuta and Maria *stilla maris*, that I experienced in real feminine, maternal images – I wove an unfinished plot. Following Sappho's vision, for me Helen has

always signified regenerating beauty and eros, but above all, androgyny, freedom and conscious choice.)

Copioli quoted in Di Palmo 2017

In Copioli's representation, Helen of Troy is a mythic manifestation of the vital power of beauty and eros modelled on Sappho. Fr. 16 is particularly salient because it juxtaposes feminine and masculine world views through the image of Helen. In various mythical accounts since Homer, Helen is often blamed for abandoning her family or shown as reticent to the erotic impulses instilled in her by the goddess Aphrodite, complying with the patriarchal norm. Sappho's fragment, however, as Di Bendetto noted, presents a feminine order in which Helen is not blamed for her actions, but justified by a grander scheme in which love overrules social constructions ([1987] 2007: 70–3). Finding this self-determination and feminine life-giving eros in several other cultures, Copioli develops a new female myth of origins aimed at reconciling various traditions.

The figure of Helen even comes to represent the feminine prefiguration of a Christian type of love:

> La sostanza femminile è consustanziale al creatore, come nello stesso corpo androgino, prima che si parli di Dio maschile e Dio femminile. La Materia [...] Mater è agli inizi, come la Madre e il Padre, Uno. Un punto vergine, né maschio né femmina.

> (Feminine substance is consubstantial with the creator, as if it belonged to the same androgynous body, before one would speak of a male or female God. The begetting Matter is at the beginning, as the Mother and the Father, One. A virgin point, neither male nor female.)

1991: 143

Helen represents a metaphysical maternal point of origin before the patriarchal symbolic order, before the feminine was differentiated from the masculine – in her words, 'the androgynous'. Copioli establishes the divine as unsexed and undifferentiated, in an attempt to represent the world before the shift from mythos to logos. She further explains the concept of the androgynous as 'una mente che non è maschio né femmina. O è tutte e due insieme. [...] [U]n qualcosa che non ha vincoli di posizioni e ruoli sociali. Qualcosa che rappresenta la libertà pura' (a mind that is neither male nor female. Or it is both together. [...] Something that is not bound by social positions and roles. Something that represents pure freedom).[38] Helen of Troy, in all its mythic variants, embodies for Copioli the unbound, life-giving power of eros, in which women are free to act and choose as they please because they have yet to become 'the Other'.

The interest in pre-Hellenic and archaic myth as a vehicle of this discourse is based on a premise analogous to Cavarero's deconstruction of Greek myths, namely that 'the classical moment of antiquity offers us the continuing presence of a transition that carries within it the fresh traces of this shift and the memory of what has been lost to patriarchal domination' (Cavarero 1995: 4–5). Within this perspective, Sappho's Helen and the erotic power expressed through her figure mean 'androgyny, freedom and conscious choice'. However, as Cavarero posits, any re-configuration of myth is born within the symbolic order and cannot ultimately escape it. Copioli's Helen does not elude this contradiction. She encapsulates the two-fold nature of eros: the feminine and life-giving power and the masculine, destructive one. In her self-determination she brings about war and death; Copioli also represents her as an insecure figure, seen rather than seeing, judged for her choice to leave her husband and family behind.

Having traced Copioli's approach to mythical revisionism, let us consider her translation of Sappho 16, where Sappho tells her version of Helen's departure from Sparta to find Paris in Troy:

> Dicono alcuni che sulla terra nera sia la cosa
> più bella un esercito di cavalieri,
> altri di fanti, altri di navi, io invece
> quel che uno ama.
>
> È così facile farlo capire
> a chiunque: perché colei che superò
> ogni umana bellezza, Elena, lasciò lo sposo
> che era valente,
>
> andò per mare a Troia;
> e non si ricordò della figlia, né dei genitori
> cari, ma Cipride la trascinò
> presa da amore.
>
> . . . .
> . . . .facilmente. . .e lei
> a me ora fa ricordare Anattoria
> che non è qui; [. . .]

Commenting on the originality of Sappho's representation of Helen's flight, in her notes to the text, Copioli states: 'L'Elena di Saffo rivela [...] una possessione dove è compresente una scelta lucida, un'adesione non ambigua né conflittuale con la sua dea' (Sappho's Helen has consciously chosen to be possessed, unambiguously and peacefully accepting the union with her goddess) (2006: 99). According to Copioli, Sappho's Helen is not only blameless because she was spurred by Aphrodite's will, but she is also consciously and readily possessed by the goddess. Helen's figure thus symbolizes the erotic union with the divine, ultimately becoming one with Aphrodite.

Aphrodite is, of course, central to Sappho's representations of eros. Yet the surviving text of fr. 16 does not explicitly mention the goddess. Copioli inserts the goddess in the lines 'ma Cipride la trascinò, / presa da amore' (but the Cyprid dragged her / who was taken by love), emphasizing Aphrodite's influence on Helen and the divine quality of her love. The line is added by Copioli on the basis of a conjecture on the lacunose Greek text, from which several words are missing. Where Voigt's text shows a lacuna, Copioli digs into the critical apparatus of Voigt's edition and reconstructs the line adopting A.S. Hunt's conjecture: 'Κύπρις ἔραι]σαν' signalled in italics within the facing Greek text of her volume. Because of her union with Aphrodite, Helen broke the patriarchal social norm, leaving her husband and her family to follow her desire. The goddess enables Helen's erotic nature, allowing beauty to arise and granting her power of self-determination.[39]

In Copioli's essay 'Il fuoco dell'Eden' (The fire of Eden) erotic desire is further posited as a necessary experience to access the divine:

> In Grecia, l'amore che avvicina uomini e dèi è Eros: [...] è l'impulso di coesione che percorre ogni essere generando la voluttà di Afrodite; e tuttavia, nel trasporto più alto, guida all'ardore della contemplazione filosofica e all'estasi della bellezza celeste. Con un brivido, Eros unisce il divino e l'umano, e solo attraverso di lui l'uomo può, per un istante, attingere al divino.
>
> (In Greece, the love that brings men and gods closer is Eros: [...] it is the cohesion instinct that is in every being, producing Aphrodite's desire; and yet, in the highest moment of rapture, it leads toward passionate philosophical contemplation and the ecstasy of heavenly beauty. With a thrill, Eros unites the divine and the human, and only through him, can man for a moment access the divine.)
>
> 2013: 10–11

This encompassing and mystical view of erotic power affects Copioli's reception of Sappho beyond fragment 16. She suggests that the eroticism of Sappho's lyrics should be considered in light of the Platonic philosophy of eros, which she regards as a form of mystic thought similar to the Christian faith in God's love:[40]

> Platone non lascia nessun cenno al caso. Alludendo a Saffo nel luogo più elevato della sua teoria dell'Eros, la via mistica più alta che i Greci hanno conosciuto nel cercare e nel toccare Dio, Platone ci suggerisce il giusto modo di leggere quella lirica che ci pare così 'soggettiva'.
>
> (In Plato no reference is made by chance. Alluding to Sappho in the most pivotal moment of his theory of Eros, the highest form of mysticism the Greeks ever reached in their search for God, Plato tells us the right way of reading her lyric poetry, which, at first, seems to be so 'subjective'.)
>
> 2006: 132

These ideas underpin her translations of Saffo, as her version fr. 31 reveals:

> Proprio sorte pari agli dèi ha per me
> quell'uomo, che ti specchia rapito,
> vicino, e la voce soave
> ti assorbe
>
> e il riso amoroso: e questo
> mi atterrisce dentro il petto il cuore.
> Oh, mi basta vederti, e di colpo di voce
> non mi resta più nulla,
>
> anzi a me la lingua s'è franta, rapido
> un fuoco sottile corre dentro la carne,
> e con gli occhi non vedo più, e le orecchie
> rombano,
>
> e il sudore m'inonda, e mi cattura
> tutta il tremore, e sono più verde
> dell'erba, e mi sento di poco lontana
> proprio dal morire.
>
> Ma tutto si può sopportare, giacché ...
> Anche un poveruomo ...

In her notes to the text, Copioli explains her translation of the first stanza. She lingers on the opening word of the poem, the verb 'Φαίνεταί', which 'in Saffo riproduce la 'manifestazione' del dio, di Eros che compare attraverso l'uomo che siede di fronte alla ragazza. E che il verbo φαίνεταί soprattutto rivela' (in Sappho's poem represents the manifestation of the god Eros, who appears through the man sitting opposite the girl) (2006: 104). She interprets the rapture of desire described by Sappho in fr. 31 as a metaphysical manifestation of love. She continues 'Saffo dice [...] che la potenza di eros, scesa in mezzo ai due, li ha trasfigurati, e che siamo dentro il divino' (Sappho says [...] that the power of eros descended has transfigured them and that we are within the divine) (104). The manifestation of erotic desire is seen as the incarnation of divine love into bodily form: eros is a religious experience.

This metaphysical conception of eros informs her translations of the vast majority of other occurrences of eros in Sappho's fragments. She translates almost every word related to love or desire with the noun 'amore' or the verb 'amare' (in English 'love' and 'to love'). Using *amare*, which in Italian mainly refers to the emotion of love, Copioli's translations do not render the sexual connotations of many words employed commonly by Sappho in her lyrics, such as the verb ἔραμαι (LSJ: to love or desire with erotic passion) and the nouns ἵμερος (LSJ: desire after something present) and πόθος (LSJ: longing, yearning for something absent or lost). By incorporating these words for desire into the undifferentiated and universal category of 'amare / amore', Copioli's translations, to an extent, intellectualize Sappho's eros as a form of divine love incarnated.

At the same time, while the Sapphic language of eros is shifted to the higher sphere of divine love, Copioli is very accurate in her rendition of the physical effects of desire on the body. Her translations cherish the physiology of eros typical of Sappho's fragments. In her version of fr. 31, the symptoms of desire in the body are described using a powerful sensual language: il sudore 'inonda' (floods), she is 'catturata dal tremore' (seized with tremor), and the flame of desire runs in her flesh, 'dentro la carne' (inside the flesh). This last occurrence gives us another insight into Copioli's syncretic method. The Greek literally reads 'under the skin', but Copioli translates 'inside the flesh' with overtones of divine incarnation. The translation thus connotes a sort of neo-Platonic separation between intellectual love and bodily desire, as Copioli establishes a continuity of symbols between the mythical figure of Eros emerging from Sappho's texts, Plato's philosophy of Eros and Christian conceptions of divine love.

So, while she rewrites myth and strives to link the mythical content of Sappho's texts to this revised tradition, Copioli's Sappho still encompasses some of the heteronormative and patriarchal ideas that inflected her reception. Superimposing platonic and Christian views of eros onto Sappho's text attenuates the homoerotic aspect of Sappho's lyrics. The first neo-platonic accounts of Sappho emerged in the Renaissance and, similarly to Copioli's translations, they strove to tone down the erotic power of Sappho's poems. As Reeser (2015: 276) points out, the suppression of the carnality of female-to-female love raises some of the issues related to representing lesbianism that have been discussed in queer studies. Copioli told me this was not deliberate, yet her translations involuntarily reproduce a general tendency in western culture to make the lesbian into a phantom, the victim of what Terry Castle calls 'a ghost effect' (Reeser 2015: 276). Her rewriting enacts the tension between classical and Catholic organizations of human sexual activity, which Cestaro outlines as inherent to the attitude of Italian culture toward homosexuality in the early 2000s (2004: 1–2).

To counterbalance the somewhat subdued homoeroticism of her translations, Sappho's love for women is given a strong voice in a poem of her last collection, *Le acque della mente* (2016). The poem, entitled 'Saffo' (Sappho) is built around Sappho 2 and 81. The former describes an epiphany of Aphrodite in her sacred apple grove, while the latter speaks of Dika, a girl whom the speaking voice encourages to wear a crown woven with dill stalks to please the Graces. The ghost of Sappho is the lyric persona of Copioli's poem, who addresses her beloved girl Dika from the underworld:

'Saffo'

Dika, da questa terra fiorita di loto,
vedo ancora i miei viaggi sulle navi assolate,
le fonti fresche con gli altari
dove Afrodite scendeva
e penso solo a te come perfetta.
Eros tra i morti non è meno blando.
Non vi manca il riso, che credevo
di Afrodite, e la luce rosa
che è dei morti
sta bene anche alla tua corona,
come a me. È una luce
bagnata di rugiada;
la madre, la Memoria
ci irrora di canti
al di là del tempo
che Oceano alimenta
senza passare dalla Terra.
Ancora, ancora, Dika,
ciò che è stato è.
I flussi di Oceano bagnano la madre,
io vivo, e tu vivi,
bagnate di eros

vinciamo il tempo.
Ora e sempre
è Mnemosine, Saffo, e Dika.

(Dika, from this land bloomed with lotus, / I still see my journeys on sunlit ships / the fresh springs with the altars / where Aphrodite descended / and I think only of you as perfect. / Eros among the dead is not less mild. / Laughter, which I thought was Aphrodite's, / is not absent, and the pink light / which is of the dead / suits your crown, too, / like me. It is a light wet with dew; / the mother, Memory, infuses us with songs / beyond time / which Oceanos feeds / without passing through Earth. / Again, again, Dika, what has been, now is. / The fluxes of Oceanos wet the mother, / I live, and you live, / wet with eros / we win over time. / Now and always / it is Mnemosyne, Sappho and Dika.)

Copioli 2016

Sappho's rapture is powerfully conveyed through the lyric persona's reminiscing of the past spent with her beloved. The world painted by the Sapphic persona is once again feminine, with mother-Mnemosyne, herself and the object of her love, Dika, living beyond time. Thanks to the divine power of eros, which completely pervades them ('wet with eros'), Sappho and Dika can be united even in death. Memory, as the mother of the Muses, allows poetry to arise and what has been in the past is carried over: 'Vinciamo il tempo' (We win over time).

This poem stands out as the symbolic representation of Copioli's views on the vital power of eros and the consoling power of memory, enabling a relationship between the living and the dead. In her commentary to fr. 2 in *Saffo. Più oro dell'oro*, Copioli links the water flowing in Aphrodite's grove to the soothing power of the water of the Lake of Memory described in orphic texts and drunk by Dionysos' initiates (2006: 90). Rewriting Sappho's own texts and invoking the power of literary memory, Copioli makes her Sapphic persona address Mnemosyne as her mother, the enabler of her poetry. Following a long tradition of modern poets making memory the primary vehicle of the literary imagination, starting with Petrarch, continuing with Leopardi, Quasimodo and the sense of cultural memory found in Pascoli and Yeats, in Copioli's poem the mystic power of eros enables the memory of one's life, one's god and one's community, lifting Sappho beyond death and toward immortality.

Sappho is thus turned into a mythical figure, a symbolic representation of primordial feminine archetypes belonging to a lost world. She becomes a figuration of the power of eros to transcend death and an embodiment of literature as the expression of an erotic power that retains the memory of the species.

6

Postmodern Sappho and Catullus

'[G]enre confuses me', Anne Carson (1950–) told me in our email interview in January 2011. Giving straight answers is not Carson's style; she is notorious for her reticence. Defined by Wilkinson a form of 'cross-genre pollinating' (2015: 2), her work manipulates genres and forms, mixing lyric fragments, essays, prose poetry, opera librettos and dramatic scripts, to striking effect. In her introduction to *Autobiography of Red* (1998) – a 'novel in verse' inspired by the *Geryoneis* of Stesichoros – she describes the fragments of the seventh-century BC poem 'as if Stesichoros had composed a substantial narrative poem then ripped it to pieces and buried the pieces in a box with some song lyrics and lecture notes and scraps of meat' ([1998] 1999: 6–7). The same definition could be easily applied to Carson's oeuvre. With a postmodern flavour, her work is realized through a continuous self-conscious rewriting of the classics, from which she extracts a complex poetics of fragmentation and multiplicity.

Living between Canada and the United States, she taught classics in various universities, until she decided to dedicate herself only to creative work;[1] today she is artist-in-residence at NYU.[2] Her reception of Sappho and Catullus reflects her scholarly background. The majority of her work engaging with the two ancient poets was published between 1986 and 2010; during this time, feminist, gender and poststructuralist approaches to Sappho and Catullus were taking centre stage in Anglo-American classical studies, while the field of classical reception was growing. At times her highly allusive work may seem to be written for academics, but she has a wide audience and she is extremely popular with the literary establishment: among her awards are a Guggenheim Fellowship in 1998, a MacArthur Fellowship in 2000 and the 2001 T. S. Eliot prize for *The Beauty of the Husband* (2001).

The works and lives of Sappho and Catullus have been central to Carson's discourse on poetry and language since the very beginning of her career. Sappho, in particular, is a fundamental prism through which Carson has developed her poetics of desire. With a mix of aesthetic and academic writing, *Eros the Bittersweet* (1986) uses Sappho's poetry to develop a book-length reflection on eros as the defining principle of ancient poetry and philosophy. Concerned with matters of desire, death and gender, the collection of miscellaneous writings *Men in the Off Hours* (2000) includes two essays dealing with Sappho, fifteen translations of Catullus's *carmina*, and a series of poems entitled 'TV Men' featuring Sappho as a character. *The Beauty of the Husband: A Fictional Essay in 29 Tangos* (2001) is a book-length poem divided into twenty-nine chapters, or 'Tangos', arranged in a narrative sequence about marriage and betrayal. Inter-textual references to Sappho are scattered throughout the book. In the 2006 collection *Decreation* she included the essay 'How Women like Sappho, Marguerite Porete and Simone Weil Tell God' (155–84). Carson also translated the entire extant Sapphic corpus in 2002 in *If Not, Winter: Fragments of Sappho*. Excerpts from this text were used as the script for her multimedia performance work 'Bracko' (2007). When the 'New' and the 'Newest Sappho' were published, she was invited to translate the new fragments.[3] She also devoted an entire book to Catullus. In 2010 she published *Nox*, an elegy for her brother inspired by Catullus 101. *Nox* is the facsimile of Carson's handmade notebook, including scraps of paper, photographs, lyrics and drawings all tied together and presented in a cardboard box.

Several of Carson's latest books strike one as artefacts of the kind produced in collaborations between artists and writers such as Burri and Villa and Baj and Merini.[4] As well as *Nox*, Carson's translation of Sophocles' *Antigone*, issued in 2012 under the comic strip title *Antigonick*, dialogues closely with the accompanying illustrations by Bianca Stone and graphic design by Robert Currie (who also contributed to the graphic and material realization of *Nox*). The blurb of her latest output, *Float* (2016), reads: 'A collection of twenty-two chapbooks whose order is unfixed and whose topics are various. Reading can be freefall.' Aiming to create book-objects 'to look at or experience as well as read' (Aitken 2004), she follows in the footsteps of Natalia Goncharova and Mikhail Larionov's expressionist experiments with text and design, modernist aesthetics at large and the comic book tradition.[5]

Also informing her reception of Sappho and Catullus, her engagement with the materiality of texts reflects her multi-media interests as well as a scholarly awareness of the troubled textual transmission of classical literature. In the hardcover edition of *If Not, Winter*, the Greek text is printed in red, enhancing its visual effect. In the introduction, Carson focuses on the fragmentariness of Sappho's work at the textual and visual levels, emphasizing how the lacunose text may affect the reading experience (xi). She ponders the fragment in its material and linguistic form: as material debris, a poem, or a linguistic manifestation. Similarly, the accordion-like shape of *Nox* makes the book as difficult to navigate as a scroll: it does not have page numbers and ultimately looks like an ancient papyrus roll in a box, hinting at the original form of Catullus's *liber*.[6] In *Antigonick*, too, page numbers are not marked, there is no punctuation throughout the book and the text is laid out in columns, like in archaic manuscripts.

By forcing the reader to become aware of the materiality of the texts, she also raises the question of who or what the names 'Sappho' and 'Catullus' signify. Highlighting the faults of transmission and of communicability, Carson invites the reader to reflect on the role of their subjective responses in defining the ancient texts' receptions. Bill Brown (2001) remarked that a malfunctioning object sheds its socially encoded value and becomes present to us in new ways through the suspension of habit. In the same way, Carson's foregrounding of the inevitably broken communicative function of the ancient fragments defamiliarizes the texts. In so doing, she also points at the multiple interpretative possibilities allowed by their fragmentariness and the partial understanding allowed by subjective interactions. Brown notes: 'As they circulate through our lives, we look through objects (to see what they disclose about history, society, nature, or culture – above all, what they disclose about us), but we only catch a glimpse of things' (2001: 4). Similarly, Carson's work is acutely aware of the partiality of a reader's gaze on the poetry of Sappho and Catullus.[7]

In our interview, she revealed that a kind of Keatsian fascination with 'negative capability' informs the aesthetics of the fragment (Keats is also the primary inter-textual presence in her book-length poem *The Beauty of the Husband*):[8]

> I love Greek and Latin and happen to know how to read them so I guess that means I am part of their legacy. the fact that the Greek and Latin poets come down to us as fragmentary traditions has perhaps influenced what you call my "aesthetic", or even justified it, but most poets find a way to justify their desire to create fragments don't they. all poems are fragments. That's why they're interesting. negative capability etc. [Carson's punctuation and capitalization]
>
> A. Carson in conversation with the author, 27 January 2011

Advocating negative capability, Carson's work exploits textual gaps and silences. The fragmentary condition of Sappho's and Catullus's verse defines the imaginative capability of their lyrics, spurring a desire to fill the gaps in the wounded text, as well as the temporal gap separating Carson from the ancient poets.

Translation, as a generative practice that bridges the temporal gap between ancients and moderns, is one of the main vehicles through which she establishes a relationship with Greek and Latin literatures. Translation and poetic faculty are articulated as equally spontaneous subjective responses to a particular feeling or 'moment in time': 'all translations are provisional (or, Homer would say, ephemeral: balanced on the day) I guess in that sense they are all "lyric" – arising out of a certain moment in time' (A. Carson in conversation with the author, 27 January 2011). Wordsworth's 'spontaneous overflow of powerful feelings' ([1802] 1963: 260) strikes one as the Romantic formulation of a similar poetics. This seemingly post-Romantic outlook is accompanied by a relentless politics of quotation. As a form of postmodern pastiche, juxtaposition is a signature trait of her work, placing ancient and modern, visual and verbal, or scholarly and poetic side by side. With an attitude to tradition and history analogous to Pound's and H.D.'s, Carson revels in the most daring associations, especially of poets, writers and thinkers who lived in very distant times. Her recreations of Sappho and Catullus chime with the work of the other writers analysed in this book, intersecting previous conceptualizations of tradition, ideas on eroticism, the relationship of lyric and ritual, and the use of Sappho and Catullus as sites of negotiation for sexual and gender identities.

For space limitations, it will not be possible to consider all occurrences of Sappho and Catullus in Carson's oeuvre in this chapter; I focus on examples that most clearly reveal the multifarious ways in which the two ancient authors inform her work and overall poetics. In the analysis, it emerges that Carson's reflection on Sappho and Catullus underpins much of her postmodern poetics and her ironic approach to the multiplicity of language. Sappho's lyrics are taken as the original expressions of creativity as an erotic desire for understanding. Yet Sappho's vexed textual tradition and biography also become paradigms of the impossibility of reaching any definitive knowledge and exemplify the idea of 'unknowing'. Catullus's poems, despite being less frequently evoked, have a structuring function analogous to Sappho's fragments; in fact, the Catullan recreations are counterparts to her considerations on Sappho. Carson's translations and rewritings of Catullus continue her exploration of the multiplicity of language by putting the idea of unknowability in relation to death. As for Pascoli, Pound, H.D., and Quasimodo, Sappho's eroticism and the Catullan contemplation of death are central interdependent themes of her work, replicating the ancient pattern of eros and thanatos.

Triangulating eros

In *Eros the Bittersweet*, Carson develops a phenomenology of desire based on Sappho's lyrics. Sapphic eros emerges as the propeller of life, art and the pursuit of understanding – always sought after, but never attained. The interplay of eros, writing and the individual imagination is explained by Carson through the figure of 'triangulation'. She traces the origin of this poetic configuration back to Sappho, who is pinpointed as the first to devise a tripartite 'stereoscopic' structure of eros in fr. 31:[9]

> We see clearly what shape desire has there: a three-point circuit is visible within Sappho's mind. The man who listens closely is no sentimental cliché or rhetorical device. He is a cognitive and intentional necessity. Sappho perceives desire by identifying it *as* a three-part structure. [...] [W]here eros is lack, its activation calls for three structural components – lover, beloved and that which comes between them. [...] The third component plays a paradoxical role for it both connects and separates, marking that two are not one, irradiating the absence whose presence is demanded by eros. When the circuit-points connect, perception leaps. [...] The difference between what is and what could be is visible. The ideal is projected on a screen of the actual, in a kind of stereoscopy.
>
> 1986: 16–17

As a defining structure of the desiring mind, triangulation implies that between lover and beloved incurs a third element, which makes the mind aware of the absence of the beloved and ignites the fiction through which the lover imagines themselves united with them. This, Carson theorizes, creates a stereoscopic view of reality, in which real and ideal coexist. Carson identifies the man in fr. 31 as the third element coming between the lyric persona and the object of her love, the girl, who is thus made more distant, fuelling her longing.

This interpretation of Sapphic desire as a form of triangulation is similar to Rene Girard's theory of 'triangular desire', or 'mimetic desire', according to which we desire an object because it is desired by the Other.[10] Carson elaborates on this structure using the model found in Sappho's poem and making the mediator of desire responsible for the 'leap in perception' that arouses the fiction of eros. Making awareness of absence, or lack, the animating, fundamental constituent of triangulation as the structure of eros,[11] Carson's view of desire is also Lacanian (Fisher 2015: 11).

The link between Eros and creative writing is made explicit in the last chapter of *Eros the Bittersweet*, entitled 'Mythoplokos'. Imaginative writing, the creation of metaphors and symbols is also spurred by desire: 'For Sappho, the desirability of desire seems to be bound up with the fictional process that she calls the "weaving of myth"' (1986: 170). The erotic drive of Sappho's lyrics represents the common ground between the spheres of loving and writing. The unfillable lack inherent in desire creates a paradox, defined for the first time by Sappho as 'γλυκύπικρον' (sweet-bitter) in fr. 130 (l. 2), provided the title for Carson's volume. Raised to an existential stance, this same paradoxical structure is essential to Carson's writing, which revels in ambiguity and defies traditional binaries by deconstructing them: light / shadow, truth / error, man / woman, inside / outside.[12] Triangulating oxymoronic eros creates a three-dimensional stereoscopic view of the text and the reality it portrays. Resisting interpretation, Sappho takes on her exemplary role once again, as a poetic archetype and an archetype of knowledge. The ancient poet is both a model for Carson's poetics and, together with Catullus, the object of her poetry. In the following section I discuss how Carson's phenomenology of eros informs her rewritings of Sappho and Catullus.

(Un)Knowing Sappho and Catullus: *Men in the Off Hours* (2000)

Sappho disappears

In *Men in the Off Hours*, Carson engages with both Sappho and Catullus; gender is a primary concern of the 2000 collection, with the subject intersecting various other themes, especially time, death and desire. Through her stereoscopic view, the works and lives of the two ancient poets are rewritten to underscore the dualism of patriarchal constructs of gender, identified, on the one hand, as fluid, polluting, internal, emotional and boundary-shattering femininity, while on the other, as arid, sanitized, external, rational and contained masculinity – a dualism that Carson strives to undermine.[13]

In the essay 'Dirt and Desire: Essay on the Phenomenology of Female Pollution in Antiquity', Carson considers women's condition within the patriarchal order as polluting others, who aroused men's fears of boundlessness. Assuming a similar position to H.D.'s in the 1930s and Copioli's in early twenty-first-century Italy, Carson launches into an anthropological exploration of femininity and sexuality by focusing on ancient ritual patterns. Sappho's poetry is an occasion to ponder the role of rituals such as marriage as a means to contain femininity within a patriarchal order. Carson 'entertain[s] the hypothesis' (2000: 151) that Sappho 31 is a literary enactment of the ancient wedding ritual of the *anakalypteria*, the unveiling of the bride, considered the 'decisive sacral action of the wedding' (149) and that, in the poem, 'Sappho has projected herself into the role of the *nympheutria* [...] [a female attendant] who stands behind the bride and helps her' (151). In the absence of any definitive knowledge on Sappho's life and on the social function of her poetry, over the years scholarship has reconstructed innumerable contexts for fr. 31, attempting to provide a coherent narrative or a plausible interpretation for the poem.[14] Carson rejects the theory, first put forward by Wilamowitz ([1896] 1913), that fr. 31 was a sort of epithalamium performed *at* a wedding, on the grounds that 'this poem does not participate in the meaning toward which it points, as ritual language must, but tropologizes it' (157). She instead argues that fr. 31 is *about* a wedding, and that the public context of the ritual is used by Sappho to express her own emotions and 'bend its ritual meaning onto herself with an irony of reference as sharp as a ray of light' (152).

Whether or not one agrees with Carson, her translation of the last two stanzas of fr. 31, included in 'Dirt and Desire' and later in *If Not, Winter*, reflects her interpretation. Prins remarked that in Sappho 31 the lyric subject is made the object of the poem itself, which is underlined in the final lines, where 'the grammatical split between subject and object persists in *phanom'em'autai*, doubling self-reflexively back on itself' (31). Carson's translation underlines precisely this aspect, 'I am and dead – or almost / I seem to me ...' (2000: 150), emphasizing through the use of pronouns the self-reflexive character of Sappho's lyric voice. As a coda to her translation, Carson further comments:

> Sappho's poem confirms everything we have been listening to the Greeks say about the female, namely that she plays havoc with boundaries and defies the rule that keep matter in its place. I suppose this is deliberate. Sappho has chosen the most solemn and authoritative of the rituals that sacralize female boundaries and used it to explode the distinction between the outside and the inside of herself.
>
> 2000: 152

Sappho's poetry is recast as the poetic enactment of the feminine self's struggle for independence from the patriarchal context of ritual, by reclaiming the private realm of eros for herself and blurring the boundaries between her interior and exterior worlds. As she 'pollutes' the ritual with her own emotions, the Sapphic poetic persona situates herself in the gap between public and private, symbolic and actual.[15] Sappho ultimately appears so impossibly irresistible to Carson because she defies interpretation as a figure of unknowing: 'Sappho is one of those people of whom the more you see the less you know' (2000: 152).

In *Men in the Off Hours*, the interplay between the private and the public spheres of desire and identity is staged in two poems, both entitled 'TV Men:

Sappho' (2000: 62–63; 118), where Sappho features as a character – an actor of a television series. In the first poem, Sappho is the speaking voice who gives her impressions of a TV-set in Place de la Concorde, as she reflects on the nature of desire. The poem's epigraph '*Avec ma main brûlée, j'écris sur la nature du feu*' (With my burnt hand, I write on the nature of fire) is taken from Ingeborg Bachmann's novel *Malina*, another story of desire and unrequited love, while the image of burning eros evokes Sappho 38: 'you burn me'. In the first part of the poem, Sappho's internal monologue is centred on law and lawfulness:

> No one knows what the laws are. That there are laws
> we know, by the daily burnings if nothing else
>
> 2000: 62

Carson first presented the idea that eros follows a divine law in an academic essay, 'The Justice of Aphrodite in Sappho I' (1996), where she argued that fr. 1 offers a non-ironic display of the dynamics underpinning the ancient Greek conception of 'erotic justice' (231) as an 'eternal principle' (232). But while in fr. 1 Sappho is favoured by Aphrodite's law, in Carson's poem, she becomes a victim of her own desire. In the second section, Sappho is tied to a rope, one end is attached to her, the other to Death:

> overlit on all fours I shall
>
> circle Him
> at a consistent focal length.
> Not too close not too far –
>
> 2000: 63

Picturing an erotic game with Death, the poem replicates the mythical pattern of eros and thanatos, in the most extreme interpretation of the bittersweet nature of desire.

In the second 'TV Men: Sappho', an unidentified third-person narrator observes Sappho getting ready to appear on set. We see Sappho 'smearing on her makeup at 5 a.m. in the woods by the hotel' and 'resembling a Beijing concubine'; on set, 'men are setting up huge white paper moons here and there' (118). As she makes Sappho play herself while wearing a mask of smeared makeup, Carson foregrounds the constructed nature of the Lesbian poet's authorial identity, ironically drawing attention to some of the most clichéd tropes associated with the name 'Sappho', such as promiscuity and moonlight. The real Sappho stands ever more distant, underscoring that 'the more you see [of her] the less you know' (Carson 2000: 152).

The rest of the poem pushes this concept even further. Every second line is composed of an unpunctuated sequence of words from Sappho 31. I quote the relevant Greek words next to Carson's lines:

> He She Me You Thou disappears
> [...]
> Laugh Breathe Look Speak Is disappears [γελαίσας, ἴδω, φώνη-ς', ἔμμεν']
> [...]
> Tongue Flesh Fire Eyes Sound disappears [γλῶσσα, χρῶι, πῦρ, ὀππάτεσσι]
> [...]
> Cold Shaking Green Little Death disappears [ἴδρως, τρόμος, χλωροτέρα, ὀλίγω, τεθνάκην]
> [...]
> Nearness When Down In I disappears [πλάσιον, ὥς, ἐν]
> [...]
> But All And Must To disappears [ἀλλὰ πᾶν, καὶ, τόλματον]
>
> 2000: 118

Turning the verbs of fr. 31 into corresponding English nouns, she disseminates them into the first six stanzas of her poem. It is as if Sappho's body and emotions have been dissected, disintegrating into fragments, like her extant work. The verb 'disappears' at the end of the lines enhances the breaking down of the lyric self, while suggesting the lacunose state of Sappho's corpus. The final word, 'Cut', abruptly interrupting Sappho soon after she has recited the last line of fragment 31, underscores the incomplete transmission of the Sapphic poem. Carson makes Sappho perform the evanescent qualities of her texts, superimposing author, works and their reception. As Sappho's character disappears, she becomes unknowable, a figure of absence as the driving force of erotic desire.

In a 2012 performance Carson explains the concept of disappearing with reference to Emily Dickinson's poem entitled 'To disappear enhances', which ends with the stanza:

> The Fruit perverse to plucking
> But leaning to the Sight
> With the ecstatic limit
> Of unobtained Delight.
>
> Carson 2012, min. 9:02–9:28[16]

The reference to Dickinson connects the ideas of disappearing and absence to the dimension of desire ('unobtained delight'). Dickinson intertextually emerges in another poem of *Men in the Off Hours*, entitled 'Sumptuous Destitution', which is structured on a string of quotations from Dickinson's letters, framed by a critique of male scholarship on female writers: '"Sumptuous destitution" [...]/ is a phrase [...]/ scholars use [...]/ of female [...]/ silence' (2000: 13).[17] This offers an interpretative key to Sappho's disappearance into silence in 'TV Men'. Sappho's destitute persona carries the weight of her male-dominated reception, as her tarnished mask of makeup suggests – a sign of her silencing and smearing through centuries of translations and rewritings within the patriarchal order. This is epitomized in the final two lines of the poem, in which Sappho, as a woman, actually disappears: 'Sappho stares into the camera and begins,'*Since I am a poor man*–' (118). The only line Sappho's character recites – a modified version of the final half-line of fr. 31 ('even a poor man') – is in the voice of a man. In one move, Sappho's femininity and sexuality are obliterated.

'TV Men – Sappho' thus dramatizes the various ways in which Sappho's male-centred reception has often ventriloquized her poetry and supressed her homoeroticism. It challenges the practise of translating fr. 31 through a male poetic persona, as in Catullus 51, or as if the *persona loquens* was expressing her love for the man of the love triangle, thus gendering Sappho as a female heterosexual subject.[18] Exemplifying the patriarchal order's silencing of women and homoeroticism, Carson's Sappho dialogues with contemporary feminist studies of the ancient poet's reception, such as Joan de Jean's *Fictions of Sappho* (1989), Margaret Williamson's *Sappho's Immortal Daughters* (1998) and Yopie Prins' *Victorian Sappho* (1999). Carson's approach is also in line with other contemporary recreations of Sappho, such as, for instance, Josephine Balmer's feminist translations in *Sappho: Poems and Fragments* (1984; rev. ed. 1992).[19] Finally, this female-centred re-evaluation of Sappho shares many of the premises of Rosita Copioli's reflection on the Lesbian poet. The two poets never engaged with each other's works, but both make Sappho's eroticism a powerful site for reclaiming female subjectivity.

Catullus beyond himself

The same deconstructive approach to subjectivity and gender characterizes Carson's creative translations of Catullus in the section 'Catullus: Carmina' in *Men in the Off Hours* (2000: 38–45). Desire, death and the realm of the mind are the main threads running through the series of fifteen Catullan rewritings. The dimension of longing is explored in all poems and it is often expressed as frustrated sexual desire or as pining for a beloved or a deceased; as in her recreations of Sappho, Carson places longing at the intersection between eros and thanatos.

The Catullan selection comprises ten poems from the Lesbia cycle (*c.* 2, 3, 43, 58, 70, 75, 76, 85, 86, 109), two for Licinius Calvus (*c.* 50 on the friendship between Catullus and Calvus and *c.* 96 for the death of Calvus's wife), two epigrammatic poems (*c.* 46, 97), and the elegiac poem for Catullus's brother (*c.* 101). Carson investigates the erotic theme in Catullus's poetry with an ironic attitude that becomes particularly bold in her rewritings of the Lesbia poems. Irony desists, however, when Carson appropriates Catullus's persona to speak of death and mourning, as in her rewritings of poems 101 and 96.

Carson's poems are only loosely modelled on the originals. In his review of *Men in the Off Hours*, John D'Agata (2000) identified the tension between scholarly approach and creative drive that is Carson's signature:

> The scholar in Carson intends to advance the conversation about translation and appropriation and the contract of artistic license between critic and poet. Carson the artist, on the other hand, is exploring the outer limits of lyric possibility.

The opening poem in the series, a recreation of *Cat.* 2, in which the poetic persona addresses his lover's pet sparrow, showcases this approach:

Passer Deliciae Meae Puellae (My Lady's Pet)

Catullus observes his love and her pet at play

On her lap one of the matted terriers.
She was combing around its genitals.
It grinned I grinned back.
It's the one she calls *Little Bottle* after Deng Xiaoping.

Carson 2000: 38

Condensing the ten Latin lines into a four-line stanza, Carson plays with the symbolic connotations of the sparrow, often understood to refer to Catullus's penis. Scholarship on this aspect is divided – many see the sexual innuendo clearly, others think it is pure fantasy.[20] Nevertheless, since the Renaissance, the erotic interpretation of *c.* 2 has been popular.[21] While in *c.* 2 Catullus's beloved feeds and plays with her pet sparrow, in Carson's rewriting the bird is substituted by a dog and the woman combs the pet around its genitals, hinting at the erotic connotations of the original *passer*. The interaction between the speaking voice and the pet suggests male innuendo, as Catullus's poetic persona gazes sardonically at the scene. The mention of Deng Xiaoping, who was in power between 1978 and 1992 in China, transports the Latin material to a modern setting. Indeed, the whole Catullan section is introduced with an epigraph referencing contemporary North America:

> I LOVE YOU JOHNNY AND I DIDN'T DO ANYTHING
> (big white letters chalked on a rock in the Mojave Desert).

Like all the other appropriations which I have so far discussed in this book, Carson's rewritings coalesce past and present dimensions. With her synchronic approach to time and tradition, in *Men in the Off Hours* Carson goes beyond the reuse of the classics as monuments of the literary tradition. Her postmodern irony and a meta-literary take on Catullus explode all such hierarchies.

Reverberating Walter Benjamin's theories in 'The Task of the Translator' (1923) in her essay 'Cassandra Float Can', first written as a performance piece and then published in *Float* (2016), she presents a view of translation that underlines its role in producing a text's afterlife. Translation becomes a bridging process, through which ancient texts are made to signify within the subjective present of the translator. 'Cassandra', the Homeric prophet whose predictions are never believed despite their being true, is the name Carson gives to the process of translation as an unveiling of meaning, 'a sensation of veils flying up' (2016: Original Cut).[22] Like prophecies, translations are also perpetually accused of being unfaithful, not true to the original; yet, for Carson, they remain revelatory. She compares translation and the arts of prophecy:

> In both cases there is some action of cutting through surfaces to a sight that has no business being underneath. What is the future doing underneath the past? Or Greek metrics inside a Trojan silence? And how does it alter it to see it there floating? And how can it float?
>
> 2016: Original Cut

Finding and revealing an ancient text's future in the present, translation is non-linear and non-narrative. This coexistence of present, past and future in literature, texts and, ultimately, language, underscores the paradoxes of a linear view of history and time. Questioning the friction between subjective and official times, Carson returns to the question of gender.[23] As Greenfield noted, in *Men in the Off Hours*, Carson's view of synchronic, horizontal time as a 'boundary-shattering potency' (2015: 94) is often associated with the feminine and juxtaposed to linear patriarchal time. From this perspective, Cassandra/translation becomes a figure of feminine synchronicity, through which Carson probes Catullan constructions of gender.

Carson's deconstructive irony is employed in her recreation of carmen 76, where she takes a critical stance on Catullus's relationship with Lesbia. In his poem, Catullus prays the gods to alleviate his suffering after Lesbia betrayed his love. In his entreaty, the Catullan speaking voice portrays himself as a virtuous man who cherishes the fundamental Roman moral values – *foedus* (bond), *fides* (faith), *pietas* (piety) and *mens grata* (gratitude)[24] – accusing his beloved of disrespecting them. The poem has been variously interpreted. Being himself adulterous, many have noted the inherent contradiction of Catullus's accusation to Lesbia, although scholars generally agree that Catullus is saying precisely that, however ambiguous the state of his love affair with Lesbia may be, the bond is as strong as a *foedus* (binding legal contract).[25] To some, Catullus's tone feels a deliberate self-aggrandizement, although any formal plea to the gods requires that Catullus depict himself as pious.[26] Others follow Fordyce, who remarked that the internal monologue 'has passed beyond recrimination and is obsessed by his own underserved suffering' (1961: 365). With a biting tone, Carson appears to engage with all these interpretations. She presents a disingenuous Catullus and deliberately takes issues with his moral code and judging eye on Lesbia:

Siqua Recordanti Benefacta Priora Voluptas
                (If for a Man Recalling Prior Benefactions)

Catullus reflects on his own piety.

Before my holy stoning in the wet kisses and the smell of sperm
I drove an ambulance for the Red Cross.
Do you think a man can be naturally pure?
In those days I kept a diary it fell out of my pocket the night
I carried you to the forge in my arms.
You grew freer and brighter with every stroke of the hammer.

Carson makes poem 76 into a lyric reflection on Catullus's own piety addressed to Lesbia. Appropriating Catullus's poetic 'I' with a scathing irony, she deconstructs his poetry and some of the assumptions of his critical reception from within, targeting in particular Catullus's moral order and his construction of Lesbia. The lyric 'I' of the poem speaks through a self-entitled tone presenting himself as pious; the truthfulness of his moral standing, however, is constantly undermined by glimpses into his life, while his narrative emerges as a self-justifying account. It is the narrative of a split subject, putting up a mask of moral standing (driving for the Red Cross), but revealing it as a public façade: 'Do you think a man can be naturally pure?' The impurity and violence of Catullus is revealed most acutely in the last two lines, in which he describes his relationship with Lesbia as a lover and as a writer. The detail on the lost diary obliquely suggests that his biographical reconstructions may be untrustworthy, perhaps also a hint at modern criticism.[27] As he creates his world, Catullus 'forges' Lesbia into his ideal woman; this is not without violence, as the eerie last line suggests. Dyson noted that 'What is peculiar to 76 is that the cries of the betrayed lover ring with all the more urgency because a moral universe is at stake' (1973: 141). Carson appears to attack the violence implicit in this patriarchal order, which enforces the ideal of the woman angel and the value of *foedus*.

The meta-poetic exploration of Catullus's split lyric self is the focus of her rewriting of *Cat.* 46, where her conceptualizations of thinking and writing as an erotic act also surface:

Iam ver egelidos refert tepores,
iam caeli furor aequinoctialis
iucundis Zephyri silescit auris.
Linquantur Phrygii, Catulle, campi
Nicaeaeque ager uber aestuosae:
ad claras Asiae volemus urbes.
Iam mens praetrepidans avet vagari,
iam laeti studio pedes vigescunt.
O dulces comitum valete coetus,
longe quos simul a domo profectos
diversae varie viae reportant.

Catullus 46 = Thomson 1997: 128

Iam Ver Egelidos Refert Tepores   (Now Spring Brings Warmths)

Catullus greets the season.

Now spring unlocks.
Now the equinox stops its blue rages quiet
As pages.
I tell you leave Troy leave the ground burning, they did.
Look we will change everything all the meanings
All the clear cities of Asia you and me.
Now the mind isn't she an avid previous hobo?
Now the feet grow leaves so glad to see whose green baits.
Awaits.
Oh sweet don't go.
Back the same way go a new way.

Carson 2000: 39

Poem 46 depicts the renewal of spring in Catullus's exterior and interior worlds during his stay in Bithynia. The season brings back warmth and calm to the world and, albeit with some melancholy, arouses a personal desire for regeneration in Catullus, who decides to leave his friends behind and return home.[28] Carson maintains these themes, anchoring her rewriting to the source texts' key-words 'ver', 'aequinoctialis', 'Phrygii', 'mens', translated as 'spring', 'equinox', 'Asia', 'mind'. The speaking voice of Carson's poem projects himself onto the external reality, blurring the boundaries between inner and outer worlds: the theme of change meets the dimension of writing as spring unlocks and winter becomes silent as a page ('blue rages quiet / as pages'); change happens beyond the natural world, opening up possibilities for the speaking persona and his own writing ('We will change everything all the meanings'); the body metamorphoses, too, with the feet growing leaves. By rendering 'vigescunt' (literally: 'feel brisk' or 'grow strong') with 'grow leaves', she appears to elaborate on Ellis's comment that 'virescunt (feel a new spring) is a natural conjecture from 'vigescunt' (Hor. *Epod.* XIII, 4)' ([1876] 2010: 131). The external and internal change occurring in Catullus's poem is thus emphasized.

The blurred boundaries between the lyric self and the addressee further heighten the sense of interference between inner and outer worlds.[29] While Catullus's poem is self-addressed, 'Linquantur Phrygii, Catulle, campi' (Catullus, it is time to leave the Phrygian fields), in the second half shifting to an address to his friends, Carson's addressee is never named. It is up to the reader to interpret the poem either as Catullus's internal monologue or as a series of dialogues with various interlocutors. The line 'I tell you leave Troy leave the ground burning, they did' may well be uttered by Catullus speaking to himself, mirroring the Latin. But Carson's translation 'Look we will change everything all the meanings / All the clear cities of Asia you and me' enhances the sense of split-self – who are 'you and me'? In the Latin, Ellis remarks, 'volemus' (l. 6) carries Catullus's self-address further, 'as if mind and body were two separate identities' ([1876] 2010: 130);[30] in her rewriting, Carson creates even more ambiguity emphasizing the exhortative and emphatic plural verb, making Catullus address himself in the second person. One may interpret Carson's poem as a series of internal focalizations in which the Catullan voice converses with his own mind, then takes a stand back to comment 'Now the mind isn't she an avid previous hobo'. The theme is already present in the Latin poem: 'iam mens praetrepidans avet vagari, / iam laeti studio pedes vigescunt' (now my mind fluttering in anticipation yearns to wander / already my happy feet grow strong in eagerness) (ll. 7–8). Carson takes the idea of wandering a step further by linking it to writing. In fact, the last line of the poem, 'back the same way go a new way', a translation of 'diversae varie viae reportant' (split paths carry home by different routes), could also be interpreted as a meta-poetic exhortation to make new verse.[31] Reflecting her poetics of triangulation, her poem ponders the desiring mind as an agent of creative writing bringing change: 'Every desiring mind reaches out toward its object by means of an imaginative action. [...] "Eros makes every man a poet" says the ancient wisdom (Eur. *Sthen.*, *TGF*, fr. 663; Pl. *Symp.* 196e)"' (Carson 1986: 169). In her rewriting of poem 46, the longing for the object and the process of creating fiction are sensitized on the plate of the poem. Catullus's lyric persona is made to speak as a postmodern subject, meta-textually reflecting on his own desire and on his own poetry.

Her thoughts on language and death emerge from her rewriting of carmen 101:

Multas per Gentes et Multa per Aequora Vectus
    (Through Peoples Through Oceans Have I Come)

Catullus buries his brother.

Multitudes brushed past me oceans I don't know.
Brother wine milk honey flowers.
Flowers milk honey brother wine.
How long does it take the sound to die away?
I a brother.
Cut out carefully the words for wine milk honey flowers.
Drop them into a bag.
Mix carefully.
Pour onto your dirty skeleton.
What sound?

Carson 2000: 45

In this poem, Catullus comes to perform a burial ritual on his brother's tomb, bringing gifts: flower, milk, honey and wine. Although the list does not feature in the source text, these are the objects that were most likely used as offerings in the ancient ritual.[32] Carson supplies the missing information, as her poem describes a personalized ritual of mourning.

First, the poetic persona cuts out all the words in the list of gifts, except the word 'brother'. Then he gathers them, drops them into a bag and pours them over the dead body. The image suggests that pronouncing the words on the brother's body would complete the ritual, thus signalling the end of mourning. Yet Carson seems to question the validity of the ritual itself. Inspired by the figure of absence evoked by the Latin 'mutam' (mute) (l. 4), the poem asks an ambiguous first question, 'How long does it take the sound to die away?' The question is left hanging unanswered. The same concept is used again in the last line, with a second question, also left hanging: 'What sound?' Denying any possibility of speaking with her brother or to hear from him again, she undermines the validity of the performative act of the ritual as a form of last salutation. When facing individual grief, the ritual fails and the communication between private and public spheres is interrupted. The ritual gathering of pieces, as a collection of words to make sense of death and loss, loses meaning when the invocation is left unanswered. Through various focalizations into Catullus's world and its reception, Carson's deconstructive rewritings in *Men in the Off Hours* dissect the triangulating relationship between language, desire and death, anticipating several of the themes later explored in *Nox*.

Floating with Sappho

If Not, Winter includes Carson's translations of the entire corpus of Sappho, as known in 2002, the parallel Greek text in Voigt's 1971 edition, some notes on the fragments, an introduction, a glossary of Greek names ('Who's Who'), and an appendix with '[s]ome exemplary testimonia' (393). The volume is intended for a scholarly or an educated general public; although it is not as experimental as some of her other works, it is similarly characterized by a mixture of academic and creative writing. The translation generally adheres to the Greek text in terms of language and form, although more often than not Carson's voice shines through. For its in-betweenness, its riding across genres, the translation has stirred mixed reactions. Daniel Mendelsohn, for instance, complained that *If Not, Winter* failed to address any particular audience as well as to portray Sapphic poetry in the accurate manner that its scholarly presentation implied; in particular, the book would fall short of informing the lay reader of ancient monodic lyric's performative context (2012: 129–30). Mendelsohn's stance, however, appears to be entrenched in the traditional and debatable assumption that translation should follow rigorous criteria of semantic equivalence. Moreover, nowhere in the book does Carson assert any didactic aim. In fact, in the paratextual material – particularly the footnotes where Carson blends explanatory comments with personal musings in her characteristic poetic-prose – she explicitly asks the reader to enter in a dialogue with both Sappho and herself. *If Not, Winter* is consistent with the rest of her work's typical oscillation between scholarly and creative modes, and the translations negotiate several key aspects of her poetics.

In her introduction to *If Not, Winter*, she calls upon Walter Benjamin's 'intention toward language' of the original (2002: xii). Benjamin envisaged a supra-historical kinship of languages, which 'rests in the intention underlying each language as a whole – an intention, however, which no single language can attain by itself, but which is realized only by the totality of their intentions supplementing each other: pure language' ([1923] 1999: 74). On these premises he further argued that '[t]he task of the translator consists in finding that intended effect upon the language into which he is translating which produced in it the echo of the original' (77). While evoking Benjamin's 'intention toward language', which frees translators from any servitude to semantic equivalence, Carson's translations and poetry make manifest the impossibility of reducing words to a single objective meaning. Her deconstructive translating process foregrounds the inherently destabilized signification of both source and target texts, whose derivative, heterogeneous and contingent qualities must be accounted for in their intersections with the translator's subjectivity.[33]

Carson admits that to step away from one's own mind is unattainable, as the translator is actively involved in the unveiling of words, the 'sensation of veils flying up' – the cognitive and creative process leading to understanding. In 'Cassandra Float Can', she further argues that translating reveals the constructed nature of the attribution of meaning:

> [Cassandra/Translation] splits open an idea of what it is to know Greek. She removes the walls and floorboards and suddenly we are in a site slated for demolition – this site which is not just her body, not just the city of Troy, not just the house of Atreus, but our whole way of knowing the truth about such things, our long-hand approach to every question and answer, our entire careers as Classicists, architects or prophets or whatever we are, the way we float and how we float and can we float. Cassandra can.
>
> Carson 2016: Original Cut

The verb 'to float' appears to describe the phenomenon of the manifestation of being like an unreachable meaning. Translation allows a temporary unveiling, which enables understanding, yet only fragmentarily. This also underlies the unlikelihood of fulfilling a semantic equivalent translation. The web of references hanging on the mind of the translator when she 'removes walls and floorboards' interfere and inform the process, as Carson remarks in her introduction to *If Not, Winter*:

> I like to think that, the more I stand out of the way, the more Sappho shows through. This is an amiable fantasy (transparency of self) within which most translators labor.
>
> 2002: x

Transparency of the self is another of Benjamin's tenets. A translator is transparent when (s)he lets the original language emerge through the target text, and 'allows the pure language, as though reinforced by its own medium, to shine upon the original all the more fully' (Benjamin [1923] 1999: 79). As Venuti points out:

> [Benjamin's] speculative approach is linked to a particular discursive strategy. The pure language is released in the translation through literalisms, especially in syntax, which result in departures from current standard usage. Benjamin is reviving Schleiermacher's notion of foreignising translation, wherein the reader of the translated text is brought as close as possible to the source text through close renderings that transform the translating language.
>
> 2012: 72

As Benjamin's, Carson's translation often performs acts of foreignization, aiming at unveiling glimpses of meaning in both the source and target languages.[34] She longs for understanding and appreciates the process that allows her quest, but she never admits to it.

An analogous meta-linguistic and meta-textual approach characterizes Carson's reception of Sappho throughout her work. It emerges clearly in her foregrounding of the materiality of Sappho's text in *If Not, Winter*, where square brackets, usually employed to signify a lacuna, are freely deployed with an aesthetic function:

> Brackets are an aesthetic gesture toward the papyrological event rather than an accurate record of it. [...] Even though you are approaching Sappho in translation, that is no reason you should miss the drama of trying to read a papyrus torn in half or riddled with holes or smaller than a postage stamp—brackets imply a free space of imaginal adventure.
>
> 2002: xi

By intervening freely on the layout of the brackets in the English text of *If Not, Winter*, she manipulates the reader's aesthetic experience of the poems to underscore textual silences and absences. The 'amiable fantasy' of the transparency of the self, advocated as a guideline to her own version of Sappho, seems to be more a rhetorical trope than a point of labour for Carson. With this operation she questions the supposed objectivity of classical textual scholarship, too: 'By grounding her translation within the historicity of loss, preservation, quotation, and repetition, Carson reframes a gendered epistemology in the interpretative and mediating work that simultaneously recorded and destroyed Sappho's legacy' (Melillo 2015: 192). Her uninhibited approach to her sources is confirmed in her interventions on Voigt's text, which she sometimes modifies substituting words with their variants, as do Pascoli and Copioli. Carson's views on language, textual instability and her notion of poetry as a manifestation of erotic desire to understand inform her playful attitude to the linguistic multiplicity of the Greek text.³⁵ For instance, in her translation of fr. 1 she emends Voigt's text inserting, instead of the commonly accepted 'Ποικιλόθρον" (with the variegated throne) (l.1), the variant 'Ποικίλοφρον" (with the variegated mind), which she translates with 'of the spangled mind'.³⁶ The most recent critical editions including Lobel and Page, Voigt and Campbell reject 'ποικίλοφρον' as a *lectio facilior*. In a rather unorthodox manner, she justifies her choice as follows:

> [I]t is Aphrodite's agile mind that seems to be at play in the rest of the poem and, since compounds of thron- are common enough in Greek poetry to make this word predictable, perhaps Sappho relied on our ear to supply the chair while she went on to spangle the mind.
>
> 2002: 357

Carson's mind clearly spangles Sappho's text, too, in *If Not, Winter*. As in *Eros the Bittersweet*, the poet is keen to trace the first connections between desire and the mind's creative fictions back to Sappho's work. Her approach to the text resembles Pascoli's and Copioli's, combing through the note apparatus to find variants that would better suit their interpretations and poetics. All three poets exploit the instability of Sappho's text to serve their own aesthetic goals in the translations.

In Carson's translations, the versification and graphic layout of the fragments is frequently altered, as in fragments 51, 53, 56 104a, 113, 114, 127, 128, 133, 134, 135, 140, 147, 149, 150, 161. Carson uses free verse and combines lines of various lengths to compose shapes on the page.³⁷ She often employs loose Sapphic stanzas, of three longer lines plus a shorter one, but with no underlining metrical pattern. Countering this free approach to form, Carson attempts to mirror the jolted syntax of the original and is rigorous in her use of lexis. Where possible, the poet keeps the word order of the source text as in a calque, adding a foreign allure to her English, à la Benjamin. She is consistent in her rendition of recurring words, which are always translated with the same English words; for instance, 'ἔρος' is translated with 'desire', 'φρήν' with 'mind', 'θῦμον' with 'heart' and 'δηῦτε' with 'now again'.

An aspect with which Carson never seems to tamper with, and refreshingly so, is the expression of sexuality. In her introduction, she briefly presents the few pieces of information scholars have gathered on Sappho's life; she underlines that 'Sappho was a musician' and a poet, signalling the importance of performativity in her own approach to Sappho (ix), and closes her remarks on a slightly polemic note:

> Controversies about her personal ethics and way of life have taken up a lot of people's time throughout the history of Sapphic scholarship. It seems that she knew and loved women as deeply as she did music. Can we leave the matter there?
>
> 2002: x

Partly blasé, partly provocative, in one sentence Carson positions herself against classical scholarship's historical fixation with Sappho's life. She takes for a truism the poet's homoeroticism and points at the inconsequence of the whole debate about it. At first, this might seem to be a revitalizing position with the aim of refocusing the critical attention on Sappho's poetry. However, considering that Carson in her meta-poetic verse exploits precisely the problematic aspects of this reception for her creative ends, the comment seems a little disingenuous. Certainly, Carson strikes a blow for feminist and queer scholars, who, by the early 2000s, had already repeatedly stated that the excessive attention reserved to Sappho's sexual mores detracted from the consideration of Sappho as a poet; it is also true, though, that almost twenty years after Carson's blasé remarks, today the work and the (textual or imagined) body of Sappho remain contentious for discourses on sexuality.

Overall, her translations of Sappho in *If Not, Winter* remain far closer to the source text than her translations of Catullus in *Men in the Off Hours*. But when they depart from the original, Carson's voice deliberately, albeit not blatantly, controls the Sapphic material, shaping it to reflect her views on poetry. The translation of fr. 22, from which Carson extracted the title-line of the collection (l.6),[38] is a good example. In the fragment, the lyric voice exhorts the girl Abanthis to sing of Gongyla in honour of the desire they shared for each other. At the beginning of the poem, Carson skips the word 'αὐάδην' (l. 5), the Aeolic form of 'ἀηδής' (literally: 'unpleasant'), and replaces it with a square bracket. She then uses West 1970's conjecture 'σ'ἀ[είδην' (West 1970: 319),[39] which she translates as 'to sing', to complement the jussive 'κέλομαι' ('I bid you'), in line 9, without signalling her integration either in the text or in her notes. The most deviant features of the translation are the rendition of 'πόθος τ. . . /

[ἀμφιπόταται᾽ (desire flutters all around you) (ll. 11–12) with 'longing / floats around you' and the rendition of the last stanza. The former instance employs two key words of Carson's aesthetic vocabulary: desire and floating. Considering the poet's theorization of writing as an unquenchable desire to grasp a floating unreachable meaning, the version of fr. 22 contains *in nuce* all the foundational elements of Carson's poetics. The relationship between longing, floating and language is elliptically established in the last lines of the fragment, too. She translates:

ὠς ἄραμα[ι
τοῦτο τῶ[
β]όλλομα[ι

(and so I pray… / this…. / I want…)

2002: 40

with:

because I prayed
this word:
I want

2002: 41

Carson cleverly fabricates a syntactically consistent sentence out of the corrupted source text, which does not signal in any way how and if the content of the three lines may have been grammatically linked to one another. From the fragmentary text, it is possible to infer that 'β]όλλομα[ι', translated with 'I want', almost certainly did not constitute a self-standing sentence in the original. It was probably the main verb of a second clause following 'ἄραμα[ι'. While the Greek verb 'β]όλλομα[ι' does express a general will, meaning 'to make a decision' or indeed 'I want', it does not indicate a sexual desire.[40] Carson's reconstruction drawing attention to 'I want', a verb left hanging, or 'floating', at the end of the fragment by the absence of punctuation, enhances the erotic connotations of the poem. She also fills the gap after the neuter article 'τῶ[' and adds 'word', which is not in Sappho. Building on the previous stanza, where the narrative voice is reproached by Aphrodite, Carson's translation drags the whole weight of the fragment down to two concepts: word and desire.

If Not, Winter reveals the mutual exchange between Sappho's fragments and Carson's phenomenology of eros and shows that, for Carson, as for all the other authors considered in this book, Sappho functions not only as a model, but also as a catalyst and a palimpsest for the development of a new poetics.

Giving thanatos back to eros: Catullus in *Nox* (2010)

Nox focuses entirely on Catullus, whose poem 101 provides the inspiration and scaffold for the volume. Translating the elegy Catullus wrote for his brother becomes a way for Carson to come to terms with the death of her own sibling.[41] Catullus's poem is dissected and appropriated in Carson's elegy, enabling her reflection on mourning. Carson refocuses the attention to the themes of brotherhood, mourning and justice, while continuing to reflect on the interrelationship among poetry, desire and understanding. *Nox* may be considered a renewed statement of poetics, in which Carson poetically and visually represents her ideas on literature via Catullus's text.

In a sort of declaration of intent, halfway through *Nox*, she tells the story of her relationship with Catullus 101:

> I have loved this poem since the first time I read it in high school Latin class and I have tried to translate it a number of times. Nothing in English can capture the passionate, slow surface of a Roman elegy. No one (even in Latin) can approximate Catullan diction, which at its most sorrowful has an air of deep festivity, like one of those trees that turns all its leaves over, silver, in the wind. I never arrived at the translation I would have liked to do of poem 101. But over the years of working at it, I came to think of translating as a room, not exactly an unknown room, where one gropes for the light switch. I guess it never ends. [...] Prowling the meanings of a word, prowling the history of a person, no use expecting a flood of light. Human words have no main switch. But all those little kidnaps in the dark. And then the luminous, big, shivering, discandied, unrepentant, barking web of them that hangs in your mind when you turn back to the page you were trying to translate.
>
> *Nox*, 7.1

In this excerpt Carson considers the idea of translation as a practice that fleetingly uncovers the unfathomable plurality of meaning or, as revisited in 'Cassandra Float Can', a word's 'floating' being. The trope of untranslatability, based on the distinctiveness of individual languages that also makes Catullus's Latin impossible to approximate in English,[42] and on the exceptional poetic skills attributed to Catullus, sustain Carson's emphasis on translation as a process, rather than a product, which, however, only affords momentary glimpses of understanding. Carson is endlessly fascinated by untranslatability, which she also associates with silence: 'There is something maddeningly attractive about the untranslatable, about a word that goes silent in transit' (Carson 2016: Variations on the Right to Remain Silent). The silent gap between source and target texts is what drives the poet-translator on her never-ending quest; it is the desire to fill this gap, the poet-translator's imaginative projection of an ideal target text, that sustains the fiction of translation and its creative process. Like all creative writing, translating is presented as driven by the 'leap' in perception produced by desire's triangulating structure, first expounded by Carson in *Eros the Bittersweet* (1986: 16–17). Faced with ungraspable silence, the poet-translator is in a constant state of in-betweenness – 'all those little kidnaps in the dark' – pulled, on the one hand, by forms of the unknown, darkness and death, and, on the other hand, by understanding, light and life. These ritualistic patterns of darkness and light, ignorance and knowledge, absence and presence, death and rebirth associated with translation bind the process to the volume's overall imagery. Carson repeatedly describes translation and elegy using images of darkness and light as the performative aspect of ancient elegy, as an accompanying song for the dead passing into the beyond, is duplicated in Carson's treatment of the process of translation as the primary vehicle through which past texts are granted an afterlife. From this perspective, Carson's translating process stands out as a life-giving ritual, conducive to (partial) illumination. As a creative process, it is comparable to Pound's definition of poetry as the expression of 'luminous details', the original qualities of a work of art that are also 'the permanent basis of psychology and metaphysics' (Pound 1973: 23) equally driven by eros' vital power.

Carson's dialectic of light and shadow refracts on both the linguistic and visual elements of *Nox*. She opens with the sentence 'I wanted to fill my elegy with light of all kinds' (2010: 1.0), while the photographs and drawings included in the volume often portray light effects and silhouettes, suggesting ghostly presences. Symbols of afterlife and mourning rituals recur, too; for example, in section 5.5, she inserts the picture of an egg, which was a symbol of the afterlife in both Greece and Roman Italy, while in 8.3 she notes that several people likened her brother to Lazarus, just before dissecting the possible meaning of the biblical story of his resurrection (2010: 8.4). Finally, *Cat.* 101, on which *Nox* is based, sees Catullus perform a funerary rite at the tomb of his brother. Carson provides both the Latin text of the Catullan poem and her translation:

Multas per gentes et multa per aequora vectus	Many the peoples many the oceans I cross –
advenio has miseras, frater, ad inferias,	I arrive at these poor, brother, burials
ut te postremo donarem munere mortis	So I could give you the last gift owed to death
et mutam nequiquam alloquerer cinerem.	And talk (why?) with mute ash.
quandoquidem fortuna mihi tete abstulit ipsum.	Now that Fortune tore you from me, you
heu miser indigne frater adempte mihi,	Oh poor (wrongly) brother (wrongly) taken from me,

nunc tamen interea haec, prisco quae more parentum	Now still anyway this – what a distant mood of parents
tradita sunt tristi munere ad inferias,	Handed down as the sad gift for burials –
accipe fraterno multum manantia fletu,	Accept! Soaked with tears of a brother
atque in perpetuum, frater, ave atque vale.	And into forever, brother, farewell and farewell.
2010: 1.0	2010: 7.2

Silence is a key element in Carson's interpretation of Catullus 101. Brian Seibert (2012) underlined the overall importance of silence in *Nox*, which, as he remarked, like all elegies, 'is a massing of words facing a muteness'. Carson's translation emphasizes the aspect of Catullus's poem that questions the validity of ritual to make sense of such muteness.[43] Her translation of line 4, 'et mutam nequiquam adloquerer cinerem' (and talk in vain to your mute ash), foregrounds the paradox of attempting to talk to the dead, 'And talk (why?) with mute ash', with the adverb 'nequiquam' (literally 'in vain') rendered with a surreptitious parenthetical 'why?' In the following lines, Carson again uses parenthetical spaces to voice the Catullan persona's intrusive thoughts, producing internal focalizations into Catullus's self-commentary. In line 6, 'Oh poor (wrongly) brother (wrongly) taken from me' the two parenthetical '(wrongly)', translating the Latin 'indigne', express Catullus's intimate reflection beyond the convention of the ritual, as if the Catullan persona momentarily let himself believe that he could enter in contact with his brother. In this way, Carson's translation intensifies the source text's tension between the fact that 'the ceremony requires [Catullus] to address his dead brother and to say certain things', yet inadequately because dictated by the conventions of the ritual, and the idea that 'there really exists between him and his brother some possibility of communication transcending normal experience' (Quinn 1969: 81).[44] At the same time, the aspect of Catullus's poem that pervades *Nox* more strongly is the impossibility of making sense of the silence left by the death of a brother. Later in the book we read: 'There is no possibility I can think my way into his muteness' (8.5). This line intra-textually circles back to her earlier reflection on translation: 'A brother never ends. He does not end. Prowling the meanings of a word, prowling the history of a person, no use expecting a flood of light' (2010: 7.2).

Nox represents various stages of the process of translation, which requires the poet to continuously face the multiplicity of meaning and the ineffable silence of words, both visually and textually. On odd pages beside the main text, Carson adds dictionary entries for each Latin word of Catullus 101, as if these were the dictionary entries she used to produce her translation of the poem.[45] For each entry, she provides a grammatical definition, the word's derivation, several meanings in English, and usage examples, which she customizes to create a web of references pivoting around the word *nox*, the Latin word for 'night', which is also used to mean 'death'. Almost every single one of Carson's dictionary entries contains a usage example employing the word 'nox'. The first entry, for the word 'multas' (many) concluded with the example '*multa nox*: late in the night, perhaps too late', which hangs ominously in the mind of the reader (1.0), while the entry for 'mutam' (mute) includes the phrase '*silentia muta noctis*, deep speechlessness of night' (4.3). Finally, in the dictionary entry for 'mortis' (death), Carson remarks: '*patiens noctis* liable to endure death, mortal: death as a personified agent of deity, Death; death as a state (usually in phrase *in nocte* when dead)'. Since reaching even a partial understanding of the other necessarily involves the uncoiling of one's own subjectivity, making the leap towards otherness entails reshuffling and reshaping the entries of one's own personal dictionary. As a process defined by contact with otherness, Carson defines translation as a room 'I can never leave, perhaps dreadful for that. At the same time, a place composed entirely of entries' (*Nox*, 7.1). In *Nox*, the self-fashioned dictionary entries underline the presence of darkness and silences within Catullus's poem and, more generally, language. Her crafted constructions of the lemmas are a way to pierce the surface of the Latin words and show the silence they carry within their floating meanings. *Nox* thus makes explicit that the gap between silence and writing, darkness and light is precisely what spurs translation's creative process, affording fleeting glimpses of understanding. Death is complementary to both the life cycle and Carson's view of language and poetry: light is followed by darkness, words contain silence, *eros* is brother to *thanatos*.

As all the other poets in this book, Carson modulates her voice against Sappho's and Catullus's poetry, while intervening on the ancient authors' reception. Her appropriations of Sappho's eros and Catullus's verse on death, mirror her views on desire and lack as two complementary forces which spur poetry and understanding. Sanctioning Sappho and Catullus as the original models for the psychological and literary structure of eros and thanatos, Carson reinforces Sappho's and Catullus' bond as a literary pair, giving new life to their twenty-first-century constellation.

Epilogue

In the introduction I set out to follow the traces of Sappho's and Catullus's slow fire in the twentieth and twenty-first centuries. I aimed to interrogate the igniting power of their interwoven works and biographies for modern poets and to illuminate some uncharted corners of their transcultural literary constellation. I asked three main questions: how does this literary pair enter into modern poetic discourses and shape key poetics of the twentieth and twenty-first centuries across Italy and North America? What are the characteristics of the supranational poetic discourse on Sappho and Catullus? How does their reception, at local and translocal levels, help to define issues of origin, gender, sexuality and national identity?

The material presented and analysed in the six chapters of this book has shown that Sappho's and Catullus's slow fire, whether running covert or out in the open, intersects various modern poetics across Italy and North America. At the turn of the twentieth century, Pascoli approaches the literary pair as an archetypal figuration central to his poetic search for the shared origins of humankind. He develops a form of poetic anthropology based on the exploration of mythical patterns of eros and thanatos, tracing them back to the poetic utterances of Sappho and Catullus; the ancient poets' works and lives are then rewritten and mythologized to create new poetry at the dawn of Italian modernism. A poetics of the fragment with a playful attitude toward poetic voices is mapped onto the reception of Sappho and Catullus in Pound's and H.D.'s Imagism in the 1920s. Albeit in different ways, the interests of the two poets in the erotic power of literature in relation to mythical narratives and rituals materialize into a re-evaluation of Sappho's and Catullus's epithalamia and hymenaic poetry, resonating with the central themes of Pascoli's poetic anthropology. The lyric fragment, modelled on Sappho's corpus, is also the trademark of Italian classical Hermeticism, coming to life in Quasimodo's and Anceschi's *Lirici greci* (1940). The Hermeticist appropriation of archaic Greek lyric as the original manifestation of a metaphysical absolute is aimed at founding a new literary humanism rooted in the first and purest poetic models. In Sappho's lyric, echoed in Roman times by the elegiac strand of Catullus's work, Hermeticist poets find the deepest and most truthful expressions of 'the heart' of humanity.

Sappho and Catullus are also linked to discourses on lyricism and subjectivity in late-modernist American poetry. Lowell and Zukofsky use the ancient poets to engender a meta-poetic reflection on the lyric voice and the objects of lyric poetry. Lowell uses Sappho and Catullus to develop his confessionalism, based on autobiographical realism and a play with authenticity; Zukofsky translates Catullus's poetry to create self-standing poetic objects through meta-linguistic experiments with Latin and English. Both Lowell and Zukofsky are particularly drawn to the popular portrayal of Catullus as an urban and 'revolutionary' character, which they re-use with aesthetic as well as political ends. In an analogous way, Ceronetti's 1969 Catullus targets uptight moral customs of middle-class Italians. In contrast with its post-war American reception, the reuse of Sappho and Catullus by Italian poets maintains a metaphysical dimension. Ceronetti employs the ancient literary pair to develop his gnostic outlook on poetry and reality. At the turn of the twenty-first century, Rosita Copioli's erotic spiritualism puts Sappho at the centre of her neo-platonic worldview. While in stark contrast with contemporary postmodern irony, her spiritualism produces a form of mythic revisionism that shares the mythopoeic inspiration of Pascoli's and H.D.'s modernist rewritings. Between the 1990s and the 2010s, postmodern irony, multiplicity and pastiche brand Carson's reception of Sappho and Catullus, which is stirred by an interest in eros as the driver of artistic creation and the search for understanding.

Key elements of the modern reception of Sappho and Catullus re-emerge transnationally and across time, tracing the figure of the ancient poets' constellation. Sappho's and Catullus's status as poetic models is unwavering. The relationship between Sappho and her first Latin translator Catullus – crystallized into an archetype of the dynamics of literary tradition and translation – repeatedly offers twentieth- and twenty-first- century poets a model to emulate or revisit. At the same time, the ancient poets' works and lives become palimpsests for the definition of new poetics, assuming multifarious shapes depending on the agent and place of their reception. As their names evoke poetic creation across time and space, Sappho and Catullus catalyze the development of transnational literary discourses.

Mythopoeic recreations of the works and lives of Sappho and Catullus have emerged throughout the twentieth and twenty-first centuries. In modernist rewritings by Pascoli, Pound and H.D., the poetry and lives of Sappho and Catullus are shaped into modern myths of origins, often taking the form of solar myths.

These mythopoeic rewritings link poetic creation, encapsulated in the authorial figures of Sappho and Catullus, to anthropological and psychological archetypal structures of eros and thanatos found in their poetry and reflected in natural cycles, such as the alternation of day and night or the seasonal rotation. Although ostensibly coincidental, Copioli's twenty-first-century mythic revisionism finds a precedent in H.D's modernist deconstructions of gender and sexuality. Copioli is adamant about her intellectual closeness not only to Pascoli's aestheticism and primitivism, but also to Yeats'. As I proposed in Chapter 5, the importance of the Irish poet's work for Pound and Anglo-American modernism might constitute an unintended transcultural bridge between Copioli's sensibility and Anglo-American modernist culture.

A common interest in Sappho's and Catullus's epithalamia emerges among the works analysed in the book, stemming from a shared view of poetry as the articulation of social rituals and the expression of primordial psychological structures. Pascoli's and Pound's verse sublimated the moment of defloration into figures of blooming and images of loss linked to youth. On the opposite end of the spectrum, H.D., and, more recently, Carson and Copioli variously call upon Sappho and Catullus to denounce the exploitative patriarchal and heteronormative power structures inherent in rituals like marriage or to advocate alternative feminine models.

Both modern and postmodern receptions of Sappho and Catullus are often made to mirror archetypal patterns of eros and thanatos as underlining forces of existence. The most compelling returning image is indeed that of eros as a life-giving principle, countered by death. Representations and engagements with forms of desire emerge almost in every reception considered in the book. Pascoli's modern myths link natural phenomena to the motif of eros and thanatos; Ezra Pound's Sapphic and Catullan personas in his short poetry and *The Cantos* are constitutive of his poetic cluster of eros, positing the erotic flow as the juice of creativity; H.D.'s rewritings and aesthetic prose identify eroticism as the source of poetry. Dynamics of desire within 1950s and 1960s social expectations in the United States and Italy are questioned by Lowell and Ceronetti respectively. In Copioli's translations, Sapphic eros, defined through a revised version of the myth of Helen, is presented as a divine manifestation. Carson's erotic phenomenology, grounded in forms of triangulating desire, is based on concepts first found in Sappho's poetry, while her elegiac Catullus constitutes a thanatic complementary force to eros.

Associated with the poetry of Sappho and Catullus, these reflections on desire also attract debates on sexuality and gender representations, bearing on constructions of 'Italianness' and 'Americanness' throughout the twentieth and twenty-first centuries. The authority of Sappho and Catullus as classics, on the one hand, and the complex eroticism and sexualities presented by their lyrics, on the other, have made their receptions into sites of political and social negotiations. The vast majority of the sightings of Sappho and Catullus from the 1890s to 2010s analysed in this book, in particular those of H.D., Lowell, Zukofsky, Ceronetti, Copioli and Carson, inevitably reflect the evolution of political and social discourses on identity. In the twentieth and twenty-first centuries, the two ancient poets are made to speak of heterosexual love, homoerotic and bisexual desires as well as unqualified, or 'androgynous', forms of eros. These recurring elements are prompted partly by a shared transcultural interpretive horizon, which places Sappho and Catullus within postromantic ideas and casts them as revolutionary poets of love, eroticism and intimacy, partly by the enhanced possibilities for transnational exchange and the increasingly faster circulation of texts in the last century.

While the comparative perspective has allowed various shared transcultural themes to emerge, individual receptions still maintain their particularities, as do the Italian and North American literary traditions. In the Italian context, Leopardi's poetic authority is felt throughout the twentieth century, up to the most recent recreations of Sappho and Catullus by Ceronetti and Copioli. Moreover, a solemn, frequently metaphysical, approach to poetry and origins characterizes the Italian receptions in ways unfamiliar to the North American sightings. This may have to do with the uninterrupted linguistic and geographic contiguity between Italian culture and Graeco-Roman antiquity, generally perceived as an un-dead presence in Italy. North American appropriations of Sappho and Catullus reveal a stronger tendency toward meta-poetic irony and demystifying attitudes, making the two ancient authors vehicles of subversive poetics and social discourses. Lowell uses Sappho and Catullus to advance a covert social criticism of the United States in the 1950s; Zukofskys' translation in the late 1960s foregrounds Catullan obscenities; in the 1990s, Carson's postmodern Sappho and Catullus stage centuries of problematic receptions.

It is possible to trace several aspects of the Italian and North American traditions back to Pascoli's and Pound's models. In Italy, in the 1940s Quasimodo and Anceschi engage with Pascoli's works, in the early 2000s Copioli (who was Anceschi's student) also reflects on Pascoli as a reference point. In post-war United States, both Lowell and Zukofsky profess themselves Pound's disciples, establishing epistolary contact with him at various points in their career. In his study of the Anglo-American reception of Catullus in the twentieth century,

David Wray identifies two traditions developing on similar lines. Wray sees two types of modern Catullus: a meditative one based on European symbolist models, epitomized in the United States by Wallace Stevens' poetry, and a (post)modern one based on Poundian juxtapositions and experimentalism (2001: 22–6). The sightings analysed in this book may be divided into works showing meditative symbolist tendencies, like those in the tradition of Pascoli, and others with experimental ironic inclinations such as those by authors in the Poundian circle. Although one should be weary of reducing the complexity of the Italian and North American literary clusters to binary linear narratives, it is essential to record that the reception of Sappho and Catullus across the twentieth and twenty-first centuries is continuously negotiated between local and translocal dimensions and aesthetic paradigms.

Finally, the book has shown that Sappho and Catullus continue to denote cultural value in both the Italian and North American literary traditions. As Casanova remarked: 'It is necessary to be old in order to have any claim of being modern or decreeing what is modern' (2004: 92). Associated with the primacy of antiquity and originality, Sappho and Catullus are employed to validate new aesthetic paradigms, whether to endorse the value of tradition or to refute it in favour of novelty. Transnationally, Sappho and Catullus are identified not only as being worthy of attention but they have also been reclaimed as models for the most disparate creative agendas of the last century.

As we enter the third decade of the twenty-first century, Sappho and Catullus remain catalysts for poetic innovation, still helping to pose fundamental questions on individual and collective identities and on the relevance of poetry to human existence. In this book, I have begun to unpack some key dynamics underpinning the development of the ancient literary pair's transnational constellation. I hope my work may offer a springboard for future studies not only on the reception of Sappho and Catullus as a literary pair of modernity, for instance beyond Europe or North America, but also on the transnational paradigm in classical reception studies. Much remains to do, as the slow fire of Sappho and Catullus continues to burn through time and space, positing new intellectual challenges.

Notes

Introduction: The Slow Fire

1. Unless otherwise stated, whenever I cite or quote Catullus's work I refer to D. F. S Thomson's 1997 edition; citations and quotations of the fragments of Sappho refer to E. M. Voigt's 1971 edition and numbering.
2. See also D'Angour (2013).
3. See also Michelakis (2009: 346–8) and DeJean (1989: 33–8).
4. The first Sapphic fragment to be published is fr. 1 in Robert Estienne's 1546 edition of Dionysius of Halicarnassus. In the same year as Sappho 31 was published by Muret, the fragment was printed by Francesco Robortello in his edition of the treatise *On the Sublime*, and fr. 168b was appended with fr. 1 by Henri Estienne in his edition of Anacreon, extending the Sapphic corpus to three fragments. See Finglass (2021b).
5. On Sappho's reception, see DeJean (1989), Prins (1999), Reynolds (2000) and (2003), Chemello (2012) and (2015), Piantanida (2021) and the reception section in Finglass and Kelly (2021). On Catullus's reception: Michelakis (2009), Gaisser (1993) and (2009) (chs 8 and 9), Vandiver (2007), Ancona and Hallett (2007), Pontani (1977), Intoppa (2002a and b).
6. Now in Valgimigli (1960).
7. On Pascoli, see Chapter 1, on Pound and H.D., see Chapter 2.
8. See Piantanida (2021).
9. Now in Yeats (1950).
10. On Quasimodo, see Chapter 3.
11. Both in Bidart and Gewanter (2003). Unless otherwise stated, all references to Lowell's poetry are from this edition.
12. On Lowell and Zukofsky, see Chapter 4.
13. On Ceronetti, see Chapter 5 and Andreotti (2012).
14. See Balmer ([1984] 1992), (2004a and b), Carson (2000), (2002), (2010), Copioli (2006). See Balmer (2013). On Copioli, see Chapter 5, on Carson, see Chapter 6.
15. See Ziolkowsky (2007).
16. Unless otherwise stated, all translations are mine. The translations are intended as literal cribs to aid understanding. I translated all non-English text, but I tried to avoid translations of translations to prevent clutter.
17. On the theoretical implications of this proposition, see Prins (1999: 19–22).

18 For a summary of this debate, see Miller (1994: 78–81). For a recent discussion of the possible context of Sappho's poetry, see Ferrari (2010).
19 For a summary, see Prins (1999: 31).
20 See Young (2015). The bibliography on Catullus 51 is vast. For a summary of scholarship between 1985 and 2015, see Skinner (2015: 265–70). See also Fo (2018: 643–56).
21 See DeJean (1989: 35); Greene (1999).
22 On Clodia, see Skinner (2011).
23 On this interpretation of Lesbia, see Miller (1994: 102); Greene (1999: 3) and Greene (2007: 132–3). On the namesake Lesbia in Catullus's work, see further Gram (2019).
24 Fordyce (1961: 219); Greene (2007: 133).
25 On meta-literary aspects, see Miller (1994: 102–3).
26 DeJean (1989: 48).
27 See Piantanida (2021).
28 The main details of Sappho's life are included in a Suida entry (Su(i)da σ 107 Adler = fr. 253 Voigt = Test. 2 Campbell), and the Parian Marble (Ep. 36 = p. 12 Jacoby = Test. 5 Campbell) which contains information on her exile, in Campbell (1982: 3 and 9). On Sappho's life and her historical context, see Aloni (1997: xcvii–ciii) and Campbell (1982: x–xiii).
29 On the use of Sappho by second-wave feminists, see Goff and Harloe (2021).
30 Scholars have reconstructed these dates following information given by Jerome in his *Chronicle*, 150 H (Ol. 173.2) and 154 H (Ol. 180.3), corresponding to Test. 11 and 12 in Wiseman (1985), which collects ancient testimonia at pp. 246–62. On dating, see Skinner (2007: 2–3). On Catullus's life and the critical debate surrounding it, see Fo (2018: xii–xvi).
31 Suetonius, *Julius* 73. Test. 50, in Wiseman (1985: 252). See Gaisser (1993: 2).
32 Suetonius, ibid. See Gaisser (1993: 2) and Skinner (2007: 3).
33 Gaisser (1993: 5).
34 On the Neoterics, see Fo (2018: xvi–xxi) and Gaisser (1993: 4).
35 See Skinner (2007: 4) and Fo (2018: xiv).
36 On the epithalamia of Sappho and Catullus, see Fedeli (1972), Ferrari (2010: 117–28), Fo (2018: 696–757).
37 Piantanida (2021), DeJean (1989: 314–15), Stead (2016).
38 On the impact of Bergk's emendation, see DeJean (1989a: 243–7), Williamson (2009: 359–60), Paradiso (1993: 54), Finglass (2021b) and Piantanida (2021).
39 See Piantanida (2021); Prins (1999: 59–61).
40 It was published as P. Berol. inv. 5006; although it is generally referred to as a papyrus, it is actually written on parchment (Finglass, (2021a).
41 On the papyri of Sappho, see Finglass (2021a). On the 'New Sappho', see West (2005), on the 'Newest Sappho', see Bierl and Lardinois (2016). See also Greene and Skinner (2009).

42 Piantanida (2021).
43 For other studies of Sappho's reception, see Williamson (1995), Greene (1996), Andreadis (2001), Reynolds (2000) and (2003), Chemello (2012) and (2015).
44 Wiseman (1985: 211–12). On the delayed UK reception, see Gaisser (2009: 194).
45 Wiseman (1985: 212).
46 On the impact of Schwabe, see Wiseman (1985: 217–18) and Martindale (1999: xiv).
47 See Gaisser (2009: 41) and Hexter (2015).
48 On idealizations of Sappho in Italian, Spanish and German receptions, see Piantanida (2021); in Victorian England, see Prins (1999: 3-4) and *passim*.
49 On the concept of 'transnational lives', see Deacon et al. (2010).
50 See H.D. (1974).
51 Blakesley (2014: 7–8) and Franco and Piantanida (2018).
52 See Camilletti (2018), Caruso (2018) and Franco and Piantanida (2018).
53 See Winterer (2002).
54 See: https://txclassics.org/old/greekschools.htm (accessed 13 April 2020).
55 See Kenner (1985). On Dante in *The Spirit of Romance,* see Riobó (2002).
56 See Casanova (2004: 328–30). On Beckett and Dante, see Caselli (2005).
57 Venuti (2000: 494–8).
58 See Rundle (2010) and Blakesley (2014: 9).
59 See Blakesley (2014).
60 On 'the long twentieth century', see Maier (2000); Stearns (2009: 226–8). For examples of the use of 'long twentieth century' in literary studies, see Perez-Sanchez (2014) or McCleery (2014).
61 Pound (1919) = Sieburth (2003: 526–45).

1 Mythical Rewritings

1 See Casa Museo Giovanni Pascoli. Available at: www.fondazionepascoli.it/museo.html (accessed 20 April 2020).
2 The poet began to study and translate the classics in primary school, he then graduated with a dissertation on the Greek lyric poet Alcaeus (G. Pascoli [1882] 2004); on Pascoli's chronology see Garboli (2002(I): 85–243) and M. Pascoli (1961). Pascoli's Latin poetry is collected in Valgimigli (1960). Del Santo (1965: 73–85; 1984: 131–7) lists six poems in Greek by Pascoli; V. Citti (1988: 49–56) published an autograph of another poem in Greek.
3 Pascoli's writings on Dante's *Commedia* are collected in *Minerva oscura* (1898), *Sotto il velame* (1900), *La mirabile visione* (1902), now in Vicinelli 1952. The poet expresses his regret for the negative reception of these works in his preface to the collection *Poemi conviviali* (1904), now in Pascoli ([1904–5] 2008: 6).

4 M. Pascoli (1961) parts 3 and 4 *passim*.
5 Ibid., part 3, chs 3 and 4. Pascoli participated in the *certamen* thirty times, won thirteen gold medals and obtained the *magna laus* fifteen times. His first victory was in 1892 with *Veianus*, the last in 1912 with *Thallusa*, cf. Favaro (2014: 280 n. 2). For the list of his works admitted to the *certamen* see Giustiniani (1979: 99–107).
6 Pascoli was professor of Greek and Latin grammar at the University of Bologna (1895–97), of Latin literature at the University of Messina (1897–1903), of Greek and Latin grammar at the University of Pisa (1903–5) and of Italian literature at the University of Bologna (1905–12). Cf. M. Pascoli (1961: Parts 3 and 4) *passim*.
7 *Myricae* (1892–1903) = Pascoli ([1892–1903] 1974) and *Canti di Castelvecchio* (1903) = Pascoli ([1903] 1907) = Vicinelli (1968). All subsequent references to these works are from the most recent editions.
8 Nava (1984) and (2008: xviii–xix).
9 The digitized Pascoli archive in Castelvecchio is an invaluable source for this material. Available at: www.pascoli.archivi.beniculturali.it/index.php?id=3 (accessed 24 April 2020). Following digitization, archival material has been recently reorganized with a new classification. For ease of consultation, when possible, I provide both old and new shelf-mark references. For a summary of unpublished autograph material on Sappho, see my article Piantanida (2013: 183–4). Most relevant for Pascoli's reception of Sappho are the notebook LXXIV, 3.8, fols 159–76 (G.74.3.8), entitled 'Studi di traduzione dal greco', which includes thirty-nine draft translations of Sappho's fragments, and the single sheet of paper in LXX, 9, fol. 8$^{r\text{-}v}$(G.70.9.1), which contains several rewritings of Sappho. For an edition and a preliminary analysis of these two documents see my 2013 article; further discussion later in the chapter. Notes and mentions of Sappho also in LXXI, 5, fols 5 and 8 (G.71.5.1); the notebook 'ΨΑΠΦΑ', in LVIII, 13, fols 7–15; another entitled 'Saffo', LXXIV, 3, fols 1–15 (G.74.3.1); LXXX, 3, fol. 11 (G.80.3.1); fol. 233 (G.80.3.6); LXXXI, 3, fols 97–9, 104–19, 128 (G.81.3.7); LXXXI, 3, fol. 129 (G.81.3.8). On autograph material on Sappho see also Citti (2010: 36–7) and Galatà (2016). On a draft translation of Catullus 76, see Lovatin (2017: 223–5) and an interesting notebook with critical notes on Catullus, dated 1886, LXXXI 4, ff. 25–71 (G.81.4.4). See also a detailed commentary of Catullus 64, LXXXI, 4, fols 187–211 (G.81.4.7). On preparatory material for the Catullan translations in *Traduzioni e Riduzioni* ([1913] 1923) see Citti (2010: 36–50).
10 Pascoli 1895 = (1904: 5–8) now in Pascoli ([1904–5] 2008: 9–20). All subsequent references to *Poemi conviviali* are from Pascoli ([1904–5] 2008).
11 Pascoli ([1899] 1915: xiii–lxxxix) now in Vicinelli (1946). The prefatory essay traces the history of the development of lyric poetry in Graeco-Roman antiquity and incorporates various poetic and prose translations of both Sappho and Catullus.
12 On 'Solon', cf. Siciliani (1906: 161–91), Bonfante (1944: 21–4), Del Grande (1955: 296–7), Debenedetti (1979: 197–264), Gibellini (1990: 209–16), V. Citti (1996: 63–80) and (1997: 104–26); the commentary by Nava in Pascoli ([1904–5] 2008: 9–20).

13 The 1897 version published in three instalments in *Marzocco* (17 January, 7 March, 11 April), then expanded and with revisions in Pascoli's collection of essays, *Miei pensieri di varia umanità* (1903), now in Pascoli ([1907] 1914: 1–55), also in Vicinelli (1946).
14 Nava (2008): x.
15 Ibid., xvii–xviii.
16 See Pascoli on imitation in ([1901] 1924: xxix).
17 See note 9 for a list of autograph material on Sappho and Catullus.
18 Archivio di Casa Pascoli, LXXIV, 3.8, fols 159–76 (G.74.3.8). On the dating of 'Studi di traduzione dal greco' see Piantanida (2013: 194–97).
19 The titles of the translations are added only in *Traduzioni e riduzioni* ([1913] 1923). In *Lyra*, the poems are introduced under the heading Sappho by the roman numerals I and II respectively ([1899] 1915: xxv–xxvi)).
20 See Finglass (2021a and b), on the Ovidian tradition and the impact of Bergk's 1843 edition of fr. 1 see the Introduction.
21 I established that Pascoli used Bergk's third edition of Sappho's fragments as his source in Piantanida (2013: 194–5).
22 On the interpretation of Sappho's stanza see Bonanno (1973), Burzacchini and Degani (1977: 131), Budelmann (2018: 120).
23 See further Piantanida (2013: 187).
24 This text was written in red ink. Letters in bold indicate later corrections in blank ink, |...| supralinea additions. For the complete text of the redrafting (fols 168–9), see Piantanida (2013) 192–3.
25 See Carson ([1980] 1996: 229–32), Aloni (1997: 5), Budelmann (2018: 120).
26 See also Piantanida (2013: 202).
27 See Welcker (1816) and Comparetti (1876a and b). In the same notebook at fols 1–4: several notes from the French translation of K. O. Müller's history of the Greeks in French translation (1866); at fol. 5: a page entitled 'Le amanti' (The lovers) with a list of Sappho's lovers; at fol. 8: notes from Domenico Comparetti's study on Sappho. References to these studies are also present in the notebook 'ΨΑΠΦΑ', LVIII, 13, fols 7–15 / G.58.13.4, probably dating from the same time, 1883–84 (Galatà 2016: 54–5).
28 MS LXXXI, 3 / G.81.3. Folio 9 contains a 'Prospetto sul lavoro sulla lirica di Lesbo, Cices e Psapfa'. Pascoli told Carducci that he intended to work on the project in a letter dated 20 August 1884 in Nencioni (1942: 149–50). The work was never completed.
29 Now in Piantanida (2013: 203–4). Another draft translation of fr. 3Bergk is found in 'Studi di Traduzione' (fol. 162) now in Piantanida (2013: 188).
30 On these autographs see also Piantanida (2015).
31 Frr. 93 and 94 are reused in 'Ὦ τὸν Ἄδωνιν' (1881) and 'Epitalamio Lesbio' (1882), too. Cf. Piantanida (2013: 208–9).

32 E.g. 'Digitale purpurea': "'E di': non lo ricordi / [...] quel segreto canto / misterioso, con quel fiore, fior di...?"', ll. 11, 14–15 ('And tell me: don't you remember / that secret song / mysterious, with that flower, flower of...'). For a discussion of the Sapphic theme in these poems see Piantanida (2013: 210). On the symbol of the woman flower see Barberi Squarotti (1966b: 59).
33 See Ebani (1997: xi) on the birth and death of Christ for the regeneration of humanity as a theme in *Primi poemetti*.
34 For the critical edition of the text and transcription of the autographs, see Capovilla (1988: 86–7; 73).
35 Villa (2012: 50–1).
36 Never published during his life but included in the posthumous anthology edited by M. Pascoli, *Traduzioni e riduzioni* ([1913] 1923).
37 Now in Garboli (2002: I, 371–3 and I, 377–9).
38 The only exception is the translation of poem 22, first published in *Lyra* ([1899] 1915: xl–xli) Citti (2010: 29).
39 Now in Vicinelli (1946). Cf. Citti (2010: 22). On Pascoli's metrical system for translating ancient languages cf. Audisio (1995) and Giannini (2010: 379).
40 M. Pascoli ([1913] 1923: 117–21) now in Vicinelli (1968).
41 Cfr. Ariosto's description of the body of Olimpia in *Orlando furioso* 11.67–9, now in Caretti (1966: I, 280–1).
42 Now in Vicinelli (1968).
43 I provide the Latin text edited by Baehrens (1876–85: 67), which Pascoli used as source text for *Lyra*.
44 Now in Santagata (1996: 969).
45 Corresponding to frr. 138, 140, 55, 2 (ll. 5–8), inc. auct. 16, 154, 168b, 136, 135, 102, 132, inc. auct. 25, 47, 105a, 105b, 104a Voigt.
46 Plato, *Phaedrus* 235c: 'δῆλον δὲ ὅτι τινῶν ἀκήκοα, ἢ τοῦ Σαπφοῦς τῆς καλῆς ἢ Ἀνακρέοντος τοῦ σοφοῦ'. See also Piantanida (2013: 181–2).
47 The first shorter edition of *Lyra* was published with the title *Lyra romana* (1895).
48 Aelian cited by Stobaeus, *Florilegium* 3.29.58 (Campbell 1982, test. 10).
49 In the first ode (ll. 41–60), at ll. 41–4 cfr. fr. 53, 3, 4, at ll. 46–8 cfr. fr. 2, l. 13 and frr. 40 and 42; in the second ode (ll. 64–83), cfr. fr. 136. Cf. Pascoli ([1904–5] 2008: 12–20).
50 I provide a shorter analysis of Sappho in 'Solon' in Piantanida (2021).
51 cf. Nava's notes in Pascoli ([1904–5] 2008: 16–17). For 'Solon' see further Debenedetti (1979: 199–264); V. Citti (1996).
52 Piantanida (2021), Nava (1984: 537; 2008: 16–17).
53 Nava (1984: 537).
54 Ibid.
55 On Pascoli's etymological reading of Sappho's name Fiorentino (1965: 98), for the meanings of 'φάος' Ciani (1974: 5–85).

56 Piantanida (2021); on the connection of Sappho and Aphrodite with the sun-god and the Leucadian rock Nagy (1973: 142; 172-7), on allegories of light and darkness Maggel (2010: 121-32).
57 Pascoli used Bergk's fourth edition (1882) as the source text for his translations in 'La poesia lirica in Roma' and 'Solon' (V. Citti 1997: 109).
58 Flora (1955: 642); Fiorentino (1965: 94-8).
59 Voigt reads Πείθω as a verb rather than a name. For a list of reconstructions of this corrupted passage see Burnett (1983: 243-4).
60 On the etymology of *persuadere*, Pianigiani (1926).
61 See Piantanida (2021), Danna (2004: 126).
62 The same Sapphics are employed in 'Cristantemi' (1895), 'Convito d'Ombre' (1906-13), in the translations from Horace and in 'La santa famiglia' by Leone XIII (1903), cf. Garboli (2002: I, 1168-9).
63 Gentili (1966: 52), Burnett (1983: 246-8). See also the 'Du-Stil' convention of prayers and sermons by which the divinity is directly addressed (Norden 2002: 261-85).
64 See 'Il dittamo', 'Sogno di Rosetta', 'Nelle nozze di Ida', 'Lo stornello', 'Calendimaggio' and the series 'Ognissanti'.
65 Now in Santagata (1996: 735).
66 Bergk (1882: 90). On line sixteen's poor textual transmission and the history of its reconstruction see Gigante (1968: 36).
67 Belponer (2010: 112) and Martini (2003).
68 The authenticity of Catullus 51's last stanza is still debated today, but all editions print it. Cf. Fo (2018: 655-66).
69 Together with *Fanum Vacunae* (1910), centred on Horace, the poem forms a microsection of Pascoli's *Carmina* entitled *Liber de poetis*.
70 On Pascoli's Latin, see Traina (2006).
71 In line 142, ref. to *Cat.* 64.251.
72 See Traina (1969: 21).

2 Modernist Rites

1 In 1929, the essay 'Psychology and the Troubadours' (first issued in 1916 in *The Quest*) was added to *The Spirit of Romance* (Sieburth 2005: xii).
2 Cf. Dante, *Purgatorio* 26.115-20 and *Rime* 52.
3 Beasley (2007: 69-71), Bell (2010: 358), Gregory (1997: 108-11).
4 Reynolds (2000: 337), Goff and Harloe (2021). On the connotations of the name of Sappho as 'The Poetess' and 'The Lesbian' in Victorian England, see Prins (1999: 14).
5 On Rilke's Sappho, see Piantanida (2021).

6   On Sapphic modernism, see Winning 2010; on H.D. and Sapphic modernism, see Collecott (1999).
7   For an account of H.D.'s life, see Stanford Friedman and Blau du Plessis (1990: 207). For H.D.'s own account of her analysis with Freud, see *Tribute to Freud* (1974).
8   *Collis O Heliconii* (1932–34) now in Fisher 2005. Unless otherwise stated, all references to H.D.'s poetry are from Martz (1986), all references to *The Cantos* are from Pound [1986] (1996).
9   Sieburth (2003: 1239). Unless otherwise stated, all references to Pound's short poetry and translations are from Sieburth (2003).
10 Cf. Edmonds (1909a) and (1909b), providing text, translation and commentary respectively of frr. 94, 96 and 3 and of frr. 95 and 92. See a later commentary in Edmonds (1916).
11 On various interpretations of this episode, see Collecott (1999: 15). On the birth of Imagism, see also Reynolds (2000: 310) and (2003: 209), Mackay (2012: 55).
12 Pound (1913: 200–6) = Pound (1954: 4–8).
13 See also Reynolds (2000: 309–14).
14 New material was added to the second edition of 1887 and the third edition of 1895. A memoir of Wharton was added in the posthumous fourth edition of 1898, reprinted in 1908 and 1974. See Prins (1999: 52). On Wharton, see also Collecott (1999: 13–14) and Reynolds (2000: 295). On Pound and Wharton, see Kenner (1991: 56, 71).
15 On Symons' Catullus, see Gaisser (2009: 208) on Symons, Pound and Yeats, see Arkins (2007: 471–3).
16 Pound (1917) = Sieburth (2003). *Lustra* was first privately printed by Elkin Mathews in September 1916, with some poems omitted from the original typescript. The volume was then printed in the United States by Alfred A. Knopf in 1917 including all but one of the poems suppressed in England, 'The Temperaments', and adding 'Three Cantos of a Poem of Some Length'. A privately printed edition of sixty copies was printed the same year, including 'The Temperaments' (Sieburth 2003: 1240).
17 First published in Pound (1916).
18 On these derivations, see Goldschmidt (2019: 20) and Kenner (1968: 212).
19 On ritualized forms of eroticism in Pound's oeuvre, see Oderman (1986).
20 On Pound's poetics of loss, see Kenner (1991: 56).
21 See also Witemeyer (1969: 63).
22 See also Sieburth (2003: 1277).
23 Ibid., 1281.
24 On 'Shop Girl' see Reynolds (2000: 311).
25 Originally published in *Poetry*, August 1914.
26 See further Beasley (2019: 78–80).
27 See also Hooper 1985: 162–78.

28 On the revisions and variants of the poem see Sieburth (2003: 1284-93); on 'non-translation' in the Ur-Cantos, see Beasley (2019: 78-83).
29 See the definition of 'Drab' in the *Oxford English Dictionary*: '1. A dirty and untidy woman; a slut, slattern; 2. A harlot, prostitute, strumpet.'
30 On 'luminous detail', see Ellmann (1987: 168-70).
31 Especially Gregory (1997) and Collecott (1999). See also Gregory (1986), (1987), (1988).
32 Gregory (1986) and (1997: 89).
33 Gregory (1986: 547) and (1988: 114-16).
34 Nagy (1973: 141).
35 On the importance of Harrison's work for H.D., see Gregory (1997: 108-22, especially 112-13).
36 On liminality in *Sea Garden*, see Collecott (2012: 99).
37 See also Buck (1991: 13).
38 See Gregory (1997: 156-60; 257) and Collecott (1999: 267-9) for a list and discussion of all fragments of Sappho alluded to in 'Hymen'. On echoes of Catullus 62, see Gregory (1997: 156-7).
39 See also Wasdin (2018: 21-3; 29-53).
40 On H.D.'s reuse of Wharton's translation, see Gregory (1997: 158-60) and Collecott (1999: 267-9).
41 For an analysis of the symbolic value of colours in *Hymen*, see Tarlo (1996: 96-102).
42 E.g. Wilamowitz (1896) = (1913: 63-78). See also Piantanida (2021).
43 Gregory draws from Stigers (1977: 92).
44 Tarlo (1996: 97-8), Collecott (1999: 36-9).
45 Du Plessis (1986: 83-4) and Buck (1991: 7-8).
46 See further Collecott (1999: 28, 195).
47 See also Collecott (1999: 26-7).
48 On echoes of this letter in H.D.'s work, see Collecott (1999: 28-9).
49 On the trope of the island as symbol in H.D.'s poetry, see Collecott (1999: 30). On H.D.'s shaping of her authorial identity, see Collecott (1999: 32).
50 On the theme of Eros in *The Cantos*, see Dekker (1963: 1-85).
51 See also Pound (1954: 8-12), ([1910-29] 2005: 40, 96, 122, 240); Paige (1950: 87); Gordon (1994: 206).On Catullus, see also (1960: 47-8, 105).
52 Gordon (1994: 207).
53 See also Hersch (2010: 141).
54 See also Kenner (1991: 64-7).
55 Paige (1950: 87); Pound (1954: 238-9); Fisher (2005: 2).
56 Fisher (2005: xix).
57 An excerpt of the scenario is transcribed by Fisher (2005: xvii).

3 Classical Hermeticism

1. Most critics indicate the period between the publication of *Lirici greci* (1940) and the collection *Ed è subito sera* (1942) as the final apex of Quasimodo's Hermeticist period, see Anceschi (1972 = Anceschi 1978); Ramat (1969: 380–3); Fortini (1976: 319-20); Lorenzini (1999: 112). Petrucciani (1986: 37) delimits the Hermeticist period of Quasimodo from 1936 to 1938; Tedesco (1959: 23–51) problematizes the Hermeticist label. All subsequent references to *Lirici greci* from Quasimodo ([1940] 2004). All subsequent references to Quasimodo's poetry are from Finzi (1996).
2. On the definition of 'letteratura come vita', Bo ([1938] 1978); on 'poesia pura', Gargiulo (1933).
3. On the history of Hermeticism, see Apollonio (1945), Petrucciani (1955), Anceschi (1972) = Anceschi (1978), Debenedetti (1974), Ramat (1969), Valli (1978), Barberi Squarotti (1966b), Barberi Squarotti and Golfieri (1984).
4. Flora coined the term 'ermetismo' in *La poesia ermetica* (1936). On the poetics of Hermeticism, see the studies cited in note 2, and Di Carlo (1981), Anceschi ([1962]1990: 218-36). See also Anceschi (1943) and (1945: 1–16).
5. The definition of 'poetica della parola' is by the Hermeticist crtic Macrí ([1938] 1969).
6. Cf. Valéry ([1928] 1958) and Anceschi ([1940] 2004: 310). On the idea of pure poetry in European poetics, see Colangelo (2001).
7. The majority of Quasimodo's translations have been collected in Finzi (1996). For a list, see the final section of this chapter and n 61.
8. On translating Catullus as an enabling process for Quasimodo, see Morelli (2015: 156).
9. See also Quasimodo (1939a) and (1939b).
10. For Foscolo's translations cf. Bezzola (1961: 277–8, 456–8), see Piantanida (2021). On Pascoli's translation method, see Giannini (2010: 379).
11. See the Introduction and DeJean (1989: 33).
12. On Quasimodo's schooling, see Finzi (1996: xci–xcvii).
13. See also Della Corte (1989: 164).
14. See also Anceschi ([1940] 2004: 307–8, 316, 318). On neoclassical metrics in the nineteenth and twentieth centuries, see Caruso (2018: 4–10).
15. See also Eliot (1920: 64–70), Paige (1950: 349, 356, 358, 361-4, 387, 390-1). On Pound and Rouse, see Culligan Flack (2015: 131–40).
16. Rundle (2010: 78–80).
17. On Quasimodo's involvement with *Circoli*, see Castelli (2003a: 94).
18. See, e.g., Hale (1919) reviewing Pound and Traverso ([1940] 1969: 293) and Valgimigli ([1946] 1969: 329) on Quasimodo.
19. Traverso ([1940] 1969: 292); La Penna (1946).

20 On this debate Paoli (2016: 30-4).
21 Paoli (2016: 33-4). Cf. Pasquali (1920: 35).
22 On Croce on untranslatability, see Steiner ([1975] 1998: 256).
23 Paoli (2016: 31-3), Jervolino (2003: 436). See also Steiner ([1975]1998: 264).
24 Elsner (2013: 138-40).
25 For a list of *Lirici*'s textual variants up to the 1958 edition, see Finzi (1996: 1326-41). 'Introduzione' (1940), 'Introduzione' (1951) and 'Altre circostanze, per il libro' (1978) are now in Quasimodo ([1940] 2004: 305-19, 321-33, 335-41). For 'Chiarimento e note alle traduzioni' see Quasimodo ([1940] 2004: 207-18).
26 The remaining eighteen fragments are mainly from iambic and elegiac poetry by ten different authors: Mimnermus' frr. 1 and 2, Archilochus' frr. 25 and 79, Theognis' lines 1197-1202, Praxilla's frr. 2 and 3, Lycophron's frr. 1 and 2, Jone of Ceos' fr. 9, Licymnius' frr. 1-2 and 3, Melanippe's fr. 1, the single fragment by Ibria; two fragments are anonymous.
27 Quasimodo ([1940] 2004: 208).
28 Valgimigli ([1946] 1969: 314). Traverso justified the exclusion of Pindar's and Bacchylides as 'manifestazioni illustri—a prima vista un po' estranee al nostro spirito' (illustrious manifestations – at first sight a little foreign to our spirit) ([1940]1969: 291).
29 Cf. Valgimigli ([1946] 1969: 318).
30 Anceschi's italics.
31 On Hermeticist views of tradition, see Verdino (1987: 97). On Quasimodo's ahistorical approach to ancient lyric, see Capra (2008: 13)
32 Horace called Sappho 'Mascula' in *Ep*.1.19.28.
33 'Salvatore Quasimodo a Luciano Anceschi', Biblioteca Comunale dell'Archiginnasio, Bologna, Fondo Speciale Luciano Anceschi, Fascicolo: Carteggio, Sottofascicolo: Salvatore Quasimodo, fol.16. I here follow the classification of Archiginnasio. At fols 1 and 17 there are two other unpublished letters documenting this exchange. In the correspondence held at Archiginnasio are also included two typescripts with autograph corrections of 'A Afrodite' and 'Come uno degli dei' (fol. 14[a-b]).
34 Luciano Anceschi, 'Cartolina Postale 20 luglio 193[7?]', Archivio del Novecento, Università La Sapienza, Roma, Fondo Enrico Falqui, Serie 'Corrispondenza', Sottoserie 'Corrispondenza con Personalità', Fascicolo 'A. F. Anceschi, Luciano (1937-63)', Sottofascicolo 'Datate'. I here follow the classification of Archivio del Novecento.
35 See also De Angelis (1983: 93).
36 See, e.g., Rissman (1983) on Homeric allusions in Sappho. Or DuBois (1996) on the myth of Helen in Sappho.
37 On the reception of *Lirici*, see Lorenzini (2004: 224-41).
38 Danna (2004: 127-8). Piantanida (2021).

39 Capra (2008) argues that Quasimodo's interpretation of ancient poetry follows the paradigm of 'lirismo solitario' (18–22).
40 On absence as an Hermeticist category, see Valli (1978: 114–15) and Bo (1945).
41 See also Zagarrio (1974: 64).
42 In his 1936 preface to Quasimodo's collection *Erato e Apollion*, the critic Sergio Solmi is one of the first to draw a line of continuity between Leopardi and Quasimodo ([1936] 1969: 116). Cf. Bevilacqua (1976).
43 See Petrucciani (1955: 155).
44 Leopardi ([1837] 1984: 71–4).
45 On Leopardi's reception of Sappho, see Piantanida (2021).
46 Note that Anceschi also echoes Leopardi as he speaks of 'idee concomitanti' (concomitant ideas), in ([1940] 2004: 311).
47 See 'Tramontata è la luna', l. 4; 'Ad Ermes', l. 2; 'Ad Attide: ricordando l'amica lontana', l. 15.
48 For other instances of this kind in Quasimodo's oeuvre, see Barberi Squarotti (2003) and Cantelmo (2003).
49 See *GDLI*: 'fanciulla'.
50 Pound employed Edmond's edition of the fragment, Quasimodo employed Diehl's. The variants between the two editions are substantive but Diehl does not alter the overall meaning of the fragment.
51 See Savoca (1986: 110; 116–18).
52 See Arrigoni (2008: 181).
53 See Morelli (2015: 156).
54 On *glubit*, see Chapter 2, p. 63.
55 The poems are: Catullus 12, 13, 26, 32, 55, 56, 105.
56 See poem 66.23 (*medullas*), 66.74 (*pectoris*), 35.15, 46.7 (*mens*), 60.3 (*mente*), 68.8 (*mens*), 76.9 (*menti*), 107.2 (*animo*), 109.4 (*animo*).
57 On Quasimodo's use of *endecasillabi*, see Finzi (2002: 18).
58 Quasimodo (1960: 32–6).
59 Bo (1947), Acrocca (1969), Paparelli (1969: 256–60).
60 See 'L'uomo e la poesia' and 'Il poeta e il politico' in Quasimodo (1960).
61 Translations of modern authors include: Ruskin (1946), Shakespeare (1948; 1952; 1956; 1959, 1966), Neruda (1952), Molière (1956), Cummings (1958), Pound (1958), Aiken (1963), Arghezi (1966), Lecomte (1968). Posthumous translations: *Iliade-episodi scelti*, with illustrations by Giorgio De Chirico; Paul Éluard, *Donner à voir*. All translations now in Finzi (1996), except St John = Quasimodo (1946), Sophocles = Quasimodo (1946) and (1954), Aeschylus = Quasimodo (1949), Ruskin ([1946] 1956), Shakespeare (1966) = Quasimodo (1966), Lecomte (1968), Moliére (1956) = Quasimodo (1958).
62 Lorenzini (2004: 216–17).

63 De Angelis (1983: 90-6).
64 See Valgimigli ([1946] 1969: 314-15), Macrí ([1954] 1956: 131) and Tondo (1976: 54).
65 See Zagarrio (1974: 117).
66 Paparelli (1969: 253-6), Zagarrio (1974: 8-9), Bo (1986).
67 Sanguineti (1969: II, 984).
68 Mengaldo (1978: 586-8), Luperini (1981: II, 603).

4 The Self and the Object

1 Hobsbaum (1988: 9).
2 Giroux (1987: 253, 261).
3 A nineteen-year-old Lowell studying at Harvard, but dissatisfied with his education, wrote to Pound to ask if he could join him in Italy and become his disciple (see 'Letter 1. To Ezra Pound, May 2 [1936]' and 'Letter 2. To Ezra Pound, [n.d. May? 1936]' in Hamilton (2005: 3-4; 4-5)). This never happened, but the two corresponded throughout their lives. Lowell visited Pound several times when he was at St Elizabeth's Hospital and he was a member of the committee when the 1949 Bollingen Prize was controversially awarded to Pound for the *Pisan Cantos* (now in Pound 1986), see Giroux (1987: 251-2). On the Bollingen Prize controversy, see Corrigan (1967).
4 Mariani (1996: 68-69), Talbot (2006: 269-70), Meyers (2011: 173).
5 Cf. 'Letter to George Santayana Feb 2 [1948]', in Hamilton (2005: 82).
6 Meyers (2011: 173); Talbot (2006: 267).
7 Hamilton (2005: 79).
8 On Lowell's time in Italy, see Hobsbaum (1988: 72-3).
9 Rosenthal coined the term 'confessional poetry' in his 1959 review of *Life Studies* and used it in his seminal 1967 study of post-war poetry, especially p. 15; on the conventions and constructions of 'confessionalism', see Perloff (1970).
10 Trilling (1972); see Maio (2005: 3).
11 On Lowell's and Zukofsky's translations, see Yao (2002: 209-10).
12 On Lowell's life, see Mariani (1996).
13 On Zukofsky's life, see Terrell (1979a and b).
14 On translation of European poetry as a creative springboard for *Life Studies*, see Van Schalkwyk (2017: 1).
15 Letter to T. S. Eliot, 28 October 1960 = Hamilton (2005: 370), cf. Mariani (1994: 294).
16 Rosenthal ([1959] 1999: 66).
17 Giroux (1987: 261).
18 Cf. Quinn ([1959] 1999). On Quinn, see Martindale (1999).

19 Allen Tate had condemned Lowell's turn to autobiography for its apparently scarce literary appeal. According to Connolly (2016: 139), 'Words for Hart Crane' may also be Lowell's way of repudiating Tate's influence.
20 Lowell was openly anti-Communist in the immediate aftermath of the Second World War. However, by the time of Eisenhower's presidency (1953–61), he was growing increasingly more sceptical of Cold War politics, turning to the opposition in the 1960s, Axelrod (1999b: 341–52).
21 On metonymy as the structural device of Lowell's realism, see Perloff (1970: 476-87).
22 Ziolkowsky (2007: 411–16).
23 Ancona and Hallett (2011: 483).
24 See Bidart and Gewanter (2003: 1045).
25 See *Cat.* 68b.143–8; 83; 109. If Lesbia is Clodia, we know that Catullus and Clodia began their relationship when her husband was still alive (Fo 2018: xxiii). On Catullus's transgressive relationship, see Fedeli (1990: 52; 89–92). On *foedus* in Roman society, see Gladhill (2016), on Catullus and *foedus amicitiae*, pp. 112–14.
26 Fo (2018: 1066–8) summarizes the main critical interpretations of love in poem 76 and gives an account of the various meanings of the values of *foedus, fides* and *pietas* in Catullus's work.
27 On 'Skunk Hour' as a vision of hell, see Gilbert (1986).
28 Meyers (2011: 187).
29 On Lowell and Latin poetry, see Meyers (2011).
30 On Lowell and Ungaretti, see Rognoni (2019).
31 Ferrari (2010: 109).
32 Snell (1953: 44, 65).
33 On heterosexual translations of fr. 31, see DeJean (1989: 57–60) and Prins (1999: 42–4).
34 On the demystification of Sappho, see further Lipking (1988: 120–1).
35 See also Reynolds (2016: 87).
36 Pound (1911) = Sieburth (2003: 236–8). Cf. Yao (2002: 225–6).
37 See, e.g., Brownjohn (1969), Raffel (1969) and Conquest (1970).
38 On *Catullus*'s foreignizing translation and its reception, see Venuti (1995: 215–23).
39 Now in Zukofsky (1991: 88). See. Wray (2004: 54).
40 See Scroggins (1998: 37) and Horáček (2014: 16).
41 The 1969 edition of *Catullus* has no page numbers. I here refer to headings and poem numbers. The translations are reprinted in Zukofsky (1991).
42 See Benjamin ([1923] 1999: 74). On Benjamin and Zukofsky, see Hooley (1988: 58).
43 On the translation of Zukofsky as a collaboration between languages, see Hooley (1988: 68).
44 See Hatlen (1979: 348–9).
45 Scroggins (1998: 37).)

46 On *Notebook* as a process poem, see Calder (1986).
47 On the poetic laboratory of *Catullus*, see Yao (2002: 228–9).
48 Zukofsky engages with Pound's translations in his essay 'Ezra Pound' (1929) = Zukofsky ([1981] 2000: 67–83), especially 71–73.
49 See Yao (2002: 220–1).
50 See Eastman (2009).
51 Scroggins (1998: 331).
52 On cross-cultural exchange, see Yao (2002: 233).
53 See Venuti (1995: 217–19).
54 Horáček (2014: 129).
55 On Catullus's poetic skills, see Fo (2018: xli–xlii).
56 See Davenport ([1973] 1979) on Zukofsky's English Catullus.
57 Hatlen (1979: 354).

5 Body vs Soul

1 Blakesley (2014: 7–8).
2 Ibid., 4.
3 Ibid., 4–5.
4 Ibid., 7–8.
5 See Franco and Piantanida (2018).
6 See Condello (2015: 96).
7 Ibid., 112.
8 Intoppa (2002a: 18–19).
9 See Masaracchia (1998: 507–15) cited in Condello (2015: 95).
10 See Piantanida (2021).
11 On Merini and Sappho, see Villani and Longo (2013).
12 Rossi (2000); Coco (2001); Savino (2002), (2008), (2014), (2015); Lenisa (2004); Di Benedetto and Ferrari (2005); Copioli (2006); Sinigaglia (2006); Guidorizzi (2007); Siracusano (2008); Rocco (2010); Marconi (2012); Raffo (2012); Avonto (2014); Fagugli (2015); Cappuccini (2016); and Neri and Cinti (2017).
13 Reprints include Dagnini (1982), (1991), (1996), (1999), (2008), (2010), (2012); Ferrari (1987), reprinted at regular intervals, most recently in 2017; Gizzi (1991), (2003), (2005), (2012); Rossi (1983), (2000), (2003). See also Pontani's 1969 anthology of Greek lyric, including Sappho, reprinted in 1975 and 2008, Cavallini (1986), Aloni (1997).
14 See the Introduction.
15 Intoppa (2001: 18) and *passim* for a survey of translations of Catullus between 1977 and 2000.

16 A quick catalogue search showed that at least forty-seven volumes of translations of Catullus were published between 2000 and 2019, including new editions, reprints and anthologies.
17 On Mazza, see Morelli (2018).
18 Now reprinted in Sanguineti (2002) with the addition of a translation of Catullus 31.
19 Ceronetti ([1991] 1969: 90).
20 Her non-fiction volumes include *I giardini dei popoli sotto le onde* (1991), *Il fuoco dell'Eden* (1992), *Ildegarda oltre il tempo* (1998), *La previsione dei sogni* (2002), *Il nostro sistema solare* (2013).
21 Bonfiglioli and Scalia (1971: viii); Morelli (2015) while recognizing its originality, still criticizes Ceronetti's translation for its lack of fidelity: 163–5. On the reception, see Andreotti (2012).
22 See Einaudi's website: www.einaudibologna.it/classici-i-millenni.html. The director of the Millenni series at the time of Ceronetti's collaboration was Carlo Carena.
23 For the same series, Ceronetti also translated Martial's epigrams (1964), the Psalms (1967) and Juvenal's satires (1971).
24 On Ceronetti's style, see Pontani (1977: 640).
25 Ceronetti ([1969] 1991: 358).
26 See n 21.
27 See Ceronetti (2008: vi) on translation as recreation.
28 See Ceronetti ([1969] 1991: 338).
29 See Ceronetti ([1988] 2015).
30 See Ceronetti ([1969] 1991: vii–viii).
31 A revised version of this translation is included in Ceronetti (2008: 25).
32 'Frammenti di poesie per vivere e non vivere' (Ceronetti 1987).
33 See also Re (1998).
34 Copioli, in conversation with the author, 29 July 2019.
35 See also Agosti (2006) and Fozzer (2006).
36 Inspired, among others, by the studies of matriarchy of Marija Gimbutas (Copioli 2006: 92–102; 144).
37 See also Copioli (1991) and (1996).
38 Copioli, in conversation with the author, 29 July 2019.
39 See also Copioli (1991: 114–15; 125).
40 For Sappho's eros as a prefiguration of sophistic and platonic philosophies, see Johnson (2012).

6 Postmodern Sappho and Catullus

1 See her biography on the Academy of American Poets' website: https://poets.org/poet/anne-carson (accessed 24 May 2020).

2   See also her personal page on NYU's website: https://as.nyu.edu/content/nyu-as/as/faculty/anne-p-carson.html (accessed 24 May 2020).
3   See Carson (2005) and her translation of the 'Newest Sappho' in *TLS* 5791 (28 March 2014). On Carson's translation of the 'Newest Sappho', see Goff and Harloe (2021).
4   On *Nox* as an artefact, see Chiasson (2010).
5   On Goncharova and Larionov, see Compton (1995); Shtrimer (2002). Steiner (2012) defines *Antigonick* as 'an *objet trouvé*, a postmodern or Dada artefact'.
6   On the form of Catullus's *liber*, see Gaisser (1993: 4–5).
7   The materiality of Sappho's text is especially foregrounded in the performance piece 'Bracko' = Carson (2012).
8   See Keats on negative capability in his 'Letter to George and Tom Keats, 21, ?27 December 1817' = Cook (1990: 369–70).
9   On stereoscopics, see Fisher (2015).
10 See Girard ([1961] 1965: 1–52), which is also included in Carson's Bibliography (1986: 177).
11 On eros as lack, see Carson (1986: 65).
12 See Battis (2003).
13 See Greenfield (2015) on constructions of gender in relation to time in *Men in the Off Hours*.
14 Prins 1999: 31. See also Burnett (1983: 233–4) and Winkler (1990: 178–80).
15 See Carson on marriage rituals in (2006: 147–54).
16 The parallelism between Sappho's poetry and Dickinson's writings is also made explicit in the notes of Carson (2002: 371). Dickinson's poem now in Franklin (1999).
17 See 'Flat Man (2nd draft)' (ll.16–29), which contains an intertextual reference to Dickinson's 'There is a Certain Slant of Light' (Carson 2000: 13, 25).
18 On these translating practices, see Prins (1999: 41).
19 See Goff and Harloe (2021).
20 On the critical debate, see, for example, Hooper (1985), Thomas (1993), Thomson (1997: 202–3), Dyson Hejduk (2007: 256–8), Fo (2018: 402–4).
21 See Gaisser (1993: 242–3).
22 *Float* does not signal page numbers. For ease of consultation, when available, I cite section titles.
23 See Carson (2000: 3).
24 On these principles in Catullus's poem and beyond, see Fo (2018: 1066–8).
25 See Dyson (1973: 138–41). On *foedus* cf. Gladhill (2016: 212–14). On Lowell's rewriting of Catullus 76, see Chapter 4, pp. 115, 117, 120–21.
26 Fo (2018: 1066–8).
27 On the non-autobiographical aspects of this poem, see Dyson (1973: 138–41).

28 See Fo (2018: 622-3).
29 On external and internal views in Catullus's poem, see Thomson (1997: 319).
30 See Fo (2018: 624).
31 On Catullus's poem as a literary reflection, see Simpson and Simpson (1989).
32 See Ellis: 'Manantia: would seem to imply the offerings were mainly solid: possibly flowers' ([1876] 2010: 382).
33 On deconstructionist approaches to translation, see Venuti (2012: 188).
34 On foreignizing translation in *If Not, Winter*, see Melillo (2015: 191).
35 On the relationship between eros and translation in *If Not, Winter*, see also Robinson (2015).
36 On this and other emendations of Voigt's text, see Yatromanolakis (2004: 271-2).
37 See Carson's use of form as a criterion for translation in her 'A Fragment of Ibykos Translated Six Ways' (2012).
38 On Carson's translation of fr. 22.6 with 'If not, winter', see Yatromanolakis (2004: 266-8).
39 Carson also follows West (1970: 319) at ll. 13-14, which she translates 'For her dress when you saw it / stirred you'. Di Benedetto (1986: 23-4) followed by Aloni (1997: 44-5) reconstructs the meaning in opposite terms and attributes the dress to the present character, Abanthis.
40 Aeolic Greek had several other words to express sexual longing, such as the verbs 'ἰμέρρω' and 'ποθήω' (with their cognate substantives: 'ἵμερος' and 'πόθος'), consistently employed by Sappho and usually translated by Carson with: 'to long', 'longing' and rarely with 'desire' or 'yearning'. For the translations 'to long' / 'longing' see *If Not, Winter*, frr. 1, 22, 36, 48, 74b, 94, 96, 102; for 'ἵμερος' translated with 'desire', see frr. 78, 137, for 'ἵμερος' translated with 'yearning', see fr. 95.
41 See Aitken (2004).
42 On the trope of untranslatability, see Steiner ([1975] 1998: 251-66).
43 C.E. Robinson noted: 'in the *quandoquidem* clause the full realization of [Catullus's] loss comes to explain and at the same time to deepen the disillusion of which *nequiquam* gave the first hint' (1965: 63).
44 See Biondi ([1976] 2007: 179-80).
45 For Carson's own description, see Aitken (2004).

List of Manuscripts

Archivio di Casa Pascoli, Castelvecchio Pascoli– Barga, Italy

Pascoli, G., MS 'ΨΑΠΦΑ', LVIII, 13, fols 7–15 (G.58.13.4).
Pascoli, G., MS LXX, 9, fol. 8^{r-v}(G.70.9.1).
Pascoli, G., MS LXXI, 5, fol. 5; fol. 8 (G.71.5.1).
Pascoli, G., MS 'Saffo', LXXIV, 3, fols 1–15 (G.74.3.1).
Pascoli, G., MS 'Studi di traduzione dal Greco', LXXIV, 3, fols 159–176 (G.74.3.8).
Pascoli, G., MS LXXX, 3, fol. 11 (G.80.3.1); fol. 233 (G.80.3.7).
Pascoli, G., MS LXXXI, 3, fols 97–99; 104–19; 128 (G.81.3.7).
Pascoli, G., MS LXXXI, 3, fol. 129 (G.81.3.8).
Pascoli, G., MS LXXXI, 4, fols 25–71 (G.81.4.4).
Pascoli, G., MS LXXXI, 4, fols 187–211 (G.81.4.7).

Biblioteca Comunale dell'Archiginnasio, Bologna, Italy

Quasimodo, S., MS 'Salvatore Quasimodo a Luciano Anceschi, Milano, 20 Novembre 1937', Fondo Speciale Luciano Anceschi, Fascicolo: Carteggio, Sottofascicolo: Salvatore Quasimodo, fol. 1.
Quasimodo, S., MS 'Salvatore Quasimodo a Luciano Anceschi, 19 Agosto 1938', Fondo Speciale Luciano Anceschi, Fascicolo: Carteggio, Sottofascicolo: Salvatore Quasimodo, fol. 16.
Quasimodo, S., MS 'Salvatore Quasimodo a Luciano Anceschi, 9 Settembre 1938', Fondo Speciale Luciano Anceschi, Fascicolo: Carteggio, Sottofascicolo: Salvatore Quasimodo, fol. 17.
Quasimodo, S., Typescript of *carte d'autore* 'A Afrodite' and 'Come uno degli dei', Fondo Speciale Luciano Anceschi, Fascicolo: Carteggio, Sottofascicolo: Salvatore Quasimodo, fol. 14^{a-b}.

Archivio del Novecento, Università La Sapienza, Rome, Italy

Anceschi, Luciano, 'Luciano Anceschi a Enrico Falqui, Cartolina Postale 20 luglio 193[7?]', Fondo Enrico Falqui, Serie: Corrispondenza, Sottoserie: Corrispondenza con Personalità, Fascicolo: A. F. Anceschi, Luciano (1937–63), Sottofascicolo: Datate.

Audio-visual Material

Carson, A. (2012), 'Anne Carson Performs "Bracko" and "Cassandra Float Can"', Schwartz Centre, Cornell University, 17 February. Available at: www.cornell.edu/video/anne-carson-performs-bracko-and-cassandra-float-can (accessed 20 May 2020).

Works Cited

Acrocca, E. F. (1969), 'I due "tempi" di Quasimodo', in G. Finzi (ed.), *Quasimodo e la critica*, 358–63, Milan: Mondadori.
Agosti, G. (2006), 'Poesia classica e tardoantica', *Semicerchio*, 35: 1–7.
Aitken, W. (2004), 'Anne Carson: The Art of Poetry No. 88', *The Paris Review*, 177. Available at: www.theparisreview.org/interviews/5420/the-art-of-poetry-no-88-anne-carson (accessed 20 May 2020).
Aloni, A., ed. (1997), *Saffo: Frammenti*, Florence: Giunti.
Anceschi, L. ([1940] 2004), 'Introduzione a *Lirici greci*' (1940), in S. Quasimodo ([1940] 2004), *Lirici greci*, ed. N. Lorenzini, 305–19, Milan: Mondadori.
Anceschi, L. (1943), 'Introduzione', in L. Anceschi (ed.), *Lirici nuovi: antologia di poesia contemporanea*, 9–24, Milan: Hoepli.
Anceschi, L. (1945), *Idea della lirica*, Milan: Edizioni di Uomo.
Anceschi, L. ([1951] 2004), 'Introduzione', in S. Quasimodo ([1940] 2004), *Lirici greci*, ed. N. Lorenzini, 321–33, Milan: Mondadori.
Anceschi, L. ([1962] 1990), *Le poetiche del novecento in Italia: studio di fenomenologia e storia delle poetiche*, Venice: Marsilio.
Anceschi, L. (1972), 'Ermetismo', in *Enciclopedia del Novecento*, II, 741–51, Milan: Treccani = Anceschi 1978.
Anceschi, L. ([1978] 2004), 'Altre circostanze, per il libro', in S. Quasimodo ([1940] 2004), *Lirici greci*, ed. N. Lorenzini, 335–41, Milan: Mondadori.
Anceschi, L. (1978), 'Luciano Anceschi: poetiche dell'Ermetismo', *Il verri*, 6th ser., 11: 10–43.
Ancona, R. and J. P. Hallett (2007), 'Catullus in the Secondary School Curriculum', in M. Skinner (ed.), *A Companion to Catullus*, 481–502, Oxford: Blackwell.
Andreadis, H. (2001), *Sappho in Early Modern England*, Chicago: University of Chicago Press.
Andreotti, R. (2012), *Classici elettrici. Da Omero al tardoantico*, Milan: BUR. Kindle Edition.
Angelini, C. (1940), 'L'ermetismo e gli ermetici', *Primato*, 1 (8), 15 June: 7–10.
Apollonio, M. (1945), *Ermetismo*, Padua: Cedam.
Arkins, B. (2007), 'The Modern Reception of Catullus', in M. Skinner (ed.), *A Companion to Catullus*, 461–78, Oxford: Blackwell.
Arrigoni, L. E. (2008), 'Il Catullo di Quasimodo e Birolli fra Parola e Immagine', *ACME: Annali della Facoltà di Lettere e Filosofia dell'Università di Studi di Milano*, 61 (1): 179–209.

Arrigoni, L. E. (2010), 'Il Carme 31: da Quasimodo a Catullo sotto il segno di "Vento a Tindari"', in M. Gioseffi (ed.), *Uso, riuso ed abuso dei testi classici*, 357–86, Milan: LED.
Audisio, F. (1995), 'Pascoli: metrica "neoclassica" e metrica italiana', *La Rassegna della Letteratura Italiana*, 8th ser., 3: 34–91
Avonto, E. (2014), *Saffo: Raccolta delle poesie con approfondimenti*. Independently Published.
Axelrod, S. G. and H. Deese, eds (1986), *Robert Lowell: Essays on the Poetry*, Cambridge: CUP.
Axelrod, S. G., ed. (1999a), *The Critical Response to Robert Lowell*, Westport: Greenwood Publishing.
Axelrod, S. G. (1999b), 'Lowell and the Cold War', *The New England Quarterly*, 72(3): 339–61.
Baehrens, E. (1876–85), *Catulli Veronensis Liber*, 2 vols, Lipsia: Teubner.
Balmer, J. ([1984] 1992), *Sappho: Poems and Fragments*, rev. edn, Tarset: Bloodaxe.
Balmer, J. (2004a), *Catullus: Poems of Love and Hate*, Tarset: Bloodaxe.
Balmer, J. (2004b), *Chasing Catullus: Poems, Translations and Transgressions*, Tarset: Bloodaxe.
Balmer, J. (2013), *Piecing Together the Fragments: Translating Classical Verse, Creating Contemporary Poetry*, Oxford: Oxford University Press.
Bàrberi Squarotti, G. (1966a), 'La continuità della poesia', in *La cultura e la poesia italiana del dopoguerra*, 69–121, Rocca San Casciano: Cappelli.
Bàrberi Squarotti, G. (1966b), *Simboli e strutture della poesia del Pascoli*, Florence: D'Anna.
Bàrberi Squarotti, G. (2003), 'Le lune di Quasimodo', *Rivista di Letteratura Italiana*, 21: 35–42.
Bàrberi Squarotti, G. and A. M. Golfieri (1984), *Dal tramonto dell'ermetismo alla neoavanguardia*, Brescia: La Scuola.
Barnard, M. (1958), *Sappho: A New Translation*, Berkeley: University of California Press.
Barnard, M. (1984), *Assault on Mount Helicon: A Literary Memoir*, Berkeley: University of California Press.
Battis, J. (2003), '"Dangling inside the word she": Confusion and Gender Vertigo in Anne Carson's Autobiography of Red', *Canadian Literature*, 176: 198–203.
Bazzocchi, M. A. (1993), *Circe e il fanciullino: interpretazioni pascoliane*, Florence: La Nuova Italia.
Beasley, R. (2007), *Theorists of Modernist Poetry: T. S. Eliot, T. E. Hulme, Ezra Pound*, London: Routledge.
Beasley, R. (2019), 'The Direct Method: Ezra Pound, Non-Translation and the International Future', in J. Harding and J. Nash (eds), *Modernism and Non-Translation*, 67–85, Oxford: Oxford University Press.
Bell, M. (2010), 'Primitivism: Modernism as Anthropology', in P. Brooker, A. Gąsiorek, D. Longworth and A. Thacker (eds), *The Oxford Handbook of Modernisms*, 353–67, Oxford: Oxford University Press.

Belponer, M. (2010), 'La *Lyra* di Giovanni Pascoli. Storia, fisionomia, e ruolo di un'antologia scolastica', PhD Thesis, Università Ca' Foscari, Venice, Italy.
Benjamin, W. ([1923] 1999), 'The Task of the Translator', in *Illuminations*, ed. H. Arendt, transl. H. Zorn, 70–82, London: Pimlico.
Bergk, T., ed. (1866–67), *Poetae Lyrici Graeci*, 3rd edn, 3 vols, III: *Poetas Melicos* (1867), Leipzig: Teubner.
Bergk, T., ed. (1878–82), *Poetae Lyrici Graeci*, 4th edn, 3 vols, III: *Poetas Melicos* (1882), Leipzig: Teubner.
Bevilacqua, M. (1976), 'La coscienza politica di Quasimodo', in *La critica e Quasimodo*, ed. M. Bevilacqua, 7–21, Bologna: Cappelli.
Bézzola, G. (1961), *Ugo Foscolo. Tragedie e poesie minori*, Edizione Nazionale delle opere di Ugo Foscolo, 2, Florence: Le Monnier.
Bidart, F. (2003), 'On Confessional Poetry', in F. Bidart and D. Gewanter (eds), *Collected Poems*, 995–1001, New York: Farrar, Straus and Giroux.
Bidart, F. and D. Gewanter (2003), *Robert Lowell, Collected Poems*, New York: Farrar, Straus and Giroux.
Bierl, A. and A. Lardinois, eds (2016), *The Newest Sappho: P. Sapph. Obbink and P.GC inv.105, frs. 1-4*, Leiden: Brill.
Biondi, G. G. ([1976] 2007), 'Poem 101', in G. H. Gaisser (ed.), *Catullus*, 177–97, Oxford: Oxford University Press.
Blakesley, J. (2014), *Modern Italian Poets: Translators of the Impossible*, Toronto: University of Toronto Press.
Bo, C. ([1938] 1978), 'Letteratura come vita', *Frontespizio*, September = Valli, D., ed. (1978), *Storia degli ermetici*, 158–65, Brescia: La Scuola.
Bo, C. (1945), *L'assenza, la poesia*, Milan: Edizioni di Uomo.
Bo, C. (1947), 'Introduzione', in S. Quasimodo, *Giorno dopo giorno*, 9–37, Milan: Mondadori.
Bo, C. (1986), 'Quasimodo: fu proprio vera gloria', in G. Finzi and G. Amoroso (eds), *Salvatore Quasimodo: la poesia nel mito e oltre*, 509–12, Rome and Bari: Laterza.
Bonanno, M.G. (1973), 'Osservazioni sul tema della "giusta" reciprocità amorosa da Saffo ai comici', *Quaderni Urbinati di Cultura Classica*, 16: 110–120.
Bonfante, G. (1944), 'Pascoli e Saffo', *Italica*, 24: 21–4.
Bonfiglioli, P. and G. Scalia (1971), 'Due voci sul tradurre', in M. Ramous (trans.), *Catullo Virgilio Orazio*, vii–xi, Bologna.
Brown, B. (2001), 'Thing Theory', *Critical Inquiry*, 28(1): *Things*: 1–22.
Brownjohn, A. (1969), 'Caesar 'ad some', *New Statesman* 78, 1 August: 151.
Buck, C. (1991), *H.D. and Freud: Bisexuality and Feminine Discourse*, New York and London: Harvester Wheatsheaf.
Budelmann, F., ed. (2018), *Greek Lyric: A Selection*, Cambridge: Cambridge University Press.
Burnett, A. P. (1983), *Three Archaic Poets: Archilochus, Alcaeus, Sappho*, London: Duckworth.
Burton, R. (1894), *The Carmina of Caius Valerius Catullus*, Privately Published.

Burzacchini, G. and F. Degani, eds (1977), *Lirici greci: antologia*, Florence: La Nuova Italia.
Calder, A. (1986), '*Notebook 1967–68*: Writing the Process Poem', in S. G. Axelrod and H. Deese (eds), *Robert Lowell: Essays on the Poetry*, 117–38, Cambridge: Cambridge University Press.
Camilletti, F. (2018), 'Italians and the Irrational', in T. Franco and C. Piantanida (eds), *Echoing Voices in Italian Literature: Tradition and Translation in the Twentieth Century*, 159–79, Newcastle-upon-Tyne: Cambridge Scholars.
Campbell, D. A., ed. (1982), *Greek Lyric*, 5 vols, I: *Sappho–Alcaeus*, Cambridge MA: Harvard University Press.
Cantelmo, M. (2003), '"Azzurra siepe a me d'intorno": sondaggi sulla riscrittura dello spazio letterario', *Rivista di Letteratura Italiana*, 21: 169–92.
Capovilla, G. (1988), *La formazione letteraria del Pascoli a Bologna*, Bologna: CLUEB.
Cappuccini, O., ed. (2016), *Saffo "La decima musa"*, trans. G. Chiademenopoulou, Rocca di Caprileone (ME): Universum.
Capra, A. (2008), 'Quasimodo e i *Lirici greci*', *I Quaderni del Vittorini*, 2: 11–40.
Caretti, L., ed. (1966), L. Ariosto, *Orlando furioso*, Turin: Einaudi.
Carson, A. ([1980]1996), 'The Justice of Aphrodite in Sappho I', in E. Greene (ed.), *Reading Sappho: Contemporary Approaches*, 226–32, Berkeley: University of California Press.
Carson, A. (1986), *Eros the Bittersweet*, Princeton: Princeton University Press.
Carson, A. ([1998] 1999), *Autobiography of Red: A Novel in Verse*, New York: Vintage.
Carson, A. (2000), *Men in the Off Hours*, London: Jonathan Cape.
Carson, A. (2001), *The Beauty of the Husband: A Fictional Essay in 29 Tangos*, New York: Knopf.
Carson, A. (2002), *If Not, Winter: Fragments of Sappho*, New York: Vintage.
Carson, A. (2005), 'The Beat Goes on', *NYRB*, 52 (15): 47.
Carson, A. (2006), *Decreation: Poetry, Essays, Opera,* London: Jonathan Cape.
Carson, A. (2010), *Nox*, New York: New Directions.
Carson, A. (2012), 'A Fragment of Ibykos Translated Six Ways', *LRB,* 34(21): 42–3.
Carson, A. (2012), *Antigonick*, New York: New Directions.
Carson, A. (2013), *Red Doc*, New York: Knopf.
Carson, A. (2016), *Float*, London: Jonathan Cape.
Caruso, C. (2018), 'Classical, Barbarian, Ancient, Archaic: The Changing Perception of the Ancient Past in Twentieth-Century Italy', in T. Franco and C. Piantanida (eds), *Echoing Voices in Italian Literature: Tradition and Translation in the Twentieth Century*, 2–28, Newcastle-upon-Tyne: Cambridge Scholars.
Casanova, P. (2004), *The World Republic of Letters*, trans. M. DeBevoise, Cambridge MA: Harvard University Press.
Caselli, D. (2005), *Beckett's Dantes: Intertexuality in the Fiction and Criticism*, Manchester: Manchester University Press.

Caselli, D. and D. La Penna, eds (2008), *Twentieth-Century Poetic Translation: Literary Cultures in Italian and English*, London: Continuum.
Castelli, R. (2003a), 'Liguria come un'infanzia: gli anni genovesi di Salvatore Quasimodo', in B. Van De Bossche (ed.), *Quasimodo e gli altri: atti del Convegno Internazionale Lovanio, 27-28 aprile 2001*, 89-100, Leuven: Leuven University Press.
Castelli, R. (2003b), 'Quasimodo e il sentimento della solitudine', *Rivista di Letteratura Italiana*, 2: 321-8.
Cavallini, E. (1986), *Saffo. Frammenti*, Parma: Guanda.
Ceronetti, G., trans. (1964), M. V. Marziale, *Epigrammi*, Turin: Einaudi.
Ceronetti, G., trans. (1967), *I salmi*, Turin: Einaudi.
Ceronetti, G. (1969), 'Il mestiere di tradurre e una nuova "querelle"', *Belfagor*, 24(1): 90-5.
Ceronetti, G., trans. ([1969] 1991), G.V. Catullo, *Le poesie*, Turin: Einaudi.
Ceronetti, G., trans. (1971), D.G. Giovenale, *Le satire*, Turin: Einaudi.
Ceronetti, G. ([1986] 2015), *Come un talismano*, Milan: Adelphi. Kindle Edition.
Ceronetti, G. (1987), *Compassioni e disperazioni: 1946-86*, Turin: Einaudi.
Ceronetti, G. ([1988] 2015), 'Poesia chiara, poesia scura', in *L'occhiale malinconico*, Milan: Adelphi. Kindle edition.
Ceronetti, G. (1988), *L'occhiale malinconico*, Milan: Adelphi.
Ceronetti, G. (1996), *La Distanza. Poesie 1946-96*, Milan: BUR.
Ceronetti, G. (2008), *Trafitture di tenerezza. Poesia tradotta 1963-2008*, Turin: Einaudi.
Ceronetti, G. (2009), *Le ballate dell'angelo ferito*, Padua: Il notes magico.
Cestaro, G.P., ed. (2004), *Queer Italia: Same-sex Desire in Italian Literature and Film*, New York: Palgrave Macmillan.
Cetrangolo, E. (1946), *Le poesie di Catullo veronese*, Venice: Neri Pozza.
Chemello, A., ed. (2012), *Saffo tra poesia e leggenda: fortuna di un personaggio nei secoli XVII e XIX*, Padua: Il Poligrafo.
Chemello, A., ed. (2015), *Saffo: Riscritture e interpretazioni dal XVI al XX secolo*, Padua: Il Poligrafo.
Chiasson, D. (2010), 'The Unfolding Elegy', *NYRB*, 7: 63-4.
Ciani, M. G. (1974), *ΦΑΟΣ e termini affini nella poesia greca: introduzione a una fenomenologia della luce*, Florence: Olschki.
Cipollini, A. (1890), *Saffo*, Milan: Fratelli Dumolard Editori.
Citti, F. (2010), 'In margine all'edizione di *Traduzioni e riduzioni* (2)', *Rivista pascoliana*, 22: 21-59.
Citti, V. (1988), 'L'eroe d'Italia: un inedito greco pascoliano', in *Testi ed esegesi pascoliana. Atti del convegno di studi pascoliani. San Mauro Pascoli. 23-24 maggio 1987*, 49-56, Bologna: CLUEB.
Citti, V. (1996), 'Solon e la ricezione dell'antico', *Rivista pascoliana*, 8: 63-80.
Citti, V. (1997), 'La ricezione dell'antico nei *Poemi conviviali*', in M. Pazzaglia (ed.), *I Poemi conviviali di Giovanni Pascoli, Atti del Convegno di studi di San Mauro Pascoli e Barga, 26-29 settembre 1996*, 99-131, Florence: La Nuova Italia.
Coco, L. (2001), *Saffo: Finché ci sia respiro. Dodici frammenti.* Novara: Interlinea.

Colangelo, S. (2001), 'Sull'idea di poesia pura', in G. M. Anselmi (ed.), *Mappe della letteratura europea e mediterranea*, 3 vols, III: *Da Gogol' al Postmoderno*, 188–94, Milan: Bruno Mondadori.
Collecott, D. (1999), *H.D. and Sapphic Modernism: 1910–50*, Cambridge: Cambridge University Press.
Collecott, D. (2012), 'H.D.'s Transformative Poetics', in J. Christodoulides and P. Mackay (eds), *The Cambridge Companion to H.D.*, 93–112, Cambridge: Cambridge University Press.
Comparetti, D. (1876a), 'Saffo e Faone dinanzi alla critica storica', *Nuova Antologia*, 31 (1): 253–88.
Comparetti, D. (1876b), 'Sulla autenticità della epistola ovidiana di Saffo a Faone e sul valore di essa per le questioni saffiche', *Pubblicazione del Regio Istituto di Studii Superiori in Firenze, Sezione di Filosofia e Filologia*, 2: 3–53.
Compton, S. (1995), 'Larionov et Gontcharova illustrateurs, 1912–29', in *Natalie Gontcharova. Michel Larionov*, 205–12, Paris: Édition du Centre Pompidou.
Condello, F. (2015), '"Cinquant'anni dopo Quasimodo": lirici greci e poeti italiani contemporanei (un dialogo tra sordi)', in F. Condello and A. Rodighiero (eds), *Un compito infinito. Testi classici e traduzioni d'autore nel Novecento italiano*, 7–36, Bologna: Bononia University Press.
Connolly, S. (2016), *Grief and Meter: Elegies for Poets after Auden*, Charlottesville: University of Virginia Press.
Conquest, R. (1970), 'The Abomination of Moab', *Encounter*, 34: 56.
Conte, G. B. (1986), *The Rhetoric of Imitation: Genre and Poetic Memory in Virgil and Other Latin Poets*, trans. C. Segal, Ithaca: Cornell University Press.
Contini, G. (1968), *Letteratura dell'Italia unita, 1861–1968*, Florence: Sansoni.
Cook, E., ed. (1990), John Keats, *The Major Works*, Oxford: Oxford University Press.
Copioli, R. (1979), *Splendida lumina solis*, Forum/Quinta Generazione.
Copioli, R., ed. (1983), 'Il flauto magico dei classici', in *Tradurre poesia, L'Altro Versante*, 1, 183–205, Brescia: Paideia Editrice.
Copioli, R., ed. (1988), W. B. Yeats, *Il crepuscolo celtico*, Rome: Theoria.
Copioli, R. (1991), *I giardini dei popoli sotto le onde: Elena, Eros, la metamorfosi*, Parma: Guanda.
Copioli, R. (1992), *Il fuoco dell'Eden*, Siracuse: Tema Celeste.
Copioli, R. (1996), *Elena*, Milan: Guanda.
Copioli, R. (1998), *Ildegarda oltre il tempo*, Rimini: Raffaelli.
Copioli, R. (2002), *La previsione dei sogni*, Milan: Medusa.
Copioli, R. (2006), *Saffo. Più oro dell'oro*, Milan: Medusa.
Copioli, R. (2013), *Il nostro sistema solare*, Milan: Medusa.
Copioli, R. (2016), *Le acque della mente*, Milan: Mondadori. Kindle Edition.
Cornish, F. W. (1904), *The Poems of Gaius Valerius Catullus*, Cambridge: Cambridge University Press.
Corrigan, R. (1967), 'Ezra Pound and the Bollingen Prize Controversy', *Midcontinent American Studies Journal*, 8(2): 43–57.

Croce, B. ([1902] 1990), *L'estetica come scienza dell'espressione e linguistica generale. Teoria e storia*, ed. G. Galasso, Milan: Adelphi.
Culligan Flack, L. (2015), *Modernism and Homer: The Odysseys of H.D., James Joyce, Osip Mandelstam, and Ezra Pound*, Cambridge: Cambridge University Press.
D'Agata, J. (2000), 'Review of *Men in the Off Hours*', *Boston Review*, 1 June. Available at: http://bostonreview.net/poetry/john-dagata-review-men-hours (accessed 20 May 2020).
D'Angour, A. (2013), 'Love's Battlefield: Rethinking Sappho Fragment 31', in E. Sanders et al. (eds), *Erôs in Ancient Greece*, 59–7, Oxford: Oxford University Press.
Dagnini, I., ed. (1982), *Saffo: Poesie*, Rome: Newton Compton.
Damrosch, D. (2003), *What is World Literature?* Princeton: Princeton University Press.
Danna, D. (2004), 'Beauty and the Beast: Lesbians in Literature and Sexual Science from the Nineteenth to the Twentieth Centuries', in G. P. Cestaro (ed.), *Queer Italia: Same-Sex Desire in Italian Literature and Film*, 117–32, New York: Palgrave Macmillan.
Davenport, G. ([1973] 1979), 'Zukofsky's English Catullus', in C. F. Terrell (ed.), *Louis Zukofsky: Man and Poet*, 365–70, Orono: The National Poetry Foundation.
Davidson, P. (1995), *Ezra Pound and Roman Poetry: A Preliminary Survey*, Amsterdam: Rodopi.
Deacon, D., P. Russell, A. Woollacott, eds (2010), *Transnational Lives: Biographies of Global Modernity, 1700–present*, Basingstoke: Palgrave Macmillan.
De Angelis, V. (1983), *L'estetica di Luciano Anceschi: prospettive e sviluppi della nuova fenomenologia critica*, Bologna: CLUEB.
Debenedetti, G. (1974), *Poesia italiana del novecento*, Milan: Garzanti.
Debenedetti, G. (1979), 'Solon', in *Pascoli: la rivoluzione inconsapevole*, 197–264, Milan: Garzanti.
DeJean, J. (1989), *Fictions of Sappho: 1546–1937*, Chicago: University of Chicago Press.
Dekker, G. (1963), *Sailing After Knowledge: The Cantos of Ezra Pound*, London: Routledge.
Del Santo, L. (1965), 'Il Carducci poeta in un epigramma greco del Pascoli', in M. Biagini (ed.), *Pascoli. Atti del convegno nazionale di studi pascoliani. San Mauro Pascoli 11-12-13 maggio 1962*, 73–85, Santarcangelo di Romagna: Maggioli.
Del Santo, L. (1984), 'La Grecia nell'opera trilingue di Giovanni Pascoli', in E. Sanguineti (ed.), *Giovanni Pascoli: poesia e poetica. Atti del convegno di studi pascoliani. San Mauro 1-2-3 aprile 1982*, 109–56, Rimini: Maggioli.
Delabroy, J., ed. (1990), C. Baudelaire, *Les Fleurs du mal*, Paris: Magnard.
Della Corte, F. (1989), 'Tre poeti traducono Catullo', *Aufidus*, 7: 159–68.
Dement, R. S. (1915), *The Lesbiad of Catullus and Pervigilium Veneris (Mood transcriptions) and Songs of a Wayfarer*, Chicago: Alderbrink.
Di Benedetto, V. (1986), 'Integrazioni al P. Oxy. 1231 di Saffo (frr. 27 e 22 V.)', *Quaderni Urbinati di Cultura Classica*, n.s. 24: 19–25.
Di Benedetto, V. ([1987] 1994), 'Introduzione', in F. Ferrari (ed.), *Saffo. Poesie*, 5–78, Milan: BUR.
Di Benedetto, V. (2005), 'La nuova Saffo e dintorni', *Zeitschrift für Papyrologie und Epigraphik*, 153, 1 January: 7–20.

Di Benedetto, V. and F. Ferrari, eds (2005), *Saffo: Frammenti d'amore*, Milan: BUR.
Di Carlo, F. (1981), *Letteratura e ideologia dell'Ermetismo*, Foggia: Edizioni Bastogi.
Di Palmo, P. (2017), 'La voce del poeta: Rosita Copioli – La mente assediata', *Succede Oggi*, January. Available at: www.succedeoggi.it/2017/01/la-mente-assediata/ (accessed 25 May 2020).
Diehl, E. (1936), ed., *Anthologia lyrica graeca*, 2nd edn, Leipzig: Teubner.
Du Plessis, R.B. (1986), *H.D.: The Career of That Struggle*, Bloomington, Indianapolis: Indiana University Press.
DuBois, P. (1996), 'Sappho and Helen', in E. Greene (ed.), *Reading Sappho: Contemporary Approaches*, 79–89, Berkeley: University of California Press.
Dyson Hejduk, J. T. (2007), 'The Lesbia Poems', in M. Skinner (ed.), *A Companion to Catullus*, 254–75, Oxford: Blackwell.
Dyson, M. (1973), 'Catullus 8 and 76', *The Classical Quarterly*, 23(1): 127–43.
Ebani, N. (1997), 'Introduzione', in G. Pascoli, *Primi poemetti*, ed. N. Ebani, ix–xxx, Parma: Guanda.
Edmonds, J. M. (1909a), 'Three Fragments of Sappho', *The Classical Review*, 23(4): 99–104.
Edmonds, J. M. (1909b), 'More Fragments of Sappho', *The Classical Review*, 23(5): 156–8.
Edmonds, J. M. (1916), 'The Berlin Sappho Again', *The Classical Review*, 30(5/6): 129–33.
Eliot, T. S. (1920), *The Sacred Wood: Essays on Poetry and Criticism*, London: Methuen & Co.
Eliot, T. S. ([1922] 2001), *The Wasteland*, ed. M. North, New York: Norton.
Eliot, T. S. ([1923] 1975), 'Ulysses, Order and Myth', in F. Kermode (ed.), *Selected Prose of T. S. Eliot*, 175–8, New York: Farrar, Straus and Giroux.
Eliot, T. S. (1943), *Four Quartets*, New York: Harcourt Brace and Company.
Ellis, R. ([1876] 2010), *A Commentary on Catullus*, Cambridge: Cambridge University Press.
Ellmann, M. (1987), *The Poetics of Impersonality: T. S. Eliot and Ezra Pound*, 168–70, Brighton: Harvester.
Elsner, J. (2013), 'Paideia: Ancient Concept and Modern Reception', *International Journal of the Classical Tradition*, 20(4): 136–52.
Elytis, O. ([1984] 1996), Σαπφώ, Ikaros: Athens.
Emmerich, K. (2017), *Literary Translation and the Making of Originals*, New York: Bloomsbury Academic.
Errante, V. (1946), *La poesia di Catullo*, Milan: Hoepli.
Fagugli, A. (2015), *Silloge delle poesie di Saffo,* Macerata: Simple.
Favaro, F. (2014), 'Destino di un poeta. Pascoli, Virgilio e il vecchio di Corico', *Lettere italiane*, 66(2): 280–93.
Fedeli, P. (1972), *Il carme 61 di Catullo*, Freiburg: Edizioni Universitarie Friburgo.
Ferrari, F., trans. (1987), *Saffo: Poesie*, Milan: BUR.
Ferrari, F. ([1987] 1994), *Saffo: poesie*, Milan: BUR.
Ferrari, F. (2010), *Sappho's Gift: The Poet and Her Community*, trans. A.H. Benjamin and L. Prauscello, Ann Arbor: Michigan Classical Press.

Finglass, P. (2021a), 'Sappho on the Papyri', in P. Finglass and A. Kelly (eds), *The Cambridge Companion to Sappho*, Cambridge: Cambridge University Press.
Finglass, P. (2021b), 'Editions of Sappho since the Renaissance', in P. Finglass and A. Kelly (eds), *The Cambridge Companion to Sappho*, Cambridge: Cambridge University Press.
Finglass, P. and A. Kelly, eds (2021), *The Cambridge Companion to Sappho*, Cambridge: Cambridge University Press.
Finzi, G., ed. (1996), S. Quasimodo, *Poesie e discorsi sulla poesia*, 10th edn, Milan: Mondadori.
Finzi, G. (2002), 'Catullo-Quasimodo', in P. Frassica (ed.), *Salvatore Quasimodo nel vento del Mediterraneo*, 13–20, Novara: Interlinea.
Fiorentino, L. (1965), 'Pascoli traduttore e riduttore', in M. Biagini (ed.) *Pascoli: atti del convegno nazionale di studi pascoliani, San Mauro Pascoli 11-12-13 maggio 1962*, 87–103, Santarcangelo di Romagna: Maggioli.
Fisher, J. (2015), 'Anne Carson's Stereoscopic Poetics', in J. M. Wilkinson (ed.), *Anne Carson: Ecstatic Lyre*, 10–16, Ann Arbor: University of Michigan Press.
Fisher, M. (2005), *Ezra Pound's Third Opera: Collis O Heliconii*, Emeryville: Second Evening Art.
Fitzgerald, R. (1995), *Catullan Provocations: Lyric Poetry and the Drama of Position*, Berkeley: University of California Press.
Fleres, U. (1929), Catullo, *Carmi*, Milan: Istituto Editoriale Italiano.
Flint, F. S. (1912), 'Canzoni by Ezra Pound', *The Poetry Review*, 1(1): 28.
Flora, F. (1936), *La poesia ermetica*, Rome and Bari: Laterza.
Flora, F. (1955), 'Classicità e impressionismo nella poesia del Pascoli', *Convivium*, n.s. (6): 641–50.
Flora, F. (1967), Giacomo Leopardi, *Zibaldone di pensieri*, 2 vols, Milan: Mondadori.
Fo, A., ed. (2018), *Gaio Valerio Catullo. Le poesie*, Turin: Einaudi.
Fordyce, C. J., (1961), *Catullus: A Commentary*, Oxford: Clarendon.
Fortini, F. (1976), 'Montale e la poesia dell'esistenzialismo storico', in *La letteratura italiana: storia e testi*, 10 vols, X (2), 347–430, Rome and Bari: Laterza.
Fozzer, G. (2006), 'Il ritorno di Saffo', *La riviera*, 24 September: 32.
Fraccaroli, G. (1910–13), *Lirici greci*, 2 vols, Turin: Fratelli Bocca.
Franco, T. and C. Piantanida (2008), 'Introduction', in T. Franco and C. Piantanida (eds), *Echoing Voices in Italian Literature: Tradition and Translation in the Twentieth Century*, viii–xviii, Newcastle-upon-Tyne: Cambridge Scholars.
Franklin, R. W., ed. (1999), *The Poems of Emily Dickinson*, Cambridge MA: Harvard University Press.
Frattini, A. (2002), 'Salvatore Quasimodo a un ventennio dal Nobel', in *Avventure di Parnaso nell'Italia del Novecento*, 5 vols, IV, 1001–8, Viareggio: Baroni.
Frazer, J. ([1880] 1994), *The Golden Bough*, Oxford: Oxford University Press.
Gaisser, J. H. (1993), *Catullus and his Renaissance Readers*, Oxford: Clarendon.
Gaisser, J. H., ed. (2007), *Catullus*, Oxford Readings in Classical Studies, Oxford: Oxford University Press.

Gaisser, J. H. (2009), *Catullus*, Blackwell Introductions to the Classical World, Oxford: Blackwell.

Galatà, F. (2016), 'Progettualità e poesia del giovane Pascoli. I «lavori artistici» di Matera', *RP*, 28: 49–70.

Garboli, C. (1997), 'Pascoli Lesbico', *Paragone: Letteratura*, 11–12: 3–8.

Garboli, C., ed. (2002), *Poesie e prose scelte di Giovanni Pascoli*, 2 vols, Milan: Mondadori.

Gardini, N. (2000), *L'antico, il nuovo, lo straniero nella lirica moderna: esempi da una storia della poesia*, Milan: Edizioni dall'Arco.

Gardini, N., trans. (2014), Catullo, *Carmina: il libro delle poesie*, Milan: Feltrinelli.

Gargiulo, A. (1933), 'Idea di lirica', in E. Falqui and A. Capasso (eds), *Il fiore della lirica italiana*, i–xiii, Lanciano: Carabba.

Gentile, G. (1920), 'Il torto e il diritto delle traduzioni', *Rivista di Cultura*, 1: 8–11.

Gentili, B. (1966), 'La veneranda Saffo', *Quaderni Urbinati di Cultura Classica*, 2: 37–62.

Ghelli, M. L., ed. (2007), 'Carteggio Pascoli-De Bosis', in M. L. Ghelli and C. Cevolani (eds), *Carteggio Pascoli-De Bosis. Carteggio Pascoli-Bianchi*, 1–157, Bologna: Patron.

Giannini, P. (2010), 'Le traduzioni metriche di G. Pascoli', in A. Carrozzini (ed.), *Teorie e forme del tradurre in versi dall'Ottocento fino a Carducci: atti del convegno internazionale, Lecce, 2–4 ottobre 2009*, 379–96, Lecce: Congedo.

Gibellini, P. (1990), 'Saffo, Catullo & Co.', in T. Kemeny (ed.), *Dicibilità del sublime*, 209–16, Udine: Campanotto.

Gigante, M. (1968), 'Invito allo studio dei risultati papirologici (Sul testo della Seconda Ode di Saffo)', *Cultura e Scuola*, 28: 30–41.

Gilbert, S. (1986), 'Mephistopheles in Maine: Rereading "Skunk Hour"', in S. G. Axelrod and H. Deese (eds), *Robert Lowell: Essays on the Poetry*, 70–9, Cambridge: Cambridge University Press.

Gioseffi, M., ed. (2010), *Uso, riuso ed abuso dei testi classici*, Milan: LED.

Girard, R. ([1961] 1965), *Deceit, Desire and the Novel: Self and Other in Literary Structure*, trans. Y. Freccero, Baltimore and London: Johns Hopkins University Press.

Giroux, R., ed. (1987), R. Lowell, *Collected Prose*, London: Faber and Faber.

Giustiniani, V. R. (1979), *Neulateinische Dichtung in Italien 1850–1950: Ein Unerforschtes Kapitel Italienischer Literatur-und Geistesgeschichte*, Tübingen: Max Niemeyer Verlag.

Gizzi, C. (1991), *Omaggio a Saffo. Variazioni*, Milan: Electa.

Gladhill, B. (2016), *Rethinking Roman Alliance: A Study in Poetics and Society*, Cambridge: Cambridge University Press.

Goff, B. and K. Harloe (2021), 'Sappho in the Twentieth Century and Beyond', in P. Finglass and A. Kelly (eds), *The Cambridge Companion to Sappho*, Cambridge: Cambridge University Press.

Goldschmidt, N. (2019), '"Orts, Scraps, and Fragments"': Translation, Non-Translation, and the Fragments of Ancient Greece', in J. Harding and J. Nash (eds), *Modernism and Non-Translation*, 49–66, Oxford: Oxford University Press.

Goold, J. P., ed. (2017) *Catullus, Tibullus and Pervigilium Veneris*, Cambridge MA: Harvard University Press.

Gordon, D. M., ed. (1994), *Ezra Pound and James Laughlin: Selected Letters*, New York: Norton.
Gram, L. M. (2019), '*Odi et Amo*: On Lesbia's Name in Catullus', in S. T. Thorsen and S. Harrison (eds), *Roman Receptions of Sappho*, 95–118, Oxford: Oxford University Press.
Greene, E. (1999), 'Re-figuring the Feminine Voice: Catullus Translating Sappho', *Arethusa*, 32(1): 1–18.
Greene, E., ed. (2006), *Re-reading Sappho: Reception and Transmission*, Berkeley: University of California Press.
Greene, E. (2007), 'Catullus and Sappho', in M. Skinner (ed.), *A Companion to Catullus*, 131–50, Oxford: Blackwell.
Greene, E. and M. Skinner, eds (2009), *The New Sappho on Old Age: Textual and Philosophical Issues*, Cambridge MA: Harvard University Press.
Greenfield, R. (2015), '"Parts of Time Fall on Her": Anne Carson's *Men in the Off Hours*', in J. M. Wilkinson (ed.), *Anne Carson: Ecstatic Lyre*, 94–100, Ann Arbor: University of Michigan Press.
Gregory, E. (1986), 'Rose Cut in Rock: Sappho and H.D.'s *Sea Garden*', *Contemporary Literature*, 27(4): 525–52.
Gregory, E. (1987), 'Scarlet Experience: H.D.'s *Hymen*', *Sagetrieb*, 6: 77–100.
Gregory, E. (1988), 'Falling from the White Rock: A Myth of Margins in H.D.', *Agenda*, 25(3–4): 113–23.
Gregory, E. (1997), *H.D. and Hellenism: Classic Lines*, Cambridge: Cambridge University Press.
Gubar, S. (1984), 'Sapphistries', *Signs*, 10(1): 43–62.
Guidorizzi, G. (2007) *Saffo: 82 poesie*, Milan: Mondadori.
H.D. ([1919] 1982), *Notes on Thought and Vision and The Wise Sappho*, San Francisco: City Light Books.
H.D. (1919), 'Hymen', *Poetry*, 15(3): 117–29.
H.D. (1974), *Tribute to Freud*, Boston: D.R. Godine.
H.D. (1979), *End to Torment: A Memoir of Ezra Pound*, ed. H. Pearson, N. and M. King, Manchester: Carcanet New Press.
H.D. (1988), 'Letter to Norman Pearson', *Agenda*, 25(3–4): 71–6.
Hale, W. G. (1919), 'Pegasus Impounded', *Poetry*, 14(1), April: 52–5.
Hamilton, S., ed. (2005), *The Letters of Robert Lowell*, London: Faber.
Harrison, J. E. ([1903] 1922), *Prolegomena to the Study of Greek Religion*, Cambridge: Cambridge University Press.
Hatlen, B. (1979), 'Zukofsky as Translator', in C. F. Terrell (ed.), *Louis Zukofsky: Man and Poet*, 345–64, Orono: National Poetry Foundation.
Hersch, K. (2010), *The Roman Wedding: Ritual and Meaning in Antiquity*, Cambridge: Cambridge University Press.
Hexter, R. (2015), 'The Kisses of Juventius, and Policing the Boundaries of Masculinity: The Case of Catullus', in J. Ingleheart (ed.), *Ancient Rome and the Construction of Modern Homosexual Identities*, 273–88, Oxford: Oxford University Press.

Hiley, F. W. C. and J. Lindsay (1929), *Catulli carmina*, London.
Hobsbaum, P. (1988), *A Reader's Guide to Robert Lowell*, London: Thames and Hudson.
Hobsbawm, E. (1994), *The Age of Extremes: A History of the World (1914-91)*, New York: Pantheon Books.
Holquist, M. (2011), 'World literature and Philology, in T. D'haen, D. Damrosch and D. Kadir (eds), *The Routledge Companion to World Literature*, 147-57, New York: Routledge.
Hooley, D. M. (1988), *The Classics in Paraphrase: Ezra Pound and Modern Translators of Latin Poetry*, Selinsgrove: Susquehanna University Press.
Hooper, R. W. (1985), 'In Defense of Catullus' Dirty Sparrow', *Greece and Rome*, 2nd ser., 32(2): 162-78.
Horáček, J. (2014), 'Pedantry and Play: The Zukofsky's *Catullus*', *Comparative Literature Studies*, 51(1), Special Issue: *Poetry Games*: 106-31.
Hudson-Williams, T. (1925), 'Review: Diehl's *Anthologia Lyrica*', *The Classical Review*, 39: 182-3.
Intoppa, L. (2002a), 'Le traduzioni italiane di Catullo dal 1977 al 2001', *Atene e Roma*, n.s. 47(1): 18-36.
Intoppa, L. (2002b), 'Le traduzioni italiane di Catullo dal 1977 al 2001, II', *Atene e Roma*, n.s. 47 (2-3): 49-79.
Jaeger, W. (1939-45), *Paideia: The Ideals of Greek Culture*, trans. Gilbert Highet, 3 vols, Oxford: Blackwell.
Jervolino, D. (2003), 'Croce, Gentile e Gramsci sulla traduzione', in G. Cacciatore, G. Cotroneo and R. Viti Cavaliere (eds), *Croce filosofo. Atti del convegno internazionale di studi in occasione del 50 anniversario della morte*, 2 vols, II, 431-41, Soveria Mannelli: Rubbettino.
Johnson, M. (2012), 'The role of Eros in Improving the Pupil, or What Socrates learned from Sappho', in *Alcibiades and the Socratic Lover-Educator*, 7-29, London: Bristol Classical Press.
Joyce, J. ([1922] 1993), *Ulysses*, Oxford: Oxford University Press.
Joyce, J. ([1939] 2002), *Finnegans Wake*, London: Faber and Faber.
Kenner, H. (1968), 'The Muse in Tatters', *Arion*, 7(2): 212-33.
Kenner, H. (1985), 'Ezra Pound's *Commedia*', in S. Y. McDougal (ed.), *Dante Among the Moderns*, 39-56, Chapel Hill: University of North Carolina Press.
Kenner, H. (1991), *The Pound Era*, London: Pimlico.
Kingsley, J., ed. (1958), *The Poems of John Dryden*, 4 vols, Oxford: Cambridge University Press.
Kunitz, S. (1964), 'Talk with Robert Lowell', *The New York Times*, 4 October: 34-8.
La Penna, A. (1946), '*Il fiore delle Georgiche* di Salvatore Quasimodo; *Catullus Veronensis Carmina* by Salvatore Quasimodo', *Belfagor*, 1(1), January: 136-7.
Laity, C. (1996), *H.D. and the Victorian Fin de Siècle: Gender, Modernism, Decadence*, Cambridge: Cambridge University Press.
Lavagnini, B. (1936), *Aglaia*, Paravia.
Lecomte, Y. (1968), *Il gioco degli astragali*, trans. S. Quasimodo, Milan: Moneta.

Lefevere, A. (1975), *Translating Poetry: Seven Strategies and a Blueprint*, Amsterdam: Van Gorcum.
Leland, B. (1992), '"Siete Voi Qui, Ser Brunetto?": Dante's Inferno 15 as a Modernist Topic Place', *ELH*, 59(4): 965–86.
Lenchantin de Gubernatis, M. (1958), *Il libro di Catullo*, Turin: Loescher.
Lenisa, M. G. (2004), *Saffo chimera*, Foggia: Bastogi.
Leopardi, G. ([1837] 1984), *Canti. Edizione critica e autografi*, ed. D. De Robertis, Milan: Polifilo.
Leopardi, G. ([1842] 1969), *Paralipomeni della Batracomiomachia*, in *Tutte le opere*, ed. W. Binni, 2 vols, I, 247–92, Florence: Sansoni.
Lipking, L. (1988), *Abandoned Women and Poetic Tradition*, Chicago and London: The University of Chicago Press.
Lorenzini, N. (1999), *La poesia italiana del novecento*, Bologna: Il Mulino.
Lorenzini, N. (2004), 'Postfazione', in S. Quasimodo, *Lirici greci*, ed. N. Lorenzini, 219–75, Milan: Mondadori.
Lovatin, F. (2017), 'Sul tavolo di Pascoli traduttore. Prove inedite da Virgilio e Catullo', in *Pascoli e le vie della tradizione. Atti del convegno internazionale di studi. Catania, 3-5 dicembre 2012*, 213–25, Messina: Centro internazionale di studi umanistici.
Lowell, R. (1953), 'Epitaph of a Fallen Poet', *Partisan Review*, 20: 39.
Lowell, R. (1969), *Notebook: 1967–68*, New York: Farrar, Straus and Giroux.
Lowell, R. (1970), *Notebook*, London: Faber and Faber.
Lunardi, E. and R. Nugent, trans. (1979), *Giovanni Pascoli: Convivial Poems*, 2 vols, Plainseville: Lake Erie College Press.
Luperini, R. (1981), *Il Novecento*, 2 vols, Turin: Loescher.
Mackay, P. (2010), 'H.D.'s Modernism', in J. Christodoulides and P. Mackay (eds), *The Cambridge Companion to H.D.*, 51–62, Cambridge: Cambridge University Press.
Macrì, O. ([1938] 1969), 'La poetica della parola e Salvatore Quasimodo', in G. Finzi (ed.), *Quasimodo e la critica*, 43–87, Milan: Mondadori.
Macrì, O. ([1954] 1956), 'Saffo e Omero', in *Caratteri e figure della poesia italiana contemporanea*, 127–39, Florence: Vallecchi.
Maggel, A. (2010), 'Tithonus and Phaon: Mythical Allegories of Light and Darkness in Sappho's Poetry', in M. Christopoulos, E. D. Karakantza and O. Levaniouk (eds), *Light and Darkness in Ancient Greek Myth and Religion*, 121–32, Lanham: Lexington.
Maier, C. (2000), 'Consigning the Twentieth Century to History: Alternative Narratives for the Modern Era', *The American Historical Review*, 105(3): 807–31.
Maio, S. (2005), *Creating Another Self: Voice in Modern American Personal Poetry*, 2nd edn, Kirksville: Truman State University Press.
Mandruzzato, E., trans. (2001), Catullo, *Canti*, Milan: BUR.
Marcolini, M. (1991), 'Gli "Elementi di Letteratura" di Giovanni Pascoli', *Lettere italiane*, 43(1): 55–80.

Marconi, G. (2012), *Saffo: Frammenti*, Alessandria: Edizioni dell'Orso.
Mariani, P. (1996), *Lost Puritan: A Life of Robert Lowell*, New York: Norton.
Martindale, C. (1999), 'Foreword to the 1999 edition', in K. Quinn ([1959] 1999), *The Catullan Revolution*, vii–xxvii, 2nd edn, Bristol: Bristol Classical Press.
Martini, S. (2003), 'Dal Carducci antologista al Pascoli antologista', *Studi e Problemi di Critica Testuale*, 1: 129–61.
Martz, L. L., ed. (1986), *H.D. Collected Poems: 1912–44*, New York: New Directions.
Mascioni, G. (1981), *Saffo*, Milan: Rusconi.
Mazza, E. (1962), Catullo, *Carmi*, Parma: Guanda.
McCleery, A. (2014), 'The Book in the Long Twentieth Century', in L. Howsam (ed.), The *Cambridge Companion to the History of the Book*, Cambridge: Cambridge University Press.
Melillo, J. (2015), 'Sappho and the "Papyrological Event"', in J. M. Wilkinson (ed.), *Anne Carson: Ecstatic Lyre*, 188–193, Ann Arbor: University of Michigan Press.
Mendelsohn, D. (2012), 'In Search of Sappho (Anne Carson's *If Not, Winter*)', in *Waiting for the Barbarians: Essays from the Classics to Pop Culture*, 121–38, New York: New York Review of Books.
Mengaldo, P. V. (1978), *Poeti italiani del Novecento*, Milan: Mondadori.
Merini, A. and E. Baj (1999–2000), *L'uovo di Saffo*, Belluno: Colophonarte.
Meyers, J. (2011), 'Robert Lowell and the Classics', *The Kenyon Review*, New Series. 33(4): 173–200.
Michelakis, P. (2009), 'Greek Lyric from the Renaissance to the Eighteenth Century', in F. Budelmann (ed.), *The Cambridge Companion to Greek Lyric*, 336–51, Cambridge: Cambridge University Press.
Miller, P. A. (1994), *Lyric Texts and Lyric Consciousness: The Birth of a Genre from Archaic Greece to Augustan Rome*, London: Routledge.
Montale, E. (1948), *Quaderno di traduzioni*, Milan: Edizioni della Meridiana.
Morelli, A. M. (2018), 'Il disunito filo che ci unisce. La traduzione catulliana di Enzo Mazza', *Paideia*, 73: 175–202.
Morelli, A. M. (2015), 'Catullo, o il *lepos* "impossibile" del secondo novecento italiano (Quasimodo e gli altri)', in F. Condello and A. Rodighiero (eds), *Un compito infinito. Testi classici e traduzioni d'autore nel Novecento italiano*, 153–78, Bologna: Bononia University Press.
Moretti, F. (2000), 'Conjectures on World Literature', *New Left Review*, 1: 54–68.
Müller, K. O., (1866), *Histoire de la littérature grecque jusqu'à Alexandre le Grand, par Otfried Müller, traduite, annotée [. . .] par K. Hillebrand,* 2 vols, Paris: August Durand.
Müller, M. (1862), *Lectures on the Science of Language: Delivered at the Royal Institution of Great Britain in April, May & June 1861*, 2nd edn, London: Longman, Green, Longman and Roberts.
Müller, M. (1870), *Introduction to the Science of Religion: Four Lectures Delivered at the Royal Institution in February and March 1879*, London: Spottiswoode & Co.

Musolino, G., ed. (2003), *I poeti devono soffrire: lettere a Giuseppe Susini (1934–50)*, Trento: Nicolodi.
Mynors, R. A. B., ed. (1958), *C. Valerii Catulli Carmina*, Oxford: Clarendon.
Nagy, G. (1973), 'Phaeton, Sappho's Phaon, and the White Rock of Leukas', *Harvard Studies in Classical Philology*, 77: 137–77
Nava, G. (1984), 'Pascoli e il folklore', *Giornale Storico della Letteratura Italiana*, 161: 507–43.
Nava, G. (2008), 'Introduzione', in G. Pascoli, *Poemi conviviali*, ed. G. Nava, vii–xx, Turin: Einaudi.
Nencioni, G., (1942) 'Da Matera a Bologna: lettere inedite di Giovanni Pascoli', *Nuova Antologia*, 1 December: 148–53.
Neri, C. and F. Cinti (2017), *Saffo: Poesie, frammenti e testimonianze*, Milan: Rusconi Libri.
Norden, E. (2002), *Dio ignoto: ricerche sulla storia della forma religiosa*, ed. C. T. Moreschini, Brescia: Morcelliana.
Oderman, K. (1986), *Ezra Pound and the Erotic Medium*, Durham: Duke University Press.
Paige, D. D., ed. (1950), *The Letters of Ezra Pound, 1907–41*, New York: Harcourt.
Paoli, C. (2016), *Greek Tragedy in Twentieth-Century Italian Literature: The Poetic Translations of Camillo Sbarbaro and Giovanna Bemporad*, DPhil Thesis, University of Oxford, Oxford.
Paparelli, G. (1969), 'Quasimodo e la critica', in G. Finzi (ed.), *Quasimodo e la critica*, 249–69, Milan: Mondadori.
Paradiso, A. (1993), 'Saffo, la poetessa', in N. Loreaux (ed.), *Grecia al femminile*, 40–70, Rome and Bari: Laterza.
Pascoli, G., ([1882] 2004), *Alceo. Tesi per la laurea*, in *Prose disperse*, ed. G. Capecchi, 79–97, Lanciano: Carabba.
Pascoli, G. ([1892–1903] 1974), *Myricae*, ed. G. Nava, 2 vols, Florence: Sansoni.
Pascoli, G., ([1894] 2002), 'Prefazione da *Lyra romana* (1894)', in *Poesie e prose scelte di Giovanni Pascoli*, ed. C. Garboli, 2 vols, I, 1042–51, Milan: Mondadori.
Pascoli, G. (1895), 'Solon', *Il Convito*, 3, April [= 1904: 5–8].
Pascoli, G. (1898), *Minerva oscura*, Livorno: Giusti.
Pascoli, G. ([1899] 1915), *Lyra*, 5th edn, Livorno: Giusti.
Pascoli, G. ([1900] 1910), *Fior da Fiore*, 6th edn, Milan: Sandron.
Pascoli, G. (1900), *Sotto il velame*, Messina: Vincenzo Muglia.
Pascoli, G. ([1901] 1924), 'Nota per gli insegnanti' (1901), in G. Pascoli ([1901] 1924), *Sul limitare: prose e poesie scelte per la scuola italiana*, 4th edn, xxix–xxxi, Milan: Sandron.
Pascoli, G., (1902), *La mirabile visione*, Messina: Vincenzo Muglia.
Pascoli, G. ([1903] 1907), *Canti di Castelvecchio*, Bologna: Zanichelli.
Pascoli, G. (1904), *Poemi conviviali*, Bologna: Zanichelli.
Pascoli, G. ([1904–5] 2008), *Poemi conviviali*, ed. G. Nava, Turin: Einaudi.

Pascoli, G. ([1904] 1997), *Primi poemetti*, ed. N. Ebani, Parma: Guanda.
Pascoli, G. ([1907] 1914), *Pensieri e discorsi. MDCCCXCV–MDCMIV*, 2nd edn, Bologna: Zanichelli.
Pascoli, M., ed. ([1913] 1923), *Traduzioni e riduzioni di Giovanni Pascoli*, Bologna: Zanichelli.
Pascoli, M. ([1933] 1943), *Giovanni Pascoli. Limpido rivo*, Milan: Mondadori.
Pascoli, M. (1961), *Lungo la vita di Giovanni Pascoli*. Milan: Mondadori.
Pasquali, G. (1920), 'Classici e antichi, traduzioni e commenti', in *Filologia e Storia*, 35–8, Florence: Le Monnier.
Pavolini, C. (1940), 'Parliamo dell'ermetismo', *Primato*, 1(7), 1 June: 7–10.
Pecci, G. (1958), 'Il Pascoli antologista e le sue relazioni col Carducci e col D'Annunzio', *Studi pascoliani*: 141–78.
Perez-Sanchez, G. (2014), 'Gay and Lesbian Literature from Spain in the Long Twentieth Century (1898–2007)', in E. L. McCallum and M. Tuhkanen (eds), *The Cambridge History of Gay and Lesbian Literature*, 438–58, Cambridge: Cambridge University Press.
Perloff, M. (1970), 'Realism and the Confessional Mode of Robert Lowell', *Contemporary Literature*, 11(4): 470–87.
Perugi, M., ed. (1981), *Giovanni Pascoli: Opere*, 2 vols, Milan: Ricciardi.
Perugi, M., ed. (1982), G. Pascoli, *Dai Canti di Castelvecchio*, Milan: Il Saggiatore.
Perugi, M. (1984), 'Fra Dante e Sully: Elementi di estetica pascoliana', in E. Sanguineti et al. (eds), *Giovanni Pascoli. Poesia e poetica. Atti del Convegno di studi pascoliani: San Mauro, 1-2-3 aprile 1982*, 383–410, Rimini: Maggioli.
Petrucciani, M. (1986), 'Quasimodo Ermetico', in *Quasimodo e l'ermetismo: atti del I incontro di studio, 15–16 febbraio 1984, Modica*, 21–39, Modica: Centro Nazionale di Studi su Salvatore Quasimodo.
Petrucciani, M., (1955), *La poetica dell'ermetismo italiano*, Turin: Loescher.
Pianigiani, O. (1926), *Dizionario etimologico della lingua italiana*, 2nd edn, Florence: Ariani.
Piantanida, C. (2013), 'Pascoli and Sappho: Two Unpublished Manuscripts', *Filologia Italiana*, 10: 181–214.
Piantanida, C. (2015), 'Le varie facce della luna nella poesia di Giovanni Pascoli: tradizione, mito ed esoterismo', *Griseldaonline*, 14(7). Available at: https://griseldaonline.unibo.it/article/view/9178 (accessed 3 October 2019).
Piantanida, C. (2021), 'Early Modern and Modern German, Italian, and Spanish Sapphos', in P. Finglass and A. Kelly (eds), *The Cambridge Companion to Sappho*, Cambridge: Cambridge University Press.
Pontani, F. M., trans. (1969), *Lirici greci*, Turin: Einaudi.
Pontani, F. M. (1977), 'Un secolo di traduzioni da Catullo', *Rivista di cultura classica e medievale*, 25: 625–44.
Pound, E. ([1910-29] 2005), *The Spirit of Romance*, ed. R. Sieburth, New York: New Directions.

Pound, E. (1913), 'A Few Don'ts by an Imagiste', *Poetry*, 1(6): 200–6 = Pound, E. (1954), *Literary Essays of Ezra Pound*, ed. T. S. Eliot, 4–8, London: Faber.
Pound, E., ed. (1914), *Des Imagistes: An Anthology*, New York: Albert and Charles Boni.
Pound, E. (1916), 'O Atthis', *Poetry*, 8: 276.
Pound, E. (1917), 'Three Cantos', *Poetry*, 10(4): 180–8.
Pound, E. (1917), *Lustra*, New York: Alfred A. Knopf.
Pound, E. (1935), *Make it New*, New Haven: Yale University Press.
Pound, E. (1954), *Literary Essays*, ed. T. S. Eliot, London: Faber.
Pound, E. (1960), *ABC of Reading*, New York: New Directions.
Pound, E. (1972), 'Letters to Viola Baxter Jordan: Edited with Commentary by Donald Gallup', *Paideuma*, 1(1): 107–11.
Pound, E. (1973), 'I Gather the Limbs of Osiris', in W. Cookson (ed.), *Selected Prose of Ezra Pound*, 19–44, London: Faber.
Pound, E. (1980), 'Arthur Symons', *Agenda*, 17–18: 54–7.
Pound, E. ([1986] 1996), *The Cantos*, New York: New Directions.
Prins, Y. (1999), *Victorian Sappho*, Princeton: Princeton University Press.
Quasimodo, A., ed. (1985), S. Quasimodo, *Lettere d'amore: 1936–59*, Milan: Spirali.
Quasimodo, S., trans. (1939a), 'A Sirmio', *Corrente*, 2 (17), 30 September: 2.
Quasimodo, S., trans. (1939b), 'A Quinto Ortensio Ortalo', *Corrente*, 2 (20), 15 November: 4.
Quasimodo, S. ([1940] 2004), *Lirici greci*, ed. N. Lorenzini, Milan: Mondadori.
Quasimodo, S. (1945), *Catullus Veronensis Carmina*, Milan: Edizioni di Uomo.
Quasimodo, S., trans. (1946), Sofocle, *Edipo re*, Milan: Bompiani.
Quasimodo, S., trans. (1946), *Il Vangelo secondo Giovanni*, Milan: Gentile.
Quasimodo, trans. (1949), *Le coefore di Eschilo*, Milan: Bompiani.
Quasimodo, S., trans. (1954), Sofocle, *Elettra*, Milan: Mondadori.
Quasimodo, S., trans. (1955), V. Catullo, *Canti*, Milan: Mondadori.
Quasimodo, S., trans. (1958), *Tartufo di Molière*, Milan: Bompiani.
Quasimodo, S. (1960), *Il poeta e il politico e altri saggi*, Milan: Schwarz.
Quasimodo, S., trans. (1966), *Antonio e Cleopatra di Shakespeare*, Milan: Mondadori.
Quinn, K. ([1959] 1999), *The Catullan Revolution*, 2nd edn, Bristol: Bristol Classical Press.
Quinn, K. (1963), *Latin Explorations: Critical Studies in Roman Literature*, London: Routledge and Kegan Paul.
Raffel, B. (1969), 'No Tidbit Love You Outdoors Far as a Bier', *Arion*, 8: 441.
Raffo, S. (2012), *Saffo: Antologia lirica*, Busto Arsizio: Nomos Edizioni.
Ramat, S. (1969), *L'ermetismo*, Florence: La Nuova Italia.
Ramazani, J. (2009), *A Transnational Poetics*, Chicago: University of Chicago Press.
Ramous, M. (1971), *Catullo Virgilio Orazio*, Bologna.
Re, L. (1998), 'Mythic Revisionism', in M. O. Marotti (ed.), *Italian Women Writers from the Renaissance to the Present: Revising the Canon*, 187–236, University Park: Pennsylvania State University Press.

Reeser, T. W. (2015), *Setting Plato Straight: Translating Ancient Sexuality in the Renaissance*, Chicago: University of Chicago Press.
Reynolds, M. (2000), *The Sappho Companion*, London: Vintage.
Reynolds, M. (2003), *The Sappho History*, Basingstoke: Macmillan.
Reynolds, M. (2011), *The Poetry of Translation: from Chaucer and Petrarch to Homer and Logue*, Oxford: Oxford University Press.
Reynolds, M. (2016), *Translation: A Very Short Introduction*, Oxford: Oxford University Press.
Reynolds, M. (2020), 'Introduction', in Reynolds, M. (ed.), *Prismatic Translation*, 1–18, Cambridge: Legenda.
Riera, C. (1975), *Te deix, amor, la mar com a penyora*, Barcelona: Editorial Laia.
Rilke, R. M. (1907), *Neue Gedichte*, Leipzig: Insel-Verlag.
Riobó, C. (2002), 'The Spirit of Ezra Pound's Romance Philology: Dante's Ironic Legacy of the Contingencies of Value', *Comparative Literature Studies*, 39(3): 201–22.
Rissman, L. (1983), *Love and War: Homeric Allusion in the Poetry of Sappho*, Königstein: Anton Hain.
Robinson, C. E. (1965), 'Multas per Gentes', *Greece and Rome*, 12: 62–3.
Robsinson, E. (2015), 'An Antipoem that Condenses Everything: Anne Carson's Translations of the Fragments of Sappho', in J. M. Wilkinson (ed.), *Anne Carson: Ecstatic Lyre*, 181–7, Ann Arbor: University of Michigan Press.
Rocco, C., ed. (2010), *Saffo: Afrodite*, Florence: Barbès.
Rognoni, F. (2019), 'Lowell and Ungaretti: Imitations and Beyond', in T. Austenfeld (ed.), *Robert Lowell in A New Century: European and American Perspectives*, 117–30, New York: Camden House.
Rosenthal, M. L. ([1959] 1999), 'Poetry as Confession', in S. G. Axelrod (ed.), *The Critical Response to Robert Lowell*, 64–8, Westport: Greenwood Publishing.
Rosenthal, M. L. (1967), *The New Poets: American and British Poetry since World War II*, Oxford: Oxford University Press.
Rossi, M., ed. (1983), *Saffo: Canti e frammenti*, Verona: Il gatto e la volpe.
Rossi, M., ed. (2000), *Saffo. Frammenti: ora tu ami un altro*, Colognola ai Colli: Demetra.
Rundle, C. (2010), *Publishing Translations in Fascist Italy*, Oxford: Peter Lang.
Ruskin, J. (1956), *La bibbia di Amiens*, trans. S. Quasimodo, Milan: Bompiani.
Saggio, C. (1928), *Il libro di Catullo*, Alpes.
Salibra, E. (1985), *Salvatore Quasimodo*, Rome: Edizioni dell'Ateneo.
Salibra, E. (2005), 'Modelli letterari e modelli linguistici nelle antologie italiane', in *Voci in fuga: poeti italiani del primo novecento*, 87–126, Naples: Liguori.
Sanders, E., C. Thumiger, C. Carey and N. J. Lowe, eds (2013), *Erôs in Ancient Greece*, Oxford: Oxford University Press.
Sanguineti, E. (1969), *Poesia italiana del Novecento*, 2 vols, Turin: Einaudi.
Sanguineti, E. (2002), *Il gatto lupesco. Poesie (1982–2001)*, Milan: Feltrinelli.
Santagata, M., ed. (1996), F. Petrarca, *Canzoniere*, Milan: Mondadori.
Savino, E., ed. (2002), *Saffo: Liriche e frammenti*, trans. S. Quasimodo and E. Savino, Milan: SE.

Savoca, G. (1986), 'Per Quasimodo traduttore di Catullo: Il Carme LXV', in *Quasimodo e l'ermetismo. Atti del 1° incontro di studio, 15–16 febbraio, Palazzo dei Mercedari, Modica*, 103–23, Modica: Centro nazionale di studi su Salvatore Quasimodo.
Schinetti, P. (1912), 'Pagine inedite di Giovanni Pascoli', *Il Secolo XX*, May: 377–92.
Schopenhauer, A. ([1818–44] 1909), *The World as Will and Idea*, ed. R. B. Haldane and J. Kemp, 7th edn, London: Kegan Paul, Trench, Trübner & Co.
Schwabe, L. (1862), *Quaestiones Catullianae*, Giessen: Ricker.
Scroggins, M. (1998), *Louis Zukofsky and the Poetry of Knowledge*, Tuscaloosa and London: University of Alabama Press.
Seibert, B. (2012), 'Movement Transforms a Poet's Elegy', *The New York Times*, 13, May. Available at: www.nytimes.com/2012/05/14/arts/dance/rashaun-mitchell-choreographs-nox-at-danspace-project.html?src=recg&_r=0 (accessed 26 May 2020).
Shtrimer, N. (2002), 'Futurist Books', in *Natalia Goncharova: the Russian Years*, 189–220, St Petersburg: Palace Editions.
Siciliani, L. (1906), 'I *Poemi conviviali* di Giovanni Pascoli', *Atene e Roma*, 90–1: 161–91.
Sieburth, R., ed. (2003), *Ezra Pound: Poems and Translations*, New York: Library of America.
Sieburth, R., (2005), 'Introduction', in E. Pound ([1910–29] 2005), *The Spirit of Romance*, vii–xii, New York: New Directions.
Simpson, C. J. and B. G. Simpson (1989), 'Catullus 46', *Latomus*, 48: 75–85.
Sinigaglia, G., trans. (2006), *Saffo: Poesie*, Acquaviva.
Siracusano, A. (2008), *Saffo: La dolce eresia di Eros*, Siena: Barbera.
Skinner, M., ed. (2007), 'Introduction', in Skinner, M. (ed.), *A Companion to Catullus*, 1–11, Oxford: Blackwell.
Skinner, M. (2011), *Clodia Metelli: The Tribune's Sister*, Oxford: Oxford University Press.
Skinner, M. (2015), 'A Review of Scholarship on Catullus 1985–15', *Lustrum*, 57: 91–360.
Snell, B. (1946), *Die Entdeckung des Geistes. Studien zur Entstehung des europäischen Denkens bei den Griechen*, Hamburg: Verlag Classen und Goverts.
Snell, B. (1953), *The Discovery of the Mind: The Greek Origins of European Thought*, trans. T.G. Rosenmeyer, Oxford: Blackwell.
Stanford Friedman, S. and R. Blau DuPlessis (1990), *Signets: Reading H.D.*, Madison: University of Wisconsin Press.
Stead, H. (2016), *A Cockney Catullus: The Reception of Catullus in Romantic Britain, 1795–1821*, Oxford: Oxford University Press.
Stearns, P. (2009), 'Long 19th Century? Long 20th? Retooling That Last Chunk of World History Periodization', *The History Teacher*, 42(2): 223–8.
Steiner, G. (2012), 'Anne Carson "translates" Antigone', *TLS*, 1 August. Available at: www.the-tls.co.uk/articles/public/anne-carson-translates-antigone/ (accessed 26 May 2020).
Steiner, G., ([1975] 1988), *After Babel: Aspects of Language and Translation*, London, 3rd edn, Oxford: Oxford University Press.
Stigers, S. E. (1977), 'Retreat from the Male: Catullus 62 and Sappho's Erotic Flowers', *Ramus*, 6: 83–102.

Sully, J. (1898), *Études sur l'enfance*, trans. A. Monod, ed. F. Alcan, Paris.
Symons, A. (1913), *Knave of Hearts: 1894–1908*, Lane Company.
Talbot, J. (2006), '"The Roman Frankness": Robert Lowell and the Classics', *International Journal of the Classical Tradition*, 13(2): 267–80.
Tarlo, H. (1996), '"Ah, could they know": The Place of the Erotic in H.D.'s *Hymen*', *Gramma: Journal of Theory and Criticism*, 4: 89–105.
Taruskin, R. (2003), 'Ezra Pound, Musical Crackpot', *New York Times*, 27 July. Available at: www.nytimes.com/2003/07/27/arts/music-ezra-pound-musical-crackpot.html?pagewanted=all&src=pm (accessed 26 May 2020).
Tedesco, N. (1959), *Salvatore Quasimodo e la condizione poetica del nostro tempo*, Palermo: Flaccovio.
Terrell, C. F. (1979a), 'Introduction', in C.F. Terrell (ed.), *Louis Zukofsky: Man and Poet*, 15–30, Orono: The National Poetry Foundation.
Terrell, C. F. (1979b), 'Louis Zukofsky: An Eccentric Profile', in *Louis Zukofsky: Man and Poet*, 31–74, Orono: The National Poetry Foundation.
Terrell, C. F. (1980), *A Companion to the Cantos of Ezra Pound*, Berkeley: University of California Press.
Thomas, R. (1983), *The Latin Masks of Ezra Pound*, Epping: Bowker.
Thomas, R. F. (1993), 'Sparrows, Hares, and Doves: A Catullan Metaphor and its Tradition', *Helios*, 20: 131–42.
Thomsen, O. (1992), *Ritual and Desire: Catullus 61 and 62, and Other Ancient Documents on Wedding and Marriage*, Aarhus: Aarhus University Press.
Thomson, D. F. S., ed. (1997), *Catullus*, Toronto: University of Toronto Press.
Traina, A., ed. (1969), G. Pascoli, *Saturae*, Florence: La Nuova Italia.
Traina, A. (2006), *Il latino del Pascoli: saggio sul bilinguismo poetico*, 3rd edn, Bologna: Pàtron.
Traverso, L. ([1940] 1969), 'Lirici Greci', in G. Finzi (ed.), *Quasimodo e la critica*, 291–94, Milan: Mondadori.
Trilling, L. (1972), *Sincerity and Authenticity*, Oxford: Oxford University Press.
Valéry, P. ([1928]1958), 'Pure Poetry: Notes for a Lecture', in J. Mathews (ed.), *The Collected Works of Paul Valéry*, 15 vols, VII: *The Art of Poetry*, trans. F. Folliot, 184–192, Princeton: Princeton University Press.
Valgimigli, M. ([1946] 1969), 'Poeti greci e Lirici nuovi', in G. Finzi (ed.), *Quasimodo e la critica*, 313–19, Milan: Mondadori.
Valgimigli, M., ed. (1960), *Carmina di Giovanni Pascoli*, 3rd edn, Milan: Mondadori, 1960.
Valli, D., ed. (1978), *Storia degli ermetici*, Brescia: La Scuola.
Van Den Bossche, B. (2003), 'Quasimodo e il mito', in *Quasimodo e gli altri: atti del Convegno Internazionale Lovanio, 27–28 aprile 2001*, 21–32, Leuven: Leuven University Press.
Van Schalkwyk, S. (2017), '"Un-American Confessions": Translation as Subversion in Robert Lowell's *Life Studies* (1959)', *European Journal of American Studies*, 12 (2): 1–18. Available at: https://journals.openedition.org/ejas/12031 (accessed 26 May 2020).

Vandiver, E. (2007), 'Translating Catullus', in M. Skinner (ed.), *A Companion to Catullus*, 523–41, Oxford: Blackwell.
Venuti, L. (1995), *The Translator's Invisibility: A History of Translation*, London: Routledge.
Venuti, L. (2000), 'Italian', in P. France (ed.), *The Oxford Guide to Literature in English Translation*, 467–502, Oxford: Oxford University Press.
Venuti, L. (2011), 'World Literature and Translation Studies', in T. D'haen, D. Damrosch and D. Kadir (eds), *The Routledge Companion to World Literature*, 180–93, New York: Routledge.
Venuti, L., ed. (2012), *The Translation Studies Reader*, 3rd edn, London: Routledge.
Verdino, S. (1987), *Luciano Anceschi: esperienza della poesia e metodo*, Genoa: Il Melangolo.
Vicinelli, A., ed. (1946), *Giovanni Pascoli. Prose*, I: *Pensieri di varia umanità*, Milan: Mondadori.
Vicinelli, A., ed. (1952), *Giovanni Pascoli. Prose*, II: *Scritti danteschi*, Milan: Mondadori.
Vicinelli, A., ed. (1968), *Poesie di Giovanni Pascoli*, 4 vols, Milan: Mondadori.
Villa, A. I. (2012), *La modernità dell'antico*. Milan: Educatt.
Villa, E. (1982), *Saffo*, with illustrations by Alberto Burri, Rome: 2RC.
Villani, A. and F. Longo (2012), *Saffo & Merini*, Trieste: Asterios.
Voigt, E. M., ed. (1971), *Sappho et Alcaeus: Fragmenta*, Amsterdam: Athenaeum-Polak & Van Gennep.
Wasdin, K. (2018), *Eros at Dusk: Ancient Wedding and Love Poetry*, Oxford: Oxford University Press.
Welcker, F. G. (1816), *Sappho von einem herrschenden Vorurtheil befreyt*, Gottingen: Vandenhoeck und Ruprecht.
West, M. L. (1970), 'Burning Sappho', *Maia*, 22: 307–30.
West, M. L. (2005), 'The New Sappho', *Zeitschrift für Papyrologie und Epigraphik*, 151: 1–9.
Wharton, H. T. (1908), *Sappho: Memoir, Text, Selected Rendering and a Literal Translation*, 5th edn, London: John Lane.
Wilamowitz-Moellendorff, U. (1913), *Sappho und Simonides. Untersuchungen über griechische Lyriker*, Berlin: Weidmann.
Wilkinson, J. M., ed. (2015), *Anne Carson: Ecstatic Lyre*, Ann Arbor: University of Michigan Press.
Williamson, M. (1995), *Sappho's Immortal Daughters*, Cambridge MA: Harvard University Press.
Williamson, M. (2009), 'Sappho and Pindar in the Nineteenth and Twentieth Centuries', in F. Budelmann (ed.), *The Cambridge Companion to Greek Lyric*, 352–70, Cambridge: Cambridge University Press.
Winkler, J. (1990), *The Constraints of Desire: The Anthropology of Sex and Gender in Ancient Greece*, New York: Columbia University Press.
Winning, J. (2010), 'Lesbian Sexuality in the Story of Modernism', in P. Brooker, A. Gąsiorek, D. Longworth and A. Thacker (eds), *The Oxford Handbook of Modernisms*, 218–34, Oxford: Oxford University Press.

Winterer, C. (2002), *The Culture of Classicism: Ancient Greece and Rome in American Intellectual Life 1780–1910*, Baltimore and London: Johns Hopkins University Press.

Wiseman, T. P. (1985), *Catullus and His World: A Reappraisal*, Cambridge: Cambridge University Press.

Witemeyer, H. (1969), *The Poetry of Ezra Pound: 1908–20*, Berkeley: University of California Press.

Wittig, M. and S. Zeig (1986), *Brouillon pour un dictionnaire des amantes*, Paris: Grasset.

Wordsworth, W. ([1802] 1963), 'Preface', in W. Wordsworth and S. T. Coleridge, *Lyrical Ballads*, ed. R. L. Brett and A. R. Jones, 235–66, London: Methuen.

Wray, D. (2001), *Catullus and the Poetics of Roman Manhood*, Cambridge: Cambridge University Press.

Wray, D. (2004), '"Cool Rare Air": Zukofsky's Breathing with Catullus and Plautus', *Chicago Review*, 50 (2/3/4): 52–100.

Yao, S. (2002), *Translation and the Languages of Modernism: Gender, Politics, Language*, New York: Palgrave Macmillan.

Yatromanolakis, D. (2004), 'Fragments, Brackets and Poetics: on Anne Carson's *If Not, Winter*', *International Journal of the Classical Tradition*, 11: 266–72.

Yeats, W. B. (1950), *Collected poems*, 2nd edn, London: Macmillan.

Yenser, S. (1975), *Circle to Circle: The Poetry of Robert Lowell*, Berkeley: University of California Press.

Young, E. M. (2015), *Translation as Muse: Poetic Translation in Catullus's Rome*, Chicago: Chicago University Press.

Zagarrio, G. (1974), *Salvatore Quasimodo*, 2nd edn, Florence: La Nuova Italia.

Ziolkowsky, T. (2007), 'Anglo-American Catullus since the Mid-Twentieth Century', *International Journal of the Classical Tradition*, 13(3): 409–430.

Zukofsky, C. (1979), 'Year by Year Bibliography of Louis Zukofsky', in C. F. Terrell (ed.), *Louis Zukofsky: Man and Poet*, 385–92, Orono: The National Poetry Foundation.

Zukofsky, C. and L. Zukofsky (1969), *Catullus: (Gai Valeri Catulli Veronensis Liber)*, London: Cape Goliard.

Zukofsky, L. (1931), 'Sincerity and Objectification: With Special Reference to the Work of Charles Reznikoff', *Poetry*, 37(5): 272–85 = Zukofsky [1981] 2000: 193–202.

Zukofsky, L. ([1981] 2000), *Prepositions +: The Collected Critical Essays*, ed. M. Scroggins, Hanover and London: Wesleyan University Press.

Zukofsky, L. (1991), *Complete Short Poetry*, Baltimore and London: Johns Hopkins University Press.

Index

absence 53, 59, 61, 97, 99, 100, 101–2, 173, 177, 184, 187, 192, 194
aesthetic (adj. and noun)
  dimension 25, 50, 85, 92, 157
  discourse 4, 8, 46, 47, 79, 83, 86, 107, 122, 125, 146, 158, 196
  eroticism 72, 78
  experience 77, 187
  fragments and 53, 171, 187
  Hermeticist 90, 92, 95, 98, 103, 104, 106
  modernist 17, 55, 67, 71, 79, 83, 89, 170
  myth and 55
  neoclassical 15
  objects 116
  prose 18, 56, 106, 169, 197
  paradigm 55, 65, 199
  translation and 90–8, 103–6, 146, 149, 159–60, 188, 190
  transnational 4
  see also Carson, A., Copioli, R., H.D., Lowell, R., myth, Pascoli, G., Pound, E., Quasimodo, S.
aestheticism 67, 145, 157–8, 197
Anceschi, L.
  Copioli, R. and 145
  correspondence with Quasimodo 93–4
  Hermeticism and 85, 88, 95, 106, 195
  Introductions to *Lirici greci* 90–4, 98, 100, 108–9
  Leopardi, G. and 100
  Pascoli, G. and 198
antiquity 7, 174
  Italy and 14–15, 198
  as model 13, 25–6, 155, 199
  North America and 15
  origins and 25–6, 53, 92, 98, 156–7, 163
  poetics and 25–6, 92, 98, 156–7
  see also Copioli, R., Italy, North America, Pascoli, G.
anthology
  literary 60
  school 24, 36, 42, 44, 98, 103, 104

translation 16, 17, 57, 72, 74, 85, 86, 88, 90–7, 100, 102, 104–6, 108, 109, 110, 123, 141, 142, 145, 155, 156
anthropology
  archetypes and 79, 197
  discipline 54, 56, 69
  poetic 24, 195
  rituals and 40, 174
appropriation 20, 159, 179
  of Catullus 8, 42, 45, 47, 56, 61–2, 65, 82, 107, 115, 120, 180, 194, 198
  fascist 15, 89, 141
  of Sappho 1, 8, 42, 45, 47, 56, 61–2, 65, 68–9, 75, 82, 87, 94, 115, 126–7, 159–60, 194, 195, 198
archetype
  Catullus as 12–13
  Lesbia as 152
  literary 34, 62, 151, 157, 174
  Sappho as 12–13, 29, 68, 168, 174
  Sappho and Catullus as 1, 24, 83, 154
  see also anthropology
Atthis 59–60, 81, 102
autobiography
  Autobiography of Red 169
  Barnard, M. 110
  Lowell, R. 113, 114, 116, 125, 128, 130, 196

Baehrens, E. 10, 44
Balmer, J. 3, 178
Barnard, M. 17, 110–11
beauty 1, 5, 25, 47, 62, 66, 68, 127, 145, 146, 156, 157, 159, 161–2, 164, 169–70, 171
Beckett, S. 15, 16
Benjamin, W. 19, 133, 180, 186–7, 188
Bergk, T. 8–9, 27, 41, 57
biography
  of Catullus 2, 6–7, 10, 17, 20, 26, 44, 64, 104, 105, 118, 120, 130, 137, 151, 182, 195

fictional 3, 6, 9, 20, 92, 120, 142
  of Sappho 2, 6–7, 9, 12, 17, 20, 26, 92,
    118, 130, 142, 172, 195
Bo, C. 85, 94, 97

canon 15, 16, 20, 26, 94, 118
  status and 6, 12–13, 108–9
Carson, A. 3, 8, 17, 169–94, 196, 197, 198
  aesthetic of 169, 171, 187, 190
  Autobiography of Red 169
  Eros the Bittersweet 169, 172, 173, 188,
    192
  Float 170, 180, 186, 191
  If Not, Winter 170, 175, 185–90
  interview with 21, 171
  Men in the Off Hours 170, 174–85, 189
  Nox 17, 179, 185, 191–4
  The Beauty of the Husband 169, 170,
    171
  see also classics, desire, eros, feminism,
    fragments, gender, genre,
    Homer, homoeroticism,
    language, poetics, scholarship,
    translation
Catullus
  Alexandrian style 7, 11, 151
  c. 10 7
  c. 24 10
  c. 28 7
  c. 31 7, 63–4, 86–7
  c. 44 7
  c. 46 7, 179, 182–4
  c. 48 10
  c. 50 2, 46, 179
  c. 51 1–2, 4–7, 41, 43–4, 47–8, 54, 63–5,
    72, 106, 125, 134–5, 153–4,
    158–60, 178
  c. 61 7, 51, 71, 72–4, 79, 80–1, 82
  c. 62 7, 48–50, 71, 72, 74, 79–81
  c. 64 33–5, 106, 134
  c. 65 7, 34, 86–7, 106
  c. 68 a 7, 103, 106
  c. 68 b 7
  c. 81 10, 136–7
  c. 99 10
  c. 101 7, 17, 34, 170, 179, 184–5, 191,
    192–4
  enfant terrible 104, 105, 151
  life 6–7, 10, 44–5, 46

  modern lyric and 7, 10–13, 14, 21, 43,
    80
  obscenities 3, 10–11, 14, 21, 58, 63, 120,
    137, 146, 147, 149–50, 198
  see also appropriation, archetype,
    biography, epithalamia,
    heterosexual, homoeroticism,
    Juventius, literary pair, model,
    rewriting, scholarship, tradition,
    translation, transnational
censorship 6, 10, 11, 85, 88, 97, 119, 120,
  151
Ceronetti, G. 3, 21, 104, 144, 160, 197, 198
  Catullo 21, 104, 146, 147–53, 196
  Come un talismano 145, 152, 155
  La distanza. Poese 1946–1996 145
  life 145
  Sappho and 21, 153–6
  see also death, fragments, language,
    translation
classicism 154–5
  Italy 14–15, 88–9, 96, 144, 167
  North America 15, 17, 133, 163
classics
  Carson A. and 169, 170, 180
  Copioli, R. and 156–8
  discipline 8–9, 11, 23, 29, 39, 88, 114,
    119, 169
  fascism and 15, 97
  Italy and 14–15, 17, 39, 141, 147
  Lowell, R. 113–15, 117, 119, 122, 123
  North America and 15, 17
  Pascoli, G. and 23, 24, 26, 42
  prestige 12–13, 14–15, 39, 91, 149, 199,
    180, 198
  publishing 104, 141, 147
  Quasimodo, S. and 86, 89, 102, 104, 107
  see also fascism, scholarship
Clodia Metelli 5, 10, 44, 151–2
comparative perspective 18, 21, 65, 198
confessionalism 2, 21, 113–15, 118, 128,
  196
consciousness 3, 20, 29, 42, 54, 60, 92, 97
convention 62, 127, 193
  literary 6, 13, 15, 28, 40, 118
Copioli, R. 3, 21, 156–68, 174, 178, 188,
  196, 197, 198
  aesthetics of 157–8, 159
  antiquity and 156–7, 163

interview with 21, 157–61
life 8, 145–6
'Saffo' 17
Saffo. Più oro dell'oro 143, 144, 146–7, 160–7, 168
see also Anceschi, L., classics, death, eroticism, homoeroticism, language, Pascoli, G., translation

Dante 3, 15–16, 23, 54, 64, 76, 107
De vulgari eloquentia 16
Divina Commedia 16, 152
Vita Nova 54
see also modernism, Pound, E.
dawn 20, 43, 49, 64, 154
death
   in Carson, A. 170, 172, 174, 176, 177, 178, 179, 184–5, 191, 192, 193, 194
   in Catullus 45, 172, 179, 184–5, 192
   in Ceronetti, G. 147, 156
   in Copioli, R. 163, 168
   in H.D. 69, 75
   love and 38, 41, 45, 75, 194, 197
   in Lowell, R. 128–9
   in Pascoli, G. 25, 32, 34, 36, 38, 45, 51
   rebirth and 20, 32, 41, 45, 54, 128
   in Sappho 1, 2, 129, 168, 177
   see also thanatos
desire 194, 197, 198
   bisexual 68, 76, 77, 198
   in Carson 169–70, 172–6, 177, 178, 184, 185, 188, 190, 191–2, 194, 197
   in Catullus 33, 61, 64, 183
   in Copioli 146, 164–6
   death and 35, 58, 170, 174, 176, 178, 185
   divine 164, 166
   female 70, 74–5
   in H.D. 68, 70–7
   life 50, 60–1, 79
   literary 1–2
   in Lowell, R. 126–7
   male 71–3
   nature and 31, 35, 50, 60–1, 183
   in Pascoli, G. 25, 27, 31, 35, 46, 50, 55
   poetics of 169–70, 172–3, 188, 194, 197
   poetry and 1–2, 50, 60–1, 65, 70, 78, 146, 171–3, 188, 191–2, 194

   in Pound, E. 55, 59–62, 64–5, 79
   in Quasimodo, S. 97, 102
   in Sappho 1, 5, 58, 61, 62, 64, 68, 75, 76, 78, 97, 126–7, 164, 166, 188, 190
   symbols of 31, 35, 77
   see also eros, homoeroticism, love

elegy 43, 45, 61, 89, 90, 91, 96, 102–3, 104, 105, 106, 107, 147, 170, 179, 191–2, 193, 196, 197
Eliot, T. S. 3, 15, 17, 55, 65, 88, 89, 93, 113, 127
   Four Quartets 16
   The Wasteland 16
Ellis, R. 10, 44, 183
epithalamia 40, 79, 80
   of Catullus 7, 71, 72, 74, 82, 104, 105, 106, 195, 197
   of Pascoli 33, 50, 101
   of Sappho 7, 30, 31, 32, 49, 71, 72, 74, 75, 101, 102, 175, 195, 197
   see also hymenaic theme
eros 1, 3, 10, 198
   bisexual 76
   Catullus and 12, 34, 43, 158, 179, 191
   in Carson, A. 172–4, 175–6, 190, 191, 192, 194, 197
   in Copioli, R. 153, 156–68, 196, 197
   divine 21, 69–70, 76, 156, 162, 164–6, 168, 176
   in H.D. 67–8, 69–70, 76
   life-giving power of 21, 35, 37, 60, 82, 162, 163, 192, 197
   nature 35, 37, 54, 60–1, 64, 69–70, 128
   neo-platonic 21, 161, 165, 166
   in Pascoli, G. 29, 31–2, 35, 37, 38, 43, 197
   poetry and 21, 29, 35, 54, 64, 67, 70, 79, 158, 159, 161, 169–70, 173, 174, 182, 184, 188, 195, 196, 197
   in Pound, E. 54, 60–1, 64, 79, 81, 197
   ritual and 31, 32, 61
   Sappho and 12, 32, 40, 61, 77, 99, 153, 158, 161–2, 164–6, 167–8, 173, 174, 175, 176, 197
   thanatos and 20, 35, 37, 38, 43, 45, 51, 54, 69, 76, 172, 176, 178, 191, 194, 195, 197

see also absence, desire, eroticism, homoeroticism, love
eroticism 2–3, 172
   Catullus 3, 33, 35, 158, 160, 198
   Copioli, R. 156–68
   H.D. and 55, 66, 72, 76, 77, 197
   Sappho 2, 12, 33, 53, 55, 142, 143, 144, 147, 160, 161, 163, 165, 168, 172, 178, 198
   symbols of 20, 31, 66, 151, 154–5, 164, 168
   see also eros, homoeroticism, love
Europe 8, 10, 12, 13, 14, 15, 18, 39, 51, 114, 142
   languages 8
   literature 11, 115, 122, 123, 141, 199
   see also homosexuality, symbol

fascism 2, 85, 86, 88, 89, 141
   classics and 15, 97
feminism 13
   Anglo-American scholarship 9–10, 142, 169, 178
   Carson and 189
   in Italy 152, 160, 161
   Sappho and 9–10, 178, 189
   see also myth, scholarship, translation
flowers (poetic symbol)
   blooming 20, 30–2, 35, 36
   in Carson, A. 184
   in Catullus 35
   in H.D. 66, 67, 68, 72, 75, 77
   in Pascoli, G. 20, 30–2, 35, 36, 50, 51
   in Pound, E. 79, 80
   in Sappho 31, 36, 51, 66, 68, 72, 79, 80
Fordyce, J.C. 11, 63, 120, 181
fragments
   lyric 2, 3, 5, 9, 12, 53, 67, 147
      Carson, A. 169, 170–1, 177
      Ceronetti, G. 145, 156
      H.D. 57, 67, 71, 76–9
      Hermeticism 85, 90, 93, 95, 98, 107, 195
      Pascoli, G. 23, 30, 32
      Pound, E. 60, 62, 81, 102
   textual 19
   see also aesthetic, fragmentation, Sappho
fragmentation 154, 186

poetics of 2, 20, 93, 169
poetry 12, 96, 98, 140, 154, 170–1, 190
   of self 78
France 9, 10, 13, 55

gender 3, 6, 12, 19, 21, 55, 147, 152
   representations in Carson, A. 170, 172, 174, 178, 180, 195
   representations in H.D. 20, 56, 68, 71, 72, 77, 78, 83, 197
   representations in Lowell, R. 116, 121, 127
   representations in Pascoli, G. 26–7
   representations in Pound, E. 61, 65
   theory 4, 9, 11, 18, 142, 169
   see also scholarship
genre 13, 40, 42–3, 141
   Carson, A. and 169, 185
   Quasimodo, S. and 90, 94, 100
Gentile, G. 14, 89
Greece 1, 6, 14, 89, 175, 176
   language 8, 14–15, 23, 26, 38, 57, 72, 81, 87, 88, 114, 131, 132, 145, 149, 154, 171, 186
   literature 15, 24, 25, 53, 57, 76, 81, 82, 86, 90, 92, 103, 108, 109, 125, 142, 180, 188, 195
   religion 69–70, 165

H.D. (Hilda Doolittle) 15, 20, 21, 53, 79, 156, 158, 172, 174, 196, 197, 198
   aesthetic of 71, 72, 77–8, 197
   Freud, S. and 13
   Heliodora 56, 70, 71, 77–8
   Hymen 56, 70, 71–6, 77, 79
   Imagism and 2, 55, 56–7, 66–70, 195
   life 13, 55
   Sea Garden 66–70
   see also death, eros, eroticism, flowers, fragments, gender, homoerotic, Imagism
Helen of Troy, 47, 95, 127–8, 161–4, 198
hendecasyllable 27, 40, 104, 106, 107
Hermeticism 20–1, 85–111, 141, 142, 195–6
   see also aesthetic, Anceschi, L. fragments, poetics, Quasimodo, S.
heteronormativity 5–6, 9, 10, 20, 144, 166
   critique of 21, 71, 75, 77, 120, 197
   Lowell, R. and 120, 125, 127

heterosexual 102, 198
  Catullus 10, 157
  desire 4, 9, 10, 76, 77, 198
  Sappho 7, 9, 20, 26, 38, 39, 68, 102,
    124–5, 178
  see also love
Homer 3, 38, 72, 86, 95, 108, 162
  Carson, A. and 172, 180
  Lowell, R. and 122, 123, 124
  in Sappho 81
  Zukofsky, L. and 132
  see also myth
homoeroticism 55, 144, 178, 198
  in Carson, A. 189
  Catullus and 10–11, 43, 137
  in Copioli, R. 166–7
  in H.D. 66, 75, 76–8
  in Lowell, R. 126–7, 129
  Sappho and 2, 6, 9, 12, 27, 28, 39, 40, 44,
    68, 97, 102, 118, 126–7, 129, 142,
    166, 189
homosexuality 6, 55, 144, 137
  in Italy 26, 97, 142–3, 144, 167
  in Europe 55
  in the United States 117–19
  see also love
hymenaic theme 20, 147, 195
  in Pascoli, G. 31–2, 34, 46, 48, 50, 51
  in Pound, E. 79–80, 82
  see also Hymen under H.D.

identity 21, 138, 175, 198, 199
  authorial 79, 118, 176
  cultural 14–15, 42
  national 3, 6, 13, 15, 16, 19, 39, 195
  sexual 9, 12
  see also gender, Italy, translation
Imagism 2, 20, 53, 55, 56–8
  H.D. and 71, 66–70, 83, 195
  Pound, E. and 58–70, 79, 113, 116
  see also language, poetics
intimacy 7, 10, 12, 74, 82, 119, 123, 137,
  193, 198
Italy 13, 18
  Anglo-American Modernists and
    15–17, 88
  Catullus and Sappho 3, 10, 18, 42, 138,
    195
  classical antiquity and 14–15, 38, 141, 198

  cultural identity 14–15, 108, 110
  education in 14
  language 15, 154
  sexuality 20, 26, 39, 143–4, 152,
    197
  translation in 16–17, 21, 85, 104, 141,
    144, 145, 152, 158, 160
  see also aesthetic, antiquity, classicism,
    classics, fascism, feminism,
    homosexuality, modernism,
    North America, Pound, E.,
    tradition

Jaeger, W. 89
Joyce, J. 15, 16
  Finnegans Wake 134
  Ulysses 16
Juventius 7, 10, 42, 55, 137

knowledge 20, 51, 78, 148, 156, 172, 174,
  192
  poetic 50

language 8, 19, 37, 77, 89, 110
  Carson, A. and 169, 172, 180, 185, 188,
    190, 194
  hybrid 136
  Imagism and 62
  poetic 13, 16, 61, 78
    Catullus 146, 151, 194
    Ceronetti, G. 147–50, 153–4
    Copioli, R. 156
    Quasimodo, S. 85, 86, 88, 91, 96,
      106–7
    Sappho 166
    Zukofsky, L. 131–3, 136, 137, 139
  pure 133, 186–7
  patriarchy and 77–8
  ritual 175
  spoken 16, 138
  see also Europe, Greece, Italy, Latin,
    poetics
Latin 3, 8, 14–15, 72, 87, 114, 133, 134, 136,
  138, 145, 152, 154, 157, 171, 191,
  194, 196
  literature 24, 42, 57, 61, 81, 82, 86,
    88, 103, 114, 122–3, 131, 142,
    171
  Neo-Latin 2, 20, 23, 24

Leopardi, G. 16, 86, 87, 89, 99–101, 107,
    123, 148, 153, 154, 168, 198
  see also Anceschi, L.
Lesbia 1, 5, 7, 10, 42–4, 45, 58, 62–3, 64–5,
    72, 105, 118, 120, 121, 137, 149,
    150–2, 159, 179, 181–2
  see also archetype
lesbian 2, 6, 9, 55, 76, 77, 97, 143, 167
Leucadian cliffs 6, 37, 68–70
literary pair
  Sappho and Catullus as 1–3, 6, 8, 13,
    18, 20, 21, 24, 43, 51, 56, 64, 71,
    79, 81, 82, 83, 86, 154, 194, 195,
    196, 199
love 1, 10, 12, 32–5, 38, 41, 43, 72, 149, 152,
    159
  betrayed 62, 118, 120–1, 181–2
  divine 70, 81, 146, 162, 164–6
  effects 123, 126
  frustrated 127
  heterosexual 5, 6, 7, 124, 167–8, 198
  homosexual 6, 7, 9, 71, 74, 78, 137, 142,
    189
  idealized 61
  Love (character in 'Hymen') 71–6
  lyric 13, 41, 42, 49–50, 94, 102
  poetry and 45–6, 47, 64–5, 68–70, 82,
    97, 127, 138, 153, 158, 173, 198
  unrequited 6, 26–9, 36, 39, 68–9, 99,
    176, 178
  see also death, eros, heterosexual,
    homoeroticism, homosexuality
Lowell, R. 115–30, 138–9, 151, 196, 197,
    198
lyric 32, 79, 172
  addressee 61–2, 97
  ancient 35, 51, 54, 91, 100, 110
  choral 90
  form 102, 179
  Greek 29, 54, 85–6, 92, 96, 97, 98, 108,
    109, 125, 142
  mode 7, 12, 82
  modern 7, 10, 11, 14, 43, 92
  monodic 85, 90–1, 92, 103, 185
  motif 26, 28, 33, 78, 81
  origins 8, 12, 92, 123, 195
  poet 7, 8, 10, 13, 17, 58, 104, 107
  pure 87, 90, 92, 95, 98, 100, 109
  Roman 42, 54, 142

self 5, 71, 76, 99, 101, 116, 118, 124, 128,
    167, 168, 173, 175, 177, 181, 182,
    183, 184
subjectivity 11, 12, 53, 138
tradition 5, 7, 10, 17, 21, 54, 56, 62, 80,
    94, 128
voice 1, 5, 6, 85, 94, 98, 107, 129, 134,
    175, 189, 196
  see also Catullus, fragment, genre, love,
    model, Sappho
  aesthetic and 122, 125
  History 115, 128, 129, 130
  Imitations 2, 16, 21, 115, 122–5, 130,
    131, 134, 141, 153
  life 8, 13, 16, 113–14, 118
  Life Studies 2, 114, 115, 116, 117–21, 128
  Notebook 129, 134
  see also autobiography, death, desire,
    gender, heteronormative,
    Homer, homoeroticism,
    translation

masculinity 10, 58, 62, 65, 121, 125, 152,
    174
  see also poetics
masculinization 6, 159
memory 57, 97–8, 161, 163, 168
  literary 6, 133, 168
metaphysical 65, 76, 85, 89, 92, 95, 148,
    151, 153, 156, 160, 161, 162, 166,
    192, 195, 196, 198
model 13, 16, 39, 62, 89, 113, 125, 127, 151,
    159, 197, 198, 199
  Catullus as 6, 10, 12, 20, 21, 44, 50, 52,
    54, 57, 79, 86, 87, 130, 138, 153,
    159, 194
  cultural 136, 144
  philological 8
  poetic 1, 3, 6, 7, 10, 12, 20, 21, 65, 67, 71,
    77, 86, 92, 138, 151, 153, 158,
    174, 190, 194, 196, 199
    lyric 3, 20, 21, 29, 38, 40–1, 68, 79,
      83, 79, 147
  Sappho as 6, 12, 20, 21, 44, 50, 54, 55,
    57, 65, 68, 71, 79, 86, 87, 92, 130,
    153, 173, 174
  see also antiquitiy
modernism 2, 122, 124, 128, 130, 138, 170,
    196

Anglo-American 2, 15, 16–17, 20, 47,
53–83, 88, 91, 113, 113, 127, 134,
136, 149, 196, 197
  Dante and 15–16
  Italy and 15–16, 88, 145, 158, 195
  see also aesthetic, Beckett, S., Eliot, T. S.,
    H.D., Imagism, Italy, Joyce, J.,
    myth, poetics, Pound E.,
    tradition, translation
Montale, E. 16, 85, 123, 141, 145
myth 2, 20, 21, 24, 25, 30, 42, 54, 71, 75,
  146, 156–7, 158, 162, 194–5
  aesthetics and 55, 145
  Apollo and Dafne 70
  Ariadne 34–5
  feminism and 160, 163
  Homeric 95
  modernism and 55, 60, 68, 79, 81
  Peleus and Thetis 33
  psychology and 53, 70, 79
  of self 118, 122, 138
  solar 20, 26, 37–8, 39, 49, 54, 68–9, 196
  Tithonos 9
  see also easthetics, eros and thanatos,
    Helen of Troy, origins, Phaon,
    poetics, rewriting, scholarship
mythopoeia 20, 21, 23, 25, 26, 29, 36, 39,
  42, 53, 54, 55, 79, 83, 92, 128, 139,
  147, 151, 154, 161, 166, 168, 173,
  196–7

nature 35, 38, 46, 49, 51, 54, 61, 62, 81, 132,
  156, 171, 183, 197
  cycles 20, 24, 32, 33, 49, 50, 60, 69, 99,
    197
  see also flowers
Neoteric 7, 150
neoclassical 15, 34, 88
neo-humanism 2, 21, 89, 97, 107, 124, 139,
  149, 196
night 5, 43, 50, 64, 78, 123, 154, 155, 181, 194
  day alternation with 20, 24, 37, 197
  wedding 48, 49, 50, 74, 80
normalization 5–7, 9, 10, 20, 26, 27–8, 125,
  127, 142
North America 3, 13, 18, 20, 180, 198
  classical antiquity in 14, 15, 138, 151,
    198
  education in 12, 15

Italian translation and 16
see also antiquity, classicism, classics,
  tradition

original 14, 37, 42, 133, 141, 153, 192, 194,
  199
  context 5
  poetry 5, 6, 17, 43, 65–6, 76, 79, 105,
    130, 146, 164, 172, 195
  text 8, 19
origins 21
  cultural 3, 8, 53, 125, 157
  human 3, 19, 20, 21, 24, 25, 37, 71, 195
  literary 2, 8, 12, 24, 26, 51, 71, 86, 89,
    119, 123, 139, 158, 198
  myth 162, 196
  see also antiquity, original, lyric
Ovid 9, 24, 28, 36, 57, 68, 86, 108, 124
  Georgics 86
  Heroides 15 6, 57, 125
  Metamorphoses 123
  tradition 27, 76, 92, 125

papyri 9, 53, 56, 58–9, 92, 171, 187
Paris 2, 13, 55, 67, 117, 119
Pascoli, G. 17, 20, 21, 23–51, 54, 56, 57, 66,
  69, 75, 79, 144, 156, 172, 188,
  195, 196, 197, 199
  aesthetics of 25–6, 46–7, 50, 55, 67,
    103
  antiquity and 24–6
  Catullocalvos 2, 24, 46–51
  Copioli, R. and 157, 168, 198
  'Il fanciullino' 24, 25–6, 44, 45, 46, 49
  life 8, 23–4, 36, 44
  Lyra 24, 26, 36, 39–40, 42–6, 47, 103
  Myricae 23
  Poemi conviviali 2, 23, 24
    'Solon' 2, 24, 36, 37–8, 40, 41, 43, 46,
      68
  Primi poemetti 31
  Quasimodo, S. and 87–8, 92, 101, 103,
    198
  Traduzioni e riduzioni 34, 36–42
  see also Anceschi, L., classics, death,
    desire, epithalamia, eros, flowers,
    fragments, gender, hymenaic
    theme, poetics, scholarship,
    translation

past 1, 7, 8, 53, 55 62, 65, 88, 89, 102, 103, 113, 121, 124, 130, 133, 168, 180
patriarchy 78, 127, 162, 164, 166, 180
   critique of 3, 21, 56, 71, 72, 74, 75, 83, 152, 160, 163, 174, 175, 178, 182, 197
Phaon 6, 9, 20, 24, 26, 28, 36–8, 39, 43, 69, 99
philology 8–9, 10, 15, 29, 56, 88, 89, 92, 142, 146, 147, 148
   see also model, textual criticism, tradition
poetics 17, 18, 19, 20, 21, 71, 110, 139, 195, 196, 198
   Carson, A. 172, 174, 188, 190, 191
   Hermeticist 21, 85–6, 92, 95, 98, 101, 106, 141
   Imagist 57, 62, 83, 146
   of language 133, 138
   lesbian 76
   of masculinity 11
   modernist 2, 61
   myth 2, 147, 159
   of the object 47
   Pascoli, G. 20, 25, 40, 46–7
   postmodern 172
   of sincerity 116, 128
   of triangulation 184, 186
   of the word 86
   see also antiquity, confessionalism, desire, fragmentation, postmodernism
poetic creation 20, 31–3, 50, 51, 66, 67–8, 116, 196–7
poetic faculty 21, 25, 49, 54
poet-translators 17, 19, 87, 89, 106, 153, 159, 192
postmodern 2, 12, 21, 156, 169, 172, 180, 184, 196, 197, 198
   see also poetics
poststructuralism 11, 13, 169
Pound, E. 3, 8, 17, 20, 21, 58–66, 67, 68, 71, 72, 79–83, 88, 110, 113, 116, 119, 120, 127, 130, 134, 152, 158, 172, 195, 196, 197, 198–9
   aesthetic and, 53–5, 79, 80, 192
   Collis o Heliconii 56, 79, 81–3
   Dante and 15–16
   Homage to Sextus Propertius 18, 88
   'Ἱμέρρω' 59–61, 62, 80, 102
   Italy and 16, 17
   life 13, 16, 56
   Lustra 58–66, 80, 81, 83
   'Papyrus' 59–61, 62, 130
   The Cantos 1, 16, 56, 63, 79–81, 83, 113, 197
   The Spirit of Romance 15, 56, 80
   'Three Cantos' 1–2, 63, 79, 80
   see also desire, eros, flowers, fragments, gender, hymenaic theme, Imagism, translation, Zukofsky

quaderno di traduzioni 141, 152
Quasimodo, S. 2, 16, 20, 85–112, 141, 144, 156, 168, 172, 198
   aesthetics of 89, 92, 98, 104, 106, 109, 139
   Canti di Catullo 86, 102, 106, 147
   Catullus Veronensis Carmina 86, 102
   correspondence 21
   Ed è subito sera 108
   Giorno dopo giorno 86, 106
   Lirici greci 17, 85–112, 142, 195
   neo-humanism 89, 97, 139, 149
   Oboe sommerso 86, 98
   see also classics, desire, genre, language, Pascoli, translation
Quinn, K.
   The Catullan Revolution 7, 11, 12, 118

rebirth 20, 30, 32, 54, 60, 128, 192
   see also death
rewriting 55, 117, 122, 169, 196–7
   of Catullus 2, 4, 15, 17, 18, 19, 20, 21, 116, 120–1, 125, 144, 146, 151, 172, 174, 178–85
   mythical 20, 21, 24–51, 147
   of Sappho 1, 2, 3, 4, 5–6, 15, 16, 17, 18, 19, 20, 60, 66, 68, 75, 81, 115, 116, 123, 125–7, 130, 134, 142–3, 167, 168, 174, 178
Rilke, R.M. 2, 55
ritual 20, 33–4, 36, 42, 53, 54, 56, 61, 70, 174, 192–3, 195, 197
   Christian 32
   language 175
   mourning 184–5, 192
   poetry and 79–80, 82, 172

see also anthropology, eros, language, wedding
Romanticism 10, 11, 12, 43, 127, 172
  Post- 26, 172, 198
Rome 7, 15, 16, 24, 63, 114, 119, 138, 143

Sappho
  'Brothers Poem' 9
  fr. 1 9, 26–7, 38–40, 64, 82, 176, 188
  fr. 2 93, 168
  fr. 16 95, 123, 124–5, 126–7, 128, 162, 164
  fr. 22 189–90
  fr. 31 1–2, 4–5, 7, 26, 38, 40–2, 43, 48, 54, 64, 76, 78, 86–7, 123–4, 126–9, 154, 158, 165–7, 173–5, 177–8
  fr. 34 29, 32
  fr. 36 98, 99
  fr. 38 176
  fr. 44 95
  fr. 47 99, 155
  fr. 51 78–9
  fr. 54 74
  fr. 58 9
  fr. 93 31
  fr. 94 31
  fr. 95 58, 79, 101
  fr. 96 59–60, 79, 81, 96–7, 102
  fr. 104a 49
  fr. 105b 79, 80
  fr. 109 79
  fr. 114 29–30, 75
  fr. 130 98, 76, 174
  fr. 146 77, 98, 99
  fr. 168b 98, 99, 101, 123, 126, 129, 155
  'Kypris Poem' 9
  life 2, 6–7, 9, 38, 68, 76, 92, 154, 175, 189
  modern lyric and 12–13, 14, 21, 80
  'New' 9, 143, 161, 170
  'Newest' 9, 143, 170
  reputation 9, 44
  see also appropriation, biography, desire, eros, eroticism, epithalamia, flowers, feminism, fragment, homoeroticism, heterosexual, Italy, literary pair, model, Phaon, rewriting, scholarship, symbol, tradition, translation

Schwabe, L. 10, 44
scholarship 87, 108, 118, 144
  Carson, A. and 169, 170, 172, 178, 179, 185, 186
  on Catullus 4, 6, 8, 9–11, 12, 26, 44, 158, 160, 179, 181
  feminist 9, 142, 189
  on gender 9, 10–11, 142
  on myth 56, 70
  Pascoli and 24, 42, 44
  on the classics and classical reception 8–9, 12, 21, 88, 89, 90, 138, 169, 187, 189, 199
  on Sappho 4, 5, 6, 8, 9, 11, 12, 26, 28, 29, 71, 175, 189
  see also philology, textual criticism, Welcker, J.
sex 10, 14, 32, 60, 77, 150
sexuality 3, 4, 6, 9, 10, 12, 18, 20
  see also desire, eros, Italy, homosexuality, homosexuality, identity
sincerity 10, 12, 113, 115, 116, 119, 121, 128, 138, 139
solitude 49, 55, 97, 98, 99–102, 106–7, 123, 124, 126, 127, 129–30, 155
sonnet 13, 54, 117, 126, 128
spiritual 69, 70, 76, 92, 98, 107, 114, 146, 156, 196
subjectivity 71, 82, 125, 128, 129, 138, 160, 178, 186, 194, 196
  see also lyric
symbol
  Catullus as 14, 47, 49, 151
  imagination and 157, 175
  poetic 14, 20, 31, 50, 51, 62, 64, 66, 73, 74, 77, 78, 85, 101, 114, 151–2, 154–5, 157, 164, 166, 168, 173, 179, 193
  Sappho as 14, 29
  symbolism European 141, 199
  see also flowers

textual criticism 4, 8, 9, 10, 18, 19, 27, 41–2, 155, 170, 187, 188
  see also fragments, philology, translation
thanatos
  see under eros
  see also death

time 2, 15, 25, 51, 68, 92, 97, 98, 101–2, 103, 123, 126, 132, 138, 156, 168, 172, 174, 180, 196
   timeless 14
tradition 38, 132, 138, 139
   of Catullus 1–3, 7, 8, 12, 21, 51
   classical 23, 24, 93, 107, 53–4, 95, 107, 158
   cultural 31, 40
   female 76, 162
   Italian 15, 17, 24, 107, 122, 198–9
   Jewish 155
   linguistic 13, 174
   literary 1, 3, 6, 12–13, 15, 17, 19, 23, 24, 29, 40, 47, 54, 55, 62, 64, 66, 73, 78, 80, 87, 88, 90, 101, 107, 113, 121, 122, 124, 133, 146, 147, 152, 153, 157, 158, 168, 170, 180, 196, 199
   medieval 15–16, 17, 54, 76
   modernist 113, 116, 172
   North American 15, 16, 17, 198–9
   Ovidian 27, 76
   philological 146, 159, 171, 172
   sapphic 77
   of Sappho 1–3, 6, 8, 12, 21, 51, 66, 125, 154, 166
   see also lyric, Ovid, translation
transcultural 13, 195, 197, 198
translation 1, 4, 5, 8, 16, 20, 21, 90, 114, 196
   academic 18, 88, 104
   Carson, A. 21, 170–2, 175, 178–94
   of Catullus 1–2, 4, 8, 10–11, 17, 18, 21, 33–5, 47, 51, 58, 62–3, 64–5, 79, 86–7, 102–7, 114, 116, 117, 120–1, 130–9, 144, 146, 147–53, 154, 178–85, 191–4
   Ceronetti, G. 21, 147–54, 148–9, 154, 156
   collaborative 19, 88, 90, 93–4, 111, 134
   Copioli, R. 156–68, 197
   creative 3, 16, 18–19, 42, 58, 102, 64–6, 86, 88, 89, 91, 114, 116, 117, 122, 130–1, 146–7, 148, 159, 171–2, 178–85
   debate 89
   domestication 26–8, 39, 107, 119
   etymological 37, 39, 42

feminist 178
foreignizing 131, 133, 135
historicist 87
homophonic 3, 21, 60, 130–9
   Lowell, R. and 114–15, 117–30
   national identity and 39
   of metre 40, 81, 144
   Pascoli, G. 24, 26–31, 33–6, 38, 39–45, 47, 49, 51
   poetic 2, 3, 87, 89, 144
   Pound, E. and 1–2, 17, 54, 58–61, 62–3, 64–5, 79
   prismatic 130
   Quasimodo, S. and 2, 17, 20, 85–111
   of Sappho 1–2, 4–6, 8, 16, 17, 18, 21, 26–31, 38, 39–42, 43, 47, 49, 53, 54, 57, 58–61, 64, 71, 72, 74, 77, 79, 86–7, 93, 96, 98–102, 110–11, 114, 122–30, 142, 143, 146–7, 153, 155, 156–68, 175, 178–90
   textual criticism and 9, 10, 19
   theory 18–19, 89, 103, 148–9, 154, 156–61, 180, 185–7, 191–2
   tradition and 19, 87
   Zukofsky, C. and L. and 130–9, 196, 198
   see also aesthetic, anthology, Barnard, M., Italy, North America, normalization, poet-translators, quaderno *di traduzioni*, untranslatability
transnational
   aesthetic 4
   discourse 8, 13, 196, 199
   networks 8, 11, 13, 17, 21, 52, 110, 198
   poetry 13, 17, 110
   reception of Sappho and Catullus 2–3, 10, 13–15, 17–18, 19, 21, 110, 196, 199

Ungaretti, G. 16, 85, 123, 141
university 8, 14, 23, 24, 33, 60, 89, 114, 116, 119, 147, 169
untranslatability 89, 149, 191

Virgil 3, 86, 122, 123, 158

wedding 33, 58, 120

poetry 3, 5, 7, 31, 40, 48, 49, 71, 74, 75, 79, 80
ritual 32, 34, 35, 40, 51, 66, 71, 72, 75, 81, 174–5
see also epithalamia
Welcker, J. 28, 38, 57, 61, 74
Wharton, H. T. 57, 71, 72, 74, 77, 111
world literature 2, 4, 18, 147

Yeats, W. B. 2, 146, 157–8, 168, 197

Zukofsky, C. 21, 116, 130, 134
Zukofsky, L. 3, 13, 115–16, 130–9, 151, 196, 198
 'A' 116, 138
 'A Statement for Poetry' 115, 132
 aesthetic objects and 116
 Catullus 19, 21, 130–9, 146
 'Ezra Pound' 133
 life 13, 116
 see also Homer, language, translation

www.ingramcontent.com/pod-product-compliance
Lightning Source LLC
Chambersburg PA
CBHW072138290426
44111CB00012B/1903